The Best American Political Writing 2006

The Best American Political Writing 2006

Edited by Royce Flippin

Thunder's Mouth Press
New York

THE BEST AMERICAN POLITICAL WRITING 2006

Published by
Thunder's Mouth Press
An Imprint of Avalon Publishing Group, Inc.
245 West 17th St., 11th Floor
New York, NY 10011

www.thundersmouth.com

AVALON
publishing group incorporated

First printing, October 2006

Library of Congress Cataloging-in-Publication Data is available.

ISBN-10: 1-56025-912-4
ISBN-13: 978-1-56025-912-1

9 8 7 6 5 4 3 2 1

Book design by Sue Canavan

Printed in the United States of America
Distributed by Publishers Group West

This book is dedicated to my wife, Alexis,
and to our brand-new baby daughter,
Lily Mazarine (Maisie) Flippin

CONTENTS

Part One: Politics in the Bush Era—The White House under Siege

Part Two: State of the Union

Part Five: Iraq and the War on Terror

Part Six: America in an Uncertain World

Acknowledgments

I'd like to gratefully acknowledge all the writers included in this book, as well as the permissions staff of their publications and literary agencies, for allowing these fine pieces of writing to appear. Thanks, too, to all who brought articles and essays of interest to my attention in the past year.

I'd like to extend special thanks to John Oakes and Lukas Volger of Thunder's Mouth Press for their help in getting this year's anthology into print, and also to the Avalon Publishing Group's design and production team and their publicity department. Finally, thank you and a big hug to my wife, Alexis Lipsitz Flippin, for her ongoing love and support.

Preface

Welcome to the fifth edition of *The Best American Political Writing*, covering the period of June 2005 through May 2006. As always, we've tried to bring you a collection of articles and essays that are both entertaining and illuminating and that also capture the essence of the past year in politics. It was a stretch that might best be described as a time of disgruntled ambivalence. Recent polls show that some two-thirds of the American populace believe the country is on the wrong track; they also indicate that the voters have little confidence in either party to right the nation's course. The Bush administration, bogged down in Iraq and presiding over an economic expansion that's mainly lining the pockets of America's wealthiest citizens, is suffering through historically low approval ratings—but Congress's approval ratings are even lower; and while the Republicans are nervously contemplating the potential loss of both houses in the midterm election, the Democrats, lacking any compelling message of their own (beyond "had enough?") aren't lighting any fires under the electorate either.

This state of affairs is reflected in this year's twenty-five selections. The book is divided into six sections. Part One, "Politics in the Bush Era—The White House under Siege," provides four different angles on the declining popularity of the Bush presidency—all depicting an administration more committed to political ideology than to pragmatic governance. "How Bush Blew It" details the government's inexplicably slow response to the devastation of Hurricane Katrina, as seen by Evan Thomas and the reporters of *Newsweek*. In "High Noon in Crawford," *Vanity Fair* writer Evgenia Peretz visits George Bush's Crawford, Texas, retreat in late summer, 2005, when his picture-perfect backdrop was invaded by Cindy Sheehan's antiwar encampment. Michael Specter of *The New Yorker* reports on the White House's ongoing efforts to spin scientific reality for political purposes in his article "Political Science." The section closes with academician Sean Wilentz's attempt to place Bush's approach to governing in historical perspective, in his *Rolling Stone* essay, "The Worst President in History?"

Part Two, "State of the Union," provides some further insight into why the U.S. public is so dissatisfied with the way the nation is currently being run. The first two articles explore the pervasive influence of money on the American political system. Elizabeth Drew's "Selling Washington" is a case study of Republican lobbyists gone wild, while Ken Silverstein's article on the proliferating use of earmarks, "The Great American Pork Barrel," goes a long way toward explaining why Congress (on both sides of the aisle) is having so much difficulty bringing federal spending under control. In "How Divided Are We?" James Q. Wilson, a professor of public policy at Pepperdine University, offers his own take on the stark divisions among today's political partisans and how those divisions have spread into the public at large. And in the last piece in this section, "Border War," John B. Judis travels to Arizona for *The New Republic* to report on the deep cultural tensions underlying Americans' current obsession with immigration.

Part Three of this year's anthology, "(Not) Politics as Usual," contains four articles that cover politics with a twist. Mark Crispin Miller's "None Dare Call It Stolen" revisits the troubling irregularities of Ohio's election results in the 2004 presidential election—and asks why the mainstream media hasn't given the subject more attention. "A New Black Power," by novelist Walter Mosley (best known for his "Easy Rawlins" mystery series), questions why African Americans don't form a political party of their own. Janet Malcolm's "The Art of Testifying," which originally appeared in *The New Yorker*, examines the recent Supreme Court confirmation hearings of John Roberts and Samuel Alito through a drama critic's eyes. The section ends with "The Third Term," in which Joe Conason profiles the peripatetic Bill Clinton for *Esquire*, as the ex-president comes to grips with life after the White House.

Part Four, "Republicans vs. Democrats," offers some red meat for political junkies. "Getting Ahead in the GOP," by Benjamin Wallace-Wells, which first ran in *The Washington Monthly*, charts the ambitious course of the Republican Party's youngest congressman. "The Framing Wars," by Matt Bai, portrays the Democrats' quest for a new way to package their ideas. The next two pieces, Ryan Lizza's analysis of the 2006 Senate races, "The Bush-Cheney Era Ends Here," and Amy Sullivan's "Not as Lame as You Think" offer behind-the-scenes glimpses of how the Democrats have relearned the art of political warfare (and improved their chances of retaking the House and Senate this November). Lest the Democrats get too confident, however, the section's concluding essay, Michael Tomasky's "Party in Search of a Notion," reprinted from *The American Prospect*, warns that improved political skills alone aren't enough to restore the Democrats to power—and goes on outline a new progressive philosophy for the twenty-first century.

In the anthology's final two sections, the focus shifts to the twin issues of foreign policy and homeland security. Part Five, "Iraq and the War on Terror," opens with "Why Iraq Has No Army," a penetrating analysis by *The Atlantic Monthly*'s James Fallows of America's mixed success in setting up an Iraqi military and security force. In "Afghanistan: The Other War," which first ran in *The Nation*, Christian Parenti gives a prescient report on the resurgence of the Taliban in southern Afghanistan. The third piece in the section, Mark Danner's "Taking Stock of the Forever War," evaluates the U.S. military efforts in Iraq and Afghanistan in the context of our country's ongoing struggle to contain Al Qaeda and other Islamic extremist groups. Last, in "Big Brother Is Listening," James Bamford turns his attention to the domestic front, as he describes how the National Security Agency monitors virtually every phone call and e-mail message going in or out of the United States.

Part Six, "America in an Uncertain World," looks at the global role of the United States. In "After Neoconservatism," Francis Fukuyama sounds the death knell of the neoconservative movement he helped to popularize—a victim, in his view, of the neocons' own overconfidence in the ability of America's military to transform the world. "The Iran Plans," by Seymour Hersh, which caused an international stir when it first appeared in *The New Yorker*, suggests that U.S. military planners are seriously contemplating the use of nuclear missiles to knock out Iran's nuclear enrichment program. In "North Korea: The War Game," Scott Stossel of *The Atlantic Monthly* oversees a simulated confrontation with that other would-be nuclear power. Finally, the book ends on a more or less optimistic note, as former U.S. Naval War College Professor Thomas P. M. Barnett explains why it's in the interests of both the United States and China to live happily ever after together, in his essay "The Chinese Are Our Friends."

Looking ahead, no one is sure how the electorate's foul mood will play out in this fall's midterm elections: Will the Republicans hold on to their edge in the House and Senate, or will the Democrats stage the congressional takeover they've been dreaming of? Either way, one thing is certain: Sooner or later, political reality inevitably trumps political philosophy. In recent weeks, Republicans in Congress have backed away from their long-held goal of permanently repealing the estate tax, while Democrats have been taking great pains to emphasize that the last thing they want to do is "cut and run" in Iraq. Even President Bush has begun listening openly to critics of his Iraq policy (reflecting the influence of his new chief of staff, Josh Bolten) and has opened the door to diplomacy with Iran and North Korea (reflecting the influence of his new secretary of state and trusted colleague, Condoleezza Rice). We're looking forward to hearing what America's political journalists make of it all.

Royce Flippin
June 2006

The Best American Political Writing 2006

Part One:
Politics in the Bush Era—
The White House under Siege

How Bush Blew It

Evan Thomas

With reporting by T. Trent Gegax, Arian Campo-Flores, Andrew Murr, Susannah Meadows, Jonathan Darman, and Catharine Skipp in the Gulf Coast region; and Richard Wolffe, Holly Bailey, Mark Hosenball, Tamara Lipper, John Barry, Daniel Klaidman, Michael Isikoff, Michael Hirsh, Eve Conant, Martha Brant, Patricia Wingert, Eleanor Clift, and Steve Tuttle in Washington

Newsweek | September 19, 2005

By any measure, the past year has been an extraordinarily rough one for President Bush and his administration. The president's approval ratings, in the low forties throughout the second half of 2005, took a dive into the thirties sometime around President's Day 2006, and haven't seen the north side of 40 percent since. One midspring poll even had him dipping down to 29 percent (tying his father's low point). Among modern presidents, only Richard Nixon has rated so poorly at this point in his second term. As this book went to press, recent good news from Iraq (the death of Abu Musab al-Zarqawi and the appointment of defense and interior ministers) and at home (the clearing of Karl Rove in the Valerie Plame leak investigation and the naming of Wall Street biggie Henry Paulson as treasury secretary) have given the president a bounce of as much as several points in some polls. Still, Bush clearly is in a tough spot, and Republicans are increasingly concerned that his lack of popularity may translate into the loss of one or both houses of Congress in the midterm elections this fall.

Invariably, the decline in any president's popularity can be traced to a multitude of causes. While the administration stoically blames Bush's swooning ratings on an unpopular-but-necessary Iraq War, other factors include a remarkably uneven economic expansion (job growth has been relatively mediocre, and real wages, as measured against inflation, have actually declined over the past two years), soaring gasoline prices, and a determinedly partisan governing style. No single event hurt the administration's reputation more, however, than Hurricane Katrina and its immediate aftermath. The images of refugees trapped in the New Orleans Superdome, a seemingly detached president, and a FEMA chief (who was clearly a crony appointment) apparently more concerned with his wardrobe than the destruction of a major U.S. city—combined with an appalling lack of preparation beforehand and inexplicably poor communication once the storm hit—all served to reinforce the general impression that the executive branch of the U.S. government was being managed incompetently.

In this article, Evan Thomas and Newsweek's *team of reporters in the field give a blow-by-blow account of what happened when the levees gave way, and how our government failed so miserably in its response.*

It's a standing joke among the president's top aides: Who gets to deliver the bad news? Warm and hearty in public, Bush can be cold and snappish in private, and aides sometimes cringe before the displeasure of the president of the United States, or, as he is known in West Wing jargon, POTUS. The bad news on this early morning, Tuesday, August 30, some twenty-four hours after Hurricane Katrina had ripped through New Orleans, was that the president would have to cut short his five-week vacation by a couple of days and return to Washington. The president's chief of staff, Andrew Card; his deputy chief of staff, Joe Hagin; his counselor, Dan Bartlett; and his spokesman, Scott McClellan, held a conference call to discuss the question of the president's early return and the delicate task of telling him. Hagin, it was decided, as senior aide on the ground, would do the deed.

The president did not growl this time. He had already decided to return to Washington and hold a meeting of his top advisers on the following day, Wednesday. This would give them a day to get back from their vacations and their staffs to work up some ideas about what to do in the aftermath of the storm. President Bush knew the storm and its consequences had been bad, but he didn't quite realize how bad.

The reality, say several aides who did not wish to be quoted because it might displease the president, did not really sink in until Thursday night. Some White House staffers were watching the evening news and thought the president needed to see the horrific reports coming out of New Orleans. Counselor Bartlett made up a DVD of the newscasts so Bush could see them in their entirety as he flew down to the Gulf Coast the next morning on Air Force One.

How this could be—how the president of the United States could have even less "situational awareness," as they say in the military, than the average American about the worst natural disaster in a century—is one of the more perplexing and troubling chapters in a story that, despite moments of heroism and acts of great generosity, ranks as a national disgrace.

President George W. Bush has always trusted his gut. He prides himself in ignoring the distracting chatter, the caterwauling of the media elites, the Washington political buzz machine. He has boasted that he doesn't read the papers. His doggedness is often admirable. It is easy for presidents to overreact to the noise around them.

But it is not clear what President Bush *does* read or watch, aside from the occasional biography and an hour or two of ESPN here and there. Bush can be petulant about dissent; he equates disagreement with disloyalty. After five years in office, he is surrounded largely by people who agree with him. Bush can ask tough questions, but it's mostly a one-way street. Most presidents keep a devil's advocate around. Lyndon Johnson had George Ball on Vietnam; President Ronald Reagan and Bush's father, George H. W. Bush, grudgingly listened to the arguments of Budget Director Richard Darman, who told them what they didn't wish to hear: that they would have to raise taxes. When Hurricane Katrina struck, it appears there was no one to tell President Bush the plain truth: that the state and local governments had been overwhelmed, that the Federal Emergency Management Agency (FEMA) was not up to the job, and that the military, the only institution with the resources to cope, couldn't act without a declaration from the president overriding all other authority.

The war in Iraq was a failure of intelligence. The government's response to Katrina—like the failure to anticipate that terrorists would fly into buildings on 9/11—was a failure of imagination. On Tuesday, within twenty-four hours of the storm's arrival, Bush needed to be able to imagine the scenes of disorder and misery that would, two days later, shock him when he watched the evening news. He needed to be able to see that New Orleans would spin into violence and chaos very quickly if the U.S. government did not take charge—and, in effect, send in the cavalry, which in this case probably meant sending in a brigade from a combat outfit, like the 82nd Airborne, based in Fort Bragg, North Carolina, and prepared to deploy anywhere in the world in eighteen hours.

Bush and his advisers in his "war cabinet" have always been action-oriented, "forward leaning," in the favorite phrase of Defense Secretary

Donald Rumsfeld. They dislike lawyers and sometimes brush aside legal-istic (and even sound constitutional) arguments. But this time "Rummy" opposed sending in active-duty troops as cops. Dick Cheney, who was vaca-tioning in Wyoming when the storm hit, characteristically kept his counsel on videoconferences; his private advice is not known.

Liberals will say they were indifferent to the plight of poor African Americans. It is true that Katrina laid bare society's massive neglect of its least fortunate. The inner thoughts and motivations of Bush and his top advisers are impossible to know for certain. Though it seems abstract at a time of such suffering, high-minded considerations about the balance of power between state and federal government were clearly at play. It's also possible that after at least four years of more or less constant crisis, Bush and his team are numb.

The failure of the government's response to Hurricane Katrina worked like a power blackout. Problems cascaded and compounded; each mistake made the next mistake worse. The foe in this battle was a monster; Katrina flattened the Gulf Coast with the strength of a vengeful god. But human beings, beginning with the elected officials of the City of New Orleans, failed to anticipate and react in time.

Congressional investigations will take months to sort out who is to blame. A *Newsweek* reconstruction of the government's response to the storm shows how Bush's leadership style and the bureaucratic culture combined to produce a disaster within a disaster.

Ray Nagin, the mayor of New Orleans, didn't want to evacuate. New Orleanians have a fatalistic streak; their joyful, jazz-blowing street funeral processions are legendary. After many near misses over the years since Hurricane Betsy flooded 20 percent of the city in 1965, longtime residents prefer to stay put. Nagin's eye had long been on commerce, not catas-trophe. A former executive at Cox Communications, he had come to office in 2002 to clear out the allegedly corrupt old guard and bring new business to the city, which has not prospered with New South metropolises like Atlanta. During Nagin's mayoral campaign, the promises were about jobs, not stronger floodwalls and levees.

But on Saturday night, as Katrina bore down on New Orleans, Nagin talked to Max Mayfield, head of the National Hurricane Center. "Max

Mayfield has scared me to death," Nagin told City Councilwoman Cynthia Morrell early Sunday morning. "If you're scared, I'm scared," responded Morrell, and the mandatory order went out to evacuate the city—about a day later than for most other cities and counties along the Gulf Coast.

As Katrina howled outside Monday morning and the windows of the Hyatt Hotel, where the mayor had set up his command post, began popping out, Nagin and his staff lay on the floor. Then came eerie silence. Morrell decided to go look at her district, including nearby Gentilly. Outside, Canal Street was dry. "Phew," Morrell told her driver, "that was close." But then, from the elevated highway, she began seeing neighborhoods under eight to fifteen feet of water. "Holy God," she thought to herself. Then she spotted her first dead body.

At dusk, on the ninth floor of city hall, the mayor and the city council had their first encounter with the federal government. A man in a blue FEMA windbreaker arrived to brief them on his helicopter flyover of the city. He seemed unfamiliar with the city's geography, but he did have a sense of urgency. "Water as far as the eye can see," he said. It was worse than Hurricanes Andrew in 1992 and Camille in 1969. "I need to call Washington," he said. "Do you have a conference-call line?" According to an aide to the mayor, he seemed a little taken aback when the answer was no. Long neglected in the city budget, communications within the New Orleans city government were poor, and eventually almost nonexistent when the batteries on the few old satellite phones died. The FEMA man found a phone, but he had trouble reaching senior officials in Washington. When he finally got someone on the line, the city officials kept hearing him say, "You don't understand, you don't understand."

Around New Orleans, three levees had overtopped or were broken. The city was doomed. There was no way the water could be stopped. But, incredibly, the seriousness of the situation did not really register, not only in Washington, but at the state emergency command post upriver in Baton Rouge. In a squat, drab cinder-block building in the state capital, full of TV monitors and maps, various state and federal officials tried to make sense of what had happened. "Nobody was saying it wasn't a catastrophe," Louisiana Senator Mary Landrieu told *Newsweek*. "We were saying, 'Thank you, God,' because the experts were telling the governor it could have been even worse."

Governor Kathleen Babineaux Blanco, a motherly but steely figure known by the nickname Queen Bee, knew that she needed help. But she wasn't quite sure what. At about 8:00 P.M., she spoke to Bush. "Mr. President," she said, "we need your help. We need everything you've got."

Bush, the governor later recalled, was reassuring. But the conversation was all a little vague. Blanco did not specifically ask for a massive intervention by the active-duty military. "She wouldn't know the 82nd Airborne from the Harlem Boys' Choir," said an official in the governor's office, who did not wish to be identified talking about his boss's conversations with the president. There are a number of steps Bush could have taken, short of a full-scale federal takeover, like ordering the military to take over the pitiful and (by now) largely broken emergency communications system throughout the region. But the president, who was in San Diego preparing to give a speech the next day on the war in Iraq, went to bed.

By the predawn hours, most state and federal officials finally realized that the 17th Street Canal levee had been breached, and that the city was in serious trouble. Bush was told at 5:00 A.M. Pacific Coast time and immediately decided to cut his vacation short. To his senior advisers, living in the insular presidential bubble, the mere act of lopping off a couple of presidential vacation days counts as a major event. They could see pitfalls in sending Bush to New Orleans immediately. His presence would create a security nightmare and get in the way of the relief effort. Bush blithely proceeded with the rest of his schedule for the day, accepting a gift guitar at one event and pretending to riff like Tom Cruise in *Risky Business*.

Bush might not have appeared so carefree if he had been able to see the fearful faces on some young police officers—the ones who actually showed up for roll call at the New Orleans Second District police headquarters that morning. The radio was reporting water nine feet deep at the corner of Napoleon and St. Charles streets. The looting and occasional shooting had begun. At two o'clock on the morning of the storm, only 82 of 120 cops had obeyed a summons to report for duty. Now the numbers were dwindling; within a day, only 28 or 30 officers would be left to save the stranded and fight the looters, recalled a sad and exhausted Captain Eddie Hosli, speaking to a *Newsweek* reporter last week. "One of my lieutenants told me, 'I was looking into the eyes of one of the officers and it was like looking into the eyes of a baby,'" Hosli recalled. "It was just terrible." (When the AWOL officers began trickling back to work last week, attracted in part by the promise of five expense-paid days in Las Vegas for all New Orleans cops, Hosli told them, "You've got your own demons to live with. I'm not going to judge you.")

At emergency headquarters in Baton Rouge, confusion raged. Though more than 100,000 of its residents had no way to get out of the city on their own, New Orleans had no real evacuation plan, save to tell people to go to the Superdome and wait for buses. On Tuesday, the state was rounding up buses; no, FEMA was; no, FEMA's buses would take too long to get there . . . and so on. On Tuesday afternoon, Governor Blanco took her second trip to the Superdome and was shocked by the rising tide of desperation there. There didn't seem to be nearly enough buses, boats, or helicopters.

Early Wednesday morning, Blanco tried to call Bush. She was transferred around the White House for a while until she ended up on the phone with Fran Townsend, the president's Homeland Security adviser, who tried to reassure her but did not have many specifics. Hours later, Blanco called back and insisted on speaking to the president. When he came on the line, the governor recalled, "I just asked him for help, 'whatever you have.'" She asked for 40,000 troops. "I just pulled a number out of the sky," she later told *Newsweek*.

The Pentagon was not sitting idly. By Tuesday morning (and even before the storm) the military was moving supplies, ships, boats, helicopters, and troops toward the Gulf Coast. But, ironically, the scale of the effort slowed it. TV viewers had difficulty understanding why TV crews seemed to move in and out of New Orleans while the military was nowhere to be seen. But a TV crew is five people in an RV. Before the military can send in convoys of trucks, it has to clear broken and flooded highways. The military took over the shattered New Orleans airport for emergency airlifts, but special teams of Air Force operators had to be sent in to make it ready. By the week after the storm, the military had mobilized some 70,000 troops and hundreds of helicopters—but it took at least two days and usually four and five to get them into the disaster area. Looters and well-armed gangs, like TV crews, moved faster.

In the inner councils of the Bush administration, there was some talk of gingerly pushing aside the overwhelmed "first responders," the state and local emergency forces, and sending in active-duty troops. But under an 1868 law, federal troops are not allowed to get involved in local law enforcement. The president, it's true, could have invoked the Insurrections Act, the so-called Riot Act. But Rumsfeld's aides say the secretary of defense was leery of sending in nineteen-year-old soldiers trained to shoot people in combat to play policemen in an American city, and he believed that National Guardsmen trained as MPs were on the way.

The one federal agency that is supposed to handle disasters—FEMA—was dysfunctional. On Wednesday morning, Senator Landrieu was standing outside the chaotic Superdome and asked to borrow a FEMA official's phone to call her office in Washington. "It didn't work," she told *Newsweek*. "I thought to myself, 'This isn't going to be pretty.'" Once a kind of petty-cash drawer for congressmen to quickly hand out aid after floods and storms, FEMA had improved in the 1990s in the Clinton administration. But it became a victim of the Iron Law of Unintended Consequences. After 9/11 raised the profile of disaster response, FEMA was folded into the sprawling Department of Homeland Security and effectively weakened. FEMA's boss, Bush's close friend Joe Allbaugh, quit when he lost his cabinet seat. (Now a consultant, Allbaugh was down on the Gulf Coast last week looking for contracts for his private clients.) Allbaugh replaced himself with his college buddy Mike Brown, whose last private-sector job (omitted from his official résumé) had been supervising horse-show judges for the International Arabian Horse Association. After praising Brown ("Brownie, you're doing a heck of job"), Bush last week removed him from honchoing the Katrina relief operation. He was replaced by Coast Guard Vice Admiral Thad Allen. The Coast Guard was one agency that performed well, rescuing thousands.

Bad news rarely flows up in bureaucracies. For most of those first few days, Bush was hearing what a good job the Feds were doing. Bush likes "metrics," numbers to measure performance, so the bureaucrats gave him reassuring statistics. At a press availability on Wednesday, Bush duly rattled them off: There were 400 trucks transporting 5.4 million meals and 13.4 million liters of water along with 3.4 million pounds of ice. Yet it was obvious to anyone watching TV that New Orleans had turned into a Third World hellhole.

The denial and the frustration finally collided aboard Air Force One on Friday. As the president's plane sat on the tarmac at New Orleans airport, a confrontation occurred that was described by one participant as "as blunt as you can get without the Secret Service getting involved." Governor Blanco was there, along with various congressmen and senators and Mayor Nagin (who took advantage of the opportunity to take a shower aboard the plane). One by one, the lawmakers listed their grievances as Bush listened. Representative Bobby Jindal, whose district encompasses New Orleans, told of a sheriff who had called FEMA for assistance. According to Jindal, the sheriff was told to e-mail his request, "and the guy was sitting in a district underwater and with no electricity," Jindal said, incredulously. "How does that make any sense?" Jindal later told *Newsweek* that "almost everybody" around the conference table had a similar story about how the federal response "just wasn't working." With each tale, "the president just shook his head, as if he couldn't believe what he was hearing," says Jindal, a conservative Republican and Bush appointee who lost a close race to Blanco. Repeatedly, the president turned to his aides and said, "Fix it."

According to Senator David Vitter, a Republican ally of Bush's, the meeting came to a head when Mayor Nagin blew up during a fraught discussion of "who's in charge?" Nagin slammed his hand down on the table and told Bush, "We just need to cut through this and do what it takes to have a more controlled command structure. If that means federalizing it, let's do it."

A debate over "federalizing" the National Guard had been rattling in Washington for the previous three days. Normally, the Guard is under the control of the state governor, but the Feds can take over—if the governor asks them to. Nagin suggested that Lieutenant General Russel Honore, the Pentagon's on-scene commander, be put in charge. According to Senator Vitter, Bush turned to Governor Blanco and said, "Well, what do you think of that, Governor?" Blanco told Bush, "I'd rather talk to you about that privately." To which Nagin responded, "Well, why don't you do that now?"

The meeting broke up. Bush and Blanco disappeared to talk. More than a week later, there was still no agreement. Blanco didn't want to give up her authority, and Bush didn't press. Jindal suggested that Bush appoint Colin Powell as a kind of relief czar, and Bush replied, "I'll take that into consideration." Bush does not like to fire people. He told Homeland

Security Secretary Michael Chertoff to go down to Louisiana and sort out the various problems. A day later FEMA's Brown was on his way back to Washington.

Late last week, Bush was, by some accounts, down and angry. But another Bush aide described the atmosphere inside the White House as "strangely surreal and almost detached." At one meeting described by this insider, officials were oddly self-congratulatory, perhaps in an effort to buck each other up. Life inside a bunker can be strange, especially in defeat.

High Noon in Crawford

Evgenia Peretz

Vanity Fair | November 2005

President Bush's ranch outside Crawford, Texas, has always been both a refuge and a statement of his Texas roots. But in the summer of 2005, as he made his forty-ninth trip to the ranch since being elected to the nation's highest office, his retreat was invaded by an unlikely visitor: Cindy Sheehan, who had become the country's most visible opponent of the Iraq War after losing her son in the conflict. While the president settled in for a five-week vacation—the longest for any chief executive in thirty-six years—Sheehan set up camp outside the ranch, demanding to speak with him personally. That meeting never happened, but "Camp Casey" quickly morphed into a stronghold of antiwar protestors and visiting media. In this piece, Vanity Fair *writer Evgenia Peretz travels to the plains of Crawford to report on the scene.*

When the 101-degree Crawford heat scorches the prairie, the dust blows through the sagebrush like a tornado, and fire ants attack your ankles like the Devil's minions, you won't see George Bush flinch. He's too busy beating the hell out of the underbrush, not caring at all whether he soils his work shirts. He doesn't talk fancy, but puts things "in English, or Texan." That's why he vowed to get Osama "dead or alive." His folks aren't

"Washington types," but the guys "down at the Coffee Station," Crawford's one tiny diner. You may have even seen him there on TV, shooting the breeze with them—his trucker and farmer buddies—telling the owner, Nick Spanos, to fire up the grill and make him a cheeseburger.

Like Ronald Reagan and Lyndon Johnson before him, Bush has been impressively successful at packaging himself as that American archetype of honesty, courage, and unshakable conviction: the cowboy. The plan to become one was hatched in the late nineties, when the Connecticut-born Texas governor, who attended Andover and Yale, worked with his close adviser, Karl Rove, to prepare a run for the presidency. The first thing Bush needed was a ranch. In 1999, he picked one, a 1,600-acre spread in Crawford, current population 705, a "dry" town with one blinking traffic light. It was one of the most conservative corners in the country, overflowing with true believers, who would turn every available wall into a Bush photo shrine and tolerate no dissenters. He'd spend roughly 20 percent of his presidency there—more than any modern president has been on vacation—so the press would get a steady diet of him in his cowboy hat, walking tall down dusty roads.

For almost five years, the plan worked—until one mother from Vacaville, California, Cindy Sheehan, camped outside his ranch for most of the month of August, demanding a face-to-face meeting about why we went to war in Iraq and why her son Casey had to die there, a month and a half before his twenty-fifth birthday. Her astonishing presence, in addition to catalyzing a nascent antiwar movement, changed the meaning of Crawford—from Bush's cowboy backdrop to the walled-off vacation compound of an out-of-touch president. Then, after ignoring Cindy, he ignored Katrina. As he squeezed out his last vacation days, a major American city drowned.

The hotbed of Bush delirium extends to Waco, the small city adjacent to Crawford, still synonymous with the 1993 Branch Davidian disaster, in which David Koresh's band of arms-hoarding religious extremists went up in flames after a fifty-one-day standoff with the FBI and the Bureau of Alcohol, Tobacco and Firearms. Within minutes of meeting a visitor to their city, Wacoans let you know that the Branch Davidians were actually fifteen miles outside of Waco—which is true. That said, the cultural center of Waco is Baylor University, a Baptist institution where, until 1996, students were not allowed to dance. To this day, women are required to cover their upper arms at the gym, because, as the girl at the front desk warns, "sleeveless shirts lead to sports bras."

When Bush was governor, Baylor president (now chancellor) Robert B. Sloan Jr. made his case that Baylor was a perfect fit for Bush's presidential library, which many Wacoans see as the best way to remove the Branch Davidian stigma. "We commented about the world of higher education and [how] the political, the majoritarian view in higher education tends not to be sympathetic to his own political outlook," says Sloan over lunch at Waco's Ridgewood Country Club. In his ten years as president, Sloan has sought to strengthen the spiritual backbone of Baylor, by demanding that its students and faculty be more devoted to faith, and by fortifying its position in the culture war. When a gay student came out of the closet, for example, his scholarship was quickly revoked. At Baylor, Sloan explains, "You couldn't advocate certain lifestyles. You couldn't advocate pedophilia or bigamy"; in contrast, he seems to be implying, to other universities, where multiple spouses and sex between adults and children are encouraged.

Not all true believers are so reasonable. Consider Bill Johnson, sixty-three, who owns the Yellow Rose, Crawford's largest gift shop. "This is God's store," says Johnson, an eerily soft-spoken, intense reed of a man with carefully parted sandy hair, a deep tan, and piercing green eyes. Outside the Yellow Rose, visitors are greeted by two giant tablets bearing the Ten Commandments and a replica of the Liberty Bell. Inside, one is greeted by a cornucopia of stuffed real tigers and bears, assorted crosses, old wagon wheels, and, mostly, Bush souvenirs: countless images of Dubya in military gear, Dubya with the Bible, Dubya flanked by eagles, Dubya bobbleheads, life-size Dubya cardboard cutouts, Western White House shot glasses—plus a sign that reads, HITLER, STALIN, CASTRO, AND QADDAFI SUPPORTED GUN CONTROL.

"Saddam Hussein—he disarmed his enemies so he could kill them," says Johnson, explaining that, although everyone has a right to his own opinion, Americans who support gun control are no different from genocidal dictators. "That's pretty much the way us folks feel about it."

Just as his store is God's store, the war in Iraq, Johnson insists, is God's war. "In the Bible, it says if you don't protect your family you're worse than an infidel," says Johnson. Jesus the pacifist needs to be seen in context, he explains. "The same Jesus that turned the other cheek is the same guy that . . . ran out the money changers. He whipped them." The Bible also holds precious wisdom about how to treat people here at home, Johnson believes. Welfare, for instance, violates the message of the Good Book that those who don't work deserve to die. "In Second Thessalonians, it says, 'That the man shall not work, he should not eat.' Just let him starve," says Johnson.

Other true believers are simply basking in the glow of having the coolest guy in the world live in town. On this day in early August, to coincide with the start of Bush's month off, Waco and Crawford society have gathered at Baylor for one of the summer's hottest tickets—a photo exhibition called "Presidential Retreat." There's Tommye Lou Davis, the stunning, extremely well-preserved right-hand woman to Robert Sloan. She's in a cream pantsuit accented with a George Bush scarf fanned out across her blouse like a bib. Over there, taking in a picture of Laura and George, is Shirley Westerfield, who became Crawford's social queen when Bush danced with her at the inaugural ball she threw for him.

"She's so *pretty*," says Westerfield, a peppy chatterbox, wearing a button-down shirt with a pattern of ferns, as she moves on to the other cheerful images on display here tonight: George giving the thumbs-up; George with his dog Barney; George with his girls; George with his top Cabinet members, enjoying a walk down Prairie Chapel Road; George charming the pants off a black woman getting a house from Habitat for Humanity. Should sixty pictures not be enough, the show is followed by a montage film of more of the same, set to music. Over the movie-soundtrack crescendos and heroic cymbal crashing, one detects "ahs" and even sniffles in the audience. "I got chills," says Westerfield, regaining her composure as she files out of the auditorium.

"He's one of us," she enthuses, over a barbecue-on-paper dinner. "I just like him. He reminds me of my father. You know—blue jeans, 'Let's get in the truck.'" His accomplishments as president—even his war in Iraq—are not only beside the point but barely on the radar. "I don't think about [the war], because I have about five or six girlfriends that I kind of stay in touch with, and we're not talking about the war when we get together."

*   *   *   *   *

Friendly and hospitable as most locals are, they can quickly turn into a lynch mob when their man is criticized, as W. Leon Smith, fifty-two, the editor of *The Lone Star Iconoclast*, discovered. Hardly your fire-breathing liberal, Smith endorsed Bush in 2000 and, in addition to editing the paper, works, unpaid, as the mayor of Clifton, a small town near Crawford.

"We monitored his first term," says Smith, a rather sober-looking grandfather type, sitting back in his decrepit office, where parts of the ceiling are being held up by cardboard and duct tape. "And at some point we needed to make a decision on who we were going to endorse, and the cards kept coming up 'not Bush.'" He and his senior staff members, Don Fisher and Nathan Diebenow, fretted over the endorsement. "I lay there some nights staring at the ceiling, thinking about what we should do," recalls Fisher. In the end, he says, "I don't think we could do anything else in all conscience."

The September 29, 2004, editorial endorsing John Kerry was a dispassionate account of how Bush had failed on a number of issues—stem-cell research, his plans for Social Security, the economy, the debt. But the local reaction was near hysteria. Letters to the editor would not suffice. The paper lost half its subscribers and most of its advertisers. Businesses in Crawford refused to sell it. "There was an active boycott put into place," says Smith, "and [shopkeepers and advertisers] have been told they will be boycotted if they support us."

It didn't stop there. Diebenow received phone calls demanding, "Are you a Christian?" (In fact, his father is a local pastor.) "We had e-mails saying, 'We hope you die,'" says Fisher. "Literally, 'We hope you die.'" One man came by the office to say that he and his buddies were going to "run you out of town." Two college students who were covering a local festival for the paper were denied admittance and were told that their names were on a list, and to wait right there so the sheriff could be summoned. Should the editors attempt to go into the Coffee Station, "you [would] have to carry your six-guns and go down, like *High Noon*," says Diebenow. "It really wouldn't surprise us if we were served the door instead of a hamburger."

"If anyone thought that the opinion of three guys in central Texas was going to sway this election one way or another, that person needs to get out more, OK?" says Fisher, able to laugh about what happened. Mainly, the three men are profoundly disappointed. "The last defense, the last defiance, that you have is your voice," Fisher says. "When you're lying helpless and injured on your deathbed, so long as you have your voice, the thing is not over."

For the true believers, handling the White House press corps—those neurotic liberal show-offs who descend on their turf for a total of about two months a year—requires a bit more finesse than hate mail and death threats. The press spend their days in the Crawford Middle School gym, sitting in a forced vigil on folding chairs at cafeteria tables beneath basketball hoops. By noon, they've usually clocked 3,000 calories, thanks to a constantly replenished feeding trough of double-smoked bacon, barbecue, and chicken-fried steak provided by local restaurants. In spite of all the food they get to eat, they are a bunch of whiners, say the true believers. They whine about the heat, they whine about the crickets, they whine about how there's nothing to do.

"I hear a lot of complaints," says Westerfield, who, as part of her volunteer work for the president, picks up his staff and the press corps from the airport and takes them to their hotels in Waco. "Especially when they're right off the plane. They're all busy, 'filing their reports.' I just keep quiet."

Locals feel free to remind the press how out of touch and wrong they are—particularly when the reporters air their opinions in public, like at restaurants. CBS's Mark Knoller found this out after he complained to his dinner partners about the security precautions now taken at airports. A fellow diner overhearing the conversation "felt my remarks were out of line," says Knoller, "and he let me know it." Some locals think such conversations are designed for them. "I was at a restaurant," says one Baylor grad, "and they were having a very grand, esoteric conversation—for my benefit. About *cancer research*," she says, rolling her eyes. Some true believers will speak up even when a reporter is quietly minding his own business. When the *New York Times*'s David E. Sanger dropped by Starbucks to get his paper, a fellow customer asked him why on earth he'd want to read that liberal nonsense. Sanger admitted that he not only reads it every day but also works there. The man advised Sanger that he ought to go home and set them straight. (For the record, Sanger's ancestors are from Waco and founded a department store there.)

Nick Spanos, whose Coffee Station is festooned with Bush cutouts and

Clinton-bashing cartoons, doesn't hesitate to let it be known he thinks journalists are idiots. "We have reporters running out of our ears," says Spanos,
his hand on a second, special cell phone he keeps on his belt, in the unlikely
event that he needs to be alerted about the arrival of a certain someone.
"*Newsweek* did a deal on where the president's money goes. And one of the
parts of the interview was: Does he pay for his cheeseburgers? *Yes*. And does
he leave a tip? This and that. Just pretty much stupid questions, you know?"

The press have also been reminded that they are considered sordid and
debauched. When they were first working out of the elementary-school
gym, unhappy parents, afraid that child-molesters might be in the group,
demanded that a large, steel door be erected between the press and the
kids. "We are the unknown . . . sort of sleazy element," says Julie Mason,
White House correspondent for the *Houston Chronicle*. "I think they feel
we're there to attack their president. . . . We're sort of these troublemakers
who make the president unhappy."

As Bush sees it, by bringing the press corps to Crawford, he's introducing
them to real America. In 2003 his conviction that the press is out of touch
with the country was articulated in an interchange at the summer barbecue at the ranch. One reporter asked him, "How do you then know what
the public thinks?" to which he responded, "You're making a huge assumption—that *you* represent what the public thinks."

"He thinks we're effete and elitist and ridiculous and consumed with
garbage," Mason says. "He calls it 'goo-goo journalism' when you ask him
something introspective, like that question about had he ever made a mistake. We're all a bunch of theater critics. . . . He'll often say, as we're
heading there, he'll say something along the lines of 'We're heading to
Texas and you're all better for it.'"

On press visits to the ranch, Bush enjoys torturing the journalists physically. He'll drive them around in his John Deere Gator, or load them into
one of his fleet of pickups like cattle, so they can feel him attack the rugged
terrain. "When you're in the back of his pickup truck and he starts
bouncing around on purpose just to watch you sort of flail in the back,"
says John King, CNN's chief national correspondent, "I think he's just
trying to see if he can ditch anybody."

According to NBC's David Gregory, whom Bush publicly ridiculed for asking Jacques Chirac a question in French, "He loves the idea that it really sort of tweaks all of us—you know, the white-wine-swilling, beach-loving East Coast elitist press corps, who would just be dying to spend time on Nantucket instead of Crawford. The fact that it puts us through our paces," says Gregory, "I think he enjoys that even more."

Bush's instinct to out-tough the press corps is so ingrained that once, when standing in front of reporters at a news conference in 106-degree heat, he said, "We've got to get in before we have a heatstroke," only to quickly correct himself: "before *you* have a heatstroke." That Sanger (a Jew from the *Times*, of all things) has Texas roots perplexes Bush. "It may not quite fit with his image of *New York Times* reporters," says Sanger, "as a bunch of Ivy League East Coasters who have little understanding of his Texas world."

The fact that they're on location doesn't mean the press can expect anything like candor. Most of the ranch visits are "off the record," and Bush makes it clear that he's not there to discuss policy. Walking tours are like "boot camp," says Gregory. "He moves so quickly, and you can tell he doesn't really want to talk about substance, so he ends up giving you this kind of Audubon Society tour of his property."

"They tell you nothing and then they slam the door," says Jean-Louis Doublet, from Agence France-Presse, over dinner at El Siete Mares, a Waco seafood restaurant. White House reporters tempted to criticize Bush do so at their own risk, Doublet explains. "Any journalist covering the White House, if they write a story saying they're a bunch of liars . . . he would do it once and he'd be gone. He'd be an outcast." Then again, feeling outcast is not uncommon among White House reporters. "This administration is so tight-lipped," says Jessica Yellin, a rising star at ABC News, "that I can't imagine the reporters who are 'frozen out' get that much less information than the rest of us."

They're left with exactly what Bush wants to give them—endless shots of him strutting around in his cowboy hat, blue jeans, short-sleeved work shirts, and question-and-answer sessions in which he's leaning on a fence rail. In the summer of 2004, the other reporters envied the AP's Scott Lindlaw when he got invited to the ranch for a one-on-one with Bush—even though his dispatch was nothing more than a play-by-play description of Bush on his mountain bike, climaxing in the president shrugging off a crash. Lindlaw noted that Bush's heart rate is in the range of Lance

Armstrong's. The *New York Times*'s Elisabeth Bumiller has devoted several columns to the president's exercise regimen, and has chronicled his problematic knee. Other Crawford dispatches, such as those from Judy Keen at *USA Today*, read like resort pamphlets. "That natural ambience is what the Bushes love so much about their ranch," Keen writes with Laurence McQuillan in one of her exclusives. "The only sounds are the chatter of birds and the murmur of the breeze through the leaves of the live oak and cedar elm trees. The 'Texas White House' is where the Bushes find peace and solitude." Meanwhile, at the Crawford Middle School, television correspondents deliver their "stand-ups" strategically placed in front of bales of hay or tractors, giving viewers the impression that they're on the ranch, because, as one cameraman explains, the executives back East love the whole ranch thing.

It has been left to Cindy Sheehan to expose the hollowness of Bush's cowboy populism. Far from the treasonous left-wing crackpot she has been painted to be by many of the right-wing pundits, Sheehan was a Catholic youth minister and until recently worked in the Napa County Health and Human Services Agency. She passed on her strong Catholic beliefs and family values to her son Casey. He was an altar boy for ten years and an Eagle Scout, and wanted to remain a virgin until he got married.

Casey enlisted in the army in 2000, with the dream of becoming a chaplain's assistant. Instead, he became a mechanic. "His recruiter promised him that even if there was a war that he wouldn't see combat because he scored so high on the military competency test," recalls Sheehan one week into her vigil, quickly eating a McDonald's breakfast in a dingy van that's swarming with flies. "He said, 'I'll only be there in support, Mom. My sergeant said you don't have to worry about me.'" Though he was skeptical about the Iraq war, says Sheehan, he went with an unwavering sense of service. "He said, 'Mom, I wish I didn't have to go to the war, but I have to. It's my duty. It's what I've trained for.'" He died on April 4, 2004, less than a month into his tour of duty. There had been intense fighting that night, and help was needed to bring wounded soldiers to safety. Although mechanics do not usually go on such missions, resources were thin, and Casey volunteered. When Cindy saw a burning Humvee on CNN the next morning, she knew somehow that her son was dead.

Together with others who'd lost loved ones in Iraq, Sheehan met with the president shortly after her son's death. The meeting left her without a shred of respect for him. Bush, who had prided himself on his compassion for military families, began the meeting, Sheehan recalls, by asking, "Who are we honoring here?" He didn't know Casey's name. He didn't look at Cindy's pictures of him. He called Cindy "Mom" throughout.

After processing that meeting Sheehan made it her mission to hold Bush's feet to the fire for a good explanation as to why the country went to war. Her quest, as she puts it, is "to make meaning out of Casey's death." In the process, she has seen her life crumble further. She lost her job due to absences. She and her husband, Pat, split up, owing in part to the difference in the way they handled Casey's death. He wanted to distract himself, she wanted to immerse herself. None of this has dimmed her determination. "I'm not afraid of anything anymore," says Sheehan. "I've already had the worst thing happen to me."

Her decision to come to Crawford was not some grand stunt to become a media star. As she tells it, it was a spur-of-the-moment decision she made with her sister, Dede Miller. Here on Prairie Chapel Road, usually a quiet spot, where a truck might drive by every ten minutes or so, Sheehan finds herself at the center of a surreal scene that's in turn exciting, heartrending, infuriating, and silly. Supporters have arrived from all over the country. Other military families have come to speak out, some who have lost children, and some who are terrified that they might any day. A few left-wing nuts roam from pup tent to pup tent, muttering about how the government was responsible for 9/11.

Over the course of the past week, Sheehan has stood in lightning storms, slept in ditches, fought fevers, and endured attacks of fire ants in the middle of the night, only to watch her character get slimed on TV day after day. But support has come from unlikely places. Republican senators Chuck Hagel, from Nebraska, and George Allen, from Virginia, both publicly announced that they believed the president should meet with Sheehan. Dozens of reporters are clamoring for just a few minutes with her. "It's a miracle," she says.

But she also harbors bitterness toward the national networks and newspapers whose reporters are now swarming around her. "I believe the media did not do its job in the run-up to the war," Sheehan says. "They did not ask the hard questions. They didn't do the investigating. I told that to CNN anchor Anderson Cooper last night, and he said, 'Well, there are only so many questions you can ask.' . . . Yesterday, a CNN producer told me I had really good timing because it was a slow news week. I said, 'Tell that to the thirty families of the Marines who died last week.'" A few minutes later, Sheehan stands before the media at a press conference and tells them she is doing the job they should have done.

This sudden jolt of ugly reality into Bush's conservative comfort zone naturally has driven the true believers bonkers. Pickup trucks routinely spray Sheehan and her supporters with mud and make sport of coming close to running them over. A local resident, Larry Northern, mowed down hundreds of crosses Sheehan and her supporters had put up, the names of fallen soldiers affixed to them. One shopkeeper remarked that she'd like to release skunks onto the whole group. Plots of land Sheehan's group had been using, which had been county property, were suddenly handed over to Crawford residents, making the protesters trespassers.

But on August 16 one Crawford landowner, Fred Mattlage, stepped in to help, by offering up his property for them to continue their protest. With this, another Crawford was put in the spotlight. This Crawford sees the growing divide between rich and poor in their community and a president who is responsible for it and accountable to no one.

One such Crawford citizen is Larry Mattlage, Fred's distant cousin, whose family has been in Crawford since 1887 and who owns a farm three-quarters of a mile from Bush's property. Mattlage is the real Crawford cowboy—with land, goats, sheep, a white beard, legs that stretch a mile—and he believes that Bush has done nothing for his beloved town except exploit it. First off, the idea that Bush is some kind of "rancher" just makes him laugh.

"He don't know dirt," says Mattlage, who is friendly with Bush's ranch foreman, Robert Blossman. All that brush clearing, Mattlage says, "is for show. It's not necessary. . . . [Brush] is where the birds live. That's birdseed. That's deer food. That's cow food. . . . [Cedar] makes cedar posts. If they're grown properly, they make a good post that will last forever." Bush's ignorance on the matter doesn't surprise him. "You don't move into these boonies and really understand the land, you know?" says Mattlage. "[They] got a lot of money, and they got access to a lot of machinery and a lot of bulldozers and a lot of destructive equipment, and before you know it, they can screw up something so damn bad. . . . A rich man with a bulldozer is a dangerous thing!" Furthermore, the notion that Bush is "friends" with anyone in Crawford is hogwash. "He's a visitor to this group of people," says Mattlage. "Nobody knows anything about him. I know *you* better than I know my neighbor."

The history of Crawford, explains Mattlage as he takes you in his white Chevy four-by-four down Prairie Chapel Road, began in the mid-nineteenth century when a bunch of German families settled and became farmers. He knows the ins and outs—which Mattlage married which Engelbrecht, which Westerfield is buried in which cemetery—and he loves every piece. He also loved the way of life he knew until Bush became his neighbor. "These people," he says, nodding toward the farms, "they like to lay their corn, their wheat. . . . Before George Bush, we knew everyone on the road. We knew who stopped on the road. We could go where we wanted."

One of Mattlage's favorite spots in Crawford is the old schoolhouse down on Prairie Chapel Road, which happens to be close to Bush's ranch. But as he approaches Mattlage Road, named after a relative, he's met by a large roadblock and an SUV. Mattlage comes to a stop. A young Secret Service man, his eyes hidden behind shades, gets out and approaches us. Mattlage rolls down the window.

"How you doing, sir?" says the young man, in Secret Service tones. Mattlage introduces himself and his visitors.

"One of the things that they're writing on is the history of this area," Mattlage says. "And there's a Prairie Chapel Schoolhouse that we would love to take a picture of, the historical markers. Anybody that can follow us there just for pictures?"

"Not while he's in town, sir."

"OK. Uh, is there anybody we can call to get permission to do that? I mean, we'll have the highway patrol follow us—"

"No. It pulls manpower away from what we already have allotted to. So, I mean, you know, it's a secure perimeter. If you want to wait, I hate to say this, but if you want to wait till September, when he goes back . . . I know that's not what you want to hear—"

"No."

"Well, these roads become open then, but until then it's a secure perimeter and it's like asking to get into the White House itself."

"Well, I understand that," says Mattlage, his frustration quietly growing.

"I know it's, this is, you know, this is your guys' home and we're visitors here, and I recognize that, and I do apologize for the inconvenience, but, uh, you know, it's, it's the job that we have to do."

Mattlage stares him in the eye, unimpressed. "That's why we're in the war, too."

"I'm sorry?" says the young man.

"That's why we're fighting the war—we're doing the job somebody wants us to do, right?"

"Yes, sir."

Mattlage pulls away and moves on. There's another road up ahead he wants to go down. This one, he explains, does not lead to Bush's ranch. When we get there, same thing.

"What the hell we got here now?" he says, getting more pissed off.

He spots Billy Westerfield, another neighbor, waiting in his pickup to get through, and he rolls down the window.

"What's going on, Billy?"

"He's riding his bicycle."

Mattlage pulls away. "Bush has got a whole ranch to ride a bicycle on. He closes the road so he can ride a *bicycle*. See, this is like the military. They took a quiet community and turned it into a base."

But it's not just that Crawford has become a police state that has Mattlage riled up. Under Bush, Mattlage has seen the country—and his own life—go downhill. For thirty years he worked in education while he ran his farm on the side. Nine years ago, when Bush was governor, Mattlage lost his job at Texas State Technical College, in Waco, where he was director of counseling. "He goes all over Texas talking about, 'We need technical education,'" says Mattlage, popping chewing tobacco into his mouth as he roams one of Crawford's cemeteries. "Hell, he's the one who cut it when we were doing it. He's the one who cut my job. He's why I don't have a job. Now he's my damned neighbor!"

Mattlage has other problems, too—a family member who is HIV-positive, addicted to cocaine, and can't get help. "To get him into treatment, I'd have to be a multimillionaire or I'd have to gamble and sell everything I

got, and he may not even get it. There's no places to go, there's no insurance for him to have, and the fact is nobody cares." Minute by minute, you
can see his Clint Eastwood stoicism giving way to rage. He gestures, fed up,
with his long arms in the direction of the ranch. "So we got a guy who can
ride a bicycle and do all the rest, but I can't get [my relative] into a drug-
treatment facility!"

Mattlage is not the only one frustrated. He sees similar struggles going
on with his friends and neighbors. "People want a job, they want a family,
they want a house, they want to work. They just want to make a living," he
says. He insists none of his neighbors would dare complain about Bush,
adding, "The things I'm telling you are just things that I know they would
say to me."

What about the true believers? "They're making money off T-shirts.
They're making money off hamburgers. Their ski lodge is open."

And Shirley Westerfield? Mattlage chuckles. "She got to dance with him
and she thinks she was dancing with Jesus Christ," he says.

If Mattlage is Crawford's real cowboy, then Robert Campbell, a thin, soft-
spoken, bespectacled, sixty-two-year-old African American, is its real president. A twenty-year air force veteran who built bases from the ground up
in Vietnam, Campbell moved from Philadelphia to Crawford in 1981 after
meeting his wife, who was from here. Upon arrival, he became the sole
maintenance worker in Crawford while he put himself through night
school, studying business administration. He followed that by earning an
advanced degree in social work from Baylor. After that, he went through
the seminary at Southern Methodist University. He's now pastor at two
churches, serving the African American communities of Crawford and
Waco. Until this past May, he was also Crawford's mayor, an unpaid position he had held since 1999.

In spite of his credentials and in spite of the enormous role he has
played in the community, he is someone the president has never shown an
interest in meeting—though foreign dignitaries, such as the president of
China and the prime minister of Australia, have. Which strikes Campbell
as odd, particularly since Bush boasted to the National Urban League Conference in July 2004 about his two black mayors, one in Washington and
one in Crawford.

"I thought, Well, that's amazing, since he hasn't had any contact with me since he's been in the White House," says Campbell, laughing as he sits in the pew of his tiny Perry Chapel United Methodist Church, his pressed yellow polo shirt tucked tidily into his jeans.

In Bush's years in Crawford, Campbell has seen the place go from a small, laid-back town where no one locked his door to an uneasy place of opportunism, where trees are being cut down to make room for shops. Car parts and home improvement projects sit in front yards and look as if they haven't been touched in years. Roofs are literally falling in. Mangy dogs roam free. Campbell can count on two hands the number of people in the African American community who have jobs. Bush has done nothing, he says. "We're his photo op."

Campbell has also seen political tension erupt when before there never was any to speak of. "Since Bush has been here, that's when political affiliation became an issue," he says. "Nobody ever worried about whether you were a Democrat or a Republican. It was a nonissue. Now it's the big thing."

Campbell knows whereof he speaks. After listening to John Kerry talk to the National Conference of Black Mayors, Campbell decided he liked what he had heard, and let it be known that he would vote for him. "That had a lot of people up in arms. They thought I had committed blasphemy because I said it publicly."

Campbell's decision had little to do with how Bush has treated Crawford. As a Vietnam veteran, he thought the war in Iraq was a mistake. "He's sending young men and young women off to war. His Cabinet and these other folks are backing it. I said, 'How many of them have children in the military? And how many of their children are going to go?'" says Campbell, whose nephew is now stationed in Germany and will soon go off to Iraq. "I've been there. I've spent five tours in Southeast Asia and Vietnam during the war. I said, 'Those people shoot real bullets, killing folks.'"

Though neighbors were enraged and he was dissed by councilmen, Campbell doesn't regret speaking up. "In church I say I believe the Lord made my shoulders broad enough and he gives me the strength to carry the load," he says. "I cannot stand in my pulpit and tell the members of my congregation what thus sayeth the Lord and how they are to live if I'm not willing to be bold enough to stand for my own convictions."

*   *   *   *   *

On the last weekend of August, marking the end of the president's vacation, the true believers and the skeptics came face-to-face when some 5,500 Sheehan supporters and 1,500 anti-Sheehan demonstrators descended on Crawford. In the 101-degree heat, the tiny town became a tinderbox for the most emotional showdown since the war began.

On one side is "Camp Casey," a giant tent located on Fred Mattlage's land, about a mile and a half from the president's ranch. For anyone who harbors a tinge of embarrassment from the peace-movement antics of the sixties, there is much here to poke fun at. The protesters, who come from Austin and San Antonio, Colorado, New York, California, and Massachusetts, are being shuttled in and out by "peace" vans provided by the Peace House, the local protest shack, which was all but defunct until Sheehan came along. Local volunteers haul around coolers of water and put out food—hamburger buns, but no hamburgers. Young people with piercings sit around tents, some playing guitars, some lazing about on top of one another. A few women are breast-feeding their sweating, unhappy babies. Some people are meditating amid the chaos. The government-was-behind-9/11 faction appears to be gaining ground. Folksinger Joan Baez, oddly clean and fresh among a crowd of the drenched and grimy, pours cold water onto the head of a young woman about to pass out. Without words, she shares lengthy embraces with whoever approaches her, including a hulking gay former marine who recently came out of the closet on Paula Zahn's show. Then there are the women of Codepink, the antiwar women's group, which is handling press. Wearing pink garments that look like they came off the racks at Barneys, they work their cell phones and BlackBerrys like Hollywood pros. As Al Sharpton and Sheehan head toward Casey's cross to kneel and pray—followed by dozens of cameras—the pink ladies become hysterical. "Media, get off the crosses! Off the crosses!" they yell, as if the crosses were not there for the media's benefit.

In a counterpoint to the silliness, more parents of fallen soldiers have joined Sheehan here, seeking answers to not just why we got into the war but why their children were put in situations they never should have seen—situations that led to their deaths. Bill Mitchell's son, Mike, a tank mechanic, had turned in all his equipment on April 3, 2004. He was one week away from going to Kuwait; two weeks from Germany; four months from his wedding day. The next day, when a group of soldiers was ambushed in Sadr City, Mike was called back to help rescue them. "Sergeant Deaton, the tank commander, said, 'Mitch, I need you to ride loader on the tank today,'" says Bill, holding the cross around his neck, in which he keeps some of Mike's ashes. "He said, 'Sarge, I'm with you.' So my son went into Sadr City that day manning a machine gun," something that was not emphasized in his training to be a mechanic.

Nadia McCaffrey, from Sunnyvale, California, never even thought her son, Patrick, who joined the National Guard after 9/11 as a way of serving his country, would have to leave the United States. "He asked if there's a war would he be deployed, because he has two children, and they told him no, you will be sent to Utah to watch a nuclear plant," recalls McCaffrey. But like about 37,000 other National Guard troops, her son was sent to Iraq, in March 2004, after just two months of boot camp. On June 22, out on a mission that likely involved a search for WMD, he was shot and killed by a group of Iraqi men he'd been training. "Patrick didn't have a chance, because he was carrying the radio," says McCaffrey. "The radio was 75 pounds. It was 125 degrees. People were dropping. Patrick was a combat lifesaver. He had evacuated two people that day by administering a saline IV. He should have been evacuated himself as well. That mission should have been called off, period." McCaffrey has repeatedly requested of the Pentagon that an autopsy of her son's body be done. None has been forthcoming.

On the anti-Sheehan side, made up of locals and people from the Sacramento-based group Move America Forward, the rage is equally palpable. Among the BUSH COUNTRY and SUPPORT THE TROOPS signs are those that read, HOW TO WRECK YOUR FAMILY IN 30 DAYS BY "BITCH IN THE DITCH" CINDY SHEEHAN. A group of teenage boys in the street yells, "Cindy, the fucking whore, get out!" Some of the prowar group have chosen a spot across the road from the original site of Sheehan's protest, which is still being maintained by a group of her supporters. As state troopers prevent them from crossing the street into each other's camp, the two groups hurl slogans across the road:

"George Bush!"

"War criminal!"

"The Rapture is coming!"

"Love your brother!"

At the end of Sunday morning's interfaith service at Camp Casey, in which clergy from Protestant, Catholic, Jewish, Buddhist, Muslim, and Unitarian groups have taken part, Rabbi Hillel Gamoran from Seattle tells the crowd that he will now lead them in Kaddish, the Jewish prayer for mourners. Just moments into it, a ferocious-looking local teenager, there with his buddy, rushes the group. "You're doing the work of Osama!" he yells, getting up in the faces of the clergy. His fists are about to fly when he is subdued by a couple of local cops.

Headquarters for the anti-Sheehan group is just outside the Yellow Rose gift shop. "We're making ground," says Bill Johnson, as he wanders rapturously around his tent, which is decorated with pictures of a muzzled Cindy Sheehan and happy Iraqi children. As at Camp Casey, small white crosses have been planted in the ground. "We got thirty crosses in one bunch and another forty coming down." Country musicians have been brought in for the day, but the music is drowned out each time a Bush supporter yanks the rope of the Yellow Rose's enormous Liberty Bell, which makes a sound that reverberates for blocks and shakes the pavement. "If you don't support George Bush, you're not supporting the troops!" yells one Waco woman over the din.

This side, too, has its share of parents in profound pain. Gregg Garvey, whose son Justin, an army sergeant with the 101st Airborne Division, was killed in July 2003 in Iraq, believes that Sheehan is trying to dishonor the troops, and he came to Crawford to set her straight. "I went up there and retrieved my son's cross from a ditch," says Garvey. "[Sheehan] made the comment that 'this country is not worth fighting or dying for.' Then why in the hell doesn't she take her protest thing and join her freedom fighters in Iraq and see how long it lasts over there?" In fact, what Sheehan said was that *Iraq* was not worth fighting for. The twisted words have been beaming from one right-wing media outlet to another.

By the end of the summer, Bush had driven past Sheehan only to go to and from a Republican fund-raising barbecue. He left Crawford on Monday, August 29—not to go to Louisiana and Mississippi, where a state of emergency had been declared three days earlier, but to Arizona, where he posed with John McCain and his birthday cake and tried to sell senior citizens on his Medicare proposal. On Tuesday, as New Orleans filled up with water, he went to Naval Air Station North Island, outside San Diego, where he messed around on a guitar with country singer Mark Wills. While conditions for about 25,000 citizens trapped in the New Orleans Superdome deteriorated into unimaginable filth, starvation, and death, and one million Gulf Coast residents found themselves homeless, Bush returned to Crawford for one more night.

It remains to be seen whether even the true believers will get all they want from Bush. Waco will likely not get its presidential library, as insiders say the president has all but decided to build his library at Southern Methodist University, in Dallas. He has been to Waco a total of six times, twice for summits at Baylor, twice to play golf, once to throw a pitch in the regional Little League game, and once for a photo op with Habitat for Humanity, which ended when Bush pinched his thumb between two boards and bled on the homeowner's new floor. As one local newspaper editor points out, "The name 'Waco' has never come out of his mouth."

What about Bill Johnson and his souvenir shop? Bush has never set foot in the Yellow Rose. But, like a doormat girlfriend, Johnson doesn't complain. Rather, he makes up lame excuses for Bush's absence. "He was going to come in here about three or four months ago, and it rained, so they couldn't get in the back door." He adds, weakly, that "the daughters have been in. And Arnie Schwartz." (That's Ari Fleischer.)

After his presidency, Bush will likely leave Shirley Westerfield and friends and buy a place in Dallas, which Laura has admitted she prefers. When Bush hangs up his cowboy hat, all that the Crawford residents will have left of him will be those souvenirs, photos, and cardboard cutouts—which, if you really think about it, was all they had in the first place.

Political Science: The Bush Administration's War on the Laboratory

Michael Specter

The New Yorker | March 13, 2006

The Bush political team has never met a subject it couldn't spin, and scientific matters have been no exception. The administration's most notorious scientific legacy is likely to be its resolute inaction in the face of growing evidence of a potential global warming crisis; White House policy makers have carefully censored any information coming from the EPA, NASA, and other agencies that might indicate that climate change is something to be concerned about—while continuing to echo the energy industry's line that "more study needs to be done" on the subject. An array of other issues have been spun in similar fashion, from mercury emissions of coal plants to the viability of existing stem cell lines to the effects of industrial activity on various forms of wildlife. President Bush's implicit endorsement of intelligent design (an unprovable concept favored by religious conservatives) as a viable alternative to the well-established theory of natural selection stands out as a singular triumph of politics over science. In short, as, New Yorker writer Michael Specter observes here, the president "appears to view science more as a political constituency than as an intellectual discipline or a way of life." (As an editorial update, it should be noted that the human papilloma virus vaccine mentioned at the start of this piece was approved by the FDA in the spring of 2006.)

On December 1 [2005], Merck & Company applied to the Food and Drug Administration for a license to sell a vaccine that it has developed to protect women against the human papillomavirus. HPV is the most common sexually transmitted disease in the United States; more than half of all Americans become infected at some point in their lives. The virus is also the primary cause of cervical cancer, which kills nearly five thousand American women every year and hundreds of thousands more in the developing world. There are at least a hundred strains of HPV, but just two are responsible for most of the cancer. Two others cause genital warts, which afflict millions of people. Merck's vaccine, designed to protect against those four strains, has been tested in thirteen countries, including the United

States. More than twelve thousand women between the ages of sixteen and twenty-six were monitored for an average of two years. The results were conclusive: twenty-one of the women who received a placebo during the trial developed the cellular abnormalities that are associated with cancer and other illnesses. Not one of those in the vaccinated group did. Another vaccine, which is being developed by GlaxoSmithKline, promises to be just as effective.

Even in the age of molecular medicine, such unqualified successes are rare. "This is a cancer vaccine, and an immensely effective one," the Nobel laureate David Baltimore, who has served for the past eight years as president of the California Institute of Technology, told me. "We should be proud and excited. It has the potential to save hundreds of thousands of lives every year."

The vaccine is now under review by the FDA and could be approved for use in the United States by June [2006]; what happens after that will depend largely on the Bush administration's Advisory Committee on Immunization Practices. The committee's recommendations are not binding, but most states rely on them in determining which vaccines a child must receive in order to attend public school. To prevent infection with HPV, and to minimize the risk of cervical cancer, girls would need inoculations before becoming sexually active. The average age of first intercourse in America is under seventeen; to insure the broadest possible coverage, the vaccines would have to be administered much earlier.

Vaccinations for contagious diseases like measles and mumps are required before a child can enter public school. That won't be the case with the HPV vaccine, however. The Bush administration, its allies on Capitol Hill, and the religious base of the Republican Party are opposed to mandatory HPV vaccinations. They prefer to rely on education programs that promote abstinence from sexual activity, and see the HPV vaccine as a threat to that policy. For years, conservatives have regarded the human papillomavirus as a kind of index of promiscuity. Many abstinence supporters argue that eliminating the threat of infection would only encourage teenagers to have sex. "I personally object to vaccinating children when they don't need vaccinations, particularly against a disease that is one hundred percent preventable with proper sexual behavior," Leslee J. Unruh, the founder and president of the Abstinence Clearinghouse, said. "Premarital sex is dangerous, even deadly. Let's not encourage it by vaccinating ten-year-olds so they think they're safe." Senator Tom Coburn, Republican of Oklahoma, a family physician and a prominent leader among those who believe that abortion should be illegal, has argued repeatedly in Congress that since condoms can fail, the nation should stop relying on them so heavily. In 2004, he made his position clear when he testified about his experience treating patients who have been infected with HPV: "Studies have indicated for years that promiscuity was associated with cervical cancer."

Bush administration health officials decline to discuss the vaccine while it is under consideration by the FDA. "I can't talk about that," Andrew Von Eschenbach said when I visited him at the National Cancer Institute, which he runs. "I would love to. But it just would not be appropriate." I had asked to speak to Von Eschenbach in his capacity as the acting commissioner of the Food and Drug Administration, a post that he has held since last fall, when his predecessor resigned suddenly. Von Eschenbach, a urological oncologist, is a friend of President Bush's from Texas, and spent twenty-five years at the University of Texas's M. D. Anderson Cancer Center. He is the first person in American history to oversee both an enormous federal bureaucracy that is responsible for discovering drugs and another, even larger agency that must approve those drugs.

Despite the official silence, the Bush administration has been relentless in its opposition to any drug, vaccine, or initiative that could be interpreted as lessening the risks associated with premarital sex. It has made every effort to diminish the use of condoms as a method of birth control in the United States and throughout the world. Government policy requires that one-third of HIV-prevention spending go to "abstinence until marriage" programs. Since George W. Bush became president, the United States has spent hundreds of millions of dollars on abstinence programs, and it has cut almost that much in aid to groups that support abortion and the use of condoms as a primary method of birth control. (Family planning organizations in the developing world are denied U.S. grants if they so much as discuss abortion with their clients.) The administration's opposition runs so deep that at one point federal health officials replaced pages from a National Cancer Institute Web site with information that suggested, without evidence, that there might be a correlation between abortion and breast cancer.

Several years ago, the Centers for Disease Control removed a fact sheet about condoms from its Web site; the sheet disappeared for more than a year, and, when it was replaced, instructions on how to use condoms had been supplanted by a message denigrating them. The CDC also removed a summary of studies that showed there was no increase in sexual activity among teenagers who had been taught about condoms. "They were the most horrific examples of manipulating science I have ever seen," a former senior official at the CDC told me. "Abstinence is the only thing that matters to this crowd. They have even brought people to Washington from Atlanta"—where the CDC is based—"just to lecture about the value of teaching abstinence. There were no scientific presentations, just speeches." He asked not to be identified because he is dependent on receiving government funds in his current job.

Nearly every group across the political spectrum supports abstinence as a first line of defense against sexually transmitted diseases as well as against unwanted pregnancies. But abstinence programs often fail. In one recent study, researchers at Columbia and Yale found that though virginity "pledge" programs helped many participants to delay sex, 88 percent of those who took such pledges and had sex before the end of the study did so before marriage. When it came to preventing sexually transmitted diseases, students in the programs fared no better than those in the control group. The study also found that students who promised to remain virgins were less likely to use contraception when they did have sex, and they were less likely to seek STD testing.

Two years ago, in one of the most contentious decisions in the history of the FDA, the agency rejected an application by Barr Pharmaceuticals to make the emergency contraceptive Plan B—commonly referred to as the morning-after pill—available over the counter, after the members of its scientific advisory committee voted, twenty-three to four, in favor of permitting the switch. Agency officials said that they did not have enough information about how easier availability of the drug would affect adolescent girls. Last year, the FDA again refused to approve the application, even after the company altered its proposal to address those concerns. The agency had never rejected a similar request against the advice of its scientific advisers and its own staff. "This just came from nowhere, and it was clearly not a decision that was made on behalf of women or families," Susan F. Wood told me. Wood, who was the director of the agency's Office of Women's Health at the time, quit in protest. "I felt there was no role—not just for me but for the people who have expertise. I lose a lot of battles; normally you go out and work to fight another day. But this time I just couldn't look in the mirror and live with myself." She was not the only scientist who felt that way: Frank Davidoff, the editor emeritus of the *Annals of Internal Medicine*, resigned as a consultant to one of the committees that voted to approve over-the-counter use of Plan B, saying that the agency had decided to place the pursuit of its moral agenda above the facts.

Religious conservatives are unapologetic; not only do they believe that mass use of an HPV vaccine or the availability of emergency contraception will encourage adolescents to engage in unacceptable sexual behavior, some have even stated that they would feel similarly about an HIV vaccine, if one became available. "We would have to look at that closely," Reginald Finger, an evangelical Christian and a former medical adviser to the conservative political organization Focus on the Family, said. "With any vaccine for HIV, disinhibition"—a medical term for the absence of fear—"would certainly be a factor, and it is something we will have to pay attention to with a great deal of care." Finger sits on the Centers for Disease Control's Immunization Committee, which makes those recommendations.

"I never thought that now, in the twenty-first century, we could have a debate about what to do with a vaccine that prevents cancer," David Baltimore said when we met in his office. Baltimore, a short, intense man, has spent much of his life studying the relationship between viruses and cancer. He stood up from the couch and crossed the room to his desk. "Politics plays a role in all these decisions, and so does belief," he said. "I have no problems with that. But this is religious zealotry masked as politics, and it runs against everything that I as a scientist believe in, that I have devoted my life to. We are talking about basic public health now. What moral precepts allow us to think that the risk of death is a price worth paying to encourage abstinence as the only approach to sex?"

Since the Enlightenment, scientific enterprise has been defined by an ethic of independent inquiry, and by reliance on data that can be observed, tested, analyzed, and repeated. The scientific method has come to shape our notion of progress and of modern life. Science largely dictated the political realities of the twentieth century. As Harold Varmus, the Nobel

Prize–winning former director of the National Institutes of Health, pointed out in a recent speech, science won the Second World War—not just with the atomic bomb but with radar, quinine, and the spectacular advances in health brought about by the use of penicillin and other antibiotics. In 1944, the engineer and entrepreneur Vannevar Bush, who oversaw military research during the war, was described on the cover of *Time* as "The General of Physics." The next year, as the war neared its end, he began to argue that if the United States was to retain its economic stability and military primacy the government would need to finance the basic research carried out at American universities.

The country has spent billions of dollars on research since then, and the investment has paid off. The United States became the most advanced nation in virtually every field of scientific endeavor, and today most researchers receive some form of federal funds—and are therefore subject to the government's political will. (Public funding reflects political realities. For 2006, President Bush proposed an increase in spending on scientific research, but 97 percent of the increase will apply to two areas: weapons development and space-exploration vehicles. This year, for the first time in thirty-six years, the budget for the National Institutes of Health, which doubled between 1998 and 2003, will be cut.)

In the past, political leaders and scientists of prominence didn't care who voted for whom: either you were good enough to do the job or you were not. (Unless, like the nuclear physicist Robert Oppenheimer, you were suspected of supporting Communists.) Vannevar Bush was a conservative who opposed the New Deal, and not quietly. Yet President Roosevelt didn't hesitate to appoint him, or to take his advice. In 1959, after Dwight Eisenhower created the position of science adviser, in the wake of Sputnik, the Harvard chemist George B. Kistiakowsky assumed the post. Jerome Wiesner, a Democrat who subsequently became president of the Massachusetts Institute of Technology, sat on the Science Advisory Committee— which met each month with Kistiakowsky and often with the president. When John F. Kennedy took office, Kistiakowsky and Wiesner simply switched roles. "In bringing scientists into the high councils of government, the presidential indifference to their politics and party affiliations reflected the belief that science and scientists were above politics," Daniel S. Greenberg wrote in *Science, Money, and Politics* (2001), his invaluable exploration of the relationship between those three elements of America's postwar success. "Scientists might consider themselves Republicans or Democrats, but, as politicians saw it, science was their true party affiliation—and scientists saw it that way, too."

During the early years of the Cold War, the country's scientific goals—winning the space race against the Russians, for instance, and eliminating deaths caused by infectious diseases like polio—were clear, so science and politics never seemed to clash. That began to change in 1964, when Barry Goldwater ran for president against Lyndon Johnson. Nearly a hundred thousand researchers, appalled by Goldwater's declared willingness to deploy nuclear weapons on the battlefield, formed a group called Scientists and Engineers for Johnson. Scientists grew more demonstrably political throughout the Vietnam War, and by 1973 Richard Nixon, outraged by academic opposition to the antiballistic-missile system and other administration programs, abolished the position of White House science adviser. (The job was reinstated by Gerald Ford, who also created the Office of Science and Technology Policy to advise the White House on scientific issues.)

If the nuclear age was difficult to understand or to accept, the molecular age has been even more so. As our knowledge about the genetic underpinnings of human life has deepened, the controversy surrounding much of the research has increased. The more we know about how human life develops, the more we seem to wonder when it truly begins. There is something decidedly unsettling about our ability to place genes from flounder into strawberries (to protect them from the cold), or to create clones of sheep, or to construct a puppy from a few cells of another dog's ear. Eventually, in all likelihood, we will be able to grow spare organs and store them in refrigerators to use as replacement parts when ours wear out. Despite the uncertainties, both George H. W. Bush and Bill Clinton supported the Human Genome Project, which identified the twenty thousand genes in our DNA and determined their chemical composition. Both invested heavily in the fundamental research that has followed.

From the start of his first term, George W. Bush seems to have been guided more by faith and ideology than by data in resolving scientific questions. He is hardly the only president to ignore the advice of federal scientists. To some degree, they all have. In 1998, for example, Clinton refused to lift a ban on federal funds for needle exchange—even after he was urged to do so by Harold Varmus, at the NIH, and Donna Shalala, his secretary of Health and Human Services. In siding with his drug czar, Barry McCaffrey, who said that it would send the wrong message to children, Clinton acknowledged that he was making the decision against the recommendation of his scientific advisers. Yet George Bush, unlike Clinton and many other presidents, appears to view science more as a political constituency than as an intellectual discipline or a way of life.

On issues ranging from population control to the state of the environment, and from how science is taught in the classroom to whether Iraq's research establishment was capable of producing weapons of mass destruction, the administration has repeatedly turned away from traditional avenues of scientific advice. In 2003, when the Environmental Protection Agency tried to loosen standards regulating mercury pollution, sections of the proposed rules were lifted directly from industry documents. Last year, the White House acknowledged that Philip A. Cooney, the administration official who once led the oil industry's efforts to prevent limits on greenhouse gases, had repeatedly altered government climate reports in order to minimize the relationship between such emissions and global warming. Over the protests of federal scientists, the administration has opened thousands of acres of pristine national forest to logging, supported drilling for oil in the Arctic National Wildlife Refuge, and weakened central provisions of the Endangered Species Act. In December, the EPA proposed new rules governing the Clean Air Act that ignore the advice of its own staff, the recommendation of the agency's scientific advisory committee, and evidence from thousands of recent studies.

In March, 2001, just after Bush took office, the administration withdrew American support for the Kyoto Protocol on climate change, saying that it would impose an unfair and unbearable financial burden on the U.S. economy. In the face of an overwhelming consensus that burning fossil fuels is a principal cause of global warming, 160 countries accepted new limits on their use. The United States, by far the world's most profligate consumer of energy, was one of only two industrialized nations to refuse. (Australia was the other.) At the time, Bush promised, "My Administration's climate-change policy will be science-based." Last year, despite pleas from hundreds of groups, and pressure from prominent allies like British Prime Minister Tony Blair, the administration declined to alter its policies, agreeing, at a G-8 summit in Scotland, only to open "a new dialogue" on the subject.

The Bush administration has worked tirelessly to control the speech and movements of American scientists. In 2004, the Department of Health and Human Services issued a policy forbidding researchers to lend their expertise to the World Health Organization (or to travel to international scientific conferences) without the department's permission. William R. Steiger, a special assistant to the secretary, told government scientists that if they wanted to act as consultants in meetings of the World Health Organization they would first have to agree to advocate U.S. policy. The practical implications were both chilling and farcical. That year, the department, saying that it needed to reduce the number of scientists attending international meetings, prevented more than 150 government researchers from traveling to the International AIDS Conference, which was held in Bangkok. Department officials said they wanted to save money; their decision came after the organizer of the conference refused a request by the United States to invite the evangelist Franklin Graham to give a speech promoting faith-based solutions to the AIDS epidemic. If an American scientist wants to attend a meeting at the Pan American Health Organization's office in Washington, just a fifteen-minute subway ride from the NIH campus, in Bethesda, Maryland, he must seek permission at least four weeks in advance.

In January, James Hansen, one of the government's most highly respected climate experts, said that the Bush administration has made several efforts to prevent him from speaking publicly since a recent lecture in which he called for the immediate reduction of greenhouse gases. "This Administration has tried to restrict the very elements of scientific success: free and open inquiry," said Margaret A. Hamburg, who was a commissioner of health in New York City under both David Dinkins and Rudolph Giuliani and worked in the Clinton administration as a senior health-policy adviser. "You can't do science without understanding that theories are public and views often clash. You resolve differences by experiments and research, not by toeing the line."

John H. Marburger, the president's science adviser, sees the restrictions more as a matter of good government than as an issue of free speech. "Many practices in government agencies have changed with the Administration," he told me. He also pointed out that when American scientists deliver papers at AIDS conferences and in other disciplines where social problems intersect with medical research, they are presenting not simply data but also, often, a point of view that should reflect U.S. policy. "This Administration is more management-oriented than others," he said. "In some cases, there has been a feeling that the ship could be run in a tighter fashion. I have no problem with that . . . I understand the need to impose more restrictive controls on things like travel to conferences which are not entirely technical. The Department of Health and Human Services is dealing with a lot of societal issues that are multidimensional—like AIDS." (It took President Bush nearly eight months to settle upon Marburger, a well-regarded physicist and a former director of the Brookhaven National Laboratory. Unlike his predecessors, he was given neither the customary title of assistant to the president nor office space in the White House.)

In the Bush administration, many types of scientific analysis and research are proscribed almost wholly on religious grounds. When the National Cancer Institute's director, Von Eschenbach, appeared at a highly technical conference on soft-tissue cancers in 2002, one of the slides he presented in his keynote address surprised many in the audience. It said simply, "We live in a country blessed by God."

On December 20 [2005], Federal District Judge John E. Jones III, a Republican who was appointed by Bush, issued a scathing decision against the Dover, Pennsylvania, school board, which had attempted to require that "intelligent design" be taught in science classes alongside the theory of evolution. Intelligent design is a school of thought that suggests that life is too complex to be ascribed to evolution and therefore that animals must have been created by a supernatural "designer." There is no evidence, no theory that could be interpreted as scientific proof. Judge Jones's ruling was not ambiguous, but opposition to Darwin remains pervasive, and schools in dozens of states still teach students about natural selection and biological evolution as if they were little more than educated guesses. President Bush has addressed intelligent design just once in public, saying that he believed "both sides ought to be properly taught." Activists who argue that educators should "teach the controversy" quickly seized on his deeply ambiguous words to bolster their cause. Even Marburger, who said that he was "extremely gratified" by the Dover decision, could not offer a fuller explanation of the president's position. "That was all he has said," Marburger noted. "It was a fairly cautious statement."

When matters involve religion and the boundaries of life, the president has never wavered. In 1998, Terri Schiavo's husband, Michael, asked that her feeding tube be removed, igniting a legal war with her parents that eventually turned into a national conflict. Last March, after the tube was removed for the third time, Congress passed an "emergency measure" that attempted to force the courts to review the Schiavo case and require that the feeding robe be reinserted. President Bush signed the bill, and when the Supreme Court—for the sixth time—declined to hear the case, he spoke out in favor of what he referred to as the "culture of life." (When Schiavo died, an autopsy supported her husband's contention that she was unaware of her condition and incapable of recovering. Within days, Jeb Bush, the governor of Florida, ordered a state prosecutor to investigate whether Schiavo's husband had purposely delayed calling an ambulance when she fell ill, in 1990. Bush produced no evidence, and his actions alarmed even his Republican allies. The investigation was quickly dropped.)

There are hundreds of advisory committees attached to scientific institutions in the United States. They are usually filled both by experts and by representatives of the public, and, while they do not make policy, they do oversee most decisions. Since President Bush took office, some of the most politically sensitive committees have been dissolved. Others have been transformed into platforms that the administration can use to pursue its social goals. When members of such boards do speak out against White House policies, they have even been removed. (In 2004, the White House dismissed Elizabeth Blackburn, a renowned cell biologist at the University of California at San Francisco, from the president's Council on Bioethics. Blackburn is a supporter of human embryonic stem-cell research. Diana Schaub, who teaches political science at Loyola College, in Baltimore, was then named to the committee. Schaub has compared the harvesting of stem cells to slavery, and once said in a speech, "Every embryo used for purposes of research is someone's blood relative.")

"I am very respectful of faith, belief, and any principled stance on abortion," Steven Hyman, the provost of Harvard University and a professor of neurobiology at Harvard Medical School, said recently when we met in his office in Harvard Square. Hyman was appointed to run the National Institute of Mental Health during the Clinton administration and remained in his job after Bush took office. He is still troubled by what he saw as the intrusion of church onto state territory. "The first inkling that things were different under Bush was when I put in a slate for my national advisory council," Hyman said. "I got a call from one of the people I had nominated and he said, 'Steve, is this normal? I was just called by somebody saying he was a White House liaison to the Department of Health and Human Services. He asked me whether I made political donations, and if so to whom, and who did I vote for.'"

Hyman said that he had "no context" in which to understand this kind of inquiry. It turned out to be an experience that others had shared. "People went to Marburger to complain about it and his answer was pretty much 'What are you guys complaining about? This is normal.'" (Marburger recently told me that he doesn't think scientists should be asked whom they voted for. He has also said, however, that "it's perfectly acceptable for the president to know if someone he's appointing to one of his advisory committees supports his policies or not.") Hyman disagrees. "This is not normal," he said. "It has never happened in anybody's memory at NIH, and, frankly, the guy who called me was a molecular biologist. I swear to you that there is no such thing as right-wing or left-wing molecular biology." Hyman became increasingly disturbed by the effects of what he saw. "It wasn't just politics, it was an unyielding bias," he said. "They were asking people if they believed in needle exchange"—which, like Clinton, President Bush has always opposed. "As a scientist, the answer has to be *I believe in data*." The data showing that shared needles are the most efficient way to spread HIV are compelling. So are the data showing that needle exchange does not turn people into heroin addicts. "Asking the question 'Do you believe in needle exchange?' is a real violation of science. It so happens that needle exchange is a good public-health measure. And we need also to understand that there are issues in society that will trump scientific information. For many people, this is one of them. That is a political decision, and I have no problem with politicians making it. But that is a terribly unfair question to put to a scientist."

In 2001, Hyman attended the World Health Assembly in Geneva. The assembly, an annual event in which the United Nations establishes its global health priorities, focuses on a particular issue each year. That year, the topic was mental health. "We took as part of the official delegation an antiabortion activist who lobbied the United Nations," Hyman said. "She was our representative of nursing. Normally, you would have brought a person from the American Nurses Association." The Bush approach to global health, which emphasizes "evidence-based" risk-reduction strategies such as fidelity for married couples, has been difficult for many countries to understand. (The administration never cites a failure rate for abstinence programs, which is many times higher than the failure rate of condoms.) "Our attitudes toward birth control and condom use are very problematic in the face of a global pandemic of AIDS," Hyman said. "The woman was affable enough, but I just do not think that people who are lobbyists ought to be representing the United States and involved in formulating global health policy."

The next morning, I went to the Boston University School of Public Health to talk with Gerald T. Keusch, who is the associate dean for global health. From 1998 to the end of 2003, he served at the NIH as the director of the Fogarty Center, which concentrates on international health. In the two years after he took the job, Keusch had seven openings on his advisory board, and he nominated seven people to fill them. "In each case, they cleared NIH in three weeks and went to the secretary of Health and Human Services to be formally appointed," Keusch recalled. "Within another month, Donna Shalala had signed all seven letters. No questions. They were the people I wanted, and, as director, it was my responsibility to pick them." When George Bush took office, the Fogarty board had four new openings. Normally, three appointments to the board of twelve went to public figures and the rest to experts in various fields of international public health. "I asked for Dikembe Mutombo"—the NBA basketball star— "as my public figure," Keusch said. "He has a foundation in Zaire and a real sense of the issues around HIV. I also wanted to appoint Torsten Wiesel"— a former president of Rockefeller University, who, in 1981, received the Nobel Prize in Medicine—"and Geeta Rao Gupta, who runs the International Center for Research on Women, and has worked extensively on issues involving abortion." His other nominee was Jane Menken, a highly regarded demographer who is now at the University of Colorado. She specializes in fertility, and has often worked in Bangladesh, which until recently had one of the highest birthrates in the world. "For weeks, and then months, I heard nothing from the department about these appointments," Keusch said. "I thought they would simply be routine. Finally, after eight months, I got a message saying they would accept Dikembe but were rejecting the three others. No explanation. No note. Nothing." Keusch was incensed, and he insisted on meeting with the people at HHS who handled the decisions.

"I was told that Torsten was rejected because he has signed open letters that were critical of the president," Keusch went on. "Geeta was rejected because her organization is not opposed to abortion—which, we should not forget, *is legal* in the United States. And Jane Menken sat on the board of the Alan Guttmacher Institute"—which has always emphasized family planning and endorses the use of condoms. "That is literally what was said to me. Then I received a bunch of CVs in the mail. One of them was from a professor emeritus of economics at an obscure college in California that I had never heard of. His entire publication record consisted of pieces in the *Christian Science Monitor* and a Catholic monthly that took politically charged positions. That was typical of the caliber: there was nothing scientific, nothing peer-reviewed." Keusch spent the next three years at war with the HHS. He had to nominate twenty-six people to find seven whom the department would accept. "The administration simply made it impossible for me to do the job I was hired for. In the end, I left and they won."

The UCLA Institute for Stem Cell Biology and Medicine is tucked into the university's medical complex—a useful location, since all significant medical research today is collaborative. Molecular biologists, cancer experts, hematologists, even chemists and physicists have joined in the attempt to fulfill the immense promise of stem-cell biology. Few scientific endeavors have generated greater expectations (or hype). Embryonic stem cells are the biological equivalent of a blank check. Soon after birth, almost every human cell is programmed to serve a single purpose: white blood cells don't become red blood cells and neurons don't become bone cells. But that comes later. In the first days after an egg is fertilized, a cluster of about a hundred cells form into a hollow ball known as a blastocyst. At that stage— before they specialize—stem cells can be turned into any tissue or organ in the body. By harvesting and growing them, scientists hope to replace damaged cells with a healthier supply produced by patients themselves. The immune system is trained to reject foreign invaders, which is one of the central problems with transplants, but these cells wouldn't be foreign and therefore shouldn't be rejected. None of this is possible yet—there are enormous obstacles—but the almost unlimited potential has electrified scientists throughout the world.

"There have been three developments in my scientific lifetime that you could look at while they were happening and say, 'This is really big,'" Owen Witte, the stem-cell institute's director and a noted microbiologist, said. Research by David Baltimore and Witte helped lay the foundation for development of the first genuinely successful cancer therapy targeted directly at the function of a protein, the leukemia drug Gleevec. "The first, without a doubt, was molecular biology," Witte said. "We didn't call it that at the time, but it was a revolution. Absolutely mind-boggling. Second, this whole understanding of viruses and what causes human cancer. The third is genomics." He paused for a moment and smiled almost wistfully. "And stem cells are the fourth. It's the same palpable feeling of excitement when you understand that this will let you make a model for a disease. That you can study its variability and investigate how a cell develops. Then you can use those cells as therapeutics and design and test new treatments. It's a sea change. All my work in my lab is related to disease—and now we have this tool. And that is when science moves forward, when you have a new tool."

Most stem cells used in biomedical research come from spare embryos generated by in vitro fertilization. However, extracting stem cells from the embryo destroys it, and in 1996 Congress prohibited the government from supporting such research. President Clinton avoided making any decisions on whether such work was morally acceptable until 1999. ("He completely punted on the issue," John Marburger told me.) Just before leaving office, Clinton came out in favor of "some" federal support, but few scientists were willing even to apply for funds until they were certain that their work could continue in the next administration. Stem-cell research was one of the first major issues that Bush addressed, and in August 2001, he announced that he would not permit federal funds to be spent to create new cell lines or to carry out research with them. Scientists were outraged at a decision that they believed did not adequately reflect the will of the American people and that could prevent the country from pursuing research in areas like cancer, diabetes, and Parkinson's disease, all of which might benefit human health at least as dramatically as antibiotics.

Bush tried to find a politically acceptable compromise, saying that research could continue on those lines which existed as of that day, "where the life-and-death decision has already been made." This, he said, would allow scientists to "explore the promise and potential of stem-cell research without crossing a fundamental moral line." His decision changed the dynamics of the way at least some major medical research is financed in the United States—shifting it from the federal government to those states and private institutions which have chosen to support such research. California was the first to revolt, passing a ballot measure in 2004 to allocate $3 billion to create the Institute for Regenerative Medicine. Proposition 71 received nearly two-thirds of the vote; several other states have also moved forward with legislation and, along with major private organizations, have provided new sources of funds.

Yet, even where money is available, the research has been hindered by federal restraints. At places like Harvard University, Memorial Sloan-Kettering Cancer Center, in New York, and UCLA's stem-cell institute, researchers have been bound by red tape since the president's decision. Every dollar spent on stem cells must be segregated from research financed with public money. "Our best young scientists, who should be thinking about their experiments, have to be very clear about which pencils they can touch and which they can't," Steven Hyman told me. "Who would want to operate in those conditions?" A modern laboratory requires equipment— electron microscopes, centrifuges, cell fractionators, and powerful computers—that costs millions of dollars, and those tools are routinely shared, except with people working on stem cells. "If we have a postdoc working on a stem-cell project and he needs to spend half an hour a week using a DNA sequencer or something else that costs a hundred thousand dollars, we cannot let him use one owned by the university," Hyman said. "We might even have to buy a new one."

There are other complications. "If we discover something exciting in a stem-cell lab and we want to test it with materials in another lab, or use it in an experiment, we can't unless those experiments and those labs have no federal money attached to them," Owen Witte said. "Then, there is the infrastructure. If portions of this building were constructed with federal dollars"—it is the rare building on a public university campus in the United States that is not—"we would be proscribed from using it, even from establishing specially segregated labs." Witte added that it was not even clear whether the results of private stem-cell research could be published in a scientific journal that receives federal funds or whether that information could then be used in other experiments by scientists who receive federal support (or work at places that do). "It is an incredible encumbrance, and it has hurt us in every possible way," he said. "If you really want science to succeed, it needs a bit of unfettered creativity. If you regulate it and restrict it and wrap it in chains, you are taking away the very essence of what science is supposed to do."

President Bush identified sixty cell lines in 2001 that he considered morally permissible to use for experiments, and that number was later expanded by government officials to seventy-eight. Witte laughed at those figures. "There aren't thirty," he said. (The Bush administration frequently contends that the lines that existed in 2001 are sufficient for current research needs. James Battey, the director of the National Institute on Deafness, has been assigned to monitor the state of stem-cell research. At a congressional hearing held to determine last year's budget appropriations, Battey was asked whether existing cell lines were sufficient for researchers in the United States. His answer, which strained the bonds of English usage, has been posted on more than one laboratory bulletin board: "It is difficult to argue that a greater number of available lines, with more potential functional diversity, would be detrimental to the research effort.")

Witte, a soft-spoken man who clearly prefers looking through a microscope to engaging in political machinations, was dressed casually in blue corduroy pants and a jean jacket. His gray hair is short and he has an easy smile, yet when he talks about the ban his facial muscles begin to clench. "If you are interested in early development, if you are interested in cell biology, if you are interested in how cells develop—this edict tells you that you may not think outside of a previously held point of view. You may not build bridges or learn anything beyond what is known. Science is a progressive field and each step leads to the next. The idea that this is enough for you guys, that nobody is going to have a new idea, that nobody is going to do it better—that is antithetical to progress and science."

Witte and most of his colleagues are aware that, too often, the promise of stem-cell science gets confused with reality. Embryonic stem cells have been advertised as cures for nearly every ailment of mankind. So far, at least, they cure nothing. (Nor has it helped that the work of Hwang Woo Suk, the South Korean scientist who had claimed to have cloned human cells—a major step toward the goal of converting a patient's cells into new tissue that can be used to treat diseases—was recently found to have been fabricated.)

Witte's lab often concentrates on bone-marrow transplants—a cure for many ailments. The technology has been established and it works, but it is not available to everyone. Marrow needs to match genetically and there is always a shortage, particularly among certain ethnic groups. Scientists are convinced that stem cells can change that. "There are examples in the literature of a cell that can be programmed to become a pancreatic cell or a liver cell," Witte said. "That is exactly what we want." Sugar, for example, is broken down by the hormone insulin, which is produced by special cells in the pancreas. People develop diabetes because those cells have been destroyed. "Now, to be able to make a pancreatic cell from a stem cell," Witte said, "that is exciting. But the more important question is 'Can you make ten to the ninth of them?'" (Ten to the ninth is the scientific notation for the number one billion.) "Because that is what we would need to make it work as a therapy. We need engineers who are experts in large-scale cell culture and other specialists. So, yes, the immediacy of this has been oversold. Absolutely. But that doesn't mean I am not excited." He went on, "Yet it simply cannot be done without a greater ability to grow a variety of stem-cell lines. Diseases usually involve many genes. You cannot study them with a random selection of cells that just happen to have existed in August of 2001."

We walked over to his lab to look at one of the "Presidential cell lines." (Each has a specific genetic fingerprint, so it can be easily identified.) Witte introduced me to Shuling Guo, a Chinese molecular biologist on the institute's staff. Shuling led me to a microscope and told me to look at a slide that she had placed beneath it. "There it is," Witte said, "the giant ethical controversy staring you in the face." I seemed to be looking at a bunch of little soccer bails packed together. "What you are seeing are thousands of human stem cells," Shuling said. Her job is to turn them into red blood cells. "Look carefully," she told me, as the cluster slowly started to become visible. "Can you see a dot of red?" I did. In fact, I saw three little red pinpoints. "The cells are sucking iron out of the environment and making hemoglobin"—a vital protein that ferries oxygen to cells around the body. "If you suffered from a fatal anemia, we should be able to cure it. But we have maybe five red cells there. We need to figure out a way to make five billion."

* * * * *

The war over the ethics of using embryos in research has proved costly to American medicine. Not only has it slowed the pace of progress but for the first time other countries have moved ahead of the United States. The United Kingdom, for example, has established several centers for stem-cell scientists. The ban has also discouraged researchers from contemplating careers in what would otherwise be considered the most exciting area of medicine. Nobody disputes the promise of stem-cell research, yet the moral complications that surround it are also real, and unlikely to soon disappear. The questions are nearly impossible to answer: Is breaking open a two-day-old stem cell murder? Is it possible to harm a blastocyst—something without nerves or human qualities? What about discarding embryos that have been left over at in vitro fertilization clinics instead of using them for research? People who oppose stem-cell research often describe embryos as potential human beings. "Like a snowflake," President Bush said in his 2001 speech, "each of these embryos is unique, with the unique genetic potential of an individual human being." Yet for many Americans it is difficult to feel the same compassion for people who don't yet exist as for those who do. According to repeated polling, a majority of Catholics, Protestants, and evangelical Christians believe that stem cells from embryos should be used for research, yet there is no consensus on the question of when life begins, or on the relative value of embryos and living human beings.

"You have to separate moral questions from the questions of science," C. Everett Koop said when I asked him recently if he could think of any way to resolve this issue. Koop is the most famously right-wing man ever appointed to a senior position in the Public Health Service. He will be ninety this year, and he has been out of government for nearly two decades, but he remains active, and runs an institute named for him at Dartmouth College's medical school. In 1981, when President Ronald Reagan nominated him to the position of surgeon general, Koop was a noted pediatric surgeon from Philadelphia with the beard of Abraham Lincoln and a strident history of opposition to abortion. Even today, his 1979 book, *Whatever Happened to the Human Race?*, remains a touchstone for those who are opposed to legal abortions. But he had no public health experience. Surgeons general are usually confirmed quickly and

tly forgotten—before Koop, few Americans could have named
ıblic health official in American history has generated more
controvers y. Liberals on Capitol Hill denounced Reagan's choice for what
it was: a blatant attempt to place ideological fealty over the demands of
public health. The battle over Koop's confirmation dragged on for nearly
a year, but in the end he took his position at the head of the Public Health
Service.

Koop then proceeded to alienate nearly every supporter he had on the
religious and political right. To fight the growing epidemic of AIDS, he recommended a program of compulsory sex education in the schools, and
argued that children should be taught how to use condoms. He cam-
paigned vigorously against smoking in public spaces, enraging tobacco
companies. When President Reagan asked him to prepare a report on the
psychological effects of abortion, conservatives finally felt certain of the
result. Yet, after meeting with activists on both sides, and reviewing hundreds of scientific publications, Koop declined to say that abortion was
always more damaging than the alternative. He even refused to issue a
report, telling the president that there weren't enough data to support
either "the preconceived notions of those pro life or those pro choice." The
administration, once again, was shocked. "You know, I never changed my
stripes during all that time, and I still haven't," Koop said. "What I did in
that job was what any well-trained doctor or scientist would do: I looked at
the data and then presented the facts to the American people. In science,
you can't hide from the data.

"I have been away for some time, and I am more of a spectator now," he
went on. "But stem-cell research is as volatile as any subject can get. People
are completely driven by their beliefs or their desires. Not the facts. Scientists have hyped it, and often they act as if there were no ethical considerations at all. That is not true. But you have to weigh the facts, and this
Administration doesn't seem to take that approach. One thing that I have
learned is that belief doesn't change reality."

The problems facing American science have not been created by a single
politician or party: they reflect a fissure in society which has grown wider
as science has edged closer to the roots of life itself. "I have never seen as
much tension between science and society," Alan Leshner, the chief exec-

utive officer of the American Association for the Advancement of Science, told me. "Some of it is religion and some of it is ideology. But science is now encroaching in areas that are too close to core human values. And it makes people afraid." Leshner was the director of the National Institute on Drug Abuse from 1994 to 2001. "Let's look at behavioral genetics. In the old days, when we talked about there being genes for schizophrenia, everybody said, 'Wow. We have to find that.' Now we know it's broader. Maybe we won't need a gene for schizophrenia; instead, it makes more sense to talk about types of schizophrenia. Fine. Then we move to where we are now: looking for individual symptoms, some of which are normal personality traits taken to the extreme—like cognition. So now we have to study the genetics of cognition. Well, cognition is intelligence. And when you say, 'Let's go back and study the genetics of intelligence,' people go batshit.

"And then that's the end of it," he said. "What we are seeing is the empowerment of ideologues who have the ability to influence the course of science far more than ever before. They say, 'I don't like the science, I don't like what it is showing,' and therefore they ignore it. And we are at a place in this country today where that can work. The basic integrity of science is under siege."

The United States now educates fewer scientists every year. In 2005, seniors in American high schools performed below the average of twenty-one countries on a test of general knowledge of mathematics and science—and in advanced courses the United States was close to the bottom. Federal research investments are shrinking as a share of the U.S. economy—just as other nations are increasing theirs. In this year's State of the Union speech, President Bush acknowledged that we need to educate more scientists to remain competitive. (He then went on the road to tell students that they ought not think of researchers as the "nerd patrol.") But China and South Korea are raising basic research budgets by 10 percent each year. This year, America's will drop by 1.5 percent. In 2004, more than 600,000 engineers graduated from Chinese universities. In India, the number was 350,000. In America, the figure was not quite 70,000. For the first time, the United States now imports more high-technology products than it exports. In fact, the U.S. share of such exports has fallen in the past twenty years, from 30 percent to 17 percent. Rather than make up for the loss of trained scientists by increasing immigration, however, the country since September 11, 2001, has invoked harsher restrictions than ever before.

"My friends in the European Union are ecstatic," Leshner said. "Between the visa problems—preventing the best students from China and India from entering this country to study or work—and the stem-cell ban, our competitors are just in heaven. While we are restricting research, the EU is working hard on ways to increase mobility. They are welcoming scientists from other countries. They are not fools."

Late last year, the American Museum of Natural History mounted the most significant exhibit ever devoted to Charles Darwin. After returning from his voyage on the *Beagle*, in 1836, Darwin waited more than two decades before he published *The Origin of Species*. As Michael Novacek, the museum's provost of science and the curator of its division of paleontology, put it when we walked through the exhibit, "Charles Darwin was a creationist when he stepped onto the *Beagle*. And he was completely aware of how his new theory would be received when he got off." In 1871, Darwin published his second book, *The Descent of Man*, in which he attempted to explain his view of how humans had evolved from other animals. That book's assertion that humans were related to monkeys became one of the most inflammatory ideas in the history of science. It remains so today, particularly in the United States. For the past two decades, polls have shown consistently that more than half of all Americans believe that humans were created directly by God. A similar number don't believe that we share a common ancestor with apes. And only 22 percent say that we evolved from an earlier species.

In Judge Jones's December ruling on intelligent design in Pennsylvania, he excoriated the Dover school board for requiring teachers to tell students that evolution is no more than a theory. He wrote that such an action "presents students with a religious alternative masquerading as a scientific theory, directs them to consult a creationist text as though it were a science resource." Judge Jones found that intelligent design is nothing but creationism with a fancy name. His argument was cogent and powerful, but will it matter? Perhaps, but for the Darwin exhibit in New York—coming eighty years after a twenty-four-year-old high-school teacher named John Scopes was put on trial in Tennessee for teaching the theory of evolution—the American Museum of Natural History failed to find even a single corporate sponsor.

Science is powerful, and it can seem miraculous. Clearly, it has transformed the way humans live, and for centuries the general view has been that science is neither good nor bad—that it merely supplies information, and that new information is always beneficial. That simplistic view makes less sense every year. The products of our most successful experiments often fill people with dread. The atomic bomb—not to mention experiments by Nazi doctors or those carried out in the United States on black men with syphilis—has demonstrated why that fear is not wholly without reason. Nor are conservatives or Christian activists the only people to misuse data or take advantage of their complexity. There are certainly risks associated with growing genetically modified products, yet, after billions of doses have been consumed, there has never been a documented case of a person dying from eating one. That has not prevented leading environmentalists from working to ban them. Nuclear energy is another idea to which liberals have been slavishly opposed, refusing to apply common sense to science, or to compare risks and benefits in any meaningful way.

Americans want to believe in "nature" in part because they have so often felt misled by science. A book called *Natural Cures "They" Don't Want You to Know About*, by Kevin Trudeau, has been on the top of the best-seller lists for almost a year. The author promises that those who read to the end will "know categorically, absolutely, with a hundred per cent certainty that there is a natural cure for your disease and you will know exactly what to do to cure yourself of your disease and remain healthy for life—all without drugs or surgery." Clearly, the Bush administration alone is not responsible for America's fear of progress. But it has widened the gulf between truth and belief immensely.

When I went to see Andrew Von Eschenbach, in his office on the NIH campus, to discuss his leadership of the cancer institute and the FDA, he didn't want to talk about data or the policies of the administration. But he did share his vision of a medical future so "profound" that he calls it the "molecular metamorphosis." He said, "It doesn't change one thing—it changes everything, and the future will look no more like the past than a butterfly looks like a caterpillar." Von Eschenbach is a pleasant and self-effacing man, and he told me, as he has often told others, that this new approach to medicine will help "eliminate suffering and death due to cancer by 2015." I asked him how we could accomplish such a remarkable feat—after all, the war on cancer has been waged for decades with only moderate success. "We are going to morph the current reality into the new reality and that will go on over the next ten years," he said.

Many of Von Eschenbach's colleagues are convinced that such unrealistic statements will weaken the position of science as the preeminent force of progress in modern society. In a recent commentary published in the journal *Cell*, Paul Nurse, a Nobel laureate and the president of Rockefeller University, addressed Von Eschenbach's statements about cancer treatment directly. They "cannot be justified even as a statement of aspiration," he wrote, "because when we fail to deliver, as we surely will . . . we will lose the confidence of both the politicians and the public." He then turned to a much larger question, the future of American science: "Present policies are set to damage a whole generation of young research workers, and the negative impact on recruitment of the next generation of scientists will be seen for years to come."

The Worst President in History?
Sean Wilentz

Rolling Stone | May 4, 2006

It's almost certainly too early to tell whether George W. Bush's languishing approval ratings are the result of a chief executive making unpopular but necessary choices or simply an indication of a failed presidency. But in this Rolling Stone *essay, which created quite a buzz when it first appeared in the spring of 2006, Princeton history Professor Sean Wilentz takes a preliminary stab at guessing how historians will end up evaluating the Bush administration. As you might have inferred from the title, his conclusion is that the nation's forty-third president will fare poorly, indeed—in large part because "he has . . . displayed a weakness common among the greatest presidential failures—an unswerving adherence to a simplistic ideology that abjures deviation from dogma as heresy, thus preventing any pragmatic adjustment to changing realities."*

George W. Bush's presidency appears headed for colossal historical disgrace. Barring a cataclysmic event on the order of the terrorist attacks of

September 11, after which the public might rally around the White House once again, there seems to be little the administration can do to avoid being ranked on the lowest tier of U.S. presidents. And that may be the best-case scenario. Many historians are now wondering whether Bush, in fact, will be remembered as the very worst president in all of American history.

From time to time, after hours, I kick back with my colleagues at Princeton to argue idly about which president really was the worst of them all. For years, these perennial debates have largely focused on the same handful of chief executives whom national polls of historians, from across the ideological and political spectrum, routinely cite as the bottom of the presidential barrel. Was the lousiest James Buchanan, who, confronted with Southern secession in 1860, dithered to a degree that, as his most recent biographer has said, probably amounted to disloyalty—and who handed to his successor, Abraham Lincoln, a nation already torn asunder? Was it Lincoln's successor, Andrew Johnson, who actively sided with former Confederates and undermined Reconstruction? What about the amiably incompetent Warren G. Harding, whose administration was fabulously corrupt? Or, though he has his defenders, Herbert Hoover, who tried some reforms but remained imprisoned in his own outmoded individualist ethic and collapsed under the weight of the stock market crash of 1929 and the Depression's onset? The younger historians always put in a word for Richard M. Nixon, the only American president forced to resign from office.

Now, though, George W. Bush is in serious contention for the title of worst ever. In early 2004, an informal survey of 415 historians conducted by the nonpartisan History News Network found that 81 percent considered the Bush administration a "failure." Among those who called Bush a success, many gave the president high marks only for his ability to mobilize public support and get Congress to go along with what one historian called the administration's "pursuit of disastrous policies." In fact, roughly one in ten of those who called Bush a success was being facetious, rating him only as the best president since Bill Clinton—a category in which Bush is the only contestant.

The lopsided decision of historians should give everyone pause. Contrary to popular stereotypes, historians are generally a cautious bunch. We assess the past from widely divergent points of view and are deeply concerned about being viewed as fair and accurate by our colleagues. When we make historical judgments, we are acting not as voters or even pundits, but as scholars who must evaluate all the evidence, good, bad, or indifferent. Separate surveys, conducted by those perceived as conservatives as well as liberals, show remarkable unanimity about who the best and worst presidents have been.

Historians do tend, as a group, to be far more liberal than the citizenry as a whole—a fact the president's admirers have seized on to dismiss the poll results as transparently biased. One pro-Bush historian said the survey revealed more about "the current crop of history professors" than about Bush or about Bush's eventual standing. But if historians were simply motivated by a strong collective liberal bias, they might be expected to call Bush the worst president since his father, or Ronald Reagan, or Nixon. Instead, more than half of those polled—and nearly three-fourths of those who gave Bush a negative rating—reached back *before* Nixon to find a president they considered as miserable as Bush. The presidents most commonly linked with Bush included Hoover, Andrew Johnson, and Buchanan. Twelve percent of the historians polled—nearly as many as those who rated Bush a success—flatly called Bush the worst president in American history. And these figures were gathered before the debacles over Hurricane Katrina, Bush's role in the Valerie Plame leak affair, and the deterioration of the situation in Iraq. Were the historians polled today, that figure would certainly be higher.

Even worse for the president, the general public, having once given Bush the highest approval ratings ever recorded, now appears to be coming around to the dismal view held by most historians. To be sure, the president retains a considerable base of supporters who believe in and adore him, and who reject all criticism with a mixture of disbelief and fierce contempt—about one-third of the electorate. (When the columnist Richard Reeves publicized the historians' poll last year and suggested it might have merit, he drew thousands of abusive replies that called him an idiot and that praised Bush as, in one writer's words, "a Christian who actually acts on his deeply held beliefs.") Yet the ranks of the true believers have thinned dramatically. A majority of voters in forty-three states now disapprove of Bush's handling of his job. Since the commencement of reliable polling in the 1940s, only one twice-elected president has seen his ratings fall as low as Bush's in his second term: Richard Nixon, during the months preceding his resignation in 1974. No two-term president since polling began has fallen from such a height of popularity as Bush's (in the neighborhood of 90 percent, during the patriotic upswell following the 2001 attacks) to such a low (now in the midthirties). No president, including Harry Truman (whose ratings sometimes dipped below Nixonian levels), has experienced such a virtually unrelieved decline as Bush has since his high point. Apart from sharp but temporary upticks that followed the commencement of the Iraq war and the capture of Saddam Hussein, and a recovery during the weeks just before and after his reelection, the Bush trend has been a profile in fairly steady disillusionment.

*   *   *   *   *

How does any president's reputation sink so low? The reasons are best understood as the reverse of those that produce presidential greatness. In almost every survey of historians dating back to the 1940s, three presidents have emerged as supreme successes: George Washington, Abraham Lincoln, and Franklin D. Roosevelt. These were the men who guided the nation through what historians consider its greatest crises: the founding era after the ratification of the Constitution, the Civil War, and the Great Depression and Second World War. Presented with arduous, at times seemingly impossible circumstances, they rallied the nation, governed brilliantly, and left the republic more secure than when they entered office.

Calamitous presidents, faced with enormous difficulties—Buchanan, Andrew Johnson, Hoover, and now Bush—have divided the nation, governed erratically, and left the nation worse off. In each case, different factors contributed to the failure: disastrous domestic policies, foreign-policy blunders and military setbacks, executive misconduct, crises of credibility and public trust. Bush, however, is one of the rarities in presidential history: He has not only stumbled badly in every one of these key areas, he has also displayed a weakness common among the greatest presidential failures—an unswerving adherence to a simplistic ideology that abjures deviation from dogma as heresy, thus preventing any pragmatic adjustment to changing realities. Repeatedly, Bush has undone himself, a failing revealed in each major area of presidential performance.

The Credibility Gap

No previous president appears to have squandered the public's trust more than Bush has. In the 1840s, President James Polk gained a reputation for deviousness over his alleged manufacturing of the war with Mexico and his supposedly covert proslavery views. Abraham Lincoln, then an Illinois congressman, virtually labeled Polk a liar when he called him, from the floor of the House, "a bewildered, confounded and miserably perplexed man" and denounced the war as "from beginning to end, the sheerest deception." But the swift American victory in the war, Polk's decision to stick by his pledge to serve only one term, and his sudden death shortly after leaving office spared him the ignominy over slavery that befell his successors in the 1850s. With more than two years to go in Bush's second term and no swift victory in sight, Bush's reputation will probably have no such reprieve.

The problems besetting Bush are of a more modern kind than Polk's, suited to the television age—a crisis both in confidence and credibility. In 1965, Lyndon Johnson's Vietnam travails gave birth to the phrase "credibility gap," meaning the distance between a president's professions and the public's perceptions of reality. It took more than two years for Johnson's disapproval rating in the Gallup Poll to reach 52 percent in March 1968—a figure Bush long ago surpassed, but that was sufficient to persuade the proud LBJ not to seek reelection. Yet recently, just short of three years after Bush buoyantly declared "mission accomplished" in Iraq, his disapproval ratings have been running considerably higher than Johnson's, at about 60 percent. More than half the country now considers Bush dishonest and untrustworthy, and a decisive plurality consider him less trustworthy than his predecessor, Bill Clinton—a figure still attacked by conservative zealots as "Slick Willie."

Previous modern presidents, including Truman, Reagan, and Clinton, managed to reverse plummeting ratings and regain the public's trust by shifting attention away from political and policy setbacks and by overhauling the White House's inner circles. But Bush's publicly expressed view that he has made no major mistakes, coupled with what even the conservative commentator William F. Buckley Jr. calls his "high-flown pronouncements" about failed policies, seems to foreclose the first option. Upping the ante in the Middle East and bombing Iranian nuclear sites, a strategy reportedly favored by some in the White House, could distract the public and gain Bush immediate political capital in advance of the 2006 midterm elections—but in the long term might severely worsen the already dire situation in Iraq, especially among Shiite Muslims linked to the Iranians. And given Bush's ardent attachment to loyal aides, no matter how discredited, a major personnel shake-up is improbable, short of indictments. Replacing Andrew Card with Joshua Bolten as chief of staff—a move announced by the president in March in a tone that sounded more like defiance than contrition—represents a rededication to current policies and personnel, not a serious change. (Card, an old Bush family retainer, was widely considered more moderate than most of the men around the president and had little involvement in policy making.) The power of Vice President Dick Cheney, meanwhile, remains uncurbed. Were Cheney to announce he is stepping down due to health problems, normally a polite pretext for a political removal, one can be reasonably certain it would be because Cheney actually did have grave health problems.

Bush at War

Until the twentieth century, American presidents managed foreign wars well—including those presidents who prosecuted unpopular wars. James Madison had no support from Federalist New England at the outset of the War of 1812, and the discontent grew amid mounting military setbacks in 1813. But Federalist political overreaching, combined with a reversal of America's military fortunes and the negotiation of a peace with Britain, made Madison something of a hero again and ushered in a brief so-called Era of Good Feelings in which his Jeffersonian Republican Party coalition ruled virtually unopposed. The Mexican War under Polk was even more unpopular, but its quick and victorious conclusion redounded to Polk's favor—much as the rapid American victory in the Spanish-American War helped William McKinley overcome anti-imperialist dissent.

The twentieth century was crueler to wartime presidents. After winning reelection in 1916 with the slogan "He Kept Us Out of War," Woodrow Wilson oversaw American entry into the First World War. Yet while the doughboys returned home triumphant, Wilson's idealistic and politically disastrous campaign for American entry into the League of Nations presaged a resurgence of the opposition Republican Party along with a redoubling of American isolationism that lasted until Pearl Harbor.

Bush has more in common with post-1945 Democratic presidents

Truman and Johnson, who both became bogged down in overseas military conflicts with no end, let alone victory, in sight. But Bush has become bogged down in a singularly crippling way. On September 10, 2001, he held among the lowest ratings of any modern president for that point in a first term. (Only Gerald Ford, his popularity reeling after his pardon of Nixon, had comparable numbers.) The attacks the following day transformed Bush's presidency, giving him an extraordinary opportunity to achieve greatness. Some of the early signs were encouraging. Bush's simple, unflinching eloquence and his quick toppling of the Taliban government in Afghanistan rallied the nation. Yet even then, Bush wasted his chance by quickly choosing partisanship over leadership.

No other president—Lincoln in the Civil War, FDR in World War II, John F. Kennedy at critical moments of the Cold War—faced with such a monumental set of military and political circumstances failed to embrace the opposing political party to help wage a truly national struggle. But Bush shut out and even demonized the Democrats. Top military advisers and even members of the president's own Cabinet who expressed any reservations or criticisms of his policies—including retired Marine Corps General Anthony Zinni and former Treasury Secretary Paul O'Neill—suffered either dismissal, smear attacks from the president's supporters, or investigations into their alleged breaches of national security. The wise men who counseled Bush's father, including James Baker and Brent Scowcroft, found their entreaties brusquely ignored by his son. When asked if he ever sought advice from the elder Bush, the president responded, "There is a higher Father that I appeal to."

All the while, Bush and the most powerful figures in the administration, Vice President Dick Cheney and Defense Secretary Donald Rumsfeld, were planting the seeds for the crises to come by diverting the struggle against Al Qaeda toward an all-out effort to topple their preexisting target, Saddam Hussein. In a deliberate political decision, the administration stampeded the Congress and a traumatized citizenry into the Iraq invasion on the basis of what has now been demonstrated to be tendentious and perhaps fabricated evidence of an imminent Iraqi threat to American security, one that the White House suggested included nuclear weapons. Instead of emphasizing any political, diplomatic, or humanitarian aspects of a war on Iraq—an appeal that would have sounded too "sensitive," as Cheney once sneered—the administration built a "Bush Doctrine" of unprovoked, preventive warfare, based on speculative threats and embracing principles previously abjured by every previous generation of U.S. foreign policy makers, even at the height of the Cold War. The president did so with premises founded, in the case of Iraq, on wishful thinking. He did so while proclaiming an expansive Wilsonian rhetoric of making the world safe for democracy—yet discarding the multilateralism and systems of international law (including the Geneva Conventions) that emanated from Wilson's idealism. He did so while dismissing intelligence that an American invasion could spark a long and bloody civil war among Iraq's fierce religious and ethnic rivals, reports that have since proved true. And he did so after repeated warnings by military officials such as General Eric Shinseki that pacifying postwar Iraq would require hundreds of thousands of American troops—accurate estimates that Paul Wolfowitz and other Bush policy gurus ridiculed as "wildly off the mark."

When William F. Buckley, the man whom many credit as the founder of the modern conservative movement, writes categorically, as he did in February, that "one can't doubt that the American objective in Iraq has failed," then something terrible has happened. Even as a brash young iconoclast, Buckley always took the long view. The Bush White House seems incapable of doing so, except insofar as a tiny trusted circle around the president constantly reassures him that he is a messianic liberator and profound freedom fighter, on a par with FDR and Lincoln, and that history will vindicate his every act and utterance.

Bush at Home

Bush came to office in 2001 pledging to govern as a "compassionate conservative," more moderate on domestic policy than the dominant right wing of his party. The pledge proved hollow, as Bush tacked immediately to the hard right. Previous presidents and their parties have suffered when their actions have belied their campaign promises. Lyndon Johnson is the most conspicuous recent example, having declared in his 1964 run against the hawkish Republican Barry Goldwater that "we are not about to send American boys nine or ten thousand miles away from home to do what Asian boys ought to be doing for themselves." But no president has surpassed Bush in departing so thoroughly from his original campaign persona.

The heart of Bush's domestic policy has turned out to be nothing more than a series of massively regressive tax cuts—a return, with a vengeance, to the discredited Reagan-era supply-side faith that Bush's father once ridiculed as "voodoo economics." Bush crowed in triumph in February 2004, "We cut taxes, which basically meant people had more money in their pocket." The claim is bogus for the majority of Americans, as are claims that tax cuts have led to impressive new private investment and job growth. While wiping out the solid Clinton-era federal surplus and raising federal deficits to staggering record levels, Bush's tax policies have necessitated hikes in federal fees, state and local taxes, and copayment charges to needy veterans and families who rely on Medicaid, along with cuts in loan programs to small businesses and college students, and in a wide range of state services. The lion's share of benefits from the tax cuts has gone to the very richest Americans, while new business investment has increased at a historically sluggish rate since the peak of the last business cycle five years ago. Private-sector job growth since 2001 has been anemic compared to the Bush administration's original forecasts and is chiefly attributable not to the tax cuts but to increased federal spending, especially on defense. Real wages for middle-income Americans have been dropping since the end of 2003: Last year, on average, nominal wages grew by only 2.4 percent, a meager gain that was completely erased by an average inflation rate of 3.4 percent.

The monster deficits, caused by increased federal spending combined with the reduction of revenue resulting from the tax cuts, have also placed Bush's administration in a historic class of its own with respect to government borrowing. According to the Treasury Department, the forty-two presidents who held office between 1789 and 2000 borrowed a combined total of $1.01 trillion from foreign governments and financial institutions. But between 2001 and 2005 alone, the Bush White House borrowed $1.05 trillion, more than all of the previous presidencies *combined*. Having inherited the largest federal surplus in American history in 2001, he has turned it into the largest deficit ever—with an even higher deficit, $423 billion, forecast for fiscal year 2006. Yet Bush—sounding much like Herbert Hoover in 1930 predicting that "prosperity is just around the corner"— insists that he will cut federal deficits in half by 2009, and that the best way to guarantee this would be to make permanent his tax cuts, which helped cause the deficit in the first place!

The rest of what remains of Bush's skimpy domestic agenda is either failed or failing—a record unmatched since the presidency of Herbert

Hoover. The No Child Left Behind educational-reform act has proved so unwieldy, draconian, and poorly funded that several states—including Utah, one of Bush's last remaining political strongholds—have fought to opt out of it entirely. White House proposals for immigration reform and a guest-worker program have succeeded mainly in dividing probusiness Republicans (who want more low-wage immigrant workers) from paleo-conservatives fearful that hordes of Spanish-speaking newcomers will destroy American culture. The paleos' call for tougher anti-immigrant laws—a return to the punitive spirit of exclusion that led to the notorious Immigration Act of 1924 that shut the door to immigrants from Southern and Eastern Europe—has in turn deeply alienated Hispanic voters from the Republican Party, badly undermining the GOP's hopes of using them to build a permanent national electoral majority. The recent proimmigrant demonstrations, which drew millions of marchers nationwide, indicate how costly the Republican divide may prove.

The one noncorporate constituency to which Bush has consistently deferred is the Christian right, both in his selections for the federal bench and in his implications that he bases his policies on premillennialist, prophetic Christian doctrine. Previous presidents have regularly invoked the Almighty. McKinley is supposed to have fallen to his knees, seeking divine guidance about whether to take control of the Philippines in 1898, although the story may be apocryphal. But no president before Bush has allowed the press to disclose, through a close friend, his startling belief that he was ordained by God to lead the country. The White House's sectarian positions—over stem-cell research, the teaching of pseudoscientific "intelligent design," global population control, the Terri Schiavo spectacle, and more—have led some to conclude that Bush has promoted the transformation of the GOP into what former Republican strategist Kevin Phillips calls "the first religious party in U.S. history."

Bush's faith-based conception of his mission, which stands above and beyond reasoned inquiry, jibes well with his administration's probusiness dogma on global warming and other urgent environmental issues. While forcing federally funded agencies to remove from their Web sites scientific information about reproductive health and the effectiveness of condoms in combating HIV/AIDS, and while peremptorily overruling staff scientists at the Food and Drug Administration on making emergency contraception available over the counter, Bush officials have censored and suppressed research findings they don't like by the Environmental Protection Agency, the Fish and Wildlife Service, and the Department of Agriculture. Far from being the conservative he said he was, Bush has blazed a radical new path as the first American president in history who is outwardly hostile to science—dedicated, as a distinguished, bipartisan panel of educators and scientists (including forty-nine Nobel laureates) has declared, to "the distortion of scientific knowledge for partisan political ends."

The Bush White House's indifference to domestic problems and science alike culminated in the catastrophic responses to Hurricane Katrina. Scientists had long warned that global warming was intensifying hurricanes, but Bush ignored them—much as he and his administration sloughed off warnings from the director of the National Hurricane Center before Katrina hit. Reorganized under the Department of Homeland Security, the once efficient Federal Emergency Management Agency turned out, under Bush, to have become a nest of cronyism and incompetence. During the months immediately after the storm, Bush traveled to New Orleans eight times to promise massive rebuilding aid from the federal government. On March 30 [2006], however, Bush's Gulf Coast recovery coordinator admitted that it could take as long as twenty-five years for the city to recover.

Karl Rove has sometimes likened Bush to the imposing, no-nonsense President Andrew Jackson. Yet Jackson took measures to prevent those he called "the rich and powerful" from bending "the acts of government to their selfish purposes." Jackson also gained eternal renown by saving New Orleans from British invasion against terrible odds. Generations of Americans sang of Jackson's famous victory. In 1959, Johnny Horton's version of "The Battle of New Orleans" won the Grammy for best country & western performance. If anyone sings about George W. Bush and New Orleans, it will be a blues number.

Presidential Misconduct

Virtually every presidential administration dating back to George Washington's has faced charges of misconduct and threats of impeachment against the president or his civil officers. The alleged offenses have usually involved matters of personal misbehavior and corruption, notably the payoff scandals that plagued Cabinet officials who served Presidents

Harding and Ulysses S. Grant. But the charges have also included alleged usurpation of power by the president and serious criminal conduct that threatens constitutional government and the rule of law—most notoriously, the charges that led to the impeachments of Andrew Johnson and Bill Clinton, and to Richard Nixon's resignation.

Historians remain divided over the actual grievousness of many of these allegations and crimes. Scholars reasonably describe the graft and corruption around the Grant administration, for example, as gargantuan, including a kickback scandal that led to the resignation of Grant's secretary of war under the shadow of impeachment. Yet the scandals produced no indictments of Cabinet secretaries and only one of a White House aide, who was acquitted. By contrast, the most scandal-ridden administration in the modern era, apart from Nixon's, was Ronald Reagan's, now widely remembered through a haze of nostalgia as a paragon of virtue. A total of twenty-nine Reagan officials, including White House national security adviser Robert McFarlane and deputy chief of staff Michael Deaver, were convicted on charges stemming from the Iran-Contra affair, illegal lobbying, and a looting scandal inside the Department of Housing and Urban Development. Three Cabinet officers—HUD Secretary Samuel Pierce, Attorney General Edwin Meese, and Secretary of Defense Caspar Weinberger—left their posts under clouds of scandal. In contrast, not a single official in the Clinton administration was even indicted over his or her White House duties, despite repeated high-profile investigations and a successful, highly partisan impeachment drive.

The full report, of course, has yet to come on the Bush administration. Because Bush, unlike Reagan or Clinton, enjoys a fiercely partisan and loyal majority in Congress, his administration has been spared scrutiny. Yet that mighty advantage has not prevented the indictment of Vice President Dick Cheney's chief of staff, I. Lewis "Scooter" Libby, on charges stemming from an alleged major security breach in the Valerie Plame matter. (The last White House official of comparable standing to be indicted while still in office was Grant's personal secretary in 1875.) It has not headed off the unprecedented scandal involving Larry Franklin, a high-ranking Defense Department official, who has pleaded guilty to divulging classified information to a foreign power while working at the Pentagon—a crime against national security. It has not forestalled the arrest and indictment of Bush's top federal procurement official, David Safavian, and the continuing

investigations into Safavian's intrigues with the disgraced Republican lobbyist Jack Abramoff, recently sentenced to nearly six years in prison—
investigations in which some prominent Republicans, including former
Christian Coalition Executive Director Ralph Reed (and current GOP aspi-
rant for lieutenant governor of Georgia) have already been implicated, and
could well produce the largest congressional corruption scandal in American history. It has not dispelled the cloud of possible indictment that hangs
over others of Bush's closest advisers.

History may ultimately hold Bush in the greatest contempt for
expanding the powers of the presidency beyond the limits laid down by
the U.S. Constitution. There has always been a tension over the constitutional roles of the three branches of the federal government. The
Framers intended as much, as part of the system of checks and balances
they expected would minimize tyranny. When Andrew Jackson took
drastic measures against the nation's banking system, the Whig Senate
censured him for conduct "dangerous to the liberties of the people."
During the Civil War, Abraham Lincoln's emergency decisions to suspend
habeas corpus while Congress was out of session in 1861 and 1862 has
led some Americans, to this day, to regard him as a despot. Richard
Nixon's conduct of the war in Southeast Asia and his covert domestic-
surveillance programs prompted Congress to pass new statutes regulating executive power.

By contrast, the Bush administration—in seeking to restore what
Cheney, a Nixon administration veteran, has called "the legitimate
authority of the presidency"—threatens to overturn the Framers' healthy
tension in favor of presidential absolutism. Armed with legal findings by
his attorney general (and personal lawyer) Alberto Gonzales, the Bush
White House has declared that the president's powers as commander in
chief in wartime are limitless. No previous wartime president has come
close to making so grandiose a claim. More specifically, this administration has asserted that the president is perfectly free to violate federal laws
on such matters as domestic surveillance and the torture of detainees.
When Congress has passed legislation to limit those assertions, Bush has
resorted to issuing constitutionally dubious "signing statements," which
declare, by fiat, how he will interpret and execute the law in question, even
when that interpretation flagrantly violates the will of Congress. Earlier
presidents, including Jackson, raised hackles by offering their own view of

the Constitution in order to justify vetoing congressional acts. Bush doesn't bother with that: He signs the legislation (eliminating any risk that Congress will overturn a veto), and then governs how he pleases—using the signing statements as if they were line-item vetoes. In those instances when Bush's violations of federal law have come to light, as over domestic surveillance, the White House has devised a novel solution: Stonewall any investigation into the violations and bid a compliant Congress simply to rewrite the laws.

Bush's alarmingly aberrant take on the Constitution is ironic. One need go back in the record less than a decade to find prominent Republicans railing against far more minor presidential legal infractions as precursors to all-out totalitarianism. "I will have no part in the creation of a constitutional double-standard to benefit the president," Senator Bill Frist declared of Bill Clinton's efforts to conceal an illicit sexual liaison. "No man is above the law, and no man is below the law—that's the principle that we all hold very dear in this country," Rep. Tom DeLay asserted. "The rule of law protects you and it protects me from the midnight fire on our roof or the 3 A.M. knock on our door," warned Rep. Henry Hyde, one of Clinton's chief accusers. In the face of Bush's more definitive dismissal of federal law, the silence from these quarters is deafening.

The president's defenders stoutly contend that wartime conditions fully justify Bush's actions. And as Lincoln showed during the Civil War, there may be times of military emergency where the executive believes it imperative to take immediate, highly irregular, even unconstitutional steps. "I felt that measures, otherwise unconstitutional, might become lawful," Lincoln wrote in 1864, "by becoming indispensable to the preservation of the Constitution, through the preservation of the nation." Bush seems to think that, since 9/11, he has been placed, by the grace of God, in the same kind of situation Lincoln faced. But Lincoln, under pressure of daily combat on American soil against fellow Americans, did not operate in secret, as Bush has. He did not claim, as Bush has, that his emergency actions were wholly regular and constitutional as well as necessary; Lincoln sought and received congressional authorization for his suspension of habeas corpus in 1863. Nor did Lincoln act under the amorphous cover of a "war on terror"—a war against a tactic, not a specific nation or political entity, which could last as long as any president deems the tactic a threat to national security. Lincoln's exceptional measures were intended to survive only as long as the Confederacy was in rebellion. Bush's could be extended indefinitely, as the president sees fit, permanently endangering rights and liberties guaranteed by the Constitution to the citizenry.

Much as Bush still enjoys support from those who believe he can do no wrong, he now suffers opposition from liberals who believe he can do no right. Many of these liberals are in the awkward position of having supported Bush in the past, while offering little coherent as an alternative to Bush's policies now. Yet it is difficult to see how this will benefit Bush's reputation in history.

The president came to office calling himself "a uniter, not a divider" and promising to soften the acrimonious tone in Washington. He has had two enormous opportunities to fulfill those pledges: first, in the noisy aftermath of his controversial election in 2000, and, even more, after the attacks of September 11, when the nation pulled behind him as it has supported no other president in living memory. Yet under both sets of historically unprecedented circumstances, Bush has chosen to act in ways that have left the country less united and more divided, less conciliatory and more acrimonious—much like James Buchanan, Andrew Johnson, and Herbert Hoover before him. And, like those three predecessors, Bush has done so in the service of a rigid ideology that permits no deviation and refuses to adjust to changing realities. Buchanan failed the test of Southern secession, Johnson failed in the face of Reconstruction, and Hoover failed in the face of the Great Depression. Bush has failed to confront his own failures in both domestic and international affairs, above all in his ill-conceived responses to radical Islamic terrorism. Having confused steely resolve with what Ralph Waldo Emerson called "a foolish consistency . . . adored by little statesmen," Bush has become entangled in tragedies of his own making, compounding those visited upon the country by outside forces.

No historian can responsibly predict the future with absolute certainty. There are too many imponderables still to come in the two and a half years left in Bush's presidency to know exactly how it will look in 2009, let alone in 2059. There have been presidents—Harry Truman was one—who have left office in seeming disgrace, only to rebound in the estimates of later scholars. But so far the facts are not shaping up propitiously for George W. Bush. He still does his best to deny it. Having waved away the lessons of history in the making of his decisions, the present-minded Bush doesn't seem to be concerned about his place in history. "History. We won't know," he told the journalist Bob Woodward in 2003. "We'll all be dead."

Another president once explained that the judgments of history cannot be defied or dismissed, even by a president. "Fellow citizens, *we* cannot escape history," said Abraham Lincoln. "We of this Congress and this administration, will be remembered in spite of ourselves. No personal significance, or insignificance, can spare one or another of us. The fiery trial through which we pass, will light us down, in honor or dishonor, to the latest generation."

Part Two:
State of the Union

Selling Washington

Elizabeth Drew

The New York Review of Books | June 23, 2005

If you want to know how government works, as Deep Throat (née Mark Felt) once said, "follow the money." In Washington, teeming with lobbyists and their clients, all seeking favors from politicians and willing to back up their requests with campaign contributions, free trips, and other giveaways, influence peddling is a way of life—and overreaching a constant temptation. The past year saw a number of high-profile heads roll for overstepping the rules: disgraced super-lobbyist Jack Abramoff pleaded guilty to several charges, including being part of a conspiracy involving the "corruption of public officials"; former House majority leader Tom DeLay (already under a cloud for accepting numerous trips and campaign contributions from Abramoff and his clients) declined to seek reelection and resigned from Congress after being indicted for allegedly laundering illegal campaign funds in Texas; former Republican Congressman Randy "Duke" Cunningham was convicted of accepting $2 million in bribes from defense contractors; and former Bush official David Safavian was convicted for lying about his efforts to assist Abramoff in real estate dealings. The Democrats had their own dirty laundry to deal with: Democratic Congressman William Jefferson is now under FBI investigation after $90,000 in alleged bribe money was found in his freezer; fellow Rep. Alan Mollohan is also being investigated by the FBI regarding the possible misappropriation of federal funds for his own benefit; and even Senate minority leader Harry Reid was forced to apologize for accepting free tickets to Las Vegas boxing matches.

In the aftermath of these and other scandals, the House and the Senate each recently passed lobbying-reform bills calling for greater disclosure of lobbying activity and of "earmarking" by elected officials (see "The Great American Pork Barrel," p. 85), and putting some restrictions on what freebies politicians can accept from lobbyists. As this anthology went to press, however, Congress had yet to reconcile the two bills—and reform advocates were warning that once they do, the resulting law will still have little effect on how business is conducted in the nation's capital. In this piece, veteran political journalist Elizabeth Drew explains how Republicans have taken Washington's pay-to-play game to new heights—and how this has affected the legislative process.

1.

As the criminal investigation of the Washington lobbyist Jack Abramoff was underway this spring, a spokesman for the law firm representing him issued a statement saying that Abramoff was "being singled out by the media for actions that are commonplace in Washington and are totally proper." Abramoff has since said much the same thing. The lawyer was half right. Like many other lobbyists, Abramoff often arranged for private organizations, particularly nonprofit groups, to sponsor pleasant, even luxurious, trips for members of Congress, with lobbyists like himself tagging along and enjoying the unparalleled "access" that such a setting provides; i.e., they get to know congressmen and sell them on legislation. They take over skyboxes at sporting events, inviting members of Congress and their staffs.

But Abramoff has differed from other lobbyists in his flamboyance (he owned two Washington restaurants, at which he entertained), and in the egregiously high fees he charged clients, in particular, Indian tribes in the casino business. The Senate Indian Affairs Committee, headed by John McCain, found last year that Abramoff and an associate, Michael Scanlon, a political consultant and former communications director for House Majority Leader Tom DeLay, received at least $66 million from six tribes over three years. Abramoff also instructed the tribes to make donations to certain members of Congress and conservative causes he was allied with. And he was careless—for example, in putting on his credit card charges for DeLay's golfing trip to the St. Andrews golf course in Scotland in 2000, with a stop in London for a bit of semiserious business to make the trip seem legitimate. It's illegal for a lobbyist to pay for congressional travel, but Abramoff is reported to have paid for three of DeLay's trips abroad. A prominent Republican lobbyist told me that the difference between what Abramoff did and what many other lobbyists do was simply "a matter of degree and blatancy."

Abramoff's behavior is symptomatic of the unprecedented corruption—the intensified buying and selling of influence over legislation and federal policy—that has become endemic in Washington under a Republican Congress and White House. Corruption has always been present in Washington, but in recent years it has become more sophisticated, pervasive, and blatant than ever. A friend of mine who works closely with lobbyists says, "There are no restraints now; business groups and lobbyists are going crazy—they're in every room on Capitol Hill writing the legislation. You can't move on the Hill without giving money."

This remark is only slightly exaggerated. For over ten years, but particularly since George W. Bush took office, powerful Republicans, among them Tom DeLay and Senator Rick Santorum, of Pennsylvania, have been carrying out what they call the "K Street Project," an effort to place more Republicans and get rid of Democrats in the trade associations and major national lobbying organizations that have offices on K Street in downtown Washington (although, of course, some have offices elsewhere).

The Republican purge of K Street is a more thorough, ruthless, vindictive, and effective attack on Democratic lobbyists and other Democrats who represent businesses and other organizations than anything Washington has seen before. The Republicans don't simply want to take care of their friends and former aides by getting them high-paying jobs: they want the lobbyists they helped place in these jobs and other corporate representatives to arrange lavish trips for themselves and their wives; to invite them to watch sports events from skyboxes; and, most important, to provide a steady flow of campaign contributions. The former aides become part of their previous employers' power networks. Republican leaders also want to have like-minded people on K Street who can further their ideological goals by helping to formulate their legislative programs, get them passed, and generally circulate their ideas. When I suggested to Grover Norquist, the influential right-wing leader and the leading enforcer of the K Street Project outside Congress, that numerous Democrats on K Street were not particularly ideological and were happy to serve corporate interests, he replied, "We don't want nonideological people on K Street, we want conservative activist Republicans on K Street."

The K Street Project has become critical to the Republicans' efforts to control all the power centers in Washington: the White House, Congress, the courts—and now, at least, an influential part of the corporate world, the one that raises most of the political money. It's another way for Republicans to try to impose their programs on the country. *The Washington Post* reported recently that House Majority Whip Roy Blunt, of Missouri, has established "a formal, institutionalized alliance" with K Street lobbyists. They have become an integral part of the legislative process by helping to get bills written and passed—and they are rewarded for their help by the fees paid by their clients. Among the results are legislation that serves powerful private interests all the more openly—as will be seen, the energy bill recently passed by the House is a prime example—and a climate of fear that is new. The conservative commentator David Brooks said on PBS's *NewsHour* earlier this year, "The biggest threat to the Republican majority is the relationship on K Street with corporate lobbyists and the corruption that is entailed in that." But if the Republicans are running a risk of being seen as overreaching in their takeover of K Street, there are few signs that they are concerned about it.

When the Republicans first announced the K Street Project after they won a majority in Congress in the 1994 election, they warned Washington lobbying and law firms that if they wanted to have appointments with Republican legislators they had better hire more Republicans. This was seen as unprecedentedly heavy-handed, but their deeper purposes weren't yet understood. Since the Democrats had been in power on Capitol Hill for a long time, many of the K Street firms then had more Democrats than Republicans or else they were evenly balanced. But the Democrats had been hired because they were well connected with prominent Democrats on Capitol Hill, not because Democratic Congresses demanded it. Moreover, it makes sense for lobbying firms that want access to members of Congress to hire people with good contacts in the majority party—especially former members or aides of the current leaders. But the bullying tactics of Republicans in the late 1990s were new.

DeLay, Santorum, and their associates organized a systematic campaign, closely monitored by Republicans on Capitol Hill and by Grover Norquist and the Republican National Committee, to put pressure on firms not just to hire Republicans but also to fire Democrats. With the election of Bush, this pressure became stronger. A Republican lobbyist told me, "Having the White House" has made it more possible for DeLay and Santorum "to enforce the K Street Project." Several Democratic lobbyists have been pushed out of their jobs as a result; business associations who hire Democrats for prominent positions have been subject to retribution. They are told that they won't be able to see the people on Capitol Hill they want to see. Sometimes the retribution is more tangible. The Republican lobbyist I spoke to said, "There's a high state of sensitivity to the partisanship of the person you hire for these jobs that did not exist five, six years ago— you hire a Democrat at your peril."

*   *   *   *   *

In one instance well known among lobbyists, the Ohio Republican Michael Oxley, chairman of the House Financial Services Committee, put pressure on the Investment Company Institute, a consortium of mutual fund companies, to fire its top lobbyist, a Democrat, and hire a Republican to replace her. According to a *Washington Post* story on February 15, 2003, six sources, both Democratic and Republican, said that members of Oxley's staff told the institute that a pending congressional investigation of mutual fund companies "might ease up if the mutual fund trade group complies with their wishes." It apparently didn't matter to them that House ethics rules prohibit congressmen or their staff "from bestowing benefits on the basis of the recipient's status as a supporter or contributor, or partisan affiliation." A Republican now holds the top job at the Investment Company Institute.

Last year retribution was taken against the Motion Picture Association of America, which—after first approaching without success a Republican congressman about to retire—hired as its new head Dan Glickman, a former Democratic representative from Kansas and secretary of agriculture in the Clinton administration. Republicans had warned the MPAA not to hire a Democrat for the job. After Glickman was hired, House Republicans removed from a pending bill some $1.5 billion in tax relief for the motion picture industry. Norquist told me, "No other industry is interested in taking a $1.5 billion hit to hire a Clinton friend." After Glickman was selected, the Capitol Hill newspaper *Roll Call* reported last year, "Santorum has begun discussing what the consequences are for the movie industry." Norquist said publicly that the appointment of Glickman was "a studied insult" and the motion picture industry's "ability to work with the House and the Senate is greatly reduced." Glickman responded by hiring prominent Republicans, including House Speaker Dennis Hastert's former spokesman, for major MPAA jobs.

Norquist's organization, Americans for Tax Reform, keeps watch on other K Street firms and calls attention on its Web site to the ones that are out of line.[1] According to a report in *The Washington Post* in 2003, an official of the Republican National Committee told a group of Republican lobbyists that thirty-three of the top thirty-six top-level K Street positions had gone to Republicans.

Despite its effectiveness, "the K Street Project is far from complete," according to Norquist, who says, "There should be as many Democrats working on K Street representing corporate America as there are Republicans working in organized labor—and that number is close to zero." He wants the project to include not just the top jobs in K Street firms, but "all of them—including secretaries."

A prominent Democratic Party fund-raiser believes that in 2001, after nineteen years as head of a trade association, he was fired because he was not a Republican. Another Democratic lobbyist told me that one of his major clients was put under pressure to drop him because he was a Democrat. A staff member in DeLay's office called the second of the two men and told him that he was "in DeLay's crosshairs," and warned him that if he attempted to work with any committees on Capitol Hill, he would get nowhere because of his political leanings.

Episodes of this kind have created a new atmosphere of fear in Washington. (Because of that atmosphere, these people as well as several others insisted on talking "on background," to protect themselves against retribution.) The Democratic lobbyist whose client was pressured by Republicans to drop him remarked, "It's a dangerous world out there," a world where, he said, "You'd better watch what you say. People in the Republican party, in the agencies, will say, 'I hear you were badmouthing X.' You know that you're being watched; you know that it's taken into account in your ability to do public policy things—[like] get a meeting with a government agency." Another lobbyist says, "It's scary now. People are afraid to say what they feel. It's had a chilling effect on debate." According to the head of a public policy group who frequently deals with lobbyists and corporations, "They don't have to say it," but he finds them now "intimidated by the atmosphere in this town—you hire Republicans."

Business groups are under heightened pressure to support the administration's policies—even those that are of no particular interest to them. A recent article in *Business Week* told of business organizations, including the Business Roundtable—an association of CEOs of major corporations—being summoned to meetings with Mike Meece, a special assistant to the president, various cabinet officers concerned with business affairs, and Karl Rove. They anticipated a friendly give-and-take about economic legislation, but instead they were told to get behind the president's plan to privatize Social Security. As a result, these organizations have spent millions of dollars promoting Bush's new program, particularly through ads.

Business groups have been notably reticent about criticizing administration policies—even ones they deeply dislike, such as the huge budget deficit. In the past, when they differed from administration policies, for example, on trade or tax issues, they spoke out. An adviser to business groups says, "They're scared of payback, of not getting their own agenda through."

2.

The connections between those who make policy and those who seek to influence it have become much stronger in recent years because of lobbyists' increasing use of nonprofit groups to sponsor trips that give them access to lawmakers, as with DeLay's trip to Scotland and England. Jack Abramoff arranged for the trips of DeLay and other members of Congress to be officially sponsored by the National Center for Public Policy Research, of which he is a member of the board. According to the congressional ethics rules, a lobbyist cannot repay the cost of a free trip for a congressman by reimbursing the nonprofit group that organized the trip. But there's nothing to prevent him from giving large contributions to the organization or encouraging his clients to do so. Abramoff urged the Indian tribes he represents to contribute to the National Center, which paid for DeLay's trips. Owing to a major loophole in the ethics rules, nonprofit groups do not have to disclose their contributors. "It's a real abuse," the Republican lobbyist told me. Such trips are also a way of getting around the ban on gifts of more than $50 to members of Congress.

For the Washington lobbyist, the most-sought-after access is to someone who writes the nation's laws and appropriates federal money. Trips offer the best opportunity for the lobbyist to make an impression on a congressman. Since congressmen can no longer make use of soft money under the McCain-Feingold campaign finance reforms, they are increasingly using golfing weekends and hunting trips for fund-raising. The politicians in effect charge the lobbyists to play golf or hunt with them. (Members of the middle class and the poor have scant opportunity to play golf with members of Congress.)

Many congressional trips have a serious purpose; some members restrict their travel to hazardous places like Iraq and Afghanistan. Such trips can be paid for out of congressional committees' funds—but they are usually less glamorous, harder to explain to the voters since the public pays for them, and they don't include lobbyists. The rules for privately funded trips, for example, that they must be "in connection with official duties," have been interpreted quite loosely. Larry Noble, executive director of the Center for Responsive Politics, a nonpartisan group that studies money in politics and its influence on public policy, says, "Even where they touch base with the rules, they don't take them seriously."

According to a study of congressional travel over the past five years paid for by nonprofit institutions, the Aspen Institute, a think tank based in Aspen, Colorado, and Washington, has spent the most on congressional travel; but Aspen is a serious organization that conducts seminars in the United States and abroad, and lobbying isn't involved.[2] More interesting is the nonprofit that spends the next highest amount: the Ripon Society, actually the Ripon Educational Fund, an offshoot of the Ripon Society, which was founded in the 1960s by liberal Republicans as a serious organization concerned with public policy. Now that liberal Republicans are virtually extinct, Ripon has become an organization for relatively moderate Republicans.

Like other policy groups that also lobby, Ripon has set up an ostensibly separate "educational" group, or 501(c)(3), to which contributors can make tax-deductible donations. The Ripon Educational Fund sponsors a large annual "Transatlantic Conference," held in such pleasant places as Rome, London, and Budapest, to which it invites between 150 and 200 U.S. citizens. These are vaguely described in the filings by the members of Congress who participated in them as "listening tour," or "fact finding."

The Ripon trips are famous among lobbyists for the opportunities they present for pressing their cases with members of Congress. A Republican lobbyist says that a Ripon Fund excursion has "become the trip to go on, because of the luxury and the access." *The Washington Post* reported that a Ripon Educational Fund trip to London in 2003 was attended by more than a hundred lobbyists, including representatives from American Express, AOL/Time Warner, and General Motors. They pay the Ripon Fund an annual membership fee of $9,500, and in addition finance their own trips abroad to Fund meetings.

Both the Ripon Society and the Ripon Educational Fund are headed by lobbyists. Former Representative Susan Molinari, of Staten Island, New York, a lobbyist whose clients now include Exxon, the Association of American Railroads, and Freddie Mac, is the chair of the Educational Fund. The president of the society itself is Richard Kessler, whose lobbying firm's clients include drug and cigarette companies. According to *The Hill*, the other Capitol Hill newspaper, Kessler's firm paid for a trip by five members of Congress to Ireland in August 2003, including four days at Ashford Castle, where the elegant grounds include a golf course. Of the members of Congress who went on Ripon Educational Fund trips, almost all took along their wives, an additional perk that contributes to the holiday atmosphere of the excursions. While lobbyists are prohibited from paying directly for congressional trips, trade associations and private corporations are allowed to do so—not much of an ethical distinction, since practically all of them engage in lobbying.

A recently released *Congressional Quarterly* study said that the disclosure forms filed by members of Congress "frequently show a direct correlation between a member's legislative interests and the sponsors of his or her trips." For example, Rep. Michael Oxley, who is particularly concerned with corporate finance, took several trips underwritten by companies such as MCI. A political observer who closely studied congressional trips concluded that the Republicans are invited so they can be "worked on" to pass pending legislation, while the Democrats are there largely for "maintenance," in case they take power in the future. Moderate, "swing" Democrats who can affect the outcome of legislation come in for special attention.

The McCain-Feingold campaign finance reform bill in 2002 didn't stop powerful companies and members of Congress from buying and selling influence. Rep. Barney Frank, a major backer of the reform bill, says, "It works about the same as it did before." But, he adds, because the new law banned large soft money contributions by individuals, corporations, and labor unions to campaigns for federal office, and maintained overall limits on how much a person can contribute to federal elections—doubling them from $2,000 to $4,000 per election cycle—everyone has to work harder to raise the money.[3] Still, congressmen are seldom heard to complain that they can't raise enough money and in fact, according to data compiled by the Center for Responsive Politics,[4] both the political parties and individual candidates are raising more money than ever. Lobbyists still manage to deliver large amounts to legislators by "bundling" smaller contributions.

They contribute most of the money they raise to incumbents who can be depended on to do favors—a major reason (in addition to gerrymandering) why there is serious competition in only 10 percent of House races, and only about five seats change hands in each congressional election. Members of Congress expect to receive contributions from local industries (and their workers)—say, the coal industry in West Virginia—and they back legislation to help them out as a matter of doing constituent work. It's illegal for a firm to compensate employees for their political contributions, but, a Republican lobbyist says, a job applicant is often told that he or she is expected to make contributions, and salaries are adjusted accordingly.

It's virtually impossible to show that a particular campaign contribution resulted in a specific vote—such quid pro quo is illegal. Fred Wertheimer, of the public advocacy group Democracy 21, told me, "The system's designed so that you don't see who gets what for their money. It's designed for me to give money to you and you do something for me in the Congress—without either of us saying a word about it. But if I give money, I know it and the candidate knows it. It's an investment, and down the road you collect on it." While much of the money buys access to a member of Congress, or key staff members, that is only the entry point to making one's case. As John McCain puts it, "You give money, you get an ear." Still, one can sometimes even trace what Larry Noble carefully calls "correlations" between contributions and legislative successes.

The energy bill passed by the House in April is a striking case in point. The oil-and-gas industry, a top contributor of campaign money—80 percent of it to Republicans—benefited from several of its new provisions. A study by the staff of Rep. Henry Waxman, Democrat of California, shows that perhaps the most indefensible provision gave a waiver against lawsuits to manufacturers of MTBE, or methyl tertiary-butyl ether, a gasoline additive that's a pollutant and suspected carcinogen. According to Waxman's staff, this waiver is worth billions to energy companies; the major beneficiaries would be Exxon, which, according to the Center for Responsive Politics, contributed $942,717 to candidates in the last election cycle; Valero Energy, $841,375; Lyondell Chemical, $342,775; and Halliburton, $243,946. The bill also exempted from the Safe Drinking Water Act the practice of hydraulic fracturing, which is used to make natural gas wells more productive and can also have an adverse effect on drinking water. Halliburton would benefit from this provision as well.

Another provision provided compensation to oil companies that bought leases, supposedly a speculative venture, on offshore sites where there is a moratorium on drilling. The compensation is worth billions of dollars to the oil industry. The bill also provided for the opening of the Arctic National Wildlife Refuge (ANWAR) to oil drilling—an invasion of the refuge that environmental groups have long tried to prevent. (Now that it contains more Republicans, the Senate passed a similar provision as part of its budget bill earlier this year.) The Democrats on the House Energy and Commerce Committee were effectively shut out of the drafting of the energy bill. House Democrat Edward Markey, a member of the Subcommittee on Energy and Air Quality, told me, "The energy companies got everything they wanted. Eight billion dollars in subsidies go to the energy companies, but to say that the conservation measures in it are modest would be a generous description."

An analysis by the Center for Responsive Politics shows that pharmaceutical manufacturers, who received a windfall from the new prescription drug program in the 2003 Medicare bill—including a provision prohibiting the federal government from negotiating with drug companies on prices—contributed more than three times as much to those who voted for the legislation as those who voted against it. A bill passed this year in the Senate and the House to tighten the rules for filing bankruptcy had long been sought by finance, insurance, and real estate interests, and particularly by credit card companies. Taken together, they all contributed $306 million to congressional campaigns, 60 percent of it to Republicans, during 2003 and 2004. The richest interests also spend the largest amounts of money on lobbying. According to a recent study by the Center for Public Integrity,[5] the makers of pharmaceuticals and health products spent the most—$759 million—on lobbying between 1998 and mid-2004, when the last lobbying reports were filed. Next came insurance companies. Oil and gas companies were seventh on the list.

The effects of the new, higher level of corruption on the way the country is governed are profound. Not only is legislation increasingly skewed to benefit the richest interests, but Congress itself has been changed. The head of a public policy strategy group told me, "It's not about governing anymore. The Congress is now a transactional institution. They don't take risks. So when a great moral issue comes up—like war—they can't deal with it." The theory that ours is a system of one-person-one-vote, or even that it's a representative democracy, is challenged by the reality of power and who really wields it. Barney Frank argues that "the political system was supposed to overcome the financial advantage of the capitalists, but as money becomes more and more influential, it doesn't work that way."

Two House Democrats, Rahm Emanuel, of Illinois, and Martin Meehan, of Massachusetts, have introduced legislation to tighten the rules on privately funded travel, strengthen the lobbying disclosure rules, and slow down the revolving door by which former members of Congress take jobs with the trade associations and, after a year, can lobby their former colleagues. Some Republicans are talking about placing more restrictive rules on trips. But the record shows that new regulations can often be evaded.

Perhaps the greatest deterrent to ethical transgression is that members of Congress don't want to read unfavorable stories about themselves. A Republican lobbyist says that the biggest factor in the growth of corruption has been "the expectation that all this goes undetected and unenforced." He added, "If Jack Abramoff goes to jail, that will be a big message to this town." Since the scandal broke over Abramoff's payments on behalf of DeLay, members of Congress have been scrambling to amend their travel reports, in some cases listing previously unreported trips, or filling in missing details. Public outrage can also have an inhibiting effect: after the Republicans changed the ethics rules earlier this year to protect DeLay, the adverse reaction in the press and from constituents was strong enough to make the Republican leadership back down.

But the public can't become outraged about something that isn't brought to its attention. The press tends to pounce on the big scandals but usually fails to cover the more common ones that take place every day. Some of the politicians I talked to hoped that the scandal over DeLay and Abramoff might lead to real changes, including more prosecutions and stricter disclosure requirements. But even they admit that, like so many other scandals, it may simply blow over.

Notes

[1] See www.atr.org/national/kstreet.

[2] See www.politicalmoneyline.com.

[3] In the 2004 presidential election, such money was paid to so-called "527 groups," which spent $500 million in the 2003-2004 election cycle. This wasn't, as widely thought, the result of a loophole in the McCain-Feingold bill but of the failure of the feckless Federal Election Committee to enforce a section of a 1974 campaign finance law.

[4] See www.opensecrets.org.

[5] See www.publicintegrity.org.

The Great American Pork Barrel
Ken Silverstein

Harper's Magazine | July 2005

As noted in the introduction to the previous selection, following a spate of recent lobbying scandals, the Senate and House both scrambled earlier this year to pass lobbying reform bills (which have yet to be reconciled in conference). One of the issues addressed in these bills is the practice of "earmarking," in which individual Congressmen anonymously insert funding for specific projects into various pieces of legislation. As Ken Silverstein reports in this Harper's *article, earmarking has grown to epidemic proportions over the past decade, and now accounts for upward of $60 billion a year in federal spending. While many in Congress defend earmarks as an important way to secure needed funds for constituents—and a time-honored prerogative of office—fiscal conservatives in the Senate and House have finally managed to convince their colleagues that something needs to be done to rein in the practice. Both reform bills would now require all earmarks inserted into spending bills to be listed publicly, along with the names of their sponsors. Congressional leaders have also promised that this provision will be extended to all types of legislation in the final reconciled bill. Of course, whether this lack of anonymity will cause lawmakers to think twice about reaching into the public till for their pet projects remains to be seen.*

*   *   *   *   *

How the $16 billion was absconded with we will never entirely know, at least not in all the particulars. What we do know is this: At approximately 2:00 P.M. last November 17, a Wednesday, a small group of senators and representatives from the congressional appropriations committees gathered in a meeting room under the Capitol dome, where they were to finalize one of thirteen bills that fund the annual affairs of the U.S. government. According to eyewitnesses, only a few members made statements about the bill in question—the Foreign Operations bill, which pays for everything from the Peace Corps to the aerial fumigation of Colombian coca. The only notable break from protocol was made by Robert Byrd of West Virginia, who delivered an impromptu speech in praise of the women of Congress; the senator was particularly fulsome in regard to Rep. Marcy Kaptur of Ohio, of whom he remarked that he "would have fallen in love with her" had he met her earlier in life. The meeting ended less than half an hour after it began, as this very straightforward piece of legislation was approved by the conferees.

Over the next seventy-two hours, by way of meetings and measures obscured from the public, this simple bill would undergo a startling metastasis. Because Congress had failed, for the third year in a row, to pass most of the bills that keep the government running, members of the appropriations committees folded eight as yet unapproved bills—those that fund the Departments of Justice, State, Energy, Labor, Commerce, Education, Agriculture, Transportation, the Treasury, the Interior, Veterans Affairs, Health and Human Services, and Housing and Urban Development, as well as the entire legislative and judiciary branches—into the Foreign Operations bill. Even to assemble the text of the resulting piece of legislation, called an omnibus appropriations bill, was an epic task. Teams of staffers labored long into the night to edit the various bills that would be folded in, after which the mass of pages was fed through copier machines across Capitol Hill. There was no time to produce a clean copy, so the version of the omnibus bill that Congress voted on was a fourteen-inch-thick clump of papers with corrections, deletions, and additions on virtually every page. Handwritten notes peppered the margins; typefaces varied from section to section and from paragraph to paragraph. First made available to lawmakers at around 12:15 A.M. on November 20 (and only to those who happened to be browsing the House Rules Committee Web site, where it was posted), the omnibus bill came to a vote before the full House some sixteen hours later, at approximately 4:00 that afternoon, and before the Senate at 8:42 that evening. For the legislators who approved it—by a margin of 344-51 in the House and 65-30 in the Senate—reading the 3,320-page bill before the vote would have been a mathematical impossibility.

Only later, after the approved bill had been shuffled off to the president for signature, could lawmakers and laymen alike peruse its contents in earnest. Scattered throughout the bill were hundreds of hastily inserted pages of "earmarks," or allocations for local projects that are tucked into federal budgets. As approved at the November 17 appropriations meeting, the Foreign Operations bill had contained a mere nine earmarks. The omnibus measure, which was completed after two feverish days of work, allocated money for 11,772 separate earmarks. There was $100,000 for goat-meat research in Texas, $549,000 for "Future Foods" development in Illinois, $569,000 for "Cool Season Legume Research" in Idaho and Washington, $63,000 for a program to combat noxious weeds in the desert Southwest, $175,000 for obesity research in Texas. In the end, the bill's earmarks were worth a combined total of nearly $16 billion—a figure almost as large as the annual budget of the Department of Agriculture and roughly twice that of the Environmental Protection Agency. It was the biggest single piece of pork-barrel legislation in American history.

Of who added these grants, no public record exists. Except in rare cases, members of Congress will refuse to discuss their involvement in establishing earmarks, and the appropriations committees have a blanket rule against commenting. Often it is difficult to discern even who is receiving the funds: earmarks are itemized in bills but generally without disclosure of the direct recipient—just a dollar amount, destination, and broad purpose. Indeed, in the matter of the $16 billion burglary, and the similar acts of mass theft plotted for this year, the only certainty seems to be this: that lawmakers and lobbyists collude to conceal, to the utmost extent possible, their actions from the American taxpayer, who serves as the ultimate benefactor to their chronic bouts of generosity.

"Pork-barreling" as a legislative epithet is a pre-Civil War coinage that referred to the custom of handing out salt pork to slaves, who would crowd around the barrels that held it; and indeed, members of Congress have raided the federal treasury for home-district boondoggles ever since the earliest days of the republic. By 1822, President James Monroe warned that financial support from Washington should henceforth be granted "to great national works only, since if it were unlimited it would be liable to abuse and might be productive of evil." The pork barrel was to become as central to our national political culture as the gerrymander or the filibuster; it has long been a foregone conclusion that whenever the federal government builds a road, or erects a dam, or constructs a power plant, members of Congress will artfully pad the bill with hometown "pork."

In the past two decades, though, the pastime has become breathtaking in its profligacy. Even as the federal deficit soars to record heights, the sums of money being diverted from the treasury have grown ever larger. Last year, 15,584 separate earmarks worth a combined $32.7 billion were attached to appropriations bills—more than twice the dollar amount in 2001, when 7,803 earmarks accounted for $15 billion; and more than three times the amount in 1998, when roughly 2,000 earmarks totaled $10.6 billion. To be sure, not every project that receives an earmark is an utter waste of money. Such appropriations can fund after-school programs, park conservation, public health. "What some people call 'pork' may be as essential as a lock on a dam that creates hydropower, or [support for] a bridge, road, or other critical infrastructure," said Zack Wamp, a Tennessee Republican on the House Appropriations Committee. "Sometimes we have to direct spending because the executive branch is not doing its job."

But the process is so willfully murky that abuse has become not the exception but the rule. Earmarks are added anonymously, frequently during last-minute, closed-door sessions of the appropriations committees. An especially attractive feature for those private interests seeking earmarks is that they are awarded on a noncompetitive basis and recipients need not meet any performance standards. In other words, applicants need not demonstrate that their project, program, or company actually delivers a useful good or service.

Although there are a number of legislative instruments that moneyed interests can use to raid the federal treasury, appropriations bills have become the vehicle of choice, both because they are regularly scheduled— they must be passed, or else the government shuts down—and because their staggering size and scope deter public scrutiny of individual line items. Unsurprisingly, seats on the appropriations committees are among the most desirable sinecures in Congress. Of the 66 seats on the House committee (37 Republican, 29 Democrat), 28 are held by members from the electoral-rich states of California, Florida, Michigan, New York, Ohio, Pennsylvania, and Texas. On the Senate committee (where Republicans hold a 15-13 advantage) sit many of the most influential members of the upper chamber: Republicans Thad Cochran of Mississippi, Ted Stevens of Alaska, and Pete Domenici of New Mexico, along with Democrats Robert Byrd of West Virginia, Minority Leader Harry Reid of Nevada, and Dianne Feinstein of California.

That appropriations bills have emerged as the premier venue for private interests also owes something to Tom DeLay, the embattled House majority leader. Traditionally, seats on the appropriations committee had been granted on the basis of seniority; but when the GOP won control of the House in 1994, DeLay (who himself served on the appropriations committee between 1987 and 2003) helped craft a new strategy under which the Republican seats were, as circumstances required, strategically assigned to "at risk" members; i.e., to those who had narrowly won office. This lent wobbly new lawmakers two vital assets: first, the ability to direct pork projects to their home districts, thereby impressing constituents with their ability to bring home federal monies; second, a fail-safe method of filling campaign war chests—namely, by tapping earmark seekers for donations.

The strategy has been eminently successful, as seen in the case of Anne Northup, a Republican from Kentucky who first won office in 1996 when she squeaked past a Democratic candidate by 1,299 votes. It was the first time in nearly three decades that a Republican had represented Kentucky's Third District, which encompasses the Democratic stronghold of Louisville. Northup was deemed to be highly vulnerable, but she was immediately assigned a slot on the appropriations committee and has held the seat ever since. In 1998, the first year she ran for reelection, Northup raised $1.9 million and won with 51.5 percent of the vote. By last November, Northup was vice-chair of one of the major pork-dispensing subcommittees—Labor, Health and Human Services, and Education—and Louisville was, not by coincidence, receiving more earmarked funds than the entire state of Delaware or Nebraska, states with no representation on the appropriations committees. Having raised $3.3 million, Northup sailed to reelection with 60 percent of the vote.

*   *   *   *   *

As earmarking has proliferated, it has become less ad hoc and more efficient; it is now an accepted Washington industry, with its own standardized rules and procedures. Whereas in the past we had isolated thefts on behalf of constituents, what we have today is a professional crime syndicate with tentacles not only in long-established pork-barrel sectors such as public works and defense but also in such relatively unspoiled fields as academic research and community programs. Those seeking government largesse no longer need to procure backroom meetings through congressional aides; most members of Congress now have simple "appropriations-request forms," which are as easy to complete as a typical job or credit-card application. The form for the office of Senator Dianne Feinstein (which is similar to the other forms I've seen) asks earmark seekers for the name of the individual making the request, a letter from that person, a description of the project, the amount sought, a budget, and the specific appropriations bill to which the request should be attached. "Multiple requests . . . must be ranked in priority," reads the instruction sheet.

By far the most significant change of recent years has been the incursion of lobbying firms, many of which have been set up expressly for this purpose. Like attorneys at hospital bedsides, earmarking lobbyists aggressively court customers with boasts of their ability to deliver easy cash. "Shepherding appropriations requests through Congress is a priority for many clients," trumpets the Web site of B&D Sagamore, one such earmarking specialist. B&D's site furthermore promises to arrange "discussions between clients and members of Congress" and track legislation so that the firm can intervene "at critical points in the process."

Last year more than 3,000 private companies or institutions hired lobbying firms such as B&D to pursue earmarks. Because federal disclosure laws are minimal, to say the least, it is difficult to estimate exactly how much money in total was doled out to lobbyists. But Keith Ashdown, of Taxpayers for Common Sense, a Washington group that tracks the earmarking process, says the typical earmark seeker pays a retainer ranging from the tens of thousands up to more than $100,000 per year, with the total easily reaching tens of millions of dollars. Large though that sum may seem, as investments such retainers are undeniably savvy: the overall payout in pork is many times that, totaling into the billions.

For the aspiring pork recipient, mastering the appropriations process is hardly a difficult task. First, one needs simply to identify the correct member of Congress to approach with one's request. Almost always this will be a member whose district or state is home to the company or entity that will receive the money. Mark McIntyre, an appropriations lobbyist at the Russ Reid Company, wrote a 2003 how-to guide to appropriations for a Web publication called *OnPhilanthropy*, in which he said that lining up the best congressional "champion" often means the difference between success and failure. "It is extremely helpful," McIntyre pointedly noted, "if your U.S. Representative or one of your U.S. Senators serves on the Appropriations Committee."

Helpful indeed, as seen in the case of Ted Stevens, the senior senator from Alaska and chairman of the Senate Appropriations Committee from 1997 to 2004. Last year's vast omnibus bill contained hundreds of earmarks for Alaska, including grants for projects on seafood waste ($160,000), salmon quality standards ($167,000), and alternative salmon products ($1.1 million, of which $443,000 was specifically set aside for the "development of baby food containing salmon"). Alaska's total haul came to $2,211.07 per capita, about twenty-two times the national average.

Mississippi, home of Senator Thad Cochran, the new chairman, also happens to be a leading recipient of appropriations bounty. Grants to his state last year included $900,000 for "cattle and nutrient management in stream crossings," $248,000 for a study to prevent the spread of cogon grass, and $2.6 million for—the surest of sure bets—Mississippi State University's Thad Cochran Research, Technology and Economic Development Park. West Virginia, home of the top Democratic appropriations mastermind, Senator Byrd, always receives ample funds as well. "You may as well slap my wife as take away my transportation funding," Byrd once remarked. The senator's most memorable achievement was when he won a Coast Guard facility for his conspicuously landlocked state.

In recent years the most daring pursuer of earmarks has been former Rep. Bob Livingston of Louisiana, who headed the House Appropriations Committee in the late 1990s before resigning from Congress in 1999; his departure, which occurred just as he was helping to spearhead the call for Bill Clinton's impeachment, became necessary when Livingston was forced to acknowledge that he himself had "on occasion" committed the sin of adultery. Livingston's disgrace proved to be short-lived: he immediately turned to lobbying and signed up a drove of clients. Among the first of these was a Louisiana firm called JRL Enterprises, which since has had remarkable success winning earmarks for its "I CAN Learn" mathematics software. Last year's omnibus bill contained three separate earmarks for JRL—none named the company, only the software program—worth a combined $5.5 million.

For JRL to have hired Livingston in the first place was a natural move: the year before he resigned, Livingston had slipped JRL's original earmark into an appropriations bill, a $7.3 million grant that provided the then-floundering firm with virtually all of its income for 1998. Since becoming a lobbyist, Livingston has received nearly $1 million in fees from JRL, which, in turn, has since received $38 million in earmarks.

Yet there is very little (excluding JRL's own extravagant claims) to suggest that I CAN Learn significantly helps the learning of anyone at all. A story last fall in the *Fort Worth Star-Telegram* found that students in the local school district, which has invested heavily in I CAN Learn, weren't learning math any more successfully than students elsewhere in the state. Meanwhile, local teachers complained that the software was freezing in the middle of lessons and sometimes provided the wrong answers to test questions. Nonetheless, Congress year after year has awarded ever more money to JRL—perhaps because company executives have year after year awarded ever more money to members of the appropriations committees. Between 1999 and 2004, of JRL's $81,460 in political contributions, at least $14,500 went to appropriations members.

The link between lawmaker and earmark is virtually impossible to make definitively. A clear paper trail, however, does exist: when requesting an earmark, lawmakers must make their request in writing to the relevant appropriations committee. But because all congressional correspondence is exempt from the Freedom of Information Act, would-be watchdogs—such as Ashdown's group, Taxpayers for Common Sense (which provided much of the hard data for this story)—have no way to obtain earmark requests unless they are leaked. Ashdown, whose whole job is to monitor the appropriations process, says he has never seen more than "a handful" of the official requests himself.

Sometimes, though, circumstantial evidence will allow for the construction of a probable scenario. For example, federal lobby-disclosure records show that last year the Rajant Corporation, based in Wayne, Pennsylvania, retained three lobbying shops to seek appropriations money for a defense contract. The campaign was successful; the defense appropriations bills approved in July awarded the company $2 million for the project.

Numerous clues suggested that Rep. Curt Weldon of Pennsylvania played a role in Rajant's earmark. Consider that Weldon is vice-chairman of the House Armed Services Committee, and Rajant is based in his district. Consider also that a former Weldon staffer, John McNichol, is now a lobbyist at Greenlee Partners, and was retained by Rajant to push for the earmark. And that Blank Rome, the second lobby shop on Rajant's payroll, is a major donor to Weldon; lobbyists at the firm, including two on the Rajant account, gave Weldon $9,300 between 2000 and 2004. And that Rajant's lobbyist at the third firm, David Urban of American Continental Group, is another Weldon donor.

Russ Caso, Weldon's chief of staff, confirmed that Weldon submitted an earmark request for Rajant but said a number of other congressional offices did as well. He added that the congressman's office "accepts all [earmark] requests and we have a vetting process." Caso said that on military-related items the office checks to see whether the product is useful and "submits requests only for items that the military wants."

Securing an earmark is never a given; only about one in four requests makes the final cut, and so steps must be taken to ensure that lawmakers are sufficiently stimulated. The most effective means is, of course, direct cash disbursements. As McIntyre forthrightly states in his how-to guide, "Money has become the oxygen supply of political campaigns. For better or for worse, perhaps the best way to show your support for a Senator or Representative is to make a campaign contribution."

And yet direct contributions to lawmakers can get one only so far. Choosing the right lobbyist is as important as choosing the right lawmaker, if not more important. Because so many lobbyists have past experience on Capitol Hill, they usually have personal ties both to members of Congress and to their key staffers, who vet and prioritize the earmark requests. "You need to hire someone who understands the process and knows the pressure points," says a Beltway lobbyist who specializes in winning appropriations money. "There's a lot of horse-trading going on, so you need someone who is hounding the staffers, calling up every week or every day if necessary."

A full taxonomy of the lobbyists of Washington would necessitate a book-length field guide, but a few of the more salient species can be considered here. The most effective ally for the earmark-seeker is a lobbyist who is actually related, by blood or marriage, to a powerful member of an appropriations committee. For years many Alaskan firms, and even huge corporations such as Lockheed Martin, have retained the services of William Bittner, brother-in-law of Senator Stevens. In one case reported by the *Los Angeles Times* in 2003, Stevens inserted a single line into an appropriations bill that awarded $9.6 million to a program whose chief beneficiary was a Hyundai subsidiary represented by Bittner. The brother of Rep. John Murtha, the top Democrat on the House Appropriations Defense Subcommittee, has lobbied for at least sixteen defense manufacturers on appropriations issues. Craig Obey, the son of Rep. David Obey, the top Democrat on the House Appropriations Committee, seeks money for the National Parks & Conservation Association.

Retired members and staffers from the appropriations committees also make particularly effective lobbyists, because they enjoy guaranteed access to the friends and colleagues they left behind. Jim Dyer, who became the Republican staff director of the House Appropriations Committee in 1995, was long considered to be one of the most powerful aides on the Hill. "Jim's job was to broker deals between members," a lobbyist and friend of Dyer's told me earlier this year. "He knew where every dime was. He's been hounded for years with big money offers." In February, just weeks after we spoke, Dyer was hired by a lobby shop called Clark & Weinstock, where he joined two former appropriations committee members, Vin Weber and Vic Fazio.

Some lobbyists specialize in winning specific types of appropriations. If your seaside community wants taxpayers to pay to have its beach restored, the man to see is Howard Marlowe. He has won dozens of such earmarks, mostly for underprivileged communities like Florida's Venice and New York's Fire Island. In late October 2001, on behalf of the American Shore & Beach Preservation Association, Marlowe's firm helped prepare a letter to Congress that bemoaned the economic toll that the events of September 11 had taken on the nation. "While these financial troubles pale in comparison with the unspeakable human losses of that day, they pose a significant problem," the letter went on. Urgent action was therefore required—specifically, lavishing money on beach communities in order to lure foreign and domestic tourists to America's shorelines. "Many national leaders have stated that increased tourism is imperative to the recovery of our economic strength," the letter claimed.

Diane Blagman, a former staffer at the House Appropriations Committee, and currently of Greenberg Traurig, was the congressional liaison for the 9/11 Memorial Concert in Washington and serves on the board of the Grateful Dead's charitable foundation. She has become adept at winning money for her entertainment-industry clients, such as the $150,000 earmark she picked up last fall to fund the Santa Monica–based Grammy Foundation's "educational activities."

Van Scoyoc Associates—headed by Stu van Scoyoc, a prominent donor to politicians of both parties—specializes in winning research money for university clients. This is an especially fast-growing field: the *Chronicle of Higher Education* estimated that academic earmarks topped $2 billion in 2003, six times more than in 1996. James Savage, a professor of politics at the University of Virginia, says academic earmarks are particularly insidious. "Academic research is supposed to be peer-reviewed, with the idea being that the best science wins out. But with earmarks, quality has nothing to do with it. Schools get research funds simply because they are in a powerful member's district or have the money to hire a lobbyist." Savage has come across cases in which universities from different states team up to submit joint requests for earmarks, knowing that their chances for funding go up by bundling together the largest number of powerful lawmakers. Many universities, he says, have received earmarks for advanced research even though they don't have graduate-studies programs in the relevant fields.

Wexler and Walker Public Policy Associates has a flourishing practice in the transportation field. One of the best-connected firms in town, Public Policy Associates' name partners are Anne Wexler, a prominent Democrat who once upon a time helped organize Eugene McCarthy's 1968 antiwar presidential campaign and who now lobbies for a fair portion of the Fortune 500, and former GOP Congressman Robert Walker, who was one of Newt Gingrich's closest allies during the latter's reign as House speaker.

Back in 1997, Public Policy Associates put together a musical revue about lobbying that it offered clients as an educational tool, and the show gives a pretty good idea of how the firm courts Washington. One skit, performed for a group of Burger King operators called the National Franchise Association (NFA), included a song performed to the tune of "Matchmaker, Matchmaker":

Congressman, senator we've formed a PAC
Now we can act, no need for tact,
Pooling resources makes very good sense
So we formed a little PAC
When NFA's membership starts to pitch in
Growing the fund, access begins
Should ever a congressman put up his guard
The PAC is our calling card . . .
Any lawmaker ignoring our PAC
Risks being fried like a Big Mac
Working together's the tried and true way to
Deliver the facts, give pats on the back
Favors attract, enemies sacked
Through NFA's brand new PAC!

Public Policy Associates knows of which it sings. During the last three election cycles, the company's own PAC doled out more than $315,000 in political contributions; its employees gave an additional $255,000.

The firm's rainmaker on transportation issues is Timothy Hannegan, a former aviation expert at the General Accounting Office. Hannegan, who is described on the firm Web site as "a prolific Democratic fund-raiser," helped secure passage of the congressional airline-aid package in the aftermath of the September 11 attacks. Another Hannegan client, the Mammoth Mountain Ski Area, in California's Sierra Nevada range, recently underwent what *Ski Magazine* termed "the biggest makeover in the history of skiing." The makeover, intended to transform the resort's image from a family oriented ski park to a retreat for the superrich, included new lodges, luxury chalets, and high-priced condominiums. Mammoth Mountain wanted to see the local transportation network upgraded to help move in the new upscale clientele, and so last year its home town won a $1 million earmark for a bus-maintenance facility that primarily services the resort. Hannegan, who is being paid a $40,000 annual retainer by Mammoth Mountain, says that he did not lobby for that earmark but acknowledges that he is currently soliciting appropriations money for a controversial new regional airport on the resort's behalf.

*   *   *   *   *

The defense appropriations bill is, as one might imagine, a particularly popular target for seekers of pork. In 1980 there were just 62 earmarks in the defense appropriations bill; last year there were 2,671, worth a combined $12.2 billion. That included $3 million to develop bathrooms made entirely of stainless steel; $3.75 million for alcoholism research (at, of all places, the Ernest Gallo Clinic and Research Center, in San Francisco); and $1 million to help eradicate brown tree snakes in Guam. It also contained $13.85 million for textile companies in North Carolina that produce clothing for the Pentagon, including Odor Signature Reduction Products for Special Forces and Smart Apparel for Warriors.

That latter line of clothing, which will be subsidized with $1 million in taxpayer money, is being developed by the Sara Lee Corp., which—though better known for its frozen cheesecake, pies, and "brownie bites"—also has an apparel division based in Winston-Salem, North Carolina, that manufactures Playtex, L'eggs, and Wonderbra. I was never able to determine exactly what Smart Apparel for Warriors is, since no one at Sara Lee's headquarters in Chicago or in Winston-Salem was willing to talk about it: they claimed that the project, as a Pentagon contract, was too sensitive to discuss. But I was able to determine, through lobby-disclosure forms, that the company obtained the money with the help (for a $20,000 retainer) of The PMA Group, a lobby shop that, according to its Web site, is "the premier Washington consulting organization in the defense arena."

Paul Magliocchetti, a former top staffer at the appropriations committees and nine-year veteran of the defense subcommittee, is the founder and president of PMA, which is strategically located on the Metro's Blue Line, two stops from the Pentagon. The move to the private sector has paid off quite handsomely for Magliocchetti, who had been forced to eke out a living on his $65,200-a-year salary at House appropriations. Since 1998, by contrast, Magliocchetti's firm has received $21.7 million in fees from large defense companies—the most paid to any lobbying firm, according to a study by the Center for Public Integrity. PMA has thirty-two lobbyists, and all but one of them are revolving-door alumni from the Defense Department or Capitol Hill. Ten have experience on one of the two appropriations committees. PMA's Web site is not terribly subtle about the company's ability to rig the system. "No one understands the inner workings of our nation's capital better than The PMA Group," it says. "Many of our associates have formulated or helped to shape the policies that are in place today."

The firm's PAC is one of the defense industry's most generous, doling out more than $975,000 to 340 House and Senate lawmakers, according to the Center for Public Integrity. Of direct contributions from PMA lobbyists, the three top recipients—Reps. Pete Visclosky, John Murtha, and James Moran—are all key players on the appropriations committees. Collectively they received about $87,250 from PMA between 1998 and 2003.

No immediate suspect emerges in the question of which member of Congress inserted Sara Lee's earmark. In the case of another winner in last year's defense-earmarks sweepstakes, Night Vision Equipment Company of Allentown, Pennsylvania, there is not only a suspect but one with motive and means as well: Arlen Specter, the third-ranking Republican on the Senate Appropriations Committee.

Night Vision won a $1.25 million earmark in the defense bill, funding lobbied for by IKON Public Affairs, to which Night Vision paid $60,000. IKON deployed two lobbyists to work the Night Vision account, Peter Grollman and Craig Snyder, both of whom previously held senior posts on Specter's staff. Between 2000 and 2004, IKON donated $13,250 to Specter, with $7,250 of that coming directly from Snyder and Grollman. During that same period, Night Vision's then president, William Grube (along with his wife), kicked in $8,000 to Specter.

Just months before the defense appropriations bill passed, Snyder helped Specter fight off a fierce primary challenge from Pat Toomey. The electoral hopes of Toomey, who favors a ban on abortion, rested on his trouncing Specter in the state's conservative heartland, where the senator's prochoice politics have made him a pariah. Shortly before the primary vote, Snyder put together a PAC called Pennsylvanians for Honest Politics, which promptly raised $17,750, with one-third coming directly from Snyder and Grube. Almost all of that money was spent to produce and air a radio ad that ran in the last few days of the campaign—on just a single Christian station that airs only in conservative areas. The ad savaged Toomey for failing to call, during an interview with Chris Matthews on *Hardball*, for criminal sanctions against a woman who gets an abortion. "Somebody who claims to be on our side had the opportunity to say abortion is murder," says the ad's protagonist. "Instead of showing the nation real pro-life leadership, Toomey shrunk like a frightened turtle." Specter won by just 17,146 votes out of more than a million ballots cast and did far better in conservative counties than expected.

Less than three months later it was Specter, along with Senator Rick Santorum, who announced that Night Vision had won the earmarks. "These projects, key to our nation's defense, will be invaluable in our continuing war against terror," he declared. So was it Specter who inserted the earmark for Night Vision? No one knows for certain, since neither the company, Specter, nor the Senate Appropriations Committee would comment.

Members of Congress are, of course, perpetually decrying the spending excesses of the body they compose; the late Illinois Senator Paul Douglas, who served between 1949 and 1967, archly likened his colleagues to "drunkards who shout for temperance in the intervals between cocktails." Just as with campaign finance, Congress in fact has little incentive to reform a system that protects incumbents, Republicans and Democrats alike. "Getting between a lawmaker and an earmark is like trying to take a ribeye away from a dog," says Keith Ashdown. "Congress sees it as one of its most fundamental rights."

Anyone who imagines that Congress could discipline itself on pork should consider the case of the $32 billion Department of Homeland Security budget. When DHS was created in 2003, congressional leaders agreed that its appropriations bill would not be earmarked, so that pork-barreling would not muddle the priorities of the incipient War on Terror. That first year the ban held—only eighteen earmarks, worth $423 million, were attached, despite the more than seven hundred lobbyists who had registered to work on homeland-security issues. The lobbyists, however, kept their chins up. "This is a stage where people are still cultivating relationships," one hopeful told a reporter for *Congressional Quarterly* in July 2003. Said another lobbyist, a former representative named Steven Kuykendall: "It's a challenge, but that's what guys like me get paid to do."

Two years of persistence have apparently paid off. This spring, as the 2006 appropriations process got under way, Capitol Hill was awash with rumors that the informal moratorium would soon be abandoned. *Congress Daily* reported in April that the heads of the appropriations subcommittees on homeland security—Rep. Harold Rogers (R., Ky.) and Senator Judd Gregg (R., N.H.)—were debating whether to end the ban, and thereby to allow earmarks to bloom within DHS with the same fecundity as elsewhere in the federal budget. One lobbyist opined, no doubt with great gravity of tone, that homeland-security agencies could benefit from "additional congressional oversight."

Congress, no doubt, will soon concur; even if the moratorium survives another year or two, its days are surely numbered. Thirty-two billion dollars, when none have been siphoned off for friends, are overdue for oversight indeed.

How Divided Are We?
James Q. Wilson

Commentary | February 2006

Historians have long embraced the concept of an underlying "consensus" in American political thought, as opposed to the class-based tensions that have characterized the politics of nations in Europe and elsewhere. A pair of selections in last year's edition of this anthology echoed this theme, using polling statistics to argue that, despite the increased polarization of our political leadership, most Americans tended to be fairly centrist in their views. In this essay, which appeared in the journal Commentary, *James Q. Wilson takes another look at the gap between conservatives and liberals, and concludes just the opposite. In his analysis, America's citizens—and the media outlets that inform them—are more intensely divided than they have been in decades. "To a degree that we cannot precisely measure, and over issues that we cannot exactly list," he writes, "polarization has seeped down into the public, where it has assumed the form of a culture war."*

The 2004 election left our country deeply divided over whether our country is deeply divided. For some, America is indeed a polarized nation, perhaps more so today than at any time in living memory. In this view, yesterday's split over Bill Clinton has given way to today's even more acrimonious split between Americans who detest George Bush and Americans who detest John Kerry, and similar divisions will persist as long as angry liberals and angry conservatives continue to confront each other across the political abyss. Others, however, believe that most Americans are moderate centrists, who, although disagreeing over partisan issues in 2004, harbor no deep ideological hostility. I take the former view.

By polarization I do not have in mind partisan disagreements alone. These have always been with us. Since popular voting began in the nineteenth century, scarcely any winning candidate has received more than 60 percent of the vote, and very few losers have received less than 40 percent. Inevitably, Americans will differ over who should be in the White House. But this does not necessarily mean they are polarized.

By polarization I mean something else: an intense commitment to a candidate, a culture, or an ideology that sets people in one group definitively apart from people in another, rival group. Such a condition is revealed when a candidate for public office is regarded by a competitor and his supporters not simply as wrong but as corrupt or wicked; when one way of thinking about the world is assumed to be morally superior to any other way; when one set of political beliefs is considered to be entirely correct and a rival set wholly wrong. In extreme form, as defined by Richard Hofstadter in *The Paranoid Style in American Politics* (1965), polarization can entail the belief that the other side is in thrall to a secret conspiracy that is using devious means to obtain control over society. Today's versions might go like this: "Liberals employ their dominance of the media, the universities, and Hollywood to enforce a radically secular agenda"; or, "conservatives, working through the religious Right and the big corporations, conspired with their hired neocon advisers to invade Iraq for the sake of oil."

Polarization is not new to this country. It is hard to imagine a society more divided than ours was in 1800, when pro-British, procommerce New Englanders supported John Adams for the presidency while pro-French, proagriculture Southerners backed Thomas Jefferson. One sign of this hostility was the passage of the Alien and Sedition Acts in 1798; another was that in 1800, just as in 2000, an extremely close election was settled by a struggle in one state (New York in 1800, Florida in 2000).

The fierce contest between Abraham Lincoln and George McClellan in 1864 signaled another national division, this one over the conduct of the Civil War. But thereafter, until recently, the nation ceased to be polarized in that sense. Even in the half-century from 1948 to (roughly) 1996, marked as it was by sometimes strong expressions of feeling over whether the presidency should go to Harry Truman or Thomas Dewey, to Dwight Eisenhower or Adlai Stevenson, to John F. Kennedy or Richard Nixon, to Nixon or Hubert Humphrey, and so forth, opinion surveys do not indicate widespread detestation of one candidate or the other, or of the people who supported him.

Now they do. Today, many Americans and much of the press regularly speak of the president as a dimwit, a charlatan, or a knave. A former Democratic presidential candidate has asserted that Bush "betrayed" America by launching a war designed to benefit his friends and corporate backers. A senior Democratic senator has characterized administration policy as a series of "lies, lies, and more lies" and has accused Bush of plotting a "mindless, needless, senseless, and reckless" war. From the other direction, similar expressions of popular disdain have been directed at Senator John Kerry (and before him at President Bill Clinton); if you have not heard them, that may be because (unlike many of my relatives) you do not live in Arkansas or Texas or other locales where the *New York Times* is not read. In these places, Kerry is widely spoken of as a scoundrel.

In the 2004 presidential election, over two-thirds of Kerry voters said they were motivated explicitly by the desire to defeat Bush. By early 2005, President Bush's approval rating, which stood at 94 percent among Republicans, was only 18 percent among Democrats—the largest such gap in the history of the Gallup poll. These data, moreover, were said to reflect a mutual revulsion between whole geographic sections of the country, the so-called Red (Republican) states versus the so-called Blue (Democratic) states. As summed up by the distinguished social scientist who writes humor columns under the name of Dave Barry, residents of Red states are "ignorant racist fascist knuckle-dragging NASCAR-obsessed cousin-marrying road-kill-eating tobacco-juice-dribbling gun-fondling religious fanatic rednecks," while Blue-state residents are "godless unpatriotic pierced-nose Volvo-driving France-loving leftwing Communist latte-sucking tofu-chomping holistic-wacko neurotic vegan weenie perverts."

*   *   *   *   *

To be sure, other scholars differ with Dr. Barry. To them, polarization, although a real enough phenomenon, is almost entirely confined to a small number of political elites and members of Congress. In *Culture War?* (2004), which bears the subtitle "The Myth of a Polarized America," Morris Fiorina of Stanford argues that policy differences between voters in Red and Blue states are really quite small, and that most are in general agreement even on issues like abortion and homosexuality.

But the extent of polarization cannot properly be measured by the voting results in Red and Blue states. Many of these states are in fact deeply divided internally between liberal and conservative areas, and gave the nod to one candidate or the other by only a narrow margin. Inferring the views of individual citizens from the gross results of presidential balloting is a questionable procedure.

Nor does Fiorina's analysis capture the very real and very deep division over an issue like abortion. Between 1973, when *Roe v. Wade* was decided, and now, he writes, there has been no change in the degree to which people will or will not accept any one of six reasons to justify an abortion: (1) the woman's health is endangered; (2) she became pregnant because of a rape; (3) there is a strong chance of a fetal defect; (4) the family has a low income; (5) the woman is not married; (6) and the woman simply wants no more children. Fiorina may be right about that. Nevertheless, only about 40 percent of all Americans will support abortion for any of the last three reasons in his series, while over 80 percent will support it for one or another of the first three.

In other words, almost all Americans are for abortion in the case of maternal emergency, but fewer than half if it is simply a matter of the mother's preference. That split—a profoundly important one—has remained in place for over three decades, and it affects how people vote. In 2000 and again in 2004, 70 percent of those who thought abortion should always be legal voted for Al Gore or John Kerry, while over 70 percent of those who thought it should always be illegal voted for George Bush.

Division is just as great over other high-profile issues. Polarization over the war in Iraq, for example, is more pronounced than any war-related controversy in at least a half-century. In the fall of 2005, according to Gallup, 81 percent of Democrats but only 20 percent of Republicans thought the war in Iraq was a mistake. During the Vietnam War, by contrast, itself a famously contentious cause, there was more unanimity across party lines, whether for or against: in late 1968 and early 1969, about equal numbers of Democrats and Republicans thought the intervention there was a mistake. Pretty much the same was true of Korea: in early 1951, 44 percent of Democrats and 61 percent of Republicans thought the war was a mistake— a partisan split, but nowhere near as large as the one over our present campaign in Iraq.

Polarization, then, is real. But what explains its growth? And has it spread beyond the political elites to influence the opinions and attitudes of ordinary Americans?

The answer to the first question, I suspect, can be found in the changing politics of Congress, the new competitiveness of the mass media, and the rise of new interest groups.

That Congress is polarized seems beyond question. When, in 1998, the House deliberated whether to impeach President Clinton, all but four Republican members voted for at least one of the impeachment articles, while only five Democrats voted for even one. In the Senate, 91 percent of Republicans voted to convict on at least one article; every single Democrat voted for acquittal.

The impeachment issue was not an isolated case. In 1993, President Clinton's budget passed both the House and the Senate without a single Republican vote in favor. The same deep partisan split occurred over taxes and supplemental appropriations. Nor was this a blip: since 1950, there has been a steady increase in the percentage of votes in Congress pitting most Democrats against most Republicans.

In the midst of the struggle to pacify Iraq, Howard Dean, the chairman of the Democratic National Committee, said the war could not be won, and Nancy Pelosi, the leader of the House Democrats, endorsed the view that American forces should be brought home as soon as possible. By contrast, although there was congressional grumbling (mostly by Republicans) about Korea and complaints (mostly by Democrats) about Vietnam, and although Senator George Aiken of Vermont famously proposed that we declare victory and withdraw, I cannot remember party leaders calling for unconditional surrender.

The reasons for the widening fissures in Congress are not far to seek. Each of the political parties was once a coalition of dissimilar forces: liberal Northern Democrats and conservative Southern Democrats, liberal coastal Republicans and conservative Midwestern Republicans. No longer; the realignments of the South (now overwhelmingly Republican) and of New England (now strongly Democratic) have all but eliminated legislators who deviate from the party's leadership. Conservative Democrats and liberal Republicans are endangered species now approaching extinction. At the same time, the ideological gap between the parties is growing: if there was once a large overlap between Democrats and Republicans—remember "Tweedledum and Tweedledee"?—today that congruence has almost disappeared. By the late 1990s, virtually every Democrat was more liberal than virtually every Republican.

The result has been not only intense partisanship but a sharp rise in congressional incivility. In 1995, a Republican-controlled Senate passed a budget that President Clinton proceeded to veto; in the loggerhead that followed, many federal agencies shut down (in a move that backfired on the Republicans). Congressional debates have seen an increase not only in heated exchanges but in the number of times a representative's words are either ruled out of order or "taken down" (that is, written by the clerk and then read aloud, with the offending member being asked if be or she wishes to withdraw them).

It has been suggested that congressional polarization is exacerbated by new districting arrangements that make each House seat safe for either a Democratic or a Republican incumbent. If only these seats were truly competitive, it is said, more centrist legislators would be elected. That seems plausible, but David C. King of Harvard has shown that it is wrong: in the House, the more competitive the district, the more extreme the views of the winner. This odd finding is apparently the consequence of a nomination process dominated by party activists. In primary races, where turnout is low (and seems to be getting lower), the ideologically motivated tend to exercise a preponderance of influence.

All this suggests a situation very unlike the half-century before the 1990s, if perhaps closer to certain periods in the eighteenth and nineteenth centuries. Then, too, incivility was common in Congress, with members not only passing the most scandalous remarks about each other but on occasion striking their rivals with canes or fists. Such partisan feeling ran highest when Congress was deeply divided over slavery before the Civil War and over Reconstruction after it. Today the issues are different, but the emotions are not dissimilar.

*   *   *   *   *

Next, the mass media. Not only are they themselves increasingly polarized, but consumers are well aware of it and act on that awareness. Fewer people now subscribe to newspapers or watch the network evening news. Although some of this decline may be explained by a preference for entertainment over news, some undoubtedly reflects the growing conviction that the mainstream press generally does not tell the truth, or at least not the whole truth.

In part, media bias feeds into, and off, an increase in business competition. In the 1950s, television news amounted to a brief thirty-minute interlude in the day's programming, and not a very profitable one at that; for the rest of the time, the three networks supplied us with westerns and situation comedies. Today, television news is a vast, growing, and very profitable venture by the many broadcast and cable outlets that supply news twenty-four hours a day, seven days a week.

The news we get is not only more omnipresent, it is also more competitive and hence often more adversarial. When there were only three television networks, and radio stations were forbidden by the fairness doctrine from broadcasting controversial views, the media gravitated toward the middle of the ideological spectrum, where the large markets could be found. But now that technology has created cable news and the Internet, and now that the fairness doctrine has by and large been repealed, many media outlets find their markets at the ideological extremes.

Here is where the sharper antagonism among political leaders and their advisers and associates comes in. As one journalist has remarked about the change in his profession, "We don't deal in facts [any longer], but in attributed opinions." Or, these days, in unattributed opinions. And those opinions are more intensely rivalrous than was once the case.

The result is that, through commercial as well as ideological self-interest, the media contribute heavily to polarization. Broadcasters are eager for stories to fill their round-the-clock schedules, and at the same time reluctant to trust the government as a source for those stories. Many media outlets are clearly liberal in their orientation; with the arrival of Fox News and the growth of talk radio, many are now just as clearly conservative.

The evidence of liberal bias in the mainstream media is very strong. The Center for Media and Public Affairs (CMPA) has been systematically studying television broadcasts for a quarter-century. In the 2004 presidential campaign, John Kerry received more favorable mentions than any presidential candidate in CMPA's history, especially during the month before election day. This is not new: since 1980 (and setting aside the recent advent of Fox News), the Democratic candidate has received more favorable mentions than the Republican candidate in every race except the 1988 contest between Michael Dukakis and George H. W. Bush. A similarly clear orientation characterizes weekly newsmagazines like *Time* and *Newsweek*.

For its part, talk radio is listened to by about one-sixth of the adult public, and that one-sixth is made up mostly of conservatives.[1] National Public Radio has an audience of about the same size; it is disproportionately liberal. The same breakdown affects cable-television news, where the rivalry is between CNN (and MSNBC) and Fox News. Those who watch CNN are more likely to be Democrats than Republicans; the reverse is emphatically true of Fox. As for news and opinion on the Internet, which has become an important source for college graduates in particular, it, too, is largely polarized along political and ideological lines, emphasized even more by the culture that has grown up around news blogs.

At one time, our culture was only weakly affected by the media because news organizations had only a few points of access to us and were largely moderate and audience-maximizing enterprises. Today the media have many lines of access, and reflect both the maximization of controversy and the cultivation of niche markets. Once the media talked to us; now they shout at us.

And then there are the interest groups. In the past, the major ones—the National Association of Manufacturers, the Chamber of Commerce, and labor organizations like the AFL-CIO—were concerned with their own material interests. They are still active, but the loudest messages today come from very different sources and have a very different cast to them. They are issued by groups concerned with social and cultural matters like civil rights, managing the environment, alternatives to the public schools, the role of women, access to firearms, and so forth, and they directly influence the way people view politics.

Interest groups preoccupied with material concerns can readily find ways to arrive at compromise solutions to their differences; interest groups divided by issues of rights or morality find compromise very difficult. The positions taken by many of these groups and their supporters, often operating within the two political parties, profoundly affect the selection of candidates for office. In brief, it is hard to imagine someone opposed to abortion receiving the Democratic nomination for president, or someone in favor of it receiving the Republican nomination.

Outside the realm of party politics, interest groups also file briefs in important court cases and can benefit from decisions that in turn help shape the political debate. Abortion became a hot controversy in the 1970s not because the American people were already polarized on the matter but because their (mainly centrist) views were not consulted; instead, national policy was determined by the Supreme Court in a decision, *Roe v. Wade*, that itself reflected a definition of "rights" vigorously promoted by certain well-defined interest groups.

Polarization not only is real and has increased, but it has also spread to rank-and-file voters through elite influence.

In *The Nature and Origins of Mass Opinion* (1992), John R. Zaller of UCLA listed a number of contemporary issues—homosexuality, a nuclear freeze, the war in Vietnam, busing for school integration, the 1990-91 war to expel Iraq from Kuwait—and measured the views held about them by politically aware citizens. (By "politically aware," Zaller meant people who did well answering neutral factual questions about politics.) His findings were illuminating.

Take the Persian Gulf War. Iraq had invaded Kuwait in August 1990. From that point through the congressional elections in November 1990, scarcely any elite voices were raised to warn against anything the United States might contemplate doing in response. Two days after the midterm elections, however. President George H. W. Bush announced that he was sending many more troops to the Persian Gulf. This provoked strong criticism from some members of Congress, especially Democrats.

As it happens, a major public-opinion survey was under way just as these events were unfolding. Before criticism began to be voiced in Congress, both registered Democrats and registered Republicans had supported Bush's vaguely announced intention of coming to the aid of Kuwait; the more politically aware they were, the greater their support. After the onset of elite criticism, the support of Republican voters went up, but Democratic support flattened out. As Bush became more vigorous in enunciating his aims, politically aware voters began to differ sharply, with Democratic support declining and Republican support increasing further.

Much the same pattern can be seen in popular attitudes toward the other issues studied by Zaller. As political awareness increases, attitudes split apart, with, for example, highly aware liberals favoring busing and job guarantees and opposing the war in Vietnam, and highly aware conservatives opposing busing and job guarantees and supporting the war in Vietnam.[2]

But why should this be surprising? To imagine that extremist politics has been confined to the chattering classes is to believe that Congress, the media, and American interest groups operate in an ideological vacuum. I find that assumption implausible.

As for the extent to which these extremist views have spread, that is probably best assessed by looking not at specific issues but at enduring political values and party preferences. In 2004, only 12 percent of Democrats approved of George Bush; at earlier periods, by contrast, three to four times as many Democrats approved of Ronald Reagan, Gerald Ford, Richard Nixon, and Dwight D. Eisenhower. Over the course of about two decades, in other words, party affiliation had come to exercise a critical influence over what people thought about a sitting president.

The same change can be seen in the public's view of military power. Since the late 1980s, Republicans have been more willing than Democrats to say that "the best way to ensure peace is through military strength." By the late 1990s and on into 2003, well over two-thirds of all Republicans agreed with this view, but far fewer than half of all Democrats did. In 2005, three-fourths of all Democrats but fewer than a third of all Republicans told pollsters that good diplomacy was the best way to ensure peace. In the same survey, two-thirds of all Republicans but only one-fourth of all Democrats said they would fight for this country "whether it is right or wrong."

Unlike in earlier years, the parties are no longer seen as Tweedledum and Tweedledee. To the contrary, as they sharpen their ideological differences, attentive voters have sharpened their ideological differences. They now like either the Democrats or the Republicans more than they once did, and are less apt to feel neutral toward either one.

How deep does this polarization reach? As measured by opinion polls, the gap between Democrats and Republicans was twice as great in 2004 as in 1972. In fact, rank-and-file Americans disagree more strongly today than did politically active Americans in 1972.

To be sure, this mass polarization involves only a minority of all voters, but the minority is sizable, and a significant part of it is made up of the college-educated. As Marc Hetherington of Vanderbilt puts it: "People with the greatest ability to assimilate new information, those with more formal education, are most affected by elite polarization." And that cohort has undeniably grown.

In 1900, only 10 percent of all young Americans went to high school. My father, in common with many men his age in the early twentieth century, dropped out of school after the eighth grade. Even when I graduated from college, the first in my family to do so, fewer than one-tenth of all Americans over the age of twenty-five had gone that far. Today, 84 percent of adult Americans have graduated from high school and nearly 27 percent have graduated from college. This extraordinary growth in schooling has produced an ever larger audience for political agitation.

Ideologically, an even greater dividing line than undergraduate education is postgraduate education. People who have proceeded beyond college seem to be very different from those who stop with a high school or college diploma. Thus, about a sixth of all voters describe themselves as liberals, but the figure for those with a postgraduate degree is well over a quarter. In mid-2004, about half of all voters trusted George Bush; less than a third of those with a postgraduate education did. In November of the same year, when over half of all college graduates voted for Bush, well over half of the smaller cohort who had done postgraduate work voted for Kerry. According to the Pew Center for Research on the People and the Press, more than half of all Democrats with a postgraduate education supported the antiwar candidacy of Howard Dean.

The effect of postgraduate education is reinforced by being in a profession. Between 1900 and 1960, write John B. Judis and Ruy Teixeira in *The Emerging Democratic Majority* (2002), professionals voted pretty much the same way as business managers; by 1988, the former began supporting Democrats while the latter supported Republicans. On the other hand, the effect of postgraduate education seems to outweigh the effect of affluence. For most voters, including college graduates, having higher incomes means becoming more conservative; not so for those with a postgraduate education, whose liberal predilections are immune to the wealth effect.

The results of this linkage between ideology, on the one hand, and congressional polarization, media influence, interest-group demands, and education on the other are easily read in the commentary surrounding the 2004 election. In their zeal to denigrate the president, liberals, pronounced one conservative pundit, had "gone quite around the twist." According to liberal spokesmen, conservatives with their "religious intolerance" and their determination to rewrite the Constitution had so befuddled their fellow Americans that a "great nation was felled by a poisonous nut."

If such wholesale slurs are not signs of polarization, then the word has no meaning. To a degree that we cannot precisely measure, and over issues that we cannot exactly list, polarization has seeped down into the public, where it has assumed the form of a culture war. The sociologist James Davison Hunter, who has written about this phenomenon in a mainly religious context, defines culture war as "political and social hostility rooted in different systems of moral understanding." Such conflicts, he writes, which can involve "fundamental ideas about who we are as Americans," are waged both across the religious/secular divide and within religions themselves, where those with an "orthodox" view of moral authority square off against those with a "progressive" view.

To some degree, this terminology is appropriate to today's political situation as well. We are indeed in a culture war in Hunter's sense, though I believe this war is itself but another component, or another symptom, of the larger ideological polarization that has us in its grip. Conservative thinking on political issues has religious roots, but it also has roots that are fully as secular as anything on the Left. By the same token, the liberal attack on conservatives derives in part from an explicitly "progressive" religious orientation—liberal Protestantism or Catholicism, or Reform Judaism—but in part from the same secular sources shared by many conservatives.

But what, one might ask, is wrong with having well-defined parties arguing vigorously about the issues that matter? Is it possible that polarized politics is a good thing, encouraging sharp debate and clear positions? Perhaps that is true on those issues where reasonable compromises can be devised. But there are two limits to such an arrangement.

First, many Americans believe that unbridgeable political differences have prevented leaders from addressing the problems they were elected to address. As a result, distrust of government mounts, leading to an alienation from politics altogether. The steep decline in popular approval of our national officials has many causes, but surely one of them is that ordinary voters agree among themselves more than political elites agree with each other—and the elites are far more numerous than they once were.

In the 1950s, a committee of the American Political Science Association (APSA) argued the case for a "responsible" two-party system. The model the APSA had in mind was the more ideological and therefore more "coherent" party system of Great Britain. At the time, scarcely anyone thought our parties could be transformed in such a supposedly salutary direction. Instead, as Governor George Wallace of Alabama put it in his failed third-party bid for the presidency, there was not a "dime's worth of difference" between Democrats and Republicans.

What Wallace forgot was that, however alike the parties were, the public liked them that way. A half-century ago, Tweedledum and Tweedledee enjoyed the support of the American people; the more different they have become, the greater has been the drop in popular confidence in both them and the federal government.

A final drawback of polarization is more profound. Sharpened debate is arguably helpful with respect to domestic issues, but not for the management of important foreign and military matters. The United States, an unrivaled superpower with unparalleled responsibilities for protecting the peace and defeating terrorists, is now forced to discharge those duties with its own political house in disarray.

We fought World War II as a united nation, even against two enemies (Germany and Italy) that had not attacked us. We began the wars in Korea and Vietnam with some degree of unity, too, although it was eventually whittled away. By the early 1990s, when we expelled Iraq from Kuwait, we had to do so over the objections of congressional critics; the first President Bush avoided putting the issue to Congress altogether. In 2003 we toppled Saddam Hussein in the face of catcalls from many domestic leaders and opinion makers. Now, in stabilizing Iraq and helping that country create a new free government, we have proceeded despite intense and mounting criticism, much of it voiced by politicians who before the war agreed that Saddam Hussein was an evil menace in possession of weapons of mass destruction and that we had to remove him.

Denmark or Luxembourg can afford to exhibit domestic anguish and uncertainty over military policy; the United States cannot. A divided America encourages our enemies, disheartens our allies, and saps our resolve—potentially to fatal effect. What General Giap of North Vietnam once said of us is even truer today: America cannot be defeated on the battlefield, but it can be defeated at home. Polarization is a force that can defeat us.

Notes

[1] The political disposition of most radio talk-show hosts is explained by William G. Mayer in "Why Talk Radio Is Conservative," *Public Interest* (Summer 2004).

[2] True, the "elite effect" may not be felt across the board. With most of the issues Zaller investigated, even well-informed citizens would have had little firsthand experience, and so their minds were of necessity open to the influence of their "betters." Results might have been different had he measured their views on matters about which most Americans believe themselves to be personally well informed: crime, inflation, drug abuse, or their local schools.

Border War
John B. Judis

The New Republic | January 16, 2006

An estimated 11 million people are currently living in the United States illegally—a situation that's existed for years. So why did illegal immigration suddenly emerge as a front-burner issue in American politics? Some trace this development to a speech by President Bush in January 2004, in which he complained that the country's immigration laws are "not working." Others point to an increased concern over the security of America's borders post-9/11, or to increased border enforcement in southern California and Texas, which has led more illegal immigrants to brave the Arizona desert (where hundreds have died), or to the rise of the Minutemen civilian border patrols over the past two years, or the growing strain illegals are placing on the healthcare system and other resources, or to call-in radio programs that have the fanned the flames of public concern.

Whatever the reason for the growing public outcry, Republicans in Congress felt bound to act—only to find their members split down the middle, between law-and-order advocates in the House of Representatives, who passed a bill last December that would make illegal immigration a crime, and more moderate, probusiness types in the Senate, who passed legislation in May (with the support of Senate Democrats) that would create a guest worker program and provide a path to citizenship for some illegal immigrants—a bill denounced by House Republicans as amounting to "amnesty." As this is being written, it appears unlikely that the two bills will be reconciled into law this year. Meanwhile, the president, who had more or less backed the Senate plan, is promising to add another 6,000 Border Patrol agents on the Mexican border.

In this New Republic *piece, John Judis suggests that what Americans are really upset about isn't illegal immigration, but immigration, period—especially of Spanish-speaking people from Latin America—and that the only way to substantially reduce this immigration is for the United States to finally get serious about helping to develop the Mexican and Central American economies.*

A battered yellow school bus rumbles up a bumpy dirt road on the outskirts of Sasabe, a small Mexican town just over the border from Arizona. At the top of the hill, the bus winds around brick and mud huts. Ragged children stand in the doorways, and emaciated dogs forage for scraps. The bus passes dented pickups and old cars without wheels and stops in a dusty clearing, where it disgorges about forty teenagers dressed in blue jeans and carrying small knapsacks. One boy's T-shirt features a picture of Che Guevara. A girl's pale blue top says ADORABLE in sequined letters. They are subdued, almost expressionless. They mill around, waiting for the *coyotes*, or smugglers, who, for a hefty fee, will take them in pickup trucks to the border.

There, they will climb through holes in the barbed wire fence separating Mexico from the United States. Some will not make it through the 100-plus-degree Arizona desert on the other side (from October 2004 to October 2005, 261 would-be migrants died in the desert before reaching Tucson or Phoenix), and about one-third of them will be apprehended by the U.S. Border Patrol. But, over the course of a year, almost 2 million will make it, sometimes after several tries, and enter the underworld of undocumented migrants: working on farms, as day-laborers in construction, as servants and maids, or in sweatshops and meatpacking plants. Unable to protest mistreatment, they will be subject to abuse and exploitation, but most of them will still fare better than if they had stayed in their native villages.

This influx of migrants into Arizona—and the fact that many stay in the state rather than moving north or west—has created a political explosion. In November 2004, anti-immigration activists won a bruising campaign to pass Proposition 200, which denies "public benefits" to people who can't prove their citizenship, despite the opposition of the state's congressional delegation, including Republican Senators John McCain and Jon Kyl, Democratic Governor Janet Napolitano, and major business groups and labor unions. Last spring, the Minuteman Project, which George W. Bush wrote off as a group of "vigilantes," set up shop in Tombstone, near the border, to dramatize the failure of the Border Patrol to prevent "illegals" from getting through. Republican state legislators, equally hostile to McCain and Napolitano, are trying to expand Proposition 200 and plan to make illegal immigration the focus of the 2006 elections. "We are ground zero" in the battle over immigration, warns former Arizona House Majority Whip Randy Graf, who spearheaded the campaign for Proposition 200 and is now running for the Tucson-area House seat to be vacated by Rep. Jim Kolbe.

The furor over illegal immigration is sweeping the country—from California and Washington to Virginia and Tennessee, and even up to Vermont, New Hampshire, and Minnesota—but Arizona is indeed ground zero, having surpassed neighboring states as the principal gateway to the United States for illegal immigrants from Mexico and Central America. Beltway politicians who want to clamp down on the border claim this furor is the result, as Colorado Republican Representative Tom Tancredo has suggested, of immigrants "taking jobs that Americans could take." And many Americans far from the Arizona border certainly believe that—in low-immigration West Virginia, for example, 60 percent of respondents in a recent poll agreed that "immigrants take jobs away from Americans." But that's not what's happening in Arizona's citrus groves or hotels or restaurants. And, in Arizona, those who are most up in arms over illegal immigration are far more concerned with its sociocultural than its economic effects. They are worried about what is commonly called the "Mexicanization" of Arizona. That kind of cultural concern extends to legal as well as illegal immigrants—and it can't be easily fixed by legislation.

Mexicans began crossing the border to Arizona in the early twentieth century to work in "the five Cs"—construction, copper, citrus, cattle, and cotton—but, until recently, the great majority of illegal immigrants came through California and Texas. In 1990, for example, about 90 percent entered through those two states, while only about 5 percent came through Arizona. But, as the uproar over "illegals" grew—in 1994, for example, California passed Proposition 187, denying public benefits to undocumented workers—the Border Patrol instituted Operation Gatekeeper in California and Operation Hold-the-Line in Texas. These programs reduced illegal immigration to those states, but not overall. Instead, illegal immigrants were simply diverted to Arizona's desert border, and, between October 2004 and October 2005, about half of the 4 million illegal immigrants who entered the United States came through Arizona. According to Princeton University sociologist Douglas Massey, about 1.5 million of them crossed the eastern part of the Arizona border, south of Tucson, and about 470,000 entered through the area around Yuma, near the California border.

Going through the desert is far more dangerous than walking over a bridge into a Texas or California border town or even fording the Rio Grande. And it's more expensive, too. But Mexicans and other Latinos are willing to pay the *coyotes*, because they hope to find well-paying jobs in the United States. And, relative to where they came from, they will. In 2000, according to the U.S. Department of Agriculture (USDA), a farm worker in Mexico could expect to make $3.60 in an eight-hour day, while his counterpart in the United States made $66.32 in the same period. The discrepancy has increased since the North American Free Trade Agreement (NAFTA) went into effect in 1994, removing tariff barriers on the importation of U.S. farm products and decimating small farmers in Mexico. Says Sandra Polaski, a trade expert at the Carnegie Endowment for International Peace, "Small farmers who produced for subsistence but also for the market lost their market access." According to the USDA, Mexican farm income fell 4.3 percent per year during the 1990s. Young men and women left in search of work, and, while some of them found jobs in U.S. factories on the border (*maquiladoras*), many of them crossed the border in search of better-paying jobs.

Most of those who make it do find jobs—92 percent of males, according to one estimate. And, with undocumented workers adding to the normal population increase, Arizona's Latino population has ballooned, going from 19 percent in 1990 to 25 percent in 2000. Phoenix, which was once a primarily Anglo town, has gone from 20 percent to about 34 percent Latino. Says former Arizona Attorney General Grant Woods, one of the state's prominent Republicans, "When I was in the first grade in 1960, Phoenix was the same distance from the border. Phoenix now feels much more like a border town than it did even ten years ago. Billboards in Spanish, a lot of people speaking Spanish. Most of us think this is great, but a lot don't." This transformation in Arizona society and culture, along with the disorder created by the dramatic rise in border crossings, has made immigration the biggest issue in Arizona politics.

In the 2002 gubernatorial election, when Napolitano barely edged out Republican Representative Matt Salmon, the two candidates rarely mentioned immigration. But, soon after Napolitano took office in 2003, she and her chief of staff, Dennis Burke, were astonished to discover that the state's voters were preoccupied with the issue. Says Burke, "The first time we looked at polling, the number-one issue was immigration, not education. Then, a year and a half ago, it got pretty visceral. It started to permeate all issues." That was largely because political activists and conservative Republican state legislators had begun organizing.

In July 2003, Phoenix resident Kathy McKee established the Protect Arizona Now Committee and got a lawyer to write what became Proposition 200, basing it on California's Proposition 187. It was put on the November 2004 ballot. And, although almost the entire Arizona political establishment opposed it, the measure still garnered 56 percent. Then, last year, the state legislature passed a raft of anti-immigrant bills, including measures to deputize local and state police officers to enforce immigration laws and to broaden the definition of the "public benefits" denied to illegal immigrants under Proposition 200. Napolitano vetoed all but one of the bills but has since backtracked in the face of growing public pressure. And Russell Pearce, the powerful chairman of the Arizona House Appropriations Committee—who, with Graf's departure in 2004, has become the leader of the legislature's anti-immigrant force—is currently championing legislation that would make English Arizona's official language and construct a wall along the entire Arizona border.

Graf, Pearce, McKee, and the Republican legislature have clearly tapped a growing sentiment among the state's white voters. Wes Gullett, a political consultant and a key adviser to John McCain, recently conducted a poll in Cochise County, south of Tucson, to test voter concerns. "Instead of asking what are the top three issues," Gullett says, "we have to ask what are the top four, because the first three are immigration. You have to ask, 'What do you care about other than immigration?' It's crazy down there."

But what, exactly, is this craziness about? In Washington, politicians and political organizations regularly attribute the obsession with immigration to illegal migrants taking the jobs of native-born Americans. Tancredo makes that claim, and so do the two leading groups advocating restrictions on immigration, the Federation for American Immigration Reform (FAIR), which bankrolled Proposition 200, and the Center for Immigration Studies. That did happen in Midwestern meatpacking plants several decades ago, and it may still be happening in some parts of the country, but it does not seem to be the case in Arizona, where unemployment hovers below 5 percent and where construction, agriculture, and tourism are plagued by acute labor shortages. Illegal immigration doesn't even seem to be having a dramatic effect on wages, with pay for unskilled work in Arizona regularly exceeding the minimum wage.

Unskilled workers currently make up 32 percent of Arizona's labor force, and they are constantly in demand. Tom Nassif of Western Growers, a trade association, recently complained that the construction industry was "siphoning off" the migrant workers that growers needed in the field. "Farms will not have enough workers to harvest their crops," he warned. Meanwhile, Arizona's tourist industry says it can't find enough workers for its hotels and restaurants. Bobby Surber, the vice president of Sedona Center, who runs three restaurants, two shopping plazas, and a resort, and employs two hundred people, says, "Even though we pay larger than average, and full medical and dental, we cannot find enough employees."

Of course, Arizonans could still believe, just as Americans in West Virginia do, that illegal immigrants threaten their jobs. And pollsters invite this response by always asking about the economic effect of immigration and refraining from raising uncomfortable cultural concerns. But, in interviewing Arizonans, one rarely encounters complaints about illegal immigrants taking jobs away. One does hear about the cost of state services for illegal immigrants. Indeed, even the Latinos who voted for Proposition 200 were worried about the burden that illegal immigrants were placing on schools and hospitals. And, in border towns, crime and disorder are pressing issues. (Some of the *coyotes* double as drug smugglers, and the migrants traipse through farms and ranches.) But, among many Arizonans, the most important issues are cultural. They fret about "Mexicanization"—about Arizona becoming a "Third World country" or "the next Mexifornia."

In interviews I conducted last fall, leaders of the movement to restrict immigration usually began by expressing concerns that illegal immigration was undermining the rule of law and allowing terrorists to sneak across the border—concerns they seem to believe are most likely to win over a national audience. But they invariably became most animated, and most candid, when talking about what they see as the unwillingness of Mexican immigrants—legal or illegal—to assimilate into American culture.

Connie, who doesn't want her last name used for fear of retaliation from immigration advocates, was one of the first members of the Minutemen. She lives in Sierra Vista, a small retirement town near the border. Barely five feet tall, with short, graying hair, she prides herself on her feistiness. She is now in charge of patrolling the Nacos area near the border. She says that, at night, she and her husband station themselves on a hill in view of the fence and watch for "illegals." She says that she became interested in the Minutemen because the organization was upholding the rule of law and keeping out terrorists. "We have many apprehensions of Pakistanis and Iraqis on the border. They are coming in disguised as Hispanics and blending in," she says. (When I ask a human rights worker in Sasabe if he had heard of Iraqis entering the United States disguised as Latinos, he laughs. "The [Mexican] army is very watchful about that kind of thing," he says.)

Connie insists that the Minutemen are neither "extremist" nor "racist," but, as we ride along the border in her Ford Navigator, Connie voices distinctly cultural and racial concerns. She says that the illegals she sees coming across the border are the "darker" Mexicans. Mexican President Vicente Fox, she says, "doesn't want them in the country." She speculates that Mexicans might want to take over Arizona: "In Mexico, they are taught this land was taken from them. They are not taught they were paid tons of money for it. There is a belief they want this back." (After defeating the Mexican army in 1848, the United States bought all of California and the Southwest from Mexico for $15 million.) When I comment that California has remained in good shape despite massive immigration, she takes exception. "California is not a shining example," she says. "You have the Chinese, the Vietnamese, the Russians, all these people immigrating. How many languages do you have to have on the ballot?" Asked if she would support McCain's proposal to allow Mexicans to enter the country legally as guest workers, Connie demurs. "Who is going to pay for it?" she asks. "When my grandmother came from Czechoslovakia, one thing she did was assimilate. She was proud to be an American. Their attitude is, 'We won't assimilate.'"

That's what bothers Graf as well. "We are talking about assimilation," says the congressional candidate, as we sit in his East Tucson campaign headquarters. "I don't have any problem about anyone who wants to salute our flag and learn our language and be a citizen. What got me into the whole issue was that I was standing in line in a Safeway, and this woman was ahead of me, and she had an infant, and was pregnant, and her mother was with her. She was paying for groceries in food stamps. And, when the clerk asked for her signature, she acted like she didn't understand English, and neither did her mother. I found it odd that an entire family could be here on welfare and not speak any English. On welfare!"

Graf's chief ally is Pearce, who lives in the Phoenix suburb of Mesa. Last fall, he complained to a reporter from *Stateline.org* about his hometown: "It's not the Mesa I was raised in. They have turned it into a Third World country," he said. By "they," Pearce means Latinos in general. On his Web site, he warns, "Over 800,000 Americans fled California last year because L.A. became a clone of Mexico City." Pearce, like Connie and Graf, envisages a cultural conflict between the white America he grew up in and an invading army of dark-skinned, Spanish-speaking immigrants from south of the border.

Ray Borane, the longtime Democratic mayor of Douglas, a border town in Cochise County, laments that Graf "represents the majority opinion" in the state. That may be an exaggeration, given Napolitano's and McCain's continued popularity, but Graf and his angry allies do represent a significant segment of voters—perhaps one-third or more—who are up in arms. And longtime observers of Arizona politics confirm that a concern with Mexicanization lies at the heart of their opposition to illegal immigration. "Nobody is afraid of jobs," says Gullett, the McCain adviser. "We have got labor demand. That's not a problem. There is no feeling that people are losing their jobs. There is a tremendous fear that our community and our way of life is changing." Dave Wagner, the former political editor of *The Arizona Republic*, who is writing a book about Arizona politics, says that, in Phoenix, "Mexicans and Mexican-Americans have their own culture and stores. It is possible if you are Spanish-speaking to disappear into that culture. That scares the hell out of some people." Says Woods: "Arizona has changed dramatically in the last 20 years, and a lot of people are uncomfortable with that."

It's a discomfort that politicians like Graf and Pearce hope to take advantage of. They want to purge the Republican Party of probusiness conservatives like McCain, Woods, Kolbe, and Phoenix Representative Jeff Flake, all of whom favor a guest-worker program and some form of amnesty for undocumented workers already in the United States. Graf ran against Kolbe, an opponent of Proposition 200, in 2004, and, in spite of being massively outspent, got 43 percent of the vote. He's running again, and, with Kolbe out of the race, he has a decent chance of winning the Republican nomination. Republicans in the legislature are also preparing a witches' brew of new anti-immigrant legislation for the term that begins in January.

And the underlying conditions that have fueled their protest and made Arizona ground zero are likely to persist. Arizona businesses have relied on migrant labor for one hundred years. Says Phoenix College political scientist Pete Dimas, author of *Progress and a Mexican American Community's Struggle for Existence*, "Immigrants have provided the cheap labor on which this whole part of the country has depended." And the demand for unskilled labor is likely to continue. According to statistics from the Department of Labor, thirteen of the twenty occupations in Arizona that will experience the highest growth from 2002 to 2012 employ unskilled workers. Many of these jobs in food processing or building service are now spurned by the native-born and are filled by illegal immigrants. And, with all of Mexico's tariffs on farm products due to disappear under NAFTA, and with the Central American Free Trade Agreement going into effect, the supply of unskilled labor looking northward is likely, if anything, to mount.

As immigrants continue to cross the border, the "culture war" is unlikely to abate. Connie is right. Mexican and Central American legal and illegal immigrants probably won't assimilate in the way her Czech grandmother did. European immigrants who came to the United States in the last century had to travel over an ocean to arrive here, and many of them came from countries undergoing political or economic upheavals. Their identification with the homeland rarely lasted past a generation. That's not as true of Mexican or other Latino immigrants, who have their own claim on the culture of the West.

Many of the migrant workers who crossed the border after 1848 did so to make money to bring back home. They retained their language and national identity. According to Douglas Massey, Jorge Duran, and Nolan J. Malone in *Beyond Smoke and Mirrors*, 23.4 million of the 28 million undocumented workers who entered the United States between 1965 and 1985 returned to Mexico. What's changed in the last decade, ironically, is that more extensive border enforcement has discouraged illegal immigrants from returning to Mexico for fear that they will be unable to get back into the United States. Still, many continue to support extended families in Mexico, call themselves Mexicans, and consider their primary language Spanish. They are contributing to a bicultural America that stirs fear and resentment among some native-born Americans and that will continue to inspire calls to close the southern border.

*   *   *   *   *

Arizonans on both sides of the controversy are looking to Washington for solutions. They know that states can't pass their own guest-worker programs; nor can they police their own borders. But there is little chance that the Bush administration and Republicans in Congress—sharply divided between social conservatives and business interests—will be able to pass legislation this year. And, even if the House, the Senate, and the White House could agree on an approach, it would not end the furor over immigration.

Last month, social conservatives in the House, led by Tancredo and Wisconsin Representative James Sensenbrenner, passed a punitive bill that would erect new walls along the border, make illegal immigration a felony, and require employers to weed out illegal workers by checking their immigration status against a national database. In the Senate, McCain and Massachusetts Democrat Edward Kennedy introduced a bill that is backed by business and by some labor groups. It would let migrant workers obtain renewable three-year visas and allow undocumented workers already in the country to stay provided they pay a fine. McCain and Kennedy probably can't get their bill through the Senate—too many Republicans fear being tagged as proponents of "amnesty" for illegal immigrants—but they could certainly muster enough votes to prevent the Senate from passing a version of the House bill.

In the past, Bush has leaned toward McCain's approach—the president encouraged McCain after the 2004 election to seek Kennedy's support for a bill—but he has recently attempted to appease social conservatives, praising the House's measures to "protect our borders and crack down on illegal entry into the United States." Bush holds out hope for a Senate bill that would somehow combine McCain's approach with Tancredo's. But that's unlikely to happen.

Even if Congress were to adopt one of these approaches—or a combination of the two—it would not quiet the controversy. Punitive approaches have either had unintended consequences (for instance, encouraging illegal immigrants to stay in the United States rather than return to Mexico) or have proved unenforceable. Border Patrol spending has increased over 1,000 percent since 1986 without reducing border crossings. McCain and Kennedy's approach is far better, acknowledging the inescapable reality of Latino immigration and its net benefit to the U.S. economy. But granting amnesty to undocumented workers, and inviting new workers in, will not satisfy Americans who are offended by the growing presence—legal or illegal—of Latinos in their midst. And combining the two proposals would more or less reproduce the Immigration Reform and Control Act of 1986, which hiked border spending, threatened employer penalties, granted amnesty to undocumented workers, *and* led to almost two decades of clamor over immigration.

That furor will not abate until at least one of two conditions is met. The first is a dramatic generational change in the cultural attitudes of non-Latino Americans—meaning the acceptance of biculturalism in large parts of the United States, including Arizona. Frank Pierson, the supervising organizer of Arizona's Valley Interfaith Network, a coalition of church and labor groups that promotes cultural integration, wants Arizonans to adopt the biblical tradition of showing "love for the stranger." But non-Latino Americans probably have to reach a point where they no longer see immigrants from south of the border as strangers at all.

The other condition is a change in the unequal economic relationship between the United States and its neighbors to the south, which would reduce the supply of unskilled laborers seeking jobs in the United States. Such a change could probably only occur if the United States were to assume the same responsibility toward Mexico and Central America that the more prosperous nations of Western Europe did toward Spain, Greece, and Portugal when they wanted to enter the European Union—granting them aid, along with protection of their industries and agriculture, over a transitional period.

But neither condition is likely to be met in the near future. Americans are not ready to embrace the teenagers who gathered in Sasabe as their own, and U.S. business is not ready to see Mexico and Central America as anything other than a platform for exports and investment. As a result, the conflict over Latino immigration will continue. And, if what's happening on the Arizona border is any gauge, that's not something to look forward to.

Part Three:
(Not) Politics as Usual

None Dare Call It Stolen: Ohio, the Election, and America's Servile Press

Mark Crispin Miller

Harper's Magazine | August 2005

There seems to be a general agreement among America's politicians and pundits that to dispute any U.S. election, once it's been declared over and done with, is somehow tacky and even undemocratic. And yet . . . certain nagging questions about the 2004 election—including the possible malfunction or manipulation of electronic voting machines as well as attempts to intimidate or mislead voters—still remain. In particular, the state of Ohio, which President Bush carried by a margin of some 100,000 votes, appeared to have far more than its share of unusual problems when it came to tallying up the presidential vote. In this Harper's *article, Mark Crispin Miller reviews the disturbing findings of a congressional inquiry on the subject, and asks why the media—not to mention the public—haven't shown more concern about these apparent assaults on the integrity of the American electoral process.*

Whichever candidate you voted for (or think you voted for), or even if you did not vote (or could not vote), you must admit that last year's presidential race was—if nothing else—pretty interesting. True, the press has dropped the subject, and the Democrats, with very few exceptions, have "moved on." Yet this contest may have been the most unusual in U.S. history; it was certainly among those with the strangest outcomes. You may remember being surprised yourself. The infamously factious Democrats were fiercely unified—Ralph Nader garnered only about 0.38 percent of the national vote—while the Republicans were split, with a vocal anti-Bush front that included anti-Clinton warrior Bob Barr of Georgia; Ike's son John Eisenhower; Ronald Reagan's chairman of the Joint Chiefs of Staff, William J. Crowe Jr.; former Air Force Chief of Staff and onetime "Veteran for Bush" General Merrill "Tony" McPeak; founding neocon Francis Fukuyama; Doug Bandow of the Cato Institute; and various large alliances of military officers, diplomats, and business professors. *The American Conservative*, cofounded by Pat Buchanan, endorsed five candidates for president, including both Bush and Kerry, while the *Financial Times* and *The*

Economist came out for Kerry alone. At least fifty-nine daily newspapers that backed Bush in the previous election endorsed Kerry (or no one) in this election. The national turnout in 2004 was the highest since 1968, when another unpopular war had swept the ruling party from the White House. And on Election Day, twenty-six state exit polls incorrectly predicted wins for Kerry, a statistical failure so colossal and unprecedented that the odds against its happening, according to a report last May by the National Election Data Archive Project, were 16.5 million to 1. Yet this ever-less-beloved president, this president who had united liberals and conservatives and nearly all the world against himself—this president somehow bested his opponent by 3,000,176 votes.

How did he do it? To that most important question the commentariat, briskly prompted by Republicans, supplied an answer. Americans of faith—a silent majority heretofore unmoved by any other politician—had poured forth by the millions to vote "Yes!" for Jesus' buddy in the White House. Bush's 51 percent, according to this thesis, were roused primarily by "family values." Tony Perkins, president of the Family Research Council, called gay marriage "the hood ornament on the family values wagon that carried the president to a second term." The pundits eagerly pronounced their amens—"Moral values," Tucker Carlson said on CNN, "drove President Bush and other Republican candidates to victory this week"— although it is not clear why. The primary evidence of our Great Awakening was a postelection poll by the Pew Research Center in which 27 percent of the respondents, when asked which issue "mattered most" to them in the election, selected something called "moral values." This slight plurality of impulse becomes still less impressive when we note that, as the pollsters went to great pains to make clear, "the relative importance of moral values depends greatly on how the question is framed." In fact, when voters were asked to "name in their own words the most important factor in their vote," only 14 percent managed to come up with "moral values." Strangely, this detail went little mentioned in the postelectoral commentary.[1]

The press has had little to say about most of the strange details of the election—except, that is, to ridicule all efforts to discuss them. This animus appeared soon after November 2, in a spate of caustic articles dismissing any critical discussion of the outcome as crazed speculation: "Election Paranoia Surfaces: Conspiracy Theorists Call Results Rigged," chuckled the *Baltimore Sun* on November 5. "Internet Buzz on Vote Fraud Is

Dismissed," proclaimed the *Boston Globe* on November 10. "Latest Conspiracy Theory—Kerry Won—Hits the Ether," *The Washington Post* chortled on November 11. The *New York Times* weighed in with "Vote Fraud Theories, Spread by Blogs, Are Quickly Buried"—making mock not only of the "postelection theorizing" but of cyberspace itself, the *fons et origo* of all such loony tunes, according to the *Times*.

Such was the news that most Americans received. Although the tone was scientific, "realistic," skeptical, and "middle-of-the-road," the explanations offered by the press were weak and immaterial. It was as if they were reporting from inside a forest fire without acknowledging the fire, except to keep insisting that there was no fire.[2] Since Kerry has conceded, they argued, and since "no smoking gun" had come to light, there was no story to report. This is an oddly passive argument. Even so, the evidence that something went extremely wrong last fall is copious, and not hard to find. Much of it was noted at the time, albeit by local papers and haphazardly. Concerning the decisive contest in Ohio, the evidence is lucidly compiled in a single congressional report, which, for the last half-year, has been available to anyone inclined to read it. It is a veritable arsenal of "smoking guns"—and yet its findings may be less extraordinary than the fact that no one in this country seems to care about them.

On January 5, Representative John Conyers of Michigan, the ranking Democrat on the House Judiciary Committee, released *Preserving Democracy: What Went Wrong in Ohio*. The report was the result of a five-week investigation by the committee's Democrats, who reviewed thousands of complaints of fraud, malfeasance, or incompetence surrounding the election in Ohio, and further thousands of complaints that poured in by phone and e-mail as word of the inquiry spread. The congressional researchers were assisted by volunteers in Ohio who held public hearings in Columbus, Cleveland, Toledo, and Cincinnati, and questioned more than two hundred witnesses. (Although they were invited, Republicans chose not to join in the inquiry.)[3]

Preserving Democracy describes three phases of Republican chicanery: the run-up to the election, the election itself, and the postelection cover-up. The wrongs exposed are not mere dirty tricks (though Bush/Cheney also went in heavily for those) but specific violations of the U.S. and Ohio constitutions, the Voting Rights Act, the Civil Rights Act of 1968, the National Voter Registration Act, and the Help America Vote Act. Although Conyers trod carefully when the report came out, insisting that the crimes did not affect the outcome of the race (a point he had to make, he told me, "just to get a hearing"), his report does "raise grave doubts regarding whether it can be said that the Ohio electors selected on December 13, 2004, were chosen in a manner that conforms to Ohio law, let alone Federal requirements and constitutional standards." The report cites "massive and unprecedented voter irregularities and anomalies" throughout the state—wrongs, moreover, that were hardly random accidents. "In many cases," the report says, "these irregularities were caused by intentional misconduct and illegal behavior, much of it involving Secretary of State J. Kenneth Blackwell, the cochair of the Bush-Cheney campaign in Ohio."[4]

The first phase of malfeasance entailed, among many other actions, several months of bureaucratic hijinks aimed at disenfranchising Democrats, the most spectacular result of which was "a wide discrepancy between the availability of voting machines in more minority, Democratic and urban areas as compared to more Republican, suburban and exurban areas." Such unequal placement had the predictable effect of slowing the voting process to a crawl at Democratic polls, while making matters quick and easy in Bush country: a clever way to cancel out the Democrats' immense success at registering new voters in Ohio. (We cannot know the precise number of new voters registered in Ohio by either party because many states, including Ohio, do not register voters by party affiliation. The *New York Times* reported in September, however, that new registration rose 25 percent in Ohio's predominantly Republican precincts and 250 percent in Ohio's predominantly Democratic precincts.)

At Kenyon College in Gambier, for instance, there were only two machines for 1,300 would-be voters, even though "a surge of late registrations promised a record vote." Gambier residents and Kenyon students had to stand in line for hours, in the rain and in "crowded, narrow hallways," with some of them inevitably forced to call it quits. "In contrast, at nearby Mt. Vernon Nazarene University, which is considered more Republican leaning, there were ample waiting machines and no lines." This was not a consequence of limited resources. In Franklin County alone, as voters stood for hours throughout Columbus and elsewhere, at least 125 machines collected dust in storage. The county's election officials had "decided to make do with 2,866 machines, even though the analysis showed that the county needs 5,000 machines."

It seemed at times that Ohio's secretary of state was determined to try every stunt short of levying a poll tax to suppress new voter turnout. On September 7, based on an overzealous reading of an obscure state bylaw, he ordered county boards of elections to reject all Ohio voter registration forms not "printed on white, uncoated paper of not less than 80 lb. text weight." Under public pressure he reversed the order three weeks later, by which time unknown numbers of Ohioans had been disenfranchised. Blackwell also attempted to limit access to provisional ballots. The Help America Vote Act—passed in 2002 to address some of the problems of the 2000 election—prevents election officials from deciding at the polls who will be permitted to cast provisional ballots, as earlier Ohio law had permitted. On September 16, Blackwell issued a directive that somehow failed to note that change. A federal judge ordered him to revise the language, Blackwell resisted, and the court was forced to draft its own version of the directive, which it ordered Blackwell to accept, even as it noted Blackwell's "vigorous, indeed, at times, obdurate opposition" to compliance with the law.

Under Blackwell the state Republican Party tried to disenfranchise still more Democratic voters through a technique known as "caging." The party sent registered letters to new voters, "then sought to challenge 35,000 individuals who refused to sign for the letters," including "voters who were homeless, serving abroad, or simply did not want to sign for something concerning the Republican Party." It should be noted that marketers have long used zip codes to target, with remarkable precision, the ethnic makeup of specific neighborhoods, and also that, according to exit polls last year, 84 percent of those black citizens who voted in Ohio voted for Kerry.[5]

The second phase of lawlessness began the Monday before the election, when Blackwell issued two directives restricting media coverage of the election. First, reporters were to be barred from the polls, because their presence contravened Ohio's law on "loitering" near voting places. Second, media representatives conducting exit polls were to remain 100 feet away from the polls. Blackwell's reasoning here was that, with voter turnout estimated at 73 percent, and with many new voters so blissfully ignorant as to have "never looked at a voting machine before," his duty was clear: the public was to be protected from the "interference or intimidation" caused by "intense media scrutiny." Both cases were at once struck down in federal court on First Amendment grounds.

Blackwell did manage to ban reporters from a postelection ballot-counting site in Warren County because—election officials claimed—the FBI had warned of an impending terrorist attack there. The FBI said it issued no such warning, however, and the officials refused to name the agent who alerted them. Moreover, as the *Cincinnati Enquirer* later reported, e-mail correspondence between election officials and the county's building services director indicated that lockdown plans—"down to the wording of the signs that would be posted on the locked doors"—had been in the works for at least a week. Beyond suggesting that officials had something to hide, the ban was also, according to the report, a violation of Ohio law and the Fourteenth Amendment.

Contrary to a prior understanding, Blackwell also kept foreign monitors away from the Ohio polls. Having been formally invited by the State Department on June 9 [2004], observers from the Organization for Security and Cooperation in Europe, an international consortium based in Vienna, had come to witness and report on the election. The mission's two-man teams had been approved to monitor the process in eleven states—but the observers in Ohio were prevented from watching the opening of the polling places, the counting of the ballots, and, in some cases, the election itself. "We thought we could be at the polling places before, during, and after" the voting, said Søren Søndergaard, a Danish member of the team. Denied admission to polls in Columbus, he and his partner went to Blackwell, who refused them letters of approval, again citing Ohio law banning "loitering" outside the polls. The two observers therefore had to "monitor" the voting at a distance of one hundred feet from each polling place. Although not technically illegal, Blackwell's refusal was improper and, of course, suspicious. (The Conyers report does not deal with this episode.)

To what end would election officials risk so malodorous an action? We can only guess, of course. We do know, however, that Ohio, like the nation, was the site of numerous statistical anomalies—so many that the number is itself statistically anomalous, since every single one of them took votes from Kerry. In Butler County the Democratic candidate for

State Supreme Court took in 5,347 more votes than Kerry did. In Cuyahoga County ten Cleveland precincts "reported an incredibly high number of votes for third party candidates who have historically received only a handful of votes from these urban areas"—mystery votes that would mostly otherwise have gone to Kerry. In Franklin County, Bush received nearly 4,000 extra votes from one computer, and, in Miami County, just over 13,000 votes appeared in Bush's column *after* all precincts had reported. In Perry County the number of Bush votes somehow exceeded the number of registered voters, leading to voter turnout rates as high as 124 percent. Youngstown, perhaps to make up the difference, reported negative 25 million votes.

In Cuyahoga County and in Franklin County—both Democratic strongholds—the arrows on the absentee ballots were not properly aligned with their respective punch holes, so that countless votes were miscast, as in West Palm Beach back in 2000. In Mercer County some 4,000 votes for president—representing nearly 7 percent of the electorate—mysteriously dropped out of the final count. The machines in heavily Democratic Lucas County kept going haywire, prompting the county's election director to admit that prior tests of the machines had failed. One polling place in Lucas County never opened because all the machines were locked up somewhere and no one had the key. In Hamilton County many absentee voters could not cast a Democratic vote for president because county workers, in taking Ralph Nader's name off many ballots, also happened to remove John Kerry's name. *The Washington Post* reported that in Mahoning County "25 electronic machines transferred an unknown number of Kerry votes to the Bush column," but it did not think to ask why.

Ohio Democrats also were heavily thwarted through dirty tricks recalling Richard Nixon's reign and the systematic bullying of Dixie. There were "literally thousands upon thousands" of such incidents, the Conyers report notes, cataloging only the grossest cases. Voters were told, falsely, that their polling place had changed; the news was conveyed by phone calls, "door-hangers," and even party workers going door to door. There were phone calls and fake "voter bulletins" instructing Democrats that they were not to cast their votes until Wednesday, November 3, the day after Election Day. Unknown "volunteers" in Cleveland showed up at the homes of Democrats, kindly offering to "deliver" completed absentee ballots to the election office. And at several polling places, election personnel or hired goons bused in to do the job "challenged" voters—black voters in particular—to produce documents confirming their eligibility to vote. The report notes one especially striking incident:

> In Franklin County, a worker at a Holiday Inn observed a team of 25 people who called themselves the "Texas Strike Force" using payphones to make intimidating calls to likely voters, targeting people recently in the prison system. The "Texas Strike Force" paid their way to Ohio, but their hotel accommodations were paid for by the Ohio Republican Party, whose headquarters is across the street. The hotel worker heard one caller threaten a likely voter with being reported to the FBI and returning to jail if he voted. Another hotel worker called the police, who came but did nothing.

The electoral fraud continued past Election Day, but by means far more complex and less apparent than the bullying that marked the day itself. Here the aim was to protect the spoils, which required the prevention of countywide hand recounts by any means necessary. The procedure for recounts is quite clear. In fact, it was created by Blackwell. A recount having been approved, each of the state's eighty-eight counties must select a number of precincts randomly, so that the total of their ballots comes to 3 percent (at least) of the county's total vote. Those ballots must then be simultaneously hand counted and machine counted. If the hand count and the new machine count match, the remaining 97 percent of the selected ballots may be counted by machine. If, however, the totals vary by as little as a single vote, all the other votes must be hand counted, and the results, once reconfirmed, must be accepted as the new official total.

The Ohio recount officially started on December 13—five days after Conyers's hearings opened—and was scheduled to go on until December 28. Because the recount (such as it was) coincided with the inquiry, Conyers was able to discover, and reveal in his report, several instances of what seemed to be electoral fraud.

On December 13, for instance, Sherole Eaton, deputy director of elections for Hocking County, filed an affidavit stating that the computer that operates the tabulating machine had been "modified" by one Michael Barbian Jr., an employee of Triad GSI, the corporate manufacturer of the county's voting machinery.

Ms. Eaton witnessed Mr. Barbian modify the Hocking County computer vote tabulator before the announcement of the Ohio recount. She further witnessed Barbian, upon the announcement that the Hocking County precinct was planned to be the subject of the initial Ohio test recount, make further alterations based on his knowledge of the situation. She also has firsthand knowledge that Barbian advised election officials how to manipulate voting machinery to ensure that [the] preliminary hand recount matched the machine count.[6]

The committee also learned that Triad similarly intervened in at least two other counties. In a filmed interview, Barbian said that he had examined machines not only in Hocking County but also in Lorain, Muskingum, Clark, Harrison, and Guernsey counties; his purpose was to provide the Board of Elections with as much information as possible—"The more information you give someone," he said, "the better job they can do." The report concludes that such information as Barbian and his colleagues could provide was helpful indeed:

Based on the above, including actual admissions and statements by Triad employees, it strongly appears that Triad and its employees engaged in a course of behavior to provide "cheat sheets" to those counting the ballots. The cheat sheets told them how many votes they should find for each candidate, and how many over and under votes they should calculate to match the machine count. In that way, they could avoid doing a full county-wide hand recount mandated by state law. If true, this would frustrate the entire purpose of the recount law—to randomly ascertain if the vote counting apparatus is operating fairly and effectively, and if not to conduct a full hand recount.

The report notes Triad's role in several other cases. In Union County the hard drive on one tabulator was replaced after the election. (The old one had to be subpoenaed.) In Monroe County, after the 3 percent hand count had twice failed to match the machine count, a Triad employee brought in a new machine and took away the old one. (*That* machine's count matched the hand count.) Such operations are especially worrying in light of the fact that Triad's founder, Brett A. Rapp, "has been a consistent contributor to Republican causes." (Neither Barbian nor Rapp would respond to

Harper's queries, and the operator at Triad refused even to provide the name of a press liaison.)

There were many cases of malfeasance, however, in which Triad played no role. Some 1,300 Libertarian and Green Party volunteers, led by Green Party recount manager Lynne Serpe, monitored the count throughout Ohio.[7] They reported that: In Allen, Clermont, Cuyahoga, Morrow, Hocking, Vinton, Summit, and Medina counties, the precincts for the 3 percent hand recount were preselected, not picked at random, as the law requires. In Fairfield County the 3 percent hand recount yielded a total that diverged from the machine count—but despite protests from observers, officials did not then perform a hand recount of all the ballots, as the law requires. In Washington and Lucas counties, ballots were marked or altered, apparently to ensure that the hand recount would equal the machine count. In Ashland, Portage, and Coshocton counties, ballots were improperly unsealed or stored. Belmont County "hired an independent programmer ('at great expense') to reprogram the counting machines so that they would only count votes for President during the recount." Finally, Democratic and/or Green observers were denied access to absentee, and/or provisional ballots, or were not allowed to monitor the recount process, in Summit, Huron, Putnam, Allen, Holmes, Mahoning, Licking, Stark, Medina, Warren, and Morgan counties. In short, the Ohio vote was never properly recounted, as required by Ohio law.

That is what the Democratic staff of the House Judiciary Committee found, that is what they distributed to everyone in Congress, and that is what any member of the national press could have reported at any time in the last half year. Conyers may or may not have precisely captured every single dirty trick. The combined votes gained by the Republicans through such devices may or may not have decided the election. (Bush won Ohio by 118,601 votes.) Indeed, if you could somehow look into the heart of every eligible voter in the United States to know his or her truest wishes, you might discover that Bush/Cheney was indeed the people's choice. But you have to admit—the report is pretty interesting.

In fact, its release was timed for maximum publicity. According to the United States Code (Title 3, Chapter 1, Section 15), the president of the

Senate—i.e., the U.S. vice president—must announce each state's electoral results, then "call for objections." Objections must be made in writing and "signed by at least one Senator and one Member of the House of Representatives." A challenge having been submitted, the joint proceedings must then be suspended so that both houses can retire to their respective chambers to decide the question, after which they reconvene and either certify or reject the vote.

Thus was an unprecedented civic drama looming on the day that Conyers's report appeared. First of all, electoral votes had been contested in the Congress only twice. In 1877 the electoral votes of several states were challenged, some by Democrats supporting Samuel Tilden, others by Republicans supporting Rutherford B. Hayes. In 1969, Republicans challenged the North Carolina vote when Lloyd W. Bailey, a "faithless elector" pledged to Richard Nixon for that state, voted for George Wallace.[8] And a new challenge would be more than just "historic." Because of what had happened—or not happened—four years earlier, it would also be extraordinarily suspenseful. On January 6, 2001, House Democrats, galvanized by the electoral larceny in Florida, tried and failed to challenge the results. Their effort was aborted by the failure of a single Democratic senator to join them, as the law requires. Al Gore—still vice president, and therefore still the Senate's president—had urged Democrats to make no such unseemly waves but to respect Bush's installation for the sake of national unity. Now, it seemed, that partisan disgrace would be redressed, at least symbolically; for a new challenge from the House, by Rep. Stephanie Tubbs-Jones of Ohio, would be cosigned by Barbara Boxer, Democratic senator from California, who, at a noon press conference on January 6, heightened the suspense by tearfully acknowledging her prior wrong: "Four years ago I didn't intervene. I was asked by Al Gore not to do so and I didn't do so. Frankly, looking back on it, I wish I had."

It was a story perfect for TV—a rare event, like the return of Halley's comet; a scene of high contention in the nation's capital; a heroine resolved to make things right, both for the public and herself. Such big news would highlight Conyers's report, whose findings, having spurred the challenge in the first place, would now inform the great congressional debate on the election in Ohio.

As you may recall, this didn't happen—the challenge was rejected by a vote of 267-31 in the House and 74-1 in the Senate. The *Boston Globe* gave the report 118 words (page 3); the *Los Angeles Times*, 60 words (page 18). It made no news in the *Wall Street Journal*, *USA Today*, *Newsweek*, *Time*, or *U.S. News & World Report*. It made no news on CBS, NBC, ABC, or PBS. Nor did NPR report it (though *Talk of the Nation* dealt with it on January 6). CNN did not report it, though Donna Brazile pointedly affirmed its copious "evidence" on *Inside Politics* on January 6. (Judy Woodruff failed to pause for an elaboration.) Also on that date, the Fox News Channel briefly showed Conyers himself discussing "irregularities" in Franklin County, though it did not mention the report. He was followed by Tom DeLay, who assailed the Democrats for their "assault against the institutions of our representative democracy." The *New York Times* negated both the challenge and the document in a brief item headlined "Election Results to Be Certified, with Little Fuss from Kerry," which ran on page 16 and ended with this quote from Dennis Hastert's office, vis-à-vis the Democrats: "They are really just trying to stir up their loony left."

Indeed, according to the House Republicans, it was the Democrats who were the troublemakers and cynical manipulators—spinning "fantasies" and "conspiracy theories" to "distract" the people, "poison the atmosphere of the House of Representatives" (Dave Hobson, R., Ohio), and "undermine the prospect of democracy" (David Dreier, R., Calif.); mounting "a direct attack to undermine our democracy" (Tom DeLay, R., Tex.), "an assault against the institutions of our representative democracy" (DeLay); trying "to plant the insidious seeds of doubt in the electoral process" (J. D. Hayworth, R., Ariz.); and in so doing following "their party's primary strategy: to obstruct, to divide and to destroy" (Deborah D. Pryce, R., Ohio).

Furthermore, the argument went, there was *no evidence* of electoral fraud. The Democrats were using "baseless and meritless tactics" (Pryce) to present their "so-called evidence" (Bob Ney, R., Ohio), "making allegations that have no basis of fact" (Candice Miller, R., Mich.), making claims for which "there is no evidence whatsoever, no evidence whatsoever" (Dreier). "There is absolutely no credible basis to question the outcome of the election" (Rob Portman, R., Ohio). "No proven allegations of fraud. No reports of widespread wrongdoing. It was, at the end of the day, an honest election" (Bill Shuster, R., Pa.). And so on. Bush won Ohio by "an overwhelming and comfortable margin," Rep. Pryce insisted, while Ric Keller (R., Fla.) said that Bush won by "an overwhelmingly comfortable margin." ("The president's margin is significant," observed Roy Blunt, R., Mo.) In short, as Tom DeLay put it, "No such voter disenfranchisement occurred in this election of 2004—and, for that matter, the election of 2000. Everybody knows it. The voters know it, the candidates know it, the courts know it, and the evidence proves it."

That all this commentary was simply *wrong* went unnoticed and/or unreported. Once Bush was reinaugurated, all inquiries were apparently concluded, and the story was officially kaput. By March talk of fraud was calling forth the same reflexive ridicule that had prevailed back in November—but only now and then, on those rare moments when somebody dared bring it up: "Also tonight," CNN's Lou Dobbs deadpanned ironically on March 8, "Teresa Heinz Kerry still can't accept certain reality. She suggests the presidential election may have been rigged!" And when, on March 31, the National Election Data Archive Project released its study demonstrating that the exit polls had probably been right, it made news only in the *Akron Beacon-Journal*.[9] The article included this response from Carlo LoParo, Kenneth Blackwell's spokesman: "What are you going to do except laugh at it?"

In the summer of 2003, Rep. Peter King (R., N.Y.) was interviewed by Alexandra Pelosi at a barbecue on the White House lawn for her HBO documentary *Diary of a Political Tourist*. "It's already over. The election's over. We won," King exulted more than a year before the election. When asked by Pelosi—the daughter of House Minority Leader Nancy Pelosi—how he knew that Bush would win, he answered, "It's all over but the counting. And we'll take care of the counting."

King, who is well known in Washington for his eccentric utterances, says he was kidding, that he has known Pelosi for years, that she is "a clown," and that her project was a "spoof." Still, he said it. And laughter, despite the counsel of Kenneth Blackwell's press flack, seems an inappropriate response to the prospect of a stolen election—as does the advice that we "get over it." The point of the Conyers report, and of this report as well, is not to send Bush packing and put Kerry in his place. The Framers could no more conceive of electoral fraud on such a scale than they could picture Fox News Channel or the Pentagon; and so we have no constitutional recourse, should it be proven, finally, that the wrong guy "won." The point of our revisiting the last election, rather, is to see exactly what the damage was so that the people can demand appropriate reforms. Those who say we should "move on" from that suspicious race and work instead on "bigger issues"—like electoral reform—are urging the impossible; for there has never been a great reform that was not driven by some major scandal.

"If a nation expects to be ignorant and free, in a state of civilization," Thomas Jefferson said, "it expects what never was and never will be." That much-quoted line foretells precisely what has happened to us since "the news" has turned into a daily paraphrase of Karl Rove's fevered dreams. Just as 2+2=5 in Orwell's Oceania, so here today the United States just won two brilliant military victories, 9/11 could not have been prevented, we live in a democracy (like the Iraqis), and last year's presidential race "was, at the end of the day, an honest election." Such claims, presented as the truth, are nothing but faith-based reiteration, as valid as the notions that one chooses to be homosexual, that condoms don't prevent the spread of HIV, and that the universe was made 6,000 years ago.

In this nation's epic struggle on behalf of freedom, reason, and democracy, the press has unilaterally disarmed—and therefore many good Americans, both liberal and conservative, have lost faith in the promise of self-government. That vast surrender is demoralizing, certainly, but if we face it, and endeavor to reverse it, it will not prove fatal. This democracy can survive a plot to hijack an election. What it cannot survive is our indifference to, or unawareness of, the evidence that such a plot has succeeded.

Notes

[1] Another poll, by Zogby International, showed that 33 percent of voters deemed "greed and materialism" the most pressing moral problems in America. Only 12 percent of those polled cited gay marriage.

[2] Keith Olbermann, on MSNBC, stood out as an heroic exception, devoting many segments of his nightly program *Countdown* to the myriad signs of electoral mischief, particularly in Ohio.

[3] The full report can be downloaded from the Judiciary Committee's Web site at

www.house.gov/judiciary_democrats/ohiostatusrept1505.pdf and is also, as of May, available as a trade paperback, titled *What Went Wrong in Ohio*. I should note here that, in a victory for family values, the publishers of that paperback are my parents, Jordan and Anita Miller.

[4] When contacted by *Harper's Magazine*, Blackwell spokesman Carlo LoParo dismissed Conyers's report as a partisan attack. "Why wasn't it more than an hour's story?" he asked, referring to the lack of media interest in the report. "Everybody can't be wrong, can they?"

[5] Let it not be said that the Democrats rose wholly above the electoral fray: in Defiance County, Ohio, one Chad Staton was arrested on 130 counts of vote fraud when he submitted voter registration forms purportedly signed by, among others, Dick Tracy, Jeffrey Dahmer, Michael Jackson, and Mary Poppins. Of course, depending on party affiliation, the consequence of election misdeeds varies. Staton, who told police he was paid in crack for each registration, received fifty-four months in jail for his fifth-degree felonies; Blackwell, for his part, is now the GOP front-runner for governor of Ohio.

[6] In May 2005, Eaton was ordered by the Hocking County Board of Elections to resign from her position.

[7] The recount itself was the result of a joint application from the Green and Libertarian parties.

[8] Offended by the president-elect's first cabinet appointments (Henry Kissinger, Daniel Patrick Moynihan, et al.), Bailey was protesting Nixon's liberalism.

[9] On the other hand, the thesis that the exit polls were flawed had been reported by the Associated Press, the *Washington Post*, the *Chicago Tribune*, *USA Today*, the *San Francisco Chronicle*, the *Columbus Dispatch*, CNN.com, MSNBC, and ABC (which devoted a *Nightline* segment to the "conspiracy theory" that the exit polls had been correct).

A New Black Power

Walter Mosley

The Nation | February 27, 2006

While the Hispanic vote in the United States has largely been split between Democrat and Republican candidates in recent elections, the African American vote has still tended to be reliably Democratic. In this Nation *essay, however, Walter Mosley, asks what either party has done for the black community lately, and suggests that it's time for African Americans to form their own political party—noting that if they did, other interest groups might well follow in their footsteps.*

Most black Americans have been Democrats for at least the fifty-three years that I've been alive. What have the Democrats done for us in all that time? We have the lowest average income of any large racial group in the nation. We're incarcerated at an alarmingly high rate. We are still segregated and profiled, and have a very low representation at the top echelons of the Democratic Party. We are the stalwarts, the bulwark, the Old Faithful of the Democrats, and yet they have not made our issues a high priority in a very long time.

Why should we be second-class members in the most important political activities of our lives? Why shouldn't the party we belong to think that our problems are the most important in this land?

I'm not saying that we should become Republicans. The Republicans don't care about us either. But at least they don't pretend to be on our side. And you have to admit that, of late, the Bush administration has put black faces into high-profile jobs that carry clout on the international playing field. I don't have to like Colin Powell or Condoleezza Rice to appreciate that once a black person has been put into a position of power, the second time around is much, much easier.

We are a racial minority in a country where racism is a fact of life, a country that was founded on economic and imperialist racism. Taking this into account and adding it to the fact that our issues are regularly put on a back burner, I believe that it is not out of order to send out a call for the formation of an African American interest group, or maybe a political unit, that would bring our issues, and others, to the forefront of American political discourse.

If we had our own political voting bloc that paid attention to issues that reflect our needs in domestic and international affairs, things would change for us. The first thing is that many more of us would be likely to vote. Imagine the interest young people would have if they felt we were organizing based on our own interests: They could work for a candidate who represented their issues; they could run for office themselves.

And even though the party would be based on the racial identity that has been shoved down our throats since the first days we came here in chains, we wouldn't work only for ourselves. We'd argue about medical care and Social Security and the good jobs that are disappearing from this nation like fleas off a dead dog's back.

America's corporations, CEOs, and portfolio managers don't have to worry about the euro and the devaluation of the dollar. They belong to an international club. It doesn't matter where the most recent SUV is being produced; what matters is that my stockholders and I own a piece of the company that makes and sells those cars.

It takes many companies working in unison to make secure the wealth of American capitalism. Two of the major-interest corporations that facilitate the needs of our wealthiest citizens are the Republican and Democratic (so-called) political parties. They exonerate their actions with numbers of votes, but the wheels they run on are greased by money, and lots of it.

If we took the vote into our own hands, we wouldn't have to ask the Democrats for their support—we could demand it. George W. Bush, or whoever takes his place, will send for our representatives to come to his home to discuss his plans. This is because they have not yet figured out how to dispose of the vote in the American political system.

Imagine it. We could actually democratize America by taking power away from the two-party system and handing it over to the people. Other special parties would arise splintering off from the centrist attendants of the rich once we show them the way.

What I'm talking about here is the beginning of an American Evolution, a movement that will create a series of political interest groups that will transform our two-party system into a kind of virtual parliament. We could construct smaller political groups based on specific interests. There could be Black Party Congress members from Watts, Harlem, the Motor City, and a dozen other inner-city bastions. All we have to do is have a fair representation in the House of Representatives to have an extraordinary impact on the wheels of government.

Farmers, women, the aged, angry young white men and, for that matter, true Republicans might create their own small parties/interest groups. These groups would not only have direct representation in the House of Representatives but would also begin to make deals with those people running for senator and president, police chief and mayor.

It's past the time when we black Americans can complain about how we are treated without ourselves trying to take the reins of power. A Black Voting Bloc would be a bold move. Some might say a radical move—too radical. But a country that incarcerates people of color at an eight-to-one ratio to whites played the race card way before Johnnie Cochran. If we could come together and see a way to put balance back in the American political landscape, then we should do it.

Why?

Because if we do not lead we will be led. And if those who have learned to despise, distrust and diminish us are the leaders, then our path will lead even farther away from our homes. We will wake up like strangers in our own beds. We, and our children, will be walking in uncomfortable shoes to poor jobs. We will be jeered on every corner, and every mirror we come across will distort our image.

Just so that it doesn't seem that I'm giving short shrift to this argument, let me try to explain why this kind of "political party" will be different from its interest-corporation counterparts. First, this kind of group will be a political unit more than a party. This unit should be patterned after interest groups that form around specific necessities of our particular community. As I've mentioned before, I would like to see many of these units evolve, but for the moment let me address the Black Voting Bloc.

What we need for this group is a short list of demands that define our political aspirations at any given point. These demands might change over time, but at any given moment we should have no more than eight expectations of the candidates or legislation we vote for. I am not positioning myself as the leader or even as a central designer of this group, but let me put forward a list of possible demands that our unit might embrace:

1. A commitment to revamping the legal system and the penal system to make sure that citizens of color are getting proper treatment and

that all inmates are given the utmost chance to rehabilitate and reestablish themselves in society. (This rehabilitation will include suffrage for all ex-convicts who have served their sentences.)

2. An expectation that there be equal distribution of all public wealth and services among the citizens, no matter their income, race, or history.

3. A demand that a true accounting for the impact of slavery be compiled by all government bodies in authority over records that give this information.

4. A universal health care system.

5. A retirement system that will assure older Americans the ability to spend their later years in relative comfort and security.

6. A commitment to assemble a general history of our nation in both its glory and its shame.

7.

8.

I left 7 and 8 blank because I think you should fill these out. This is, after all, a communal effort meant to bring our intelligences together. And if you don't feel that you're an affiliate of the Black Voting Bloc, write your own demands and see what kind of group you might attract. I believe that any group concerned with the rights of Americans will have at least half of these demands in common.

One last comment on the idealistic part of this notion:

All black people don't have to join right off. If we can put together just 10 percent of the voting black population, we will be wielding a great deal of power. Others will join us if our political strategy works. In time we might tip the scales against the rich and the ultra-rich. If we do that we might very well make this a better world.

*   *   *   *   *

I know many of you will say that we don't have the time to allow the United States to evolve politically. Like many Americans, you believe that our nation faces urgent problems that must be solved by the next election and the elections after that. My answer is, that is just what they want you to think. Our so-called political parties want you to believe that only they can save you when, really, they have no intention of doing so. The Democrats, the Republicans—they're in business for themselves in this vast religion of capitalism. They will never solve Americans' problems, not fully. We have to strive against the system, change it, make it reflect our inexpert visions of right and good. As long as you vote Democratic, as long as you vote Republican, you will be assuring that true democracy has no chance to exist. As long as we believe in the fearmongers' light show, the world will suffer under our misguided convictions.

There's no question that a Black Voting Bloc would be a fine context for us and for people of the black diaspora around the world. It would be a forum that would express perceptions from the underbelly of the American experience. That experience, I believe, would find resonance on an international scale and help to bring our maverick nation into concert with certain other countries that would like to get along with us.

But how do we get our people to feel strongly about political unity? What in our experience will bring us together? Should we turn to a charismatic leader to guide us safely through the minefield of fanaticism? I've been told so many times that the problem in this world is that so-and-so died too young. A couple of years ago I heard another public figure say that it was because Robert Kennedy died that American liberalism lost its way. What might Martin Luther King Jr. or Malcolm X have achieved if assassins' bullets had not cut them down in their prime?

If only we had leaders now like we did back then, so many lament. It's hard for me to write these words without a hint of sarcasm. Nostalgia belongs in the retirement home. Any organization, movement, or people who rely solely (or even greatly) on a charismatic leader for their strength and their motivation are in the most precarious position possible.

"Cut off the head and the body will fall," their enemies murmur. This is a way to let those enemies dissolve your context. Just put all your belief in one leader, and sooner or later you will be lost.

Some might say that I should end this section with those words. This may be true, but I think they open the door to other considerations. We do need leadership. We have to have people who will make decisions and blaze trails; people who will stand up to warmongers and moneylenders; people who might create context, illuminate the darkness with an electronic billboard; people who could organize our vote.

I could spend a lot of time and space here criticizing our current leaders. But what would be the purpose? These leaders, no matter how much they have lost their way, are not our enemies. If I follow a man or woman who is leading me astray, then I have to accept my own culpability and blindness.

"Didn't you see the millions dying in Africa while your leaders argued about the references and jokes in the movie *Barbershop*?" someone in a later year may ask. And how will we answer? If we don't lie we might say, "I knew what was happening, but I didn't know how to act. I felt powerless and helpless and so I did nothing."

The truth hurts. We all know that. But if we can see that we need leadership and that we don't have the leadership we need, then we might begin to question why. I believe a vacuum in our leadership has been caused by a natural conservatism in the black community that echoes the smug confidence of America in general. This conservatism harbors a deep dread of our young people.

This problem has to be approached by using a two-tiered process. First, we (the elders) have to realize how we exclude young people from taking leadership roles in our community. Why do we celebrate the blues but denigrate hip-hop? Why don't we distinguish between the major thinkers among our youth and the thugs? What are the young people telling us when they talk about bitches and ho's, motherfuckers and niggahs and bling? These are questions we shouldn't gloss over. We bear the responsibility for the lost generations of our people. Even if we see their actions as self-defeating and self-hating, we have to take responsibility for having allowed this situation to occur.

On the other hand, why do we get so upset when young men and women of African descent also want to identify with their other racial sides? Are we afraid that they're trying to abandon us? Do we want to hold them back so that they don't have a broader and more sophisticated view of their identities? Don't we know that this is their world, and it is our job to support them while they gain a solid footing?

These are only the first few questions we should ask, and answer. And as we respond we should edit out all cynicism and derogatory notions from our voices and words. These young people are our only hope. We have to liberate them where we can, decriminalize them when necessary, detoxify them if possible—but most important we have to hear what they're telling us and make way for their leadership.

And to the youth I say, You have to take the reins. You have to realize that many members of the older generation have gotten what they wanted out of the Struggle. They aren't worried about the problems of America's urban youth; at least not enough to, once again, charge the ramparts and put what they have on the line. Revolutions (both violent and nonviolent) are manned by the young. Older people have retirement accounts and diseases to support, weak constitutions, and a justified fear of imprisonment. We have fallen to the rear of the column. You, the urban youth of America, must lead us.

If you, the youth, do not forgive us for fumbling, our race will be very far behind in the twenty-first century. And if we lose, the world suffers because most of America is on the wrong road already.

America has carried the notion of property and power to such an intensely negative degree that we have very little room left for humanity and art in our hearts. We work long hours, eat bad food, close our eyes to the atrocities committed in our name and spend almost everything we make on the drugs that keep us from succumbing to the emptiness of our spiritual lives. We gobble down antidepressants, sleeping pills, martinis, sitcoms and pornography in a desperate attempt to keep balance in this soulless limbo.

In a world where poetry is a contest at best and a competition at worst, where the importance of a painting is gauged by the price it can be sold for—we are to be counted among the lost. And so when I say that we need leaders and that those leaders must come from our youth, it is no idle statement. We need our young people because without their dreams to guide us we will have only cable TV and grain alcohol for succor.

The Art of Testifying: The Confirmation Hearings as Theatre

Janet Malcolm

The New Yorker | March 13, 2006

After eleven years during which the composition of the Supreme Court remained unchanged—the longest such stretch since the 1820s—Justice Sandra Day O'Connor's announcement in July 2005 that she was retiring, followed by the death of Chief Justice William Rehnquist from thyroid cancer two months later, suddenly left two positions to fill on the Court. With a Republican majority in the Senate and the threat of a filibuster by Democrats taken off the table, there was never any doubt about the confirmation of John Roberts as the new Chief Justice (in September 2005) or—once Harriet Miers's disastrous nomination was withdrawn—of Samuel Alito as O'Connor's replacement (in January 2006). But as Janet Malcolm observes in this engaging New Yorker *article, the two confirmation hearings could still be enjoyed for what they were: political theater in its highest form.*

On the second day of David Souter's appearance before the Senate Judiciary Committee, in September 1990, Gordon Humphrey, a Republican senator from New Hampshire, with something of the manner of a boarding school headmaster in a satiric novel, asked the nominee, "Do you remember the old television program 'Queen for a Day'?"

"Well, it wasn't something that I spent much of my youth watching," Souter said, "but I've heard the term."

Humphrey fussed with papers and went on, "Yes, well, going back to the days of black-and-white TV, let's play 'Senator for a Day.'"

"I still have a black-and-white TV," Souter put in.

"I don't doubt it," Humphrey said, and continued:

I hope you don't watch it much. My theory is that nothing would do more good for this country than for everyone to smash his television set; . . . because people would begin—especially parents and children—would begin talking and children would begin doing their homework instead of watching—having their minds filled with rubbish every evening from our wonderful networks.

Humphrey collected himself and went on to propose that Souter put himself in the shoes of a senator interrogating a Supreme Court nominee and asked him what he would be most concerned about. He added that he was asking not so much for his own benefit as for that of "the young people who are tuned in—"

"On television," the voice of a quick-witted Joseph Biden, the chairman of the committee, rang out.

"On television, yes," Humphrey conceded, as Souter smiled puckishly and the audience burst into laughter.

1.

During the confirmation hearings for John Roberts last September, old black-and-white movies came to mind unbidden. Watching Roberts on television was like watching one of the radiantly wholesome heroes that Jimmy Stewart, Joel McCrea, and Henry Fonda rendered so incisively in the films of Capra, Lubitsch, and Sturges. They don't make men like that anymore. But Roberts had all their anachronistic attributes: the grace, charm, and humor of a special American sort in which decency and kindness are heavily implicated, and from which sexuality is entirely absent. It was out of the question that such a man be denied a place on the Supreme Court. The plot of the hearing hinged not on whether Roberts would be confirmed but on how the eight Democrats on the committee—Patrick Leahy, of Vermont; Edward Kennedy, of Massachusetts; Joseph Biden, of Delaware; Dianne Feinstein, of California; Russell Feingold, of Wisconsin; Charles Schumer, of New York; Herbert Kohl, of Wisconsin; and Richard Durbin, of Illinois—would perform.

In his opening statement, Roberts offered a baseball analogy to illustrate his notion of judicial seemliness. He likened judges to umpires, who "don't make the rules; they apply them. . . . They make sure everybody plays by the rules, but it is a limited role." He added, "Nobody ever went to a ballgame to see the umpire." At the game of Senate confirmation, however, Roberts was precisely the person everybody had come to see: he was the batter to whom eighteen pitchers would pitch. Eight of them would try to strike him out while ten (Arlen Specter, of Pennsylvania; Orrin Hatch, of Utah; Charles Grassley, of Iowa; Jon Kyl, of Arizona; Mike DeWine, of Ohio; Jeff Sessions, of Alabama; Lindsey Graham, of South Carolina; John Cornyn, of Texas; Sam Brownback, of Kansas; and Tom Coburn, of Oklahoma) would insure that he got on base.

The fastballs that the Democrats hurled were fueled largely by memorandums that Roberts had written as a young attorney in the Reagan administration advising his superiors on how best to undermine civil rights, voting rights, affirmative action, and antidiscrimination legislation. The written record of what Kennedy called "a narrow and cramped and, perhaps, even a mean-spirited view of the law" was the focus of the Democrats' pointed questioning. The Democrats invited Roberts to disavow the misguided views of his youth—Surely you don't believe such stuff now? they asked him in not so many words. And in not so many words Roberts indicated that he still did. But words were not decisive in this hearing. Roberts's dazzlingly sympathetic persona soared over the proceedings and enveloped them in its aura. In the third round of questions, Charles Schumer looked over his glasses at Roberts and said, "You did speak at length on many issues and sounded like you were conveying your views to us, but when one went back and read the transcript each evening, there was less than met the ear that afternoon." But in fact it was the eye that created the illusion.

Roberts had a wonderful way of listening to questions. His face was exquisitely responsive. The constant play of expression on his features put one in mind of nineteenth-century primers of acting in which emotions—pleasure, agreement, dismay, uncertainty, hope, fear—are illustrated on the face of a model. When it was his turn to speak, he did so with equal mesmerizing expressiveness. Whenever he said "With all due respect, Senator"—the stock phrase signaling disagreement—he looked so genuinely respectful, almost regretful, that one could easily conclude that he was agreeing with his interlocutor rather than demurring. During the first round of questions, Biden flashed his famous insincere smile and said, "This shouldn't be a game of gotcha." In point of fact, the Democrats—notably Biden himself—"got" Roberts a number of times, but no matter what disagreeable things were said to him he maintained his invincible pleasantness. Biden scored heavily, for example, when he said:

In 1999 you said in response to a question . . . "You know, we've gotten to a point these days where we think the only way we can show we're serious about a problem is if we pass a federal law, whether it's the Violence Against Women Act or anything else. The fact of the matter is conditions are different in different states, and state laws are more relevant . . . more attuned to different situations in New York as opposed to Minnesota. And that's what the federal system is based upon."

Judge, tell me how a guy beating up his wife in Minnesota is any different condition in New York.

What could Roberts say? He could only flounder, but he floundered so prettily that Biden had to laugh and say "OK." Schumer, too, repeatedly won debating points but never penetrated Roberts's armor of charm. In the second round of questioning, Schumer offered this inspired set piece:

> You agree we should be finding out your philosophy and method of legal reasoning, modesty, stability, but when we try to find out what modesty and stability mean, what your philosophy means, we don't get any answers.
>
> It's as if I asked you: What kind of movies do you like? Tell me two or three good movies. And you say, "I like movies with good acting. I like movies with good directing. I like movies with good cinematography." And I ask you, "No, give me an example of a good movie." You don't name one. I say, "Give me an example of a bad movie." You won't name one. Then I ask you if you like *Casablanca*, and you respond by saying, "Lots of people like *Casablanca*." You tell me it's widely settled that *Casablanca* is one of the great movies.

Arlen Specter, the chairman of the committee, intervened to say that Schumer's time was up, and that there would be a fifteen-minute break. Roberts meekly asked if he could respond before the break, and, when given permission to do so, he said, "First, *Dr. Zhivago* and *North by Northwest*"—bringing down the house. Roberts went on to give an unconvincing defense of his evasiveness, but it was too late—there was too much good feeling wafting through the room like lavender air-freshener—for the weakness of his argument to matter. Roberts's performance gave the word "disarming" new meaning. In the end, three Democrats—who had been no less pointed in their questioning than their fellow-Democrats—voted to confirm Roberts. "I will vote my hopes and not my fears," Herbert Kohl said, confessing, "I was troubled by parts of Judge Roberts's record, but I was impressed by the man himself." The two other Democrats who voted for Roberts—Patrick Leahy and Russell Feingold—similarly allowed Roberts's persona to lull them into unguarded optimism. Even Democrats who voted against Roberts acknowledged his spectacular winningness.

But no performance can be entirely without flaw, and there was one extraordinary moment when Roberts was taken by surprise and propelled into uncharacteristic, unattractive at-a-lossness. Dianne Feinstein—a thirties' movie character in her own right, with her Mary Astor loveliness, and air of just having arrived with a lot of suitcases—was questioning him. As she later recalled, "When I couldn't get a sense of his judicial philosophy, I attempted to get a sense of his temperament and values, and I asked him about the end-of-life decisions, clearly decisions that are gut-wrenching, difficult, and extremely personal." Feinstein looked at Roberts and said:

> I have been through two end of life situations, one with my husband, one with my father, both suffering terrible cancers, a lot of pain, enormous debilitation. Let me ask you this question this way: If you were in that situation with someone you deeply love and saw the suffering, who would you want to listen to, your doctor or the government telling you what to do?

Roberts, his brow furrowed with concern and empathy, replied:

> Well, Senator, in that situation, obviously, you want to talk and take into account the views and heartfelt concerns of the loved one that you're trying to help in that situation, because you know how they are viewing this. You know what they mean when they're saying things like what their wishes are and their concerns are and, of course, consulting with their physicians.

Huh? For once, the ear trumped the eye. What was Roberts saying? What had happened to his syntax? Why all those "you"s and "they"s when the answer clearly called for an "I"? As Roberts went on speaking in this unsettling language of avoidance, Feinstein coldly interrupted, "That wasn't my question." "I'm sorry," Roberts said demurely. "I'm trying to see your feelings as a man," Feinstein said. But she wasn't able to sustain the moment. She fell into the trap of rephrasing her question in a way that allowed Roberts to say, "Well, that's getting into a legal question." Feinstein quickly backed off. "OK. I won't go there," she said, as the split screen showed Roberts smiling with relief and perhaps a bit of triumph.

The Republican bridesmaids performed their ceremonial function with varying degrees of perfunctoriness. Specter, who had the role of chairman to play as well, played it as a courtly old man. A recent battle with cancer had left him thin and almost without hair. It was hard to see in this diminished figure the dark-haired man who fifteen years earlier had interrogated Anita Hill with such arrogant ruthlessness. No one who watched the Clarence Thomas hearings will forget the look of hatred that Hill directed toward Specter as she parried his assault on her credibility with her weapon of steely truthfulness. Specter no longer inspires hatred, of course, but he remains an obscurely sour figure. Some fundamental unlovableness adheres. It doesn't help that he speaks with excruciating slowness, as if he were a Southerner.

Lindsey Graham, who is a Southerner, speaks at Northern speed, and to highly entertaining effect. When it was his turn to question Roberts, he didn't just stroke him. He cut to the chase:

> You were picked by a conservative president because you have associated yourself with the conservative administrations in the past, advising conservative presidents about conservative policies. And there's another selection to be made, and you're going to get the same type person. And you can—I'm not even talking to you now—to expect anything else is just not fair. I don't expect—I didn't expect President Clinton to pick you.

I'm not even talking to you now. Graham brought to the surface what is always lying just below it at televised Supreme Court confirmation hearings: namely, that the Judiciary Committee members are never merely talking to the nominee; they are always talking to their constituents as well.

The confirmation hearing as we know it today evolved over the past century. In his excellent book *The Selling of Supreme Court Nominees* (1995), John Anthony Maltese lays stress on the inescapably political character of the nomination process. Since the early days of the Republic—starting with the Borking of George Washington's appointee for chief justice, John Rutledge—Supreme Court nominations have been fiercely fought over by rival senatorial factions. However, only in the twentieth century did these fights become public spectacles. A pivotal event, in Maltese's account, was the passage of the Seventeenth Amendment, in 1913, which changed the method by which senators come into office—from appointment by the state legislature to direct election—and intensified their activity as jumpy instruments of public will. The first public confirmation hearing took place in 1916, for Louis Brandeis (the first Jew to be named to the high court). Dozens of witnesses, pro and con, flocked to the hearing, but Brandeis himself did not choose to come. His advisers felt, Maltese writes, that "to do so would give the appearance that Brandeis was on trial." Not until 1925 did a nominee—Harlan Fiske Stone—testify before the Judiciary Committee, and thirty more years went by before it became customary, if not obligatory, for the nominee to testify. Between 1930 and 1955, four nominees testified and fifteen didn't. Since 1955, when the second John Marshall Harlan was nominated, every nominee has testified.

Brandeis's advisers were right: the Supreme Court nominee, sitting alone at a table facing a tribunal of legislators seated above him on a dais, is on trial. But so, of course, are the legislators. Each one knows that when he is up for reelection voters will remember (or someone will remind them of) his words and his demeanor. Graham presently abandoned all pretense of examining Roberts. "Let's talk about righting wrongs here," he said to the folks back home, and went on:

> I think it stinks that somebody can burn the flag and that's called speech. What do you think about that?
>
> ROBERTS: Well [laughter]. We had the Flag Protection Act after the Supreme Court concluded that it was protected speech.
>
> GRAHAM: Show me where their term "symbolic speech" is in the Constitution.
>
> ROBERTS: Well, it's not.
>
> GRAHAM: It's not. They just made it up, didn't they? And I think it stinks that a kid can't go to school and say a prayer if he wants to voluntarily. What do you think about that?
>
> ROBERTS: That's something that's probably inappropriate for me to comment on.
>
> GRAHAM: What do you think Ronald Reagan thought about that?
>
> ROBERTS: His view was that voluntary school prayer was appropriate.
>
> GRAHAM: I think it's not right for elected officials to be unable to talk about or protect the unborn. What do you think about that?
>
> ROBERTS: Well, again, Senator . . .

The fifty-year-old Graham has a gift for comedy—he delivers his lines as if he were working a nightclub crowd—and exudes an air of cynicism that right-wing politicians do not usually permit themselves, and that is very refreshing. The right-wing politician Sam Brownback has a more conventional style. During his questioning of Roberts, he paused to say that because of *Roe v. Wade* "we now have forty million fewer children in this country to bless us with" and that "eighty per cent to ninety per cent of children prenatally diagnosed with Down's Syndrome never get here—never get here." Roberts as gracefully declined to engage with the antiabortion Republicans as he had declined to engage with the prochoice Democrats. He was like the host of a successful and elegant party. Everybody could go home feeling good and good about himself. No one had spilled his champagne or been rude. When, four months later, Roberts joined Scalia and Thomas in their dissent to the majority opinion in *Gonzalez v. Oregon*, which upheld the state's law permitting assisted suicide, no one even seemed to feel betrayed. Good parties cast lovely long shadows.

2.

The Democrats came home from the hearing for Samuel Alito as if they had been beaten up by a rival gang in a bar. At the Roberts hearing, they had been vigorous and assured, sometimes even magnificent, in their defense of liberal values. At the Alito hearing, they were erratic and disoriented, as if suffering from a malaise they had fallen into between the two proceedings. In fact, what they were suffering from was the nominee. In his opening statement, Alito told this story:

> During the previous weeks, an old story about a lawyer who argued a case before the Supreme Court has come to my mind, and I thought I might begin this afternoon by sharing that story. The story goes as follows. This was a lawyer who had never argued a case before the court before. And when the argument began, one of the justices said, How did you get here? Meaning how had his case worked its way up through the court system. But the lawyer was rather nervous and he took the question literally and he said—and this was some years ago—he said, "I came here on the Baltimore and Ohio Railroad."

Throughout the hearing, in answer to almost every question, Alito said, in effect, that he had come here on the Baltimore and Ohio Railroad—and thus defeated every attempt to engage him in a dialogue. Each answer ended the matter then and there. He was like a chauffeur who speaks only when spoken to, and doesn't presume to converse. While Alito listened to questions, his face was expressionless. When giving answers, he spoke in a mild, uninflected voice. His language was ordinary and wooden. His manner was sober and quiet. He was a negligible, neutral presence.

It seemed scarcely believable that, in his fifteen years on the federal bench, this innocuous man had consistently ruled against other harmless individuals in favor of powerful institutions, and that these rulings were sometimes so far out of the mainstream consensus that other conservatives on the court were moved to protest their extremity. Or that in 1985, on an application for a job in the Reagan Justice Department, he had written, "I am particularly proud of my contributions in recent cases in which the government has argued in the Supreme Court that . . . the Constitution does not protect a right to an abortion." And, further, that "in college I developed a deep interest in constitutional law, motivated in large part by disagreement with Warren Court decisions, particularly in the areas of criminal procedure, the Establishment Clause, and reapportionment."

If Roberts was a pill the Democrats could agree to swallow even before tasting its delicious sugar coating, and Harriet Miers was a pig in a poke that some Democrats were prepared to buy, Alito was a nominee no Democrat could accept. But no Democrat could touch him. The impassive Alito paralyzed the Democrats. Their hopes of blocking the nomination by bringing forward two stains on his character—his membership in a notorious organization called Concerned Alumni of Princeton, which opposed the admission of women and minorities; and his failure to recuse himself in a case involving the Vanguard company, in which he had a financial stake—were decisively dashed. The stains proved too small—the garment remained presentable.

Twenty years ago, William Rehnquist, at the hearing for his elevation to chief justice, offered a model for how to parry embarrassing questions about your past. When asked about reports that as a young poll watcher he had harassed minority voters, Rehnquist shook his head sadly and said, "No, I don't think that's correct," and when asked about a restrictive clause in the lease to his country house barring "members of the Hebrew race," he said, "I certainly don't recall it." Alito, similarly, didn't recall joining the Concerned Alumni. "I have racked my memory," he said each time he was asked why he had joined. Nor could he explain why he hadn't recused himself in the Vanguard case. The Democrats realized too late that their pursuit of the Concerned Alumni and Vanguard matters was a trap. This time, the Republican bridesmaids didn't merely simper. They hastened to close ranks and attack the Democrats for their cruel badgering of Alito.

Lindsey Graham rose joyfully to the occasion. Rules of seniority placed him late on the program (he was elected to the Senate in 2002) and gave him the material for great shtick. He did a little preliminary routine with Vanguard ("Why would Judge Alito sit down in the corner of a room and say, I think I've got a conflict, but I'm just going to let it go and hear the case anyway?") and moved on to the Concerned Alumni:

> GRAHAM: Now this organization that was mentioned very prominently earlier in the day; did you ever write an article for this organization?
>
> ALITO: No, I did not.
>
> GRAHAM: OK. And some quotes were shown, from people who did write for this organization, that you disavowed. Do you remember that exchange?
>
> ALITO: I disavow them. I deplore them. They represent things that I have always stood against and I can't express too strongly . . .
>
> GRAHAM: If you don't mind the suspicious nature that I have is that you may be saying that because you want to get on the Supreme Court; that you're disavowing this now because it doesn't look good. And really what I would look at to believe you're not—and I'm going to be very honest with you—is: how have you lived your life? Are you really a closet bigot?

Is Lindsey Graham really a closet liberal? The sense of double entendre that always faintly hovers over Graham's speech is almost palpable in this passage. "I'm not any kind of a bigot, I'm not," Alito said. Graham assured Alito that he believed him, not because of his good reputation but because of "the way you have lived your life and the way you and your wife are raising your children." Then Graham had the audacity to cite—not by name—the Abramoff scandal as an instance of the kind of guilt by association that Alito was being subjected to:

> We're going to go through a bit of this ourselves as congressmen and senators. People are going to take a fact that we got a campaign donation from somebody who's found to be a little different than we thought they were—and our political opponent's going to say, "Aha, I gotcha!" And we're going to say,

"Wait a minute. I didn't know that. I didn't take the money for that reason."
. . . We have photos taken with people—and sometimes you wish you didn't have your photo taken. But that doesn't mean that you're a bad person because of that association. Judge Alito, I am sorry that you've had to go through this. I am sorry that your family has had to sit here and listen to this.

It was at this moment that Mrs. Alito got up and left the hearing room to have her famous cry. The TV camera barely caught the image of her figure brushing past two seats, and the TV watcher would have attached no significance to the sight. Unlike the forbiddingly beautiful and elegant Mrs. Roberts—who sat motionless during her husband's hearing, with a look of intense, almost anxious concentration on her face—the buxom Mrs. Alito fidgeted and looked around and never seemed to be fully engaged by the proceedings. As it was later reported (around the globe), Mrs. Alito had been so upset by the bad things the Democrats had said about her husband, and so moved by Graham's defense, that she had to leave in tears. But to anyone who had observed Mrs. Alito's demeanor in the days before the incident, Charles Isherwood's comment in the *Times*—"Surely grinding boredom may also have played a part in her scene-stealing eruption and flight from the Senate chamber"—had the ring of truth.

The Alito hearings were indeed grindingly boring. Although subjects of the highest interest were introduced—spying on citizens, torture, abortion, the right to privacy, civil rights, discrimination, executive power—the talk was never interesting, since Alito could never be drawn. Like Roberts, he eluded the Democrats' attempts to pry his judicial philosophy out of him, but, unlike Roberts, he offered no compensatory repartee. He was always just a guy answering questions *very carefully*. Over and over, the Democrats quizzed Alito on his pro-police, pro-prosecution, and pro-employer opinions. (The legal scholar Cass Sunstein analyzed forty-five of Alito's dissents in cases where individual rights and institutions were in conflict and found that in thirty-eight of them Alito took the side of the institution.) And over and over—like an accountant patiently explaining why the figures on a tax return are correct—Alito spared no dry detail in justifying his reasoning.

As the hearings wore on, and the fight between the Democratic and Republican committee members took on heat, Alito became an almost peripheral figure. The charge that the Democrats were cruelly badgering Alito was in fact unfounded. They had been a lot tougher on Roberts. At

one point in the Roberts hearing, Joe Biden pushed Roberts so hard—
indeed, was so fresh to him—that Specter had to intervene and say, "Let
him finish his answer, Joe." But, when questioning Alito, Joe practically
tugged his forelock. "Presumptuous of me to say this," "You'd know better
than I, Judge," "I don't mean to suggest I'm correcting you," "I'm not pre-
suming to be as knowledgeable about this as you," "All I'm suggesting is,"
"You've been very gracious" are among the examples of Biden's nervous
servility. (In the second round of questioning, in a gesture of propitiation
that can only be called deranged, Biden put on a Princeton cap.) But the
very idea of questioning Alito's probity left the Democrats open to charges
of bullying. Where the fair Roberts had been fair game, the mousy Alito
was out of bounds. Why don't you pick on someone your own size? By the
time the Democrats realized their tactical error, it was too late to correct it.
That the judge who consistently rules against little guys should become the
confirmation hearing's own little guy was one of the proceedings' more
delicious (and, for the Democrats, bitterest) ironies.

On the Senate floor two weeks later, with Alito no longer there to drain
their blood, the eight Democrats spoke their fears with forceful urgency.
Kennedy, Leahy, Durbin, and Feinstein were especially eloquent, and
Biden behaved himself. Over the days of debate, the flame of filibuster
flickered and subsided, and the ten Republicans, smelling victory,
showed the losers no mercy. Jeff Sessions, who had been one of the quieter presences in both the Roberts and the Alito hearings, now came to
demonic life:

> It is almost amusing as we have gone through the committee process to see
> them grasp in desperation to find something to complain about with Judge
> Alito. None of them could agree on what they didn't like. They bounced all
> over the place mostly. It sounded like they didn't like President Bush. They
> were having grievances about Abu Ghraib prison, which President Bush had
> nothing to do with.

Sessions went on:

They have been hankering for Harriet Miers, which is rather odd, I think. They have suggested somehow that some right-wing cabal caused President Bush to withdraw her nomination. . . . They have complained steadfastly that Judge Alito somehow is a tool of President Bush to defend his national policy and his war on terrorism and that Judge Alito is going to be a part of his efforts to arrogate powers to the executive branch. Who has been at President Bush's right arm for 5 years? It is Harriet Miers. . . . She has been involved in every one of these decisions about executive branch powers, National Security Agency wiretaps of Al Qaeda telephone conversations. She has been part of all of that. You think they would have let her come through here? They say: Oh we think she would be a fine nominee. What would they have done to her?

(Sessions had a point. The Democrats' tears for the martyred Harriet Miers had something of the crocodile quality of the Republicans' tears for Mrs. Alito's. The Democrats' outrage over Alito's dissent in the case of *Doe v. Groody* was similarly transparent. The case involved the warrantless strip search of a ten-year-old girl and her mother during a drug bust. Alito sided with the police, who argued that an affidavit gave them the authority to search the mother and daughter. The Democrats treated the incident as if it were the Rape of Nanking.) Other Republicans made other gloating speeches about the hapless Democrats, and, of course, none of it mattered because there would be no filibuster and Alito would be confirmed by the Republican majority in the Senate. John Kerry arrived exhausted from an economic conference in Davos to try to rally the minority troops. Sessions, apparently unaware of Kerry's return, jeered at the "international" filibuster "hatched in Davos, Switzerland, where Senator Kerry now is with those masters of the universe trying to figure out the world economy. Maybe they ought to spend more time trying to get the oil prices down than worrying about conjuring up a filibuster of a judge as able as Judge Alito."

When it was Biden's turn to speak, he quoted a remark that Alito had made during the hearing that he had not been alone in finding striking. Biden had been questioning the nominee about his position in a case involving the Family and Medical Leave Act, and had asked whether he and his fellow-judges on the panel had taken into consideration the fact that pregnant women sometimes need leave for bed rest during the last two months of pregnancy. Alito replied that, no, they had not considered that, and added, "We can't know everything about the real world." The remark leaped out of the gray blur of Alito's technocratic speech like a confession that can no longer be withheld. It confirmed what we already felt we knew about this dour and oddly innocent man.

Perhaps nowhere is the sense of Alito's alienation more palpable than in his dissent in *Riley v. Taylor* (2001), the case of a black man who was convicted of murder (and condemned to die) by an all-white jury, and who had appealed the verdict on the ground of discrimination. The appeals court, ruling en banc, accepted the possibility of discrimination and reversed the conviction. But Alito couldn't see what the majority saw. He argued that his colleagues had been wrong to be influenced by the fact that within a year three other murder cases in the county had been tried by all-white juries. He wrote:

> "An amateur with a pocket calculator," the majority writes, can calculate that "there is little chance of randomly selecting four consecutive all-white juries." Statistics can be very revealing—and also terribly misleading in the hands of "an amateur with a pocket calculator." The majority's simplistic analysis treats the prospective jurors who were peremptorily challenged as if they had no relevant characteristics other than race, as if they were in effect black and white marbles in a jar from which the lawyers drew. In reality, however, these individuals had many other characteristics, and without taking those variables into account, it is simply not possible to determine whether the prosecution's strikes were based on race or something else.
>
> The dangers in the majority's approach can be easily illustrated. Suppose we asked our "amateur with a pocket calculator" whether the American people take right- or left-handedness into account in choosing their Presidents. Although only about 10% of the population is left-handed, left-handers have won five of the last six presidential elections. Our "amateur with a calculator" would conclude that "there is little chance of randomly selecting" left-handers in five out of six presidential elections. But does it follow that the voters cast their ballots based on whether a candidate was right- or left-handed?

Judge Dolores K. Sloviter, the author of the majority opinion, dryly replied to Alito, "The dissent has overlooked the obvious fact that there is no provision in the Constitution that protects persons from discrimination based on whether they are right-handed or left-handed. To suggest any comparability to the striking of jurors based on their race is to minimize the history of discrimination against prospective black jurors and black defendants."

The facts that Alito overlooks are, of course, facts that his fellow right-wing ideologues also can't see from the mysterious planet—even farther away than Davos, Switzerland—they inhabit. During the Roberts and the Alito hearings, it was almost amusing to hear the nominees ritually denounce discredited Supreme Court decisions, such as *Plessy v. Ferguson* (1896), which refused a Creole named Homer Plessy the right to sit where he wanted on a train, and established the separate-but-equal doctrine; and *Korematsu v. U.S.*, which countenanced the internment of Americans of Japanese descent during the Second World War. Is there any reason to think that, had he been on the Court when these cases came before it, Alito or Roberts would have opposed the majority? Roberts was much given to affirming his fealty to "the rule of law." He said, "Somebody, asked me . . . 'Are you going to be on the side of the little guy?' And you obviously want to give an immediate answer, but, as you reflect on it, if the Constitution says that the little guy should win, the little guy's going to win in court before me. But if the Constitution says that the big guy should win, well, then the big guy's going to win, because my obligation is to the Constitution." The cases that are the glory of Supreme Court history are the cases where the little guy won; the cases that are its shame are those where he lost. The Constitution doesn't say who should win. Nine people do.

3.

Another memorable passage in the David Souter confirmation hearings occurred while he was being questioned by the Democratic senator from Ohio, Howard Metzenbaum. Metzenbaum asked Souter, as fifteen years later Feinstein asked Roberts, to give a personal rather than a legal response to a question about a controversial issue—abortion, in this case. Metzenbaum described in gruesome detail cases of illegal abortion from the pre-Roe era, and then said, "My real question to you isn't how you will rule on *Roe v. Wade* . . . but what does a woman face, when she has an unwanted pregnancy, a pregnancy that may be the result of rape or incest or failed contraceptives or ignorance of basic health information? And I would just like to get your own view and your own thoughts of that woman's position under those circumstances."

Souter paused before replying. Then he said, "Senator, your question comes as a surprise to me. I wasn't expecting that kind of question, and you have made me think of something that I have not thought of for twenty-four years." Souter went on to tell a story from his days at Harvard Law School. He had an appointment as a resident proctor (a student adviser) in a Harvard College freshman dormitory, and one day a student came to him for counsel. "He was in pretty rough emotional shape," Souter recalled,

> and we shut the door and sat down, and he told me that his girlfriend was pregnant and he said, "She's about to try to have a self-abortion and she doesn't know how to do it." He said, "She's afraid to tell her parents what has happened and she's afraid to go to the health services," and he said, "Will you talk to her?" and I did. . . . I will not try to say what I told her. But I spent two hours in a small dormitory bedroom that afternoon, in that room because that was the most private place we could get . . . listening to her and trying to counsel her to approach her problem in a way different from what she was doing, and your question has brought that back to me, and I think the only thing I can add to that is I know what you were trying to tell me, because I remember that afternoon.

As Souter spoke—gravely and slowly (but not too slowly), with his strong New England accent (he said "lore" for "law" and "sore" for "saw" and "floor" for "flaw")—one had the feeling of lights dimming on a set. One of the characters would soon get up to draw the curtains and turn on a lamp. This was not the only time in the Souter hearing that one felt as if one were seeing a well-wrought play rather than witnessing a piece of left-to-chance reality. In his opening statement, Souter told the senators that he was looking forward to "our dialogue," and dialogue did indeed take place—often very gripping dialogue. As Alito had unnerved, you could almost say unmanned, his questioners, so Souter gave his interlocutors to know that this was a play in which all the roles had good lines. If Souter—a slight man (his thinness had a mildly ascetic cast) of enormous, subtle intelligence and a moving absence of self-regard—was the star turn, he permitted the supporting cast of senators to perform no less brilliantly. Watching tapes of the Souter hearings makes one feel how things have deteriorated.

But not so fast. When the stately Shavian drama of the questioning of Souter ended, a new and entirely different drama began. The furies arrived. Molly Yard, the president of NOW, Fay Wattleton, of Planned Parenthood, Eleanor Smeal, of the Fund for the Feminist Majority, Kate Michelman, the executive director of NARAL, and Elizabeth Holtzman, the New York City comptroller, testified against Souter with fierce disdain. They assumed (as Michelman assumed about Alito when she testified against his confirmation in January) that Souter would cast a decisive vote to overturn *Roe v. Wade*. "I tremble for this country if you confirm David Souter," said Molly Yard. "Women's lives are literally on the line." She sneered at Souter's account of the scene in the freshman dorm: "This shows empathy? How do we know but what he may have cold-bloodedly told her she would be a murderer if she ended her pregnancy?"

Souter's record on civil rights, voting rights, gay rights, and victim rights and his bias toward law enforcement was similarly mocked and denounced by the feminists. Had these angry witnesses been able to see into the future, would they have testified as they did? Of course not. And had I *not* known how things turned out with Souter would I have watched the tape of his confirmation hearing with the same charmed delight? Of course not. We read what we can into reality's impassive face. Alan Simpson, a prescient prochoice Republican senator from Wyoming, said to Michelman and Wattleton, "I really believe you are making a big mistake on this one. . . . These things are going to come up again. There are going to be other Supreme Court choices when you are really going to need to be in the trenches. This is not one of those cases." He went on to say that Souter was "bright, intelligent, studious, caring, chivalrous, patient, probative, civilized, and a great listener and if that ain't enough for you, I think you are making a real mistake." "I think we have a difference of opinion," Wattleton said. After the furies left, a little parade of law enforcement officials went by who said that when Souter was attorney general of New Hampshire he had shown the police unfailing courtesy and kindness.

Then came another twist of the plot. Howard Phillips, the chairman of an organization called the Conservative Caucus, took the stand and compared Souter to Adolf Eichmann. After Souter performed his aria of the freshman dorm, Metzenbaum had said that's nice, it shows "you have empathy for the problem." But was there any reason to think that Souter could empathize with *both* sides of the abortion debate? His record showed strong antiabortion leanings. Was there anything he could show on the "other" side? To which Souter replied that he was a trustee of a hospital in Concord where abortions were performed. Now Phillips accused Souter of being "an accomplice" to "the shedding of innocent blood." "I would say that there is a fundamental distinction between the position of the groups such as NOW and NARAL and Planned Parenthood and so forth which urge a 'no' vote on Judge Souter," Phillips said. "Their position is that they are not absolutely certain that Judge Souter is going to be with them to their satisfaction. I, on the other hand, am absolutely certain on the basis of the record that Justice Souter does have a permissive view toward abortion." (Phillips went on to say that he was "troubled by his answers to other questions," above all by "one he gave to Senator Thurmond at the very beginning of the hearings, when he said that the power of the law comes from the people. I don't believe that. I believe it comes from God.")

After the debacle of the Alito hearing, Joseph Biden said that confirmation hearings should be abolished. (During the Roberts hearing, he had already remarked, "These hearings have become sort of a Kabuki dance" and "I am moving to the view that I'm not sure these hearings are the proper way to determine how to vote for a judge.") Biden is not the first to make such a proposal. In 1988, in response to the noisy Bork hearings, a Twentieth Century Fund Task Force on Judicial Selection recommended that the confirmation process be restored to a quieter former mode, whereby the nominee was judged solely on his written record and on the testimony of legal experts. These recommendations were ignored, as we know. As John Anthony Maltese points out, they were posited on the dubious idea of

> a golden age when Supreme Court nominees were not required to testify, when the factious whims of public opinion were ignored by senators, when the legal qualifications of nominees were considered without the taint of political motivation and when senators deliberated behind closed doors rather than posturing in the glare of television lights. The problem is that the apolitical nature of that golden age is largely fictitious.

Maltese's book is devoted to the political fights by which Supreme Court nominations are by their very nature dogged. Another book could be written about Supreme Court nominations since television lights first glared at them, in 1981, when Sandra Day O'Connor appeared before the Judiciary Committee. The televised hearings have not been uniformly edifying—the Alito hearing may be the least instructive of the lot—but each has its atmosphere and, so to speak, plot. The hearing for the nomination of Ruth Bader Ginsburg had the atmosphere of a garden party held to fête a beloved aunt about to embark on a wonderful journey. Ted Kennedy, who usually sits at confirmation hearings looking as if he had a toothache, was charming and funny. The Republicans were polite and deferential. During the recent hearings, the Republicans repeatedly boasted of their gracious acceptance of Ginsburg in contrast to the Democrats' sulky resistance to Roberts and Alito. Lindsey Graham was particularly mordant in his description of Ginsburg as an ACLU Commie whom, nevertheless, the Republicans manfully swallowed because Clinton had won the election. So why don't the Democrats manfully swallow Bush's appointees? Why are they being such poor sports? "Elections matter," Graham said. As the Democrats might have retorted—but didn't think or know to do until Senate debate on Alito was under way—Ginsburg had not been thrust on the Republicans the way Roberts and Alito had been thrust on the Democrats. She had been pre-approved by Orrin Hatch. Hatch recalls the circumstances in his book *Square Peg: Confessions of a Citizen Senator*. He writes that when Byron White resigned from the Court, Bill Clinton called him to ask how his secretary of the interior, Bruce Babbitt, would go over as a nominee. Hatch, then chairman of the Judiciary Committee, told Clinton that Babbitt was too liberal and would be hard to confirm, and gave him two names as alternatives: Ginsburg and Stephen Breyer. (In a footnote, Hatch writes that Ginsburg's record as a federal appeals court judge was "very similar to that of another subsequent Supreme Court Justice, Antonin Scalia.")

The Thomas hearings, in contrast, with their incredible final act, had a dark character—though it wasn't until Jane Mayer and Jill Abramson published their tour de force of reporting, *Strange Justice: The Selling of Clarence Thomas*, that we understood just how dark. Thomas's "high-tech lynching" speech, in which he denied Anita Hill's accusations with moving vehemence, was one of the great performances of its time. But Mayer and Abramson's research—their interviews with confidants of Hill who corroborated her account and with schoolmates of Thomas who recalled his crude sexual humor and regular attendance at pornographic movies—makes it all but impossible to believe that the zealot who sits in Thurgood Marshall's place on the high court didn't say those crassly dirty things to Anita Hill. Even more disturbing is the book's account of how the far right, the lesson of Bork fresh in its memory, stopped at nothing to get this nominee on the Court.

Since Bork, nominees have played their cards close to their chests. Bork could conceivably have saved his nomination by not constantly shorting his losing hand, but more likely the combination of powerful organized opposition on the left and the Democratic majority in the Senate was always enough to defeat it. By the time of Thomas, the right had mobilized, and has never again failed a stricken nominee. The so-I-lied convention, established by Thomas (who told the senators that he believed in a constitutional right to privacy and when safely on the Court said that, well, actually, he didn't), along with the mantra of "If I talk about recent Supreme Court cases, the sky will fall," has been firmly in place since the Thomas hearing. Biden's misgivings about the hearings are justified: when they are over we know no more about the nominee's judicial philosophy than we did before they started. But they yield another kind of knowledge: a portrait of the nominee emerges from them that may be as telling as any articulation of his judicial philosophy. When Alan Simpson asked David Souter whether he would be able to remove his personal feelings from his judgments, Souter said, "We always ask, we constantly ask ourselves, Senator, whether we can do that. We have no guarantee of success, but we know that the best chance of success comes from being conscious of the fact that we will be tempted to do otherwise." Neither Alito nor Roberts showed himself capable of such fineness of mind. In the light of Souter's testimony before the Judiciary Committee, his opinions on the high court should not have been surprising. And, in the light of theirs, Roberts's and Alito's probably will not be, either.

Biden also left out what may be the most compelling reason of all for the continued life of confirmation hearings: the intimate glimpse they give us of eighteen of our legislators. Which ones we love and which ones we hate is determined by our partisanship, of course. But as we watch them playing their big-league game we may sometimes forget to root, and just sit transfixed by their remarkable athleticism.

The Third Term: The Dawning of a Different Sort of Post-Presidency

Joe Conason

Esquire | December 2005

What does a two-term ex-president, still in the prime of his life, do after he leaves office (besides supporting his wife as she runs for reelection to the Senate and ponders a possible presidential bid of her own)? In Bill Clinton's case, the answer appears to involve staying incredibly busy and raising a ton of money. Just don't expect him to bail out his fellow Democrats by spending a whole lot of time bashing George W. Bush and the Republicans. As this Esquire *profile by Joe Conason makes clear, Clinton has been there and done that—and these days he's got bigger fish to fry.*

With lights dimmed in the late afternoon, the grand ballroom of the Sheraton Hotel in midtown Manhattan feels like an oversized television studio. Hundreds of men and women in dark suits are milling about, slowly seating themselves in rows facing a bright white stage accented with sky blue. Over loudspeakers comes the smooth baritone of a professional announcer, politely admonishing the crowd to be seated and be quiet. A few moments later the announcer says simply, "Bill Clinton."

To the cool techno hum of Moby's "Porcelain"—most often played as background sound in car and liquor commercials—the forty-second president of the United States ambles out from behind the set. Everyone rises to applaud as he opens his three-day conference of government leaders, business moguls, activists, and experts from around the world, gathered on this day in mid-September to discuss what can be done about poverty, corruption, climate change, and religious conflict.

Lean and at ease in a fine blue suit that happens to coordinate with the decor, Clinton is brandishing a wireless microphone, obviously comfortable in the role of host and impresario. Soon he is to be joined onstage by Tony Blair, Condoleezza Rice, and the king of Jordan for a rambling and agreeable chat. Prompted by Clinton, they will talk about the Mideast peace process, terrorism, international trade, alternative energy, and nuclear proliferation, sounding like guests on a high-minded chat show. Lurking not so inconspicuously in the reserved seats are current and former heads of state as well as rock legends and movie stars, and waiting for their turn to palaver with the former president are the chief executives of several of the world's largest corporations.

Of course, this looks exactly like what his die-hard critics assumed the Clinton Global Initiative would turn out to be: just another elaborate occasion for him to seize the spotlight and shine it on himself. The theme music, the fancy set, the mood lighting, the production values, and the political and business celebrities, indeed all of what might be called the "optics" of this event, certainly suggest an immodest purpose. Produced by the same firm that manages the fabulous World Economic Forum of moguls, activists, and stars in Davos, Switzerland, the opening of the CGI brings to mind an unflattering term that has often been applied to the host.

It looks slick.

In an era when celebrity dominates culture and consciousness, highly publicized events like the Clinton Global Initiative inevitably acquire the sheen of showbiz. With Angelina Jolie, Brad Pitt, Mick Jagger, Barbra Streisand, Tony Bennett, and Leonardo DiCaprio decorating the premises, the shiny surface is almost blinding. To glimpse the serious purpose underneath requires a closer attention.

If all Bill Clinton desires in his post-presidency is publicity, status, or the chance to hang out with power brokers and other actors, then he need not have gone to the effort and expense on display in Manhattan. All of those perks and more are easily available to him, regardless of whether he spends months planning and executing the heavy responsibilities he has taken on, which will keep him running, flying, meeting, plotting—and strenuously raising money—for the next decade.

Before the wave of news coverage surrounding the global initiative, not much attention had been paid to Clinton since the successful marketing of *My Life*, the thousand-page memoir that became a worldwide best-seller.

What coverage there was didn't delve much beneath the surface. Most Americans would have no reason to know, for instance, that while he was starting to draft his memoir in 2002, Clinton had committed himself to bring medical treatment to the millions dying from AIDS in the underdeveloped world. Most probably didn't notice the announcement, a year later, that the William J. Clinton Foundation had negotiated agreements to drastically reduce the cost of HIV/AIDS drugs and diagnostics—an achievement that is already saving hundreds of thousands of lives and promises to save millions more.

And until then nobody—perhaps not even Clinton himself—had yet understood the unprecedented aspirations of his life after the presidency.

At the Clinton house in Chappaqua, New York, an hour's drive north of his Harlem office, the big living room and formal dining room look immaculate and unused. As in most suburban homes, the action is out back in the kitchen, where the former president's press secretary and two of his senior aides hover around the center island, helping themselves to a smorgasbord of Chinese chicken, broiled salmon, and fruit salad. All three are in business attire, but Clinton glides in pretty casual in jeans and running shoes.

"Hey," he says, taking a plate with a chunk of salmon, and continues walking out to the glass-enclosed breakfast nook, a sun-filled octagonal room that overlooks the garden. He settles down at the oversized table and puts his feet up on another chair.

Nearly a week has passed since the closing session of the Clinton Global Initiative. As he talks about it now, his blue eyes widen and he allows himself the hint of a satisfied smile. Producing pledges of almost $2 billion to finance more than two hundred new projects around the world, the conference almost instantly proved to be more than just another "talkathon," as he feared it might be, more than another gust of hot air.

"I don't know what I expected, but I didn't think it would do this well. Maybe not half as well," he says. "Because there weren't speeches; everybody was serious, everybody was working on very specific things, and they really did feel like they had the power to make a difference."

The smile broadens when he is asked about those who dismissed the initiative as his latest bid to win the spotlight for himself and his wife. "Most people don't even fully understand their own motives, so when they make judgments about others', it's always dicey." He pauses, as if considering whether to continue. "I always figure when somebody goes after your motives, they're on their last leg, because they actually think you're doing something good that's gonna have good consequences. Attacking somebody's motives is the last refuge of somebody who's on the short end of the stick."

His words come faster, signaling irritation. "That's pretty lame, I think.

I could think of all kinds of ways to get publicity. I could get lots of publicity if I just sat right out on the street."

When his presidency ended, he says, "I wondered whether I would feel useless." Friends of his say that even before he became president, Clinton had imagined life after the White House. He more or less expected to emulate the post-presidential career of Jimmy Carter, human-rights advocate and Nobel laureate, whom he credits with accomplishing more than any ex-president, with the possible exception of the abolitionist John Quincy Adams. Toward the end of his second term, he invited Carter up to Camp David and the White House to talk about the years to come.

Clinton recalled those consultations late one night in Nairobi, Kenya, a stop on his seven-day tour through southern and eastern Africa in late July, when he alternated meetings in presidential palaces with visits to hospitals and AIDS clinics. Stationed at the end of a long table in the luxurious, heavily guarded Serena Hotel, he was playing hearts with four of his aides after finishing a lavish catered meal of steaks and curry and a glass or two of red wine. He talked, his aides muttered their bids and cursed their cards.

"I've never met anyone who did more with the gifts God gave him than Jimmy Carter," he said, holding up the unlit stub of a thick cigar in his right hand while fanning the cards in his left. "He declared what he was interested in and where he thought he could make a difference. They were superficially disparate, but all helped people have a better life. He eradicated river blindness in Africa, he worked on the green revolution to help people become more agriculturally self-sufficient, he's advanced human rights and monitored elections. . . . He has things that he plans to do, and things that come up."

For Clinton, the "things that come up" have ranged from last winter's tsunami in South Asia, where he is helping direct relief and reconstruction efforts with former president George Herbert Walker Bush, and Hurricane Katrina, where the former presidents have joined again to raise and direct funds along the Gulf Coast, to his own heart surgery, which led him to forge an alliance with the American Heart Association in a new crusade against unhealthy diets and childhood obesity. He has done scholarship drives for the 9/11 families and helped Harlem's small businesses. And while these projects seem to lack any unifying theme, he is hoping his ten-year global initiative may yet provide a means to make his work more coherent.

Unlike Carter, Clinton had to confront extraordinary financial challenges before he could embark on a life of good works. After twenty-two years of holding elective office, the man was totally in hock. He needed to pay off millions of dollars in legal bills left over from the Paula Jones lawsuit and the Whitewater investigation. He had to buy houses in Washington, D.C., and Westchester County, two of the costliest real estate markets in the country. He had to raise another $100 million—no, make that $165 million—to complete his sprawling presidential library in Little Rock, and still more to fund his new foundation, with staff and offices in Harlem.

For the first time in his life, Clinton concentrated on making money as well as raising money. As a politician, he had conjured up tens of millions of dollars, sometimes by controversial means, but he'd never earned much for himself and his family.

Ironically, all the controversies of his presidency only enhanced his earning potential upon leaving the White House. His bulky, engrossing memoir, which brought him at least $10 million in publishing advances, sold many more copies, both in America and around the world, than comparable books written by politicians. He charged as much as $250,000 for speaking engagements and filled auditoriums everywhere.

He became popular again. And after three years, suddenly, he was also rich. As one of the few American presidents who has in his life been poor, this is a status that, at age fifty-nine, he is still getting used to.

"It tickles me. I've enjoyed the fact that I can pay all my debts," he says, grinning and leaning back in his chair. "I've enjoyed the fact that I could give us nice homes in Washington and New York, and it's been really important for me and for Hillary, hard as she's been working. . . . I enjoy the protection that being financially self-sufficient gives me." He clips off the chewed end of the cigar stub and lifts it to his mouth.

"I've enjoyed it as much as anything else—having some security for my family, and knowing that if I drop dead, they'll be all right and I'll be able to leave a little something, but also having the freedom to speak out against policies that concentrate wealth and power, which I passionately disagree with. Now I have more credibility 'cause I've got money. I've tried to give away my tax cut and then some, every year since I got my debts paid."

The price of Clinton's fortune, earned with constant travel and work, turned out to be a near heart attack last fall, emergency quadruple-bypass heart surgery, and then another operation to repair his injured chest cavity. His face, close up, shows that he has aged a decade in the past year. And he has, those close to him say, "good days and bad days." Still, he looks good, considering. "I think I'm in as good a shape now as I've been in in years and years and years," he says. At dinner he still sneaks a few french fries when he thinks nobody is looking, but he has lost almost forty pounds and exercises daily. He's got his gym in the converted barn behind his house and a favorite hiking trail in Chappaqua.

While many heart patients experience a psychological letdown or worse after surgery, he says, "I didn't have any depression in my recovery, and I think it's 'cause I haven't had any real time off in thirty-five years, since I've been in politics. So I loved being home all day, every day, and being more or less incapacitated. I had a long rest. I got to watch movies, which I hadn't done in a long time. I got to read books. In my house in New York, I've got nearly five thousand books. I could stay a year up there."

Yet when his enforced rest ended, jarring intimations of the inevitable left him, he says, with a sense of moral urgency. He knows he doesn't have an unlimited horizon before him anymore. Now when he talks about changing the world, whether he happens to be in Nairobi or New York, the subject is inextricably tied to his own mortality. "I've reached an age now where it doesn't matter whatever happens to me. I just don't want anyone to die before their time anymore."

Moral urgency, it seems, causes one to travel a lot. His life is a never-ending succession of rich men and their jets. Clinton often says that he is "obsessed with this AIDS thing," and he sometimes seems to think he can drive progress toward his goal by sheer momentum. Just before the debut of his global initiative in New York, he set off on a weeklong, world-spanning jaunt from Houston to Glasgow to Beijing. "You should have been with us on that trip to China," he later boasted in the hallway of the Sheraton, stopping to sign an autograph. "We were in the air for ninety hours!"

Hours before dawn on September 5, he and Senator Hillary Rodham Clinton showed up at the local airport in Westchester County to board a jet loaned by John Catsimatidis, a New York supermarket magnate and long-time Democratic donor. They arrived in Houston a few hours later to join

Oprah Winfrey, several members of Congress, and an assortment of ministers visiting the Gulf Coast evacuees at the Astrodome.

Aside from the chance to throw his arms around the devastated evacuees of Hurricane Katrina, the purpose of this brief flyby was to announce a joint effort with his old nemesis George Herbert Walker Bush to raise money for those affected. It is an odd partnership, cemented during the aftermath of the Asian tsunami. Clinton gets along with the Bushes, father and son, he says, and however deep their political differences, he never speaks of them in a "hateful" tone.

"For whatever reason, we get along fine," he says of the president. "And I kinda get him now. I understand him better than I did. We have a good personal rapport and we can be very candid.

"When we went to the pope's funeral, he asked me to come in and talk to him. And he said, 'Tell me what you're doin' on AIDS.' And he said, 'Well, how do you relate to our program?' And I told him the truth, I said, 'Well, in the first place, it was terrible because your people thought we were the enemies of the drug companies, and they didn't want to work with us at all,' and we worked it out."

Speaking of Bush on another occasion, he said, "I've always been a big fan of his political skills, I've always thought he was an exceptional politician, even though I don't agree with him. But when you've been president and troops are committed and lives are on the line, I think we have to be very careful what we say. I remember when we went into Kosovo and the Republicans were practically rooting for us to lose. And I just don't approve of that. You know, I have an interesting relationship with President Bush, and I believe when a president asks you to do something, if in good conscience you can do it, you should do it.

"I have never thought he wasn't sincere. That is, in general he's done what he thinks is right. I think he's the most conservative president we've had since the twenties. More conservative than Reagan."

Clinton found his political voice long enough to blast the administration's mishandling of the Katrina catastrophe in early September, but only after seeming to give them cover in the storm's immediate aftermath. His turnabout came after protests from fellow Democrats—including a private but passionate admonishment from his wife.

That some Democrats still expect him to lead opposition to the Bush administration irritates Clinton: "I have to chart my own course, I have to do things that I think are important. I'm not the leader of the opposition anymore. I will always be loyal to my party, but if I spend time being a leader of the opposition, I won't be able to save lives doing what I'm doing. . . . That's something we have to have congressional leaders for, we have to have people like Hillary for, we have to have people like [Delaware senator] Joe Biden and all these people who want to run for president—and I can be supportive where it's appropriate. But I have a different life now, and I've got to lead it."

And that means perpetual motion. By early afternoon on September 5, the Clintons were in the air again, on their way home from Houston. After dropping the senator off in Chappaqua, the motorcade brought Clinton back to the airport. Idling there was another private jet, owned by Frank Giustra, the former chairman of Lions Gate Entertainment. It waited to transport Clinton and his entourage, including Giustra, to Central Asia and then on to China.

On the way, however, they stopped in Scotland for a few hours to refuel and to take a breakfast meeting at 4:00 A.M. with Tom Hunter, a Glasgow investor and philanthropist who has decided that he wants to get involved in African development. Hunter had accompanied the former president on part of the July trip to southern Africa, and, impressed with the performance of Clinton's HIV/AIDS Initiative in those countries, he had tentatively agreed to donate $100 million to health and education projects over the coming decade. Clinton had touched down to confirm that commitment, which Hunter agreed to announce in person at the Clinton Global Initiative in New York.

Late in the evening on September 6, the Clinton party landed in Almaty, the mountainous former capital of Kazakhstan, and from the airport proceeded directly to a meeting with President Nursultan Nazarbayev, much as if this were an official diplomatic visit.

At a joint nighttime press conference, Clinton praised Nazarbayev for dismantling the nuclear arsenal he inherited from the Soviets, who used to test weapons in the remote republic. Then, before sitting down to a midnight banquet, Clinton signed an agreement with the Kazakh health minister that permits the government to buy heavily discounted HIV/AIDS drugs through the Clinton foundation's procurement consortium. Sometime around 2:30 A.M., he met with the Kazakh opposition leaders to hear their complaints about the authoritarian Nazarbayev. Within an hour he was in the air again, heading to Lucknow, India.

This disorienting forty-eight hours was only the prelude to four more days of plane-hopping across China, where his foundation has established an active HIV/AIDS program, from Zhengzhou to Kunming to Urumqi to Hangzhou and finally to Beijing, where he marked the anniversary of September 11 with the U.S. embassy staff.

Only four days later he was back in Manhattan, waiting to walk out onto the stage of the Sheraton ballroom. For much of the two days that followed, he would hold court in a hotel suite, conferring and cajoling these great and good world citizens to commit themselves and their resources to his vision of global improvement.

And when the Clinton Global Initiative concluded, after two very full days of panels and workshops and reports, he would be able to announce that the participants—an extraordinary group that included the presidents of South Africa, Ukraine, Nigeria, and the Dominican Republic, the prime minister of Turkey, the CEOs of General Electric, Sony, Time Warner, Swiss Re, Goldman Sachs, and Starbucks, the president of the World Bank, a handful of Nobel Prize winners, and the leaders of several of the world's largest nonprofit organizations—had signed agreements to sponsor and finance more than two hundred separate projects valued at nearly $2 billion. They pledged to invest hundreds of millions in renewable-energy projects, in credit for small businesses in developing nations, in democracy initiatives in Arab and African countries, in clean water for Ghana and in terrorism insurance for Gaza, in environmental protection for Tierra del Fuego and in youth employment for the Balkans.

For his part, Clinton vowed that his foundation would monitor the fulfillment of each of these brave promises and report the findings next year. Those who deliver surely will be praised, and those who don't will be noted, and not invited back. The question that lingers is whether any of this activity can generate substantial improvement in the lives of those so distant and so disconnected from these very important people. Two billion dollars is a decent down payment, but two billion dollars won't go far on a sweltering planet where more than a billion human beings exist in conditions of extreme poverty and untreated disease.

Understanding why Clinton thinks he can accomplish something important as leader of the world's nongovernmental sector is easier after seeing what his foundation's three hundred employees and volunteers are doing on the ground. The best place to observe that is in Africa, a continent of special meaning for America's "first black president," as Toni Morrison famously called him. It is the home of his most venerable friend, who inspired him to make a rash promise.

On a bright morning last July, a short motorcade passed through the gates of Nelson Mandela's walled home in a leafy suburb of Johannesburg. Traveling through Africa on a typical seven-day, seven-country business trip, Bill Clinton had arrived to lunch with the great statesman on the occasion of his eighty-seventh birthday. From within the mustard stucco walls of Mandela's large house, his booming, cheerful voice could be heard quite clearly as he walked slowly out to the stone portico to greet the Clinton entourage, which included four aides, six Secret Service agents, and a few potential foundation donors. Mandela now uses a cane and a hearing aid, but his eyes were clear and his mind focused as he greeted everyone personally. He was happy to see Clinton again.

That night, in an enormous wood-paneled hall in downtown Johannesburg, Clinton joined thousands of South Africans of all races to pay homage to the man who led his nation peacefully out of apartheid. The well-dressed crowd whistled and cheered as "Madiba"—the Xhosa clan name that is his popular nickname—carefully bent over onstage to blow out the candles on a bombe-shaped cake.

When Mandela was seated, he beckoned Clinton over to sit beside him, and as the speeches and celebrating continued, they whispered to each other. Mandela seems to regard Clinton, whom he defended ferociously during his impeachment, as a political son. In *My Life*, Clinton recalls how Mandela counseled him to refuse to reciprocate the hatred of his enemies. Mandela's embrace has affected Clinton deeply.

Three years ago, at an international conference in Barcelona, the South African urged him to devote his post-presidential energies to fighting HIV/AIDS. Specifically, he asked Clinton to do what Western governments had deemed wildly impractical: provide effective treatment for the millions of HIV-infected poor in Africa, Asia, and Latin America, who had essentially been consigned to death because saving them would cost too much. At a minimum of roughly $1,600 per person, including diagnostic tests, the annual pharmacy bill alone would have come to about $40 billion.

It seemed impossible to imagine how this could be done, and yet it was also impossible for Clinton to turn Mandela down.

To conceive and run the Clinton HIV/AIDS Initiative, he brought in Ira Magaziner, an old friend and management consultant who had worked on Hillary's ill-fated health care plan during his first term. Magaziner came up with a plan to reduce the costs of treatment by driving down the price of drugs and testing, while Clinton lobbied government leaders in Europe and Canada to fund his program.

Political pressures had already reduced the price of some AIDS treatments in the Third World by the time Clinton got involved. Generic manufacturers were producing the antiretroviral drug combinations at lower costs, but the price still had to be reduced much further to permit any real progress.

Essentially, Clinton and Magaziner argued that if the companies cut prices enough, Western governments would appropriate funds to buy the drugs in volume. They worked with the suppliers all the way down the production process to reduce real costs. Moreover, they promised to make sure that the money would be available, that there would be no kickbacks or black market sales, and that the companies would be paid reliably and on time. And after a year of difficult negotiations, Clinton announced in October 2003 that his foundation would license countries to purchase HIV/AIDS drugs at an annual cost of $140 per person.

According to Magaziner, CHAI and its partners—including several NGOs and the governments of Ireland, Norway, Sweden, France, Canada, and the U.K.—have helped put almost 400,000 people in treatment and expect to provide care to 1 million people by the end of 2006 and 2 million by 2008. This has been possible, Magaziner says, through a "partnership" with the drug manufacturers, the governments that provide financing, and the major nonprofits that are fighting AIDS, such as the Gates Foundation and the Global Fund, as well as the United Nations and the World Bank.

The hope that he can fulfill his promise to Mandela keeps Clinton moving from one dusty, humid African capital to another. Sometimes he confesses that the continuing death toll from AIDS is depressing, or denounces the combined efforts of the Western governments and nongovernmental organizations as "pathetic" and "unacceptable." When he talks about his foundation's progress before audiences, he sometimes tells them not to applaud, because so few of the suffering are being treated.

But he reverts instantly to his usual optimism when it is suggested that the numbers must be daunting. "Yes, they are," he says. "But let's assume we need six million people getting their medicine. If our foundation alone can account for two million of that, if we can do a third of that by 2008, then we've done a heck of a lot there. That's the only point I'm making. We think we can go from three hundred thousand to two million in two more years, and so if we can do that, then . . ."

As fluent as Clinton sounded when reciting statistics, however, the numbers alone don't feed his determination. What seemed to motivate him, as ever, was human contact. Day after day in Africa, in visits to the grimmest rooms, in dingy hospital wards where doctors and nurses persevere in the worst circumstances, and in clinics where patients must confront the overwhelming social stigma of their disease just to show up for treatment, Clinton's energy did not flag.

At Mnazi Mmoja Hospital on the edge of the sea in Zanzibar, the peeling walls and dark, muddy floors contrasted starkly with the gorgeous blues of the water and sky. Green scrubs hung on an outdoor clothesline, and odors hinted of poor sanitation. Until three months earlier, this place offered no AIDS treatment at all—a situation that reflected traditional prejudices among the island's overwhelmingly Muslim population.

Clinton climbed the stairs to the second floor to meet patients, talked quietly with their doctors, and inspected the hospital's new clinic. Currently treating fifty-six HIV-infected patients, its program will scale up to two thousand by the end of the year. One doctor showed him a boxy machine that looked like a large computer printer. This essential item, purchased by the Clinton Foundation and the Swedish government, is a CD4 T-cell counter, which measures the health of a patient's immune system. Clinton recognized the electronic box and knew how to interpret the readout from it.

Downstairs in the hospital parking lot, he held an impromptu press conference. Dressed in a custom-made navy suit, red tie, and black Gucci loafers, he delivered his upbeat message to the local media. "I am thrilled to be in Zanzibar for the first time in my life," he exclaims. "Just now, I shook hands with an eleven-year-old orphan child who knows that he is HIV-positive. His circumstances have changed. He doesn't have to be stigmatized. And he doesn't have to resign himself to an early death." Later that afternoon, in another old building in Stone Town, the island's ancient Moorish city, he held sick children on his lap and promised their sick mothers that he would continue to send them the medicine that keeps them alive, for free.

This scene was repeated in Lesotho, Mozambique, Tanzania, Kenya. In every country, the visits to clinics and hospitals alternated with visits to presidents and ministers, with whom he ostentatiously shared credit and praise, whether they deserved it or not.

Clinton cultivates these relationships with the same care he once devoted to governors and mayors in America—although at a long afternoon ceremony at Tanzania's State House, Clinton seemed to be blinking away sleep. "It has been my great honor to work with you," he said to the Tanzanian president when it was finally his turn, "and to be your friend."

The African leaders tend to treat him as if he were still the world's most powerful head of state. He is, after all, perhaps the most famous person in the world, an emissary from a rich country that they love and sometimes hate, and in Africa they seem to regard Clinton as still being the leader of the part of America that is more agreeable to them. The presidents stand proudly next to him, as if his presence reflects their own legitimacy. And they listen when he urges them to help remove the stigma from their HIV-infected citizens, to expand health services in rural areas—and to cooperate with the United Nations, Western governments, and nongovernmental organizations.

His trip's final destination was Kigali, the capital of Rwanda, where he solemnly laid a wreath on the mass tomb that commemorates the 800,000 victims of the genocide that Clinton did nothing to stop. He has apologized for that failure before, but it may not be possible to apologize enough. That day, before visiting one of the AIDS clinics that his foundation operates there, Clinton went to a formal state luncheon in his honor at the presidential palace.

For a while, he held forth while Paul Kagame, Rwanda's thin, reticent president, sat on the opposite side of the table and listened. Then the room went quiet. Clinton realized that Kagame wanted to speak. Without the sound of Clinton's voice, the whole room was suddenly silent. Kagame finally spoke. "Mr. President," he said, facing Clinton, "you are welcome in our country anytime."

The corners of Clinton's mouth turned up slightly, a gratified look, as if he had gotten something he had wanted very much.

To Clinton, his foundation's HIV/AIDS Initiative has implications that go beyond the delivery of medical treatment to the poor. The CHAI model points toward a new system of relationships that brings together governments, nonprofit groups, investors, donors, and international organizations. He is seeking ways to leverage the money and power of states with the flexibility and skills of the NGOs. And he sees the enthusiastic response to the launch of his global initiative as a signal that the world in which he operates is ready for new kinds of cooperation, and perhaps is ready for global leadership.

Although he knows that nobody else wields that kind of influence, he is too politically astute to stake any explicit claims for himself. Back in Chappaqua, he speaks in more modest terms, but his voice is emphatic: "This movement has grown so rapidly, and there's so many people doing it, and it's so entrepreneurial that I think it would profit from better coordination, more information sharing, and combining efforts. There's no association of NGOs, there's no United Nations of NGOs, there's no coordination. I think that since so much money is going out there, and since on the whole it's fairly cost-efficient, I think that it would be beneficial if we all worked together more."

Before the CGI ended, he agreed to continue sponsoring the meetings annually for a decade to come. "It's kind of an arbitrary figure, but I figured that if we could do this for ten years, we would have a real significant body of achievements to show what we had done," he said, then laughed. "And I thought there'd be a reasonable chance I would survive ten years and be alert and cognizant. Hopefully I won't be in a coffin by then."

Strong and vital and happy as he appears, he often speaks these days in the voice of a man who feels his own death. It is a voice made more credible by his physical aging—the snowy hair, the thinner face and frame, the lines in his cheeks and brow, the scar that runs the length of his chest. When Clinton took the stage at the final session of his global initiative, he sounded more philosophical than political.

Our near-human forefathers were making tools 2 million years ago, he said. People have been walking around as *Homo sapiens* for 130,000 years. It's just 15,000 years since the big Ice Age moved away and enabled people to move across the earth. "So if we had a huge cataclysmic event from global warming, it would just be about 15,000 years from the last Ice Age, which is the blink of an eye in the life of the planet—or the life of humanity on the planet."

And in that moment at least, ten years didn't seem like very much time at all.

Part Four:
Republicans vs. Democrats

Getting Ahead in the GOP
Benjamin Wallace-Wells

The Washington Monthly | October/November 2005

Do you ever get the feeling that the current breed of young Republicans are tougher, better focused, and more politically savvy then their Democratic counterparts? Chances are, you're right—as this Washington Monthly *profile by Benjamin Wallace-Wells of a rising young GOP star makes abundantly clear.*

His name, you notice immediately, is nearly an American hero's.

Rep. Patrick McHenry, twenty-nine-years-old and a freshman Republican congressman, is sitting calmly in front of an *ABC World News Tonight* camera, his prematurely gray hair parted on the side and pulled thick over his scalp. He is waiting for the show to begin. It is mid-July and a particularly perilous political moment. The House majority leader and conservative power broker, Rep. Tom DeLay (R-Texas), is in hot water for taking a series of ethically sketchy trips—to the Mariana Islands, to Scotland, and to Russia—funded by lobbyists whose clients happen to have benefited from loopholes DeLay helped write into federal law. Even for Congress, this is shameless stuff and, with rumors of an indictment imminent, many conservatives are backing away from DeLay. But if the House leader has a more committed supporter on the planet Earth than Patrick McHenry, he is certainly not an elected member of the United States Congress. McHenry is one of only twenty Republican representatives who signed on with DeLay's ultimately failed attempt to rewrite the House ethics process to grant himself effective immunity from indictment. DeLay needs something—a diversion, dynamite in the distance. And here is McHenry. As the camera turns on, his face snaps into a bank teller's automatic smile. McHenry is the kind of young person whom other young people can't stand because he comes across as if he's been prepping his whole life to be forty. His voice is high-pitched, his tone world-weary, measured, sighingly cynical. Twenty-nine years old, he's seen it all before. "This is just the pot calling the kettle black," he says, arguing that Democratic leader Nancy Pelosi (D-Calif.) also took a trip she didn't fund herself. This is the Republican line of the day, even though Pelosi's trip was a nonprofit-funded visit to a U.S. naval base while DeLay's was a St. Andrews golf vacation financed by indicted lobbyist Jack Abramoff. Nevertheless, McHenry's eyebrows temple upward, neat geometries of piety. "They call their own failure to disclose travel a mere oversight. But when Republicans do it, they call it an ethical scandal." *Dynamite in the distance.* The news report pivots, and ABC correspondent Brian Ross spends most of the rest of the segment affirming that Democrats, too, have taken some trips they haven't paid for. *A pox on both their houses.* For McHenry, this is mission accomplished.

No political movement can survive on talking points alone. It requires an endless succession of faces, flesh and bone, elected officials willing to impose their smiling mugs in front of the camera even when the talking points are ridiculous. In the nine months since he came to Washington, McHenry has cultivated a role as a kind of fraternity pledge for the House leadership, willing to do the dirty work on behalf of crusades that the rest of his caucus will no longer touch. He was still pumping Social Security privatization this summer, months after the GOP leadership had given up on the bill. He was still attacking Terri Schiavo's husband after other Republicans, with an eye toward opinion polls, clammed up. And in June, he was summoned by the cable networks to defend Karl Rove after it began to appear likely that the president's chief strategist had identified Valerie Plame as a CIA agent while talking to reporters.

McHenry is perhaps the most successful and precocious of the endless string of *those guys*, the youngish Republican representatives who show up on cable television to defend the indefensible. But McHenry has also mastered, far more quickly than most, the inside game, the art of cultivating personal relationships with the powerful. Soon after moving to Congress, McHenry hired Grover Norquist's press secretary as his own. More recently, he's been dating Karl Rove's executive assistant.

For his labors and for his promise, McHenry has won committee assignments and leadership positions like a row of shined medals, commemoratives for heroisms rendered. He's the only freshman to be part of the majority whip's team. He is cochair for communications of the National Republican Congressional Committee, an exalted post that entitles him to help frame the national message for GOP candidates around the country. "He's got an awful lot of promise," House Majority Whip Eric Cantor (R-Va.) told *National Journal* for a profile headlined "Boy Wonder." He has shared the stage with President Bush at the insurance industry's annual convention. Both DeLay and the man who replaced him as House Majority Leader, Rep.

Roy Blunt (R-Mo.), have hosted fund-raisers for McHenry, a rare privilege for a freshman. A puffy *Weekly Standard* piece praised McHenry's "tenacity."

When Newt Gingrich brought the Republican Party back to power in the House in 1994, he did it with a phalanx of gate crashers—dentists, insurance agents, small businessmen—political rookies and ideologues, many of whom have recently been at odds with DeLay and the spendthrift House leadership. A decade on, the revolution has calcified into what is less an ideology than a system, a cluster of organizations that manage power and careers—a political machine. Like most of the post-Gingrich generation, McHenry's ultimate loyalty is less to principle or ideology than to the machine itself.

To understand the values and pathologies of an organization, it often helps to follow the career path of its most precocious stars. Henry Blodget, the famous late-1990s Wall Street TV analyst, made it by grasping that his employer, Merrill Lynch, wanted him to talk up stocks that his firm had an extra hidden financial interest in selling to an investing public eager to believe the normal rules of share prices were suspended. Similarly with Sammy Glick, the fictional young Hollywood up-and-comer in Budd Schulberg's satirical novel about the 1930s movie business *What Makes Sammy Run?*, who figures out that stealing scripts and snitching on members of the nascent screenwriter's union is the way to get ahead in the studio system. Patrick McHenry is the Henry Blodget, the Sammy Glick of Republican power in Washington. "What Patrick understands is the same thing that George Bush understood," the omnipresent conservative power broker Grover Norquist told me, "which is how the modern Republican Party works."

Taking Credit

You had to hand it to him. He was always improving. I mean, he was becoming more and more expert at being Sammy Glick. The way he was telling this story, for instance. He wasn't outlining it, he was acting it. What the story lacked in character and plot his enthusiasm and energy momentarily overcame.

—Budd Schulberg, *What Makes Sammy Run?*

McHenry represents North Carolina's 10th congressional district, an in-between place where the hollows and dipping roads of Appalachia drop down into the golf courses and big lawns that spiral out from Charlotte.

The district is caught in an aspirational middle zone, too: On a dark back road with a house maybe every half mile, with the lawns only mowed now and then and fingers of grass lingering listless upright in the heat like the unemployed, there's a wood sign tacked to a tree, the kind of sign that in a Bugs Bunny cartoon would say, "Moonshine this-away." But instead it says, "Cherryville Golf Shop." *The Almanac of American Politics* has called the 10th the "most blue-collar district in America."

Historically, at least, that's on account of the old textile mills, great long brick masses with broken windows, slung along the train tracks. The mills have been shut down for decades now, the work long since sent off to Mexico or China. But they have left this district with a particular quirk. The people who live here, many of them descendents of the mill workers who now commute to service jobs in Charlotte suburbs, still bank with the credit unions that originated in the mills, taking advantage of the better loan terms that tend to come from nonprofit financial institutions. This is significant because one of the first bills authored by McHenry, whose district has 172,000 credit union members, would make it much harder for government to regulate or block the conversion of credit unions into banks, a process that tends to benefit the credit union's directors (who get to cash in stock options and can sometimes make millions) and hurt the union's members, who can no longer borrow and save at the same generous terms.

McHenry's credit union bill, a high priority for the banking lobby, has received strong backing from DeLay. The Republican leadership awarded McHenry a seat on the House Financial Services Committee upon his arrival in Washington. "Most people would say it's the most plum assignment you can get," one conservative lobbyist told me, "because you can leverage it to do so much in fund-raising." But first you have to prove yourself. Asking McHenry to author a bill that undermines the interest of half his constituents is the political equivalent of demanding a young Mafia enforcer kill his cousin as a test of loyalty. "It's a bill that a lot of us are watching," a conservative activist from Mecklenberg County who has been skeptical about McHenry told me. "It's pretty clear that here McHenry is picking Washington over his district, and we're interested to see if he pays any price for it."

The crowd that fills an old textile mill in Morganton, N.C., in early August to meet with McHenry is comprised mostly of elderly supporters, with one exception: a clutch of young, well-dressed women at the back, stickers pasted to their lapels, the hand-printed word "bank" with a crude red slash through it. During the question-and-answer session, they stand up and speak, a few in turn. They're members of local credit unions, they tell McHenry, and worry that their credit union could now convert to a bank, leaving them high and dry. The older ladies and gents at the front of the room turn around, a little befuddled; so far, they've been nodding agreeably every time the sweet-faced young man tells them he's been cutting their taxes; this is an unexpected bit of controversy.

McHenry handles it expertly. As the women at the back of the room speak, he nods constantly to show he's taking them seriously; and when he begins to speak, McHenry commands the room, his hands moving forward to punctuate each essential word, model UN-style. He's spoken with the leadership of their particular credit unions, the congressman says, and the leadership strongly supports the bill. (That these credit union managers stand to benefit financially if their institutions convert into banks, he does not mention.) Credit union members may not be completely aware of the provisions of his bill; in any event, he'd be happy to "get with you" afterward, to talk through the technical details of bank conversion. Then, with the room still unsettled, McHenry smoothly moves the discussion back to safe ground, focusing on big, national topics—the plans Republicans have for major tax cuts, for Social Security reform, for defending marriage. The room bursts into spontaneous and lavish applause. There's something openly paternal about the way the crowd reacts to him—they want to like him, want him to be doing good, this kid with their values, their politics, these hills in his veins.

Exile in Cherryville

The first time I saw him he couldn't have been much more than sixteen years old, a little ferret of a kid, sharp and quick. Sammy Glick . . . Always ran. Always thirsty.

—Budd Schulberg, *What Makes Sammy Run?*

As it happens, McHenry's not even really from this district. He grew up in suburban Charlotte, the son of the owner of the Dixie Lawn Care Company, and after high school enrolled at North Carolina State. There, involved in politics, he displayed an early aptitude for translating conservative politics into street theater; in 1997, a sophomore, he stood on a Raleigh avenue as President Clinton's motorcade passed, a bearded Abe Lincoln mask over his head, and held a sign saying, "Who's sleeping in my bed?"

Halfway through his college career, McHenry left N.C. State, transferred to tiny Belmont Abbey College, and moved into a house off campus in the small nearby town of Cherryville. For a young man on the make, the move seemed an odd choice. Cherryville is a little, unprosperous town with nowhere to go and nothing to do, a place where middle-aged men walk along the side of the highway because the car broke down again. The town, in other words, is the kind of place that animates the nightmares of college juniors. As a long-term political strategy, however, the move made sense. The part of suburban Charlotte where McHenry had grown up was and is represented by a young, well-liked conservative, Rep. Sue Myrick (R-N.C.) who figured to be around for a while. Cherryville was just across the border in a solidly conservative district whose man in Washington, Rep. Cass Ballenger (R-N.C.), was into his eighth decade and whose career seemed to be winding down. And this very conservative town was represented in the State House by a Democrat.

At Belmont Abbey, McHenry moved quickly. "He always managed to get his work done . . . but he made it clear from the beginning that he was going to miss a lot of classes, that his political work came first," McHenry's adviser, history professor Francis Murray, told me. Soon after arriving at Belmont Abbey, McHenry founded the school's College Republican (CR) chapter, then launched a winning campaign for chairman of the state CR organization.

The College Republicans have legendarily been the starting point, the training and networking ground, for the careers of all of the party's most influential activists: Lee Atwater, Grover Norquist, Jack Abramoff, Karl Rove. And producing Roves and Atwaters, tactical geniuses and election winners, is exactly what the organization is set up to do: The organization is a four-year crash course in how to win votes from conservatives, in electioneering, with its members running endlessly for College Republican state board, College Republican state treasurer, College Republican national committee. There's a balls-out element to these contests, to the infighting; when I talked to College Republicans in North Carolina, I heard constant, ridiculous allegations thrown at rivals within the organizations. This rival had an illegitimate son in Tennessee, that one paid for an abortion for some poor girl from Missouri. When I asked an innocent question about a network of political consultants in Raleigh, one College Republican stopped me immediately: "Surely you must have heard," he said ominously, his drawl thick, "about them *bisexual orgies*."

This training served McHenry well when, midway through his junior year, he declared his candidacy for the state House of Representatives. His opponent in the primary was a man named David Cline, a former county commissioner. McHenry prevailed upon College Republicans from around the state to volunteer, going door-to-door, and claimed in the course of his campaign that he was the most conservative candidate. The proof? He'd never voted to raise taxes, and once, as a county commissioner, Cline had. Cline said, essentially, *of course* he's never voted to raise taxes, he's a *college junior*. Didn't matter; the charge stuck—McHenry won. In the general election, he faced off against a connected, conservative Democrat, a businessman, Rotarian and ex-county commissioner named John Bridgeman. McHenry, who seems to have been working from a limited bag of political tricks, claimed he was the most conservative candidate in the race. When that didn't work, he tried to link Bridgeman to the scandal-ridden Bill Clinton, charging that because Bridgeman was a Democrat, "he supported selling out the Lincoln bedroom." McHenry—keep in mind, a twenty-one-year-old college student—lost. Bridgeman had managed to raise far more money, and one of the critical lessons McHenry's friends and advisors drew from the race, one told me, was that "Patrick had to get better at fund-raising." Soon after he graduated from Belmont Abbey, he moved to Washington.

Political Finishing School

It's queer to think how many little guys there are like that, with more ability than push, sucked in by one wave and hurled out by the next, for every Sammy Glick who slips through and over the waves like a porpoise.
                    —Budd Schulberg, *What Makes Sammy Run?*

"It wasn't like he was a Bill Gates, someone who was the smartest guy in the room or the most charismatic guy in the room or something like that," Dee Stewart, McHenry's former chief of staff and longtime political consultant, told me. "But he did something else just as special: He figured out what the system was, and he worked it harder than anyone I've ever met."

McHenry's first full-time job in Washington was with the conservative communications group DCI. It was quite a choice. If there is a center to Washington conservative dark arts, DCI is pretty much it. They were paid consultants, for instance, to the Swift Boat Veterans for Truth last year, although they are most known for attacking fellow Republicans. DCI's founder is Thomas Synhorst; his expertise lies in "astroturfing"—developing fake grassroots groups to front for conservative and corporate causes—and "push-polling," a subtle technique that can impart damaging information about a rival candidate in the guise of a hypothetical question for a poll. Synhorst conducted, for instance, push-polls for Bob Dole's presidential campaign in 1996, in which Iowans were asked if they would be more or less likely to vote for Steve Forbes if they knew that the candidate had a "promiscuously homosexual father."

This was McHenry's political finishing school. The recent graduate started work at DCI's New Media division in the fall of 1999; his main project was running a Web site, *NotHillary.com*, which peddled rumors that Hillary Clinton would run for president in 2000 in order to drum up conservative campaign contributions. Meanwhile, DCI was working for Karl Rove; Synhorst's group helped defeat Senator John McCain in South Carolina that year with a series of notorious push-polls that, among other things, called McCain "a liar, a cheat, and a fraud." By June, with McCain no longer a factor and Bush breezing toward the nomination, McHenry used his connections to get an interview with Rove, who hired him to be the National Coalition Director for the Bush-Cheney campaign.

After the election, McHenry looked around for his next step. When a new administration sweeps into power, young partisans start looking for plum jobs—flipping through a book that is literally plum-colored to search for political appointee slots. The most coveted are jobs as "special assistants." Such positions require no substantive experience but put a young person in the room with an agency's principal decision makers. They are also assignments that cannot be won without highly placed contacts. So, when McHenry soon turned up as special assistant to the new secretary of labor, Elaine Chao, the wife of influential Senator Mitch McConnell (R-Ky.), it caught the attention of some powerful conservatives. "He had a reputation that preceded him," Norquist told me. "I was hearing from friends that Patrick was a rising star long before I met him."

There is a streak of impatience, urgency, get-aheadness that runs throughout McHenry's young career; he habitually stays at jobs for six or eight months, long enough to add a line to his résumé, make the necessary contacts, and then move on. McHenry stayed with Chao for less than six months; his credential in hand, he returned to North Carolina and began scoping out a second run for the State House. He used the same tactic—claiming he was the most conservative candidate in the race—and with a weak field of candidates, he won. He spent the first half of 2003 attacking the moderates who ran the State House when, almost as if on schedule, the local congressional seat opened up. The incumbent Ballenger had been making increasingly odd public statements (among other things, he attributed the breakup of his fifty-year marriage to the presence of an American-Islamic relations association next door to his house) and soon was coaxed into retirement. Congressional seats don't come open too often in the one-party precincts of the South. Six months after he had taken his seat in Raleigh, McHenry announced that he was running for Congress.

I Shot the Sheriff

At twenty-seven, McHenry was only two years above the constitutional age requirement for running for Congress, though with his prematurely graying hair he could pass for thirty-five. His real problem was that he had never worked a day in his life in the district as an adult. McHenry needed to get something relevant into his résumé, quickly. So he took an alternate route: In the fall of 2003, he sat for the real estate licensure exam and, almost instantly, Patrick McHenry the political operative became Patrick McHenry the realtor, proprietor of "McHenry Real Estate." He didn't appear to do much business—local newspapers list no transactions and note that the "company phone number" he listed for state records was actually his personal cell phone—but "McHenry Real Estate" gave his campaign room to claim that he was the "one small businessman in the race."

Most politicians also need a local reputation, an organization, contacts, and a profile. McHenry didn't have much local profile—he was, his consultant Stewart says, "virtually unknown" in the district when his campaign began, having represented only 2 percent of it in the State

House. In contrast, also running for the Republican nomination were two local businessmen—Sandy Lyons and George Moretz—who were able to self-finance their campaigns, as well as David Huffman, the popular, twenty-four-year sheriff of Catawba County.

That, according to the old rules of politicking, would have been that. The young up-and-comer would have been told—or made—to wait his turn while the more experienced men fought to claim their right to the district. But McHenry understood the new, emerging set of political rules. He may have been unknown in the district, but McHenry was known in Washington. Soon after he officially declared his candidacy, checks were coming in from conservative godfathers such as Norquist and from the PACs of powerful lobbies such as the American Medical Association and the National Home Builders Association. And while McHenry couldn't count on much of a local volunteer base, he could draw on his national contacts to staff his campaign with College Republicans. Volunteers from Alabama, Texas, and Missouri came to help out. In the North Carolina chapter, he brought in "what must have been every CR in the state," one volunteer told me, to knock on doors. When this seemed as if it might be coming up short, he applied another rule of Rove's GOP: Rules are made to be broken. His friends at the College Republican National Committee arranged to send seventy paid field operatives to work the district—a trip that may have violated the group's bylaws, which forbid the organization from taking a position in primaries. McHenry snuck into second place and a runoff against Sheriff Huffman.

Sheriff Huffman occupies a position on the political spectrum that might fairly be called lethally conservative. "Patrick's people called me antigun," he complained to me, "but I was the only sheriff in the state to vote to make it legal to carry a concealed weapon without a permit." This is an obvious point of pride for the sheriff. In the two-man race, he was the more established, the more well known, and had staked out a political slot that was almost unimaginably right.

So how did McHenry convince voters he was the most conservative candidate? He simply *said so*. "It was our mantra," Elizabeth Beck, a former campaign worker and then-president of the UNC-Charlotte College Republicans, told me. "We told voters Patrick was the most conservative candidate in the race, that he was antitax, antigun control, and antiabortion." The swarms of College Republicans also hustled: "We'd go knock on doors at nine in the morning, and a lot of these places up in the rural areas seemed like it had been years since someone had knocked on their door—I never got turned away." Once inside, the College Republicans opened up campaign-bought portable DVD players and let McHenry's recorded address play away.

McHenry, a Catholic in an overwhelmingly Protestant district, also started attending Baptist youth groups. "I knew he was against abortion and against the homosexual agenda," Pastor Ruffin Snow, a Baptist minister from Hickory who is considered a major power broker in McHenry's district, explained to me. "But with him being Catholic, the most important thing was I asked him, actually, the same question I'm fixin' to ask you, Ben. I asked him, Patrick, if God were to call you today and ask you whether you deserved to go to heaven, would you be able in your heart to tell him you did? Because," the pastor added with a sly hint of the deep and dark, "everyone spends eternity *someplace*." Pastor Snow let that sink in and continued: "And Patrick said to me, 'yes, because even though I'm Catholic I'm also born-again, I've accepted Christ into my heart.' And that was good enough for me."

After a bitter election campaign, in which Bob Novak echoed the McHenry campaign's cooked-up charges of ethical improprieties against Huffman and the sheriff charged his challenger with throwing beer parties for underage students, McHenry won the runoff by eighty-five votes out of 30,000 cast, and trounced his Democratic opponent in November to win the congressional seat.

"No rules in a knife fight"

There is no word in English to describe it. You could say gloat, smile, leer, grin, smirk, but it was all of those and something more, a look of deep sensual pleasure.

—Budd Schulberg, *What Makes Sammy Run?*

Congress! McHenry arrived already a celebrity, thanks to his youth. C-SPAN recorded McHenry and his staff—virtually all of whom were fellow former College Republicans—setting up their office. In a first-day profile, the *Winston-Salem Journal* noted that McHenry had been more or less waiting for this moment since high school. When the youngest member of the 109th Congress headed for his first vote, "That's when it hits you like a freight train," he told the paper. "This is the first time you realize the responsibility voters have given you." The first vote he had to cast was for speaker, a foregone conclusion. "When they called out my name," McHenry told the *Journal*, "I stood up and said loudly, 'Hastert.'"

"What stood out about Patrick from the beginning," Charles Symington, the influential head of Independent Insurance Agents and Brokers of America's government affairs program, told me, "was he was interested not only in policy but also in politics, that he was willing to work hard and fight on behalf of the Republican leadership." The only thing that seemed strange, a conservative activist in North Carolina told me, was that "Patrick and his staff still seemed to have what you could call an obsessive involvement in College Republicans—this was a sitting Congressman and his staff, mind you, and they were making calls to try to go behind the scenes and figure out who was getting elected to the state board, kid stuff like that, what seemed like every week. It was odd."

The shape of the College Republican national organization was beginning to shift, mud underfoot, the friends and allies McHenry had made were losing influence and power. During the lead-up to the 2004 election, the College Republican National Committee (CRNC) sent out a fund-raiser that specifically targeted, as *The Washington Post* put it, "elderly people with dementia," and misled them into thinking they were sending money to President Bush's reelection campaign. The letter became a low-level scandal in the national press, a story helped along by the pathos of the victims: elderly conservatives with little to live on who were sending their savings on to a bunch of bow-tied college kids, smirking at their swelling bank accounts. But things really hit the fan when the letter's author, a University of South Dakota senior named Paul Gourley (a close friend and ally of McHenry's), announced he was running for national chairman, and a series of quick endorsements by the outgoing CRNC National Chair and the leaders of major state delegations followed. An outraged caucus within the CRNC came together behind an insurgent, Michael Davidson.

College Republican campaigns are big money—costs can run in the hundreds of thousands of dollars. But the rewards are big, too: The chairman, who gets a $75,000 salary and benefits, manages a paid staff with an annual budget of $2 million in salary and expenses. And the fund-raiser was seamy stuff, the kind of thing that elected officials fight like hell to distance themselves from. National political figures from Senator John McCain (R-Ariz.) and California Governor Arnold Schwarzenegger, to Senator Richard Burr

(R-N.C.) and Texas Governor Rick Perry endorsed Davidson. The House Ways and Means Committee Chairman, Rep. Bill Thomas (R-Calif.), even held a fund-raiser for him. At the convention, things got competitive, then grotesque. Convention speakers were deleted out of the program at the last minute, replaced by figures who supported Gourley. Delegations switched allegiances for mysterious reasons in the dead of night; virtually everybody accused virtually everybody else of being gay. As *The New Republic*'s Franklin Foer reported in a recent account of the CRNC convention, the Gourley-Davidson contest began in earnest after Norquist reminded delegates from the podium that "there are no rules in a knife fight."

This was when Patrick McHenry, sitting in his congressional office, picked up the phone. The tradition in Congress has been that it's perfectly fine to endorse candidates, but it's a little below the office to get personally involved in the organization's races. But like his mentors in the Republican leadership, McHenry wasn't much for tradition. North Carolina's College Republicans had endorsed Davidson, and so McHenry and his chief of staff, Jason Deans, began to phone the leaders of the North Carolina College Republican chapters, asking for them to change their vote. "Patrick said that he had only won the election because of the field reps the [College Republican National Committee] had sent, that Davidson wouldn't send them again, and that Patrick wouldn't win reelection without the field reps, and if we wanted Patrick to stay in Congress, we'd back Gourley," Elizabeth Beck, then the chair of the College Republican chapter at UNC-Charlotte, told me. In other phone calls, McHenry was more blunt: "He told me, and several of my friends that we were done in politics if we didn't support him," another College Republican chapter president told me. (McHenry has admitted that he and Deans made the calls but denied that they threatened anyone's career.) Over the course of two weeks, after a couple of a dozen calls, McHenry prevailed upon those in the North Carolina delegation to change their votes, removing three votes from Davidson's column and putting them in Gourley's. Gourley ended up winning by six votes; had North Carolina voted the other way, Davidson might have won.

Not Dead Yet

In late September, the day after Tom DeLay was indicted for criminally conspiring to funnel corporate money into state elections, *New York Times* columnist David Brooks tried to cast a hopeful spin on the situation, declaring: "The old team is dead." He meant that the indictment signaled an end to the kind of political world in which McHenry had ascended, where "loyalty to the team matters more than loyalty to the truth."

Dead? Well, maybe. But there remains a whole generation of conservatives in Washington who came up through that system and who have rallied to defend it. That includes McHenry, who appeared on Fox News the night that the indictment was announced to debate his sixty-eight-year-old Democratic congressional colleague Rep. Bill Pascrell (D-N.J.). The two batted their talking points back and forth—"it's a culture of corruption"; "no, it isn't"—when McHenry hit a little lower. Interrupting Pascrell, McHenry said he couldn't believe someone from New Jersey had the nerve to talk about ethics. Pascrell blew up, as did most of the Garden State delegation. McHenry later apologized to Pascrell privately, but never publicly. And the attack did nothing but burnish his image among fellow conservatives as a nervy team player.

"You know, I see him as someone who could someday be vice president," McHenry's political consultant Dee Stewart tells me. "Not president, because you've got to be more bipartisan for that, but a vice president, someone who could become a conservative legend."

The Framing Wars
Matt Bai

The New York Times Magazine | July 17, 2005

One of the questions that's bedeviled Democrats in recent election cycles is why the Republicans have been so much more effective at packaging their positions into compelling sound bites. Whether they're railing against the "death tax" and "big government," accusing their opponents of "hating America," decrying the "war against Christmas" or pushing the "defense of marriage," GOP partisans have a knack for the succinct, evocative phrase. Democrats, on the other hand, often seem incapable of summing up their views in a way that average Americans can understand—preferring instead to give long-winded, convoluted explications of their views (think Al Gore and John Kerry). Perhaps that's why linguist George Lakoff became an instant celebrity with his book Don't Think of an Elephant! *which is basically a primer aimed at reeducating Democrats on how to talk about politics. Here,* The New York Times Magazine's *political reporter Matt Bai analyzes Lakoff's message and its potential impact on the 2006 midterm elections.*

After last November's defeat, Democrats were like aviation investigators sifting through twisted metal in a cornfield, struggling to posit theories about the disaster all around them. Some put the onus on John Kerry, saying he had never found an easily discernable message. Others, including Kerry himself, wrote off the defeat to the unshakable realities of wartime, when voters were supposedly less inclined to jettison a sitting president. Liberal activists blamed mushy centrists. Mushy centrists blamed Michael Moore. As the weeks passed, however, at Washington dinner parties and in public postmortems, one explanation took hold not just among Washington insiders but among far-flung contributors, activists, and bloggers, too: the problem wasn't the substance of the party's agenda or its messenger as much as it was the Democrats' inability to communicate coherently. They had allowed Republicans to control the language of the debate, and that had been their undoing.

Even in their weakened state, Democrats resolved not to let it happen again. And improbably, given their postelection gloom, they managed twice in the months that followed to make good on that pledge. The first instance was the skirmish over the plan that the president called Social Security reform and that everybody else, by spring, was calling a legislative disaster. The second test for Democrats was their defense of the filibuster (the time-honored stalling tactic that prevents the majority in the Senate from ending debate), which seemed at the start a hopeless cause but ended in an unlikely stalemate. These victories weren't easy to account for, coming as they did at a time when Republicans seem to own just about everything in Washington but the first-place Nationals. (And they're working on that.) During the first four years of the Bush administration, after all, Democrats had railed just as loudly against giveaways to the wealthy and energy lobbyists, and all they had gotten for their trouble were more tax cuts and more drilling. Something had changed in Washington—but what?

Democrats thought they knew the answer. Even before the election, a new political word had begun to take hold of the party, beginning on the

West Coast and spreading like a virus all the way to the inner offices of the Capitol. That word was "framing." Exactly what it means to "frame" issues seems to depend on which Democrat you are talking to, but everyone agrees that it has to do with choosing the language to define a debate and, more important, with fitting individual issues into the contexts of broader story lines. In the months after the election, Democratic consultants and elected officials came to sound like creative-writing teachers, holding forth on the importance of metaphor and narrative.

Republicans, of course, were the ones who had always excelled at framing controversial issues, having invented and popularized loaded phrases like "tax relief" and "partial-birth abortion" and having achieved a kind of *Pravda*-esque discipline for disseminating them. But now Democrats said that they had learned to fight back. "The Democrats have finally reached a level of outrage with what Republicans were doing to them with language," Geoff Garin, a leading Democratic pollster, told me in May.

By the time Washington's attention turned to the Supreme Court earlier this month, rejuvenated Democrats actually believed they had developed the rhetorical skill, if it came to that, to thwart the president's plans for the court. That a party so thoroughly relegated to minority status might dictate the composition of the Supreme Court would seem to mock the hard realities of history and mathematics, but that is how much faith the Democrats now held in the power of a compelling story. "In a way, it feels like all the systemic improvements we've made in communications strategy over the past few months have been leading to this," Jim Jordan, one of the party's top strategists, said a few days after Sandra Day O'Connor announced her resignation. "This will be an extraordinarily sophisticated, well-orchestrated, intense fight. And our having had some run-throughs over the past few months will be extremely important."

The most critical run-through for Democrats, in light of the test ahead, was the defense of the filibuster, and for that reason, it offers some useful clues to how Democrats may try to frame the Supreme Court fight as well. The battle began late last fall, when Senate Republicans, feeling pretty good about themselves, started making noises about ramming judges through the Senate by stripping Democrats of their ability to filibuster, a plan the Republican senators initially called "the nuclear option." The fight was nominally over Bush's choices for the federal bench, but everyone knew it was in fact merely a prelude to the battle over the Supreme Court;

the only way for Democrats to stop a confirmation vote would be to employ the filibuster.

In January, Geoff Garin conducted a confidential poll on judicial nominations, paid for by a coalition of liberal advocacy groups. He was looking for a story—a frame—for the filibuster that would persuade voters that it should be preserved, and he tested four possible narratives. Democratic politicians assumed that voters saw the filibuster fight primarily as a campaign to stop radically conservative judges, as they themselves did. But to their surprise, Garin found that making the case on ideological grounds— that is, that the filibuster prevented the appointment of judges who would roll back civil rights—was the least effective approach. When, however, you told voters that the filibuster had been around for over two hundred years, that Republicans were "changing rules in the middle of the game" and dismantling the "checks and balances" that protected us against one-party rule, almost half the voters strongly agreed, and seven out of ten were basically persuaded. It became, for them, an issue of fairness.

Garin then convened focus groups and listened for clues about how to make this case. He heard voters call the majority party "arrogant." They said they feared "abuse of power." This phrase struck Garin. He realized many people had already developed deep suspicions about Republicans in Washington. Garin shared his polling with a group of Democratic senators that included Harry Reid, the minority leader. Reid, in turn, assigned Stephanie Cutter, who was Kerry's spokeswoman last year, to put together a campaign-style "war room" on the filibuster. Cutter set up a strategy group, which included senior Senate aides, Garin, the pollster Mark Mellman, and Jim Margolis, one of the party's top ad makers. She used Garin's research to create a series of talking points intended to cast the filibuster as an American birthright every bit as central to the Republic as Fourth of July fireworks. The talking points began like this: "Republicans are waging an unprecedented power grab. They are changing the rules in the middle of the game and attacking our historic system of checks and balances." They concluded, "Democrats are committed to fighting this abuse of power."

Cutter's war room began churning out mountains of news releases hammering daily at the GOP's "abuse of power." In an unusual show of discipline, Democrats in the Senate and House carried laminated, pocket-size message cards—"DEMOCRATS FIGHTING FOR DEMOCRACY, AGAINST ABUSE OF

POWER," blared the headline at the top—with the talking points on one side and some helpful factoids about Bush's nominees on the other. During an appearance on *This Week with George Stephanopoulos* in April, Senator Charles Schumer of New York needed all of thirty seconds to invoke the "abuse of power" theme—twice.

By the time Reid took to the airwaves in late May, on the eve of what looked to be a final showdown on the filibuster ("This abuse of power is not what our founders intended," he told the camera solemnly), the issue seemed pretty well defined in the public mind. In a typical poll conducted by *Time* magazine, 59 percent of voters said they thought the GOP should be stopped from eliminating the filibuster. Perhaps feeling the pressure, a group of seven Republicans joined with seven Democrats in a last-minute compromise. Bill Frist, the Senate majority leader, and his team, smarting from crucial defections, had no choice but to back down from a vote. The truce meant that several of Bush's judges would be confirmed quickly, but it marked a rare retreat for Republicans and infuriated conservative activists, who knew that a Supreme Court battle would now be messier than they had hoped.

For their part, Democrats were euphoric at having played the GOP to a draw. The facts of the filibuster fight hadn't necessarily favored them; in reality, the constitutional principle of "checks and balances" on which the Democrats' case was based refers to the three branches of government, not to some parliamentary procedure, and it was actually the Democrats who had broken with Senate tradition by using the filibuster to block an entire slate of judges. ("An irrelevancy beyond the pay grade of the American voter," Garin retorted when I pointed this out.) And yet it was their theory of the case, and not the Republicans', that had won the argument. As Garin explained it, Republicans had become ensnared in a faulty frame of their own making. The phrase "nuclear option"—a term Frist and his colleagues had tried gamely, but unsuccessfully, to lose—had made Dr. Frist sound more like Dr. Strangelove. "It's a very evocative phrase," Garin said. "It's blowing up the Senate. It's having your finger on the button."

Garin was gloating, but it was hard to blame him. On the eve of what promises to be a historic debate over the direction of the nation's highest court, Democrats on Capitol Hill seemed to have starkly reversed the dynamic of last fall's election. Then, they had watched helplessly as George W. Bush and his strategists methodically twisted John Kerry into a hopeless tangle of contradictions and equivocations, using words and imagery to bend him into a shape that hardly resembled the war hero he had been. Now, Democrats believed, they had deciphered the hieroglyphics of modern political debate that had so eluded them in the campaign, and in doing so they had exacted some small measure of revenge. As one of the party's senior Senate aides told me a few days after the filibuster compromise was reached, "We framed them the way they framed Kerry."

The father of framing is a man named George Lakoff, and his spectacular ascent over the last eight months in many ways tells the story of where Democrats have been since the election. A year ago, Lakoff was an obscure linguistics professor at Berkeley, renowned as one of the great, if controversial, minds in cognitive science but largely unknown outside of it. When he, like many liberals, became exasperated over the drift of the Kerry campaign last summer—"I went to bed angry every night," he told me—Lakoff decided to bang out a short book about politics and language, based on theories he had already published with academic presses, that could serve as a kind of handbook for Democratic activists. His agent couldn't find a publishing house that wanted it. Lakoff ended up more or less giving it away to Chelsea Green, a tiny liberal publisher in Vermont.

That book, *Don't Think of an Elephant!* is now in its eighth printing, having sold nearly 200,000 copies, first through liberal word of mouth and the blogosphere and then through reviews and the lecture circuit. (On the eve of last fall's election, I came across a Democratic volunteer in Ohio who was handing out a boxful of copies to her friends.) Lakoff has emerged as one of the country's most coveted speakers among liberal groups, up there with Howard Dean, who, as it happens, wrote the foreword to *Don't Think of an Elephant!* Lakoff has a DVD titled *How Democrats and Progressives Can Win: Solutions from George Lakoff*, and he recently set up his own consulting company.

When I first met Lakoff in April, at a UCLA forum where he was appearing with Arianna Huffington and the populist author Thomas Frank, he told me that he had been receiving an average of eight speaking invitations a day and that his e-mail account and his voice mailbox had been full for months. "I have a lot of trouble with this life," Lakoff confided wearily as we boarded a rental-car shuttle in Oakland the following morning. He is a short and portly man with a professorial beard, and his rumpled suits are a size too big. "People say, 'Why do you go speak to all these little groups?' It's because I love them. I wish I could do them all." Not that most of Lakoff's engagements are small. Recently, in what has become a fairly typical week for him, Lakoff sold out auditoriums in Denver and Seattle.

How this came to be is a story about the unlikely intersection of cognitive science and political tumult. It began nearly forty years ago, when, as a graduate student, Lakoff rebelled against his mentor, Noam Chomsky, the most celebrated linguist of the century. The technical basis of their argument, which for a time cleaved the linguistics world in two, remains well beyond the intellectual reach of anyone who actually had fun in college, but it was a personal and nasty disagreement, and it basically went like this: Chomsky said that linguists should concern themselves with discovering the universal rules of syntax, which form the basis for language. Lakoff, on the other hand, theorized that language was inherently linked to the workings of the mind—to "conceptual structures," as a linguist would put it—and that to understand language, you first had to study the way that each individual's worldview and ideas informed his thought process.

Chomsky effectively won this debate, at least in the sense that most American linguistics departments still teach it his way. (To this day, the two men don't speak.) Undeterred, however, Lakoff and his like-minded colleagues marched off and founded the field of cognitive linguistics, which seeks to understand the nature of language—how we use it, why it is persuasive—by exploring the largely unconscious way in which the mind operates.

In the 1970s, Lakoff, verging into philosophy, became obsessed with metaphors. As he explained it to me one day over lunch at a Berkeley cafe, students of the mind, going back to Aristotle, had always viewed metaphor simply as a device of language, a facile way of making a point. Lakoff argued instead that metaphors were actually embedded in the recesses of the mind, giving the brain a way to process abstract ideas. In other words, a bad relationship reminds you on an unconscious level of a cul-de-sac, because both are leading nowhere. This results from what might be called a "love as journey" frame in the neural pathways of your brain—that is, you are more likely to relate to the story of, say, a breakup if it is described to you with the imagery of a journey. This might seem intuitive, but in 1980, when Lakoff wrote *Metaphors We Live By*, it was considered fairly radical. "For 2,500 years, nobody challenged Aristotle, even though he was wrong,"

Lakoff told me, sipping from a goblet of pinot grape juice. Humility is not his most obvious virtue.

Through his work on metaphors, Lakoff found an avenue into political discourse. In a seminal 1996 book, *Moral Politics*, he asserted that people relate to political ideologies, on an unconscious level, through the metaphorical frame of a family. Conservative politicians, Lakoff suggests, operate under the frame of a strict father, who lays down inflexible rules and imbues his family with a strong moral order. Liberals, on the other hand, are best understood through a frame of the nurturant parent, who teaches his child to pursue personal happiness and care for those around him. (The two models, Lakoff has said, are personified by Arnold Schwarzenegger on one side and Oprah Winfrey on the other.) Most voters, Lakoff suggests, carry some part of both parental frames in the synapses of their brains; which model is "activated"—that is, which they can better relate to—depends on the language that politicians use and the story that they tell.

The most compelling part of Lakoff's hypothesis is the notion that in order to reach voters, all the individual issues of a political debate must be tied together by some larger frame that feels familiar to us. Lakoff suggests that voters respond to grand metaphors—whether it is the metaphor of a strict father or something else entirely—as opposed to specific arguments, and that specific arguments only resonate if they reinforce some grander metaphor. The best evidence to support this idea can be found in the history of the 2004 presidential campaign. From Day 1, Republicans tagged Kerry with a larger metaphor: he was a flip-flopper, a Ted Kennedy–style liberal who tried to seem centrist, forever bouncing erratically from one position to the other. They made sure that virtually every comment they uttered about Kerry during the campaign reminded voters, subtly or not, of this one central theme. (The smartest ad of the campaign may have been the one that showed Kerry windsurfing, expertly gliding back and forth, back and forth.) Democrats, on the other hand, presented a litany of different complaints about Bush, depending on the day and the backdrop; he was a liar, a corporate stooge, a spoiled rich kid, a reckless warmonger. But they never managed to tie them all into a single, unifying image that voters could associate with the president. As a result, none of them stuck. Bush was attacked. Kerry was framed.

According to Lakoff, Republicans are skilled at using loaded language, along with constant repetition, to play into the frames in our unconscious minds. Take one of his favorite examples, the phrase "tax relief." It presumes, Lakoff points out, that we are being oppressed by taxes and that we need to be liberated from them. It fits into a familiar frame of persecution, and when such a phrase, repeated over time, enters the everyday lexicon, it biases the debate in favor of conservatives. If Democrats start to talk about their own "tax relief" plan, Lakoff says, they have conceded the point that taxes are somehow an unfair burden rather than making the case that they are an investment in the common good. The argument is lost before it begins.

Lakoff informed his political theories by studying the work of Frank Luntz, the Republican pollster who helped Newt Gingrich formulate the Contract with America in 1994. To Lakoff and his followers, Luntz is the very embodiment of Republican deception. His private memos, many of which fell into the hands of Democrats, explain why. In one recent memo, titled "The 14 Words Never to Use," Luntz urged conservatives to restrict themselves to phrases from what he calls, grandly, the "New American Lexicon." Thus, a smart Republican, in Luntz's view, never advocates "drilling for oil"; he prefers "exploring for energy." He should never criticize the "government," which cleans our streets and pays our firemen; he should attack "Washington," with its ceaseless thirst for taxes and regulations. "We should never use the word outsourcing," Luntz wrote, "because we will then be asked to defend or end the practice of allowing companies to ship American jobs overseas."

In Lakoff's view, not only does Luntz's language twist the facts of his agenda, but it also renders facts meaningless by actually reprogramming, through long-term repetition, the neural networks inside our brains. And this is where Lakoff's vision gets a little disturbing. According to Lakoff, Democrats have been wrong to assume that people are rational actors who make their decisions based on facts; in reality, he says, cognitive science has proved that all of us are programmed to respond to the frames that have been embedded deep in our unconscious minds, and if the facts don't fit the frame, our brains simply reject them. Lakoff explained to me that the frames in our brains can be "activated" by the right combination of words and imagery, and only then, once the brain has been unlocked, can we process the facts being thrown at us.

This notion of "activating" unconscious thought sounded like something out of *The Manchurian Candidate* ("Raymond, why don't you pass the time by playing a little solitaire?"), and I asked Lakoff if he was suggesting that Americans voted for conservatives because they had been brainwashed.

"Absolutely not," he answered, shaking his head.

But hadn't he just said that Republicans had somehow managed to rewire people's brains?

"That's true, but that's different from brainwashing, and it's a very important thing," he said. "Brainwashing has to do with physical control, capturing people and giving them messages over and over under conditions of physical deprivation or torture. What conservatives have done is not brainwashing in this way. They've done something that's perfectly legal. What they've done is find ways to set their frames into words over many years and have them repeated over and over again and have everybody say it the same way and get their journalists to repeat them, until they became part of normal English."

I asked Lakoff how he himself had avoided being reprogrammed by these stealth Republican words. "Because I'm a linguist, I recognize them," he said. Even to him, this sounded a little too neat, and a moment later he admitted that he, too, had fallen prey to conservative frames now and then. "Occasionally," he said with a shrug, "I've caught myself."

In May 2003, Senator Byron Dorgan, the North Dakota Democrat, read *Moral Politics* and took Lakoff to a Democratic Senate retreat in Cambridge, Maryland. Lakoff had never met a senator before. "I knew what they were up against, even if they didn't know what they were up against," Lakoff says. "They were just besieged. My heart went out to them."

Lakoff gave a presentation, and in the parlance of comedians, he killed. Hillary Clinton invited him to dinner. Tom Daschle, then the minority leader, asked Lakoff if he would rejoin the senators a few days later, during their next caucus meeting at the Capitol, so that he could offer advice about the tax plan they were working on. Lakoff readily agreed, even though he had come East without so much as a jacket or tie. "I went in there, and it was just this beautiful thing," he told me, recalling the caucus meeting. "All these people I'd just met applauded. They gave me hugs. It was the most amazing thing."

Of course, the idea that language and narrative matter in politics shouldn't really have come as a revelation to Washington Democrats. Bill Clinton had been an intuitive master of framing. As far back as 1992, Clinton's image of Americans who "worked hard and played by the rules," for instance, had perfectly evoked the metaphor of society as a contest that relied on fairness. And yet despite this, Democrats in Congress were remarkably slow to grasp this dimension of political combat. Having ruled Capitol Hill pretty comfortably for most of the past sixty years, Democrats had never had much reason to think about calibrating their language in order to sell their ideas.

"I can describe, and I've always been able to describe, what Republicans stand for in eight words, and the eight words are lower taxes, less government, strong defense, and family values," Dorgan, who runs the Democratic Policy Committee in the Senate, told me recently. "We Democrats, if you ask us about one piece of that, we can meander for five or ten minutes in order to describe who we are and what we stand for. And frankly, it just doesn't compete very well. I'm not talking about the policies. I'm talking about the language."

Dorgan has become the caucus's chief proponent of framing theory. "I think getting some help from some people who really understand how to frame some of these issues is long overdue," he says, which is why he invited Lakoff back to talk to his colleagues after the 2004 election. Meanwhile, over on the House side, George Miller, a Democrat from the San Francisco area, met Lakoff through a contributor and offered to distribute copies of *Don't Think of an Elephant!* to every member of the caucus. The thin paperback became as ubiquitous among Democrats in the Capitol as Mao's Little Red Book once was in the Forbidden City. "The framing was perfect for us, because we were just arriving in an unscientific way at what Lakoff was arriving at in a scientific way," says Representative Nancy Pelosi, the minority leader in the House.

In fact, though Lakoff started the framing discussion, he was by no means the only outside expert whom Democrats were consulting about language. To the contrary, a small industry had blossomed. Even before the 2004 election, Pelosi had enlisted John Cullinane, a software entrepreneur in Boston, to help the caucus develop the wording for a vision statement. Cullinane spent an hour and a half with members of the caucus one afternoon, while his aide scrawled suggestions on a white board. Among his recommendations was that they come up with a list that had six parts—either six principles or six values or six ideas. When we spoke, I asked Cullinane why it had to be six. "Seven's too many," he replied. "Five's too few."

Then there was Richard Yanowitch, a Silicon Valley executive and party donor, who worked with Senate Democrats, providing what he calls "private-sector type marketing." Last December, at Dorgan's request, Reid put Yanowitch in charge of a "messaging project" to help devise new language for the party. Another adviser who became a frequent guest on the Hill after the election was Jim Wallis, a left-leaning evangelical minister who wrote *God's Politics: Why the Right Gets It Wrong and the Left Doesn't Get It.* In January, after addressing a Senate caucus retreat at the Kennedy Center, Wallis wrote a memo to the Democratic Policy Committee titled "Budgets Are Moral Documents," in which he laid out his argument that Democrats needed to "reframe" the budget in spiritual terms.

What all of these new advisers meant by "framing," exactly, and whether their concepts bore much resemblance to Lakoff's complex cognitive theories wasn't really clear. The word had quickly become something of a catchall, a handy term to describe anything having to do with changing the party's image through some new combination of language. So admired were these outside experts that they could hardly be counted as outsiders anymore. In May, for instance, Roger Altman, Clinton's former deputy treasury secretary, held a dinner for the former president to discuss the party's message with about fifteen of its most elite and influential thinkers, including James Carville, Paul Begala, the pollster Mark J. Penn, and John Podesta, president of the Center for American Progress, the liberal think tank. Lakoff sat at Clinton's table; Wallis, at the next one over.

Bush's plan to reform Social Security provided, last winter, the first test of the Democrats' new focus on language and narrative. In retrospect, it shows both the limits of framing and, perhaps, the real reason that Democrats have managed to stymie critical pieces of the Bush agenda.

Almost as soon as Bush signaled his intention to overhaul the existing program, Democrats in Congress, enamored of Lakoff's theories, embarked on a search for a compelling story line. Yanowitch's highly secretive messaging group met for months on the topic and came up with two "sample narratives" that Democrats might use. The first, titled "Privatization: A Gamble You Can't Afford to Take," stressed the insecurity of middle-class families and compared Bush's plan to a roll of the dice. The second, "The Magical World of Privatization," spun out a metaphor that centered on Bush as "an old-fashioned traveling salesman, with a cart full of magic elixirs and cure-all tonics." Some of this imagery found its way into the dialogue, for better or worse; Pelosi and other House members, never too proud to put their dignity above the greater good, held an outdoor news conference standing next to a stack of giant dice.

As they would later with the filibuster fight and with the Supreme Court, Senate Democrats, under Reid's direction, set up a war room and a strategy group, this one run by Jim Messina, chief of staff for Senator Max Baucus of Montana. Eschewing all the lofty metaphors, the war room stuck to two simple ideas: Bush's plan relied on privatizing the most popular government benefit in America, and it amounted to benefit cuts coupled with long-term borrowing. In addition to keeping members focused on their talking points, Messina's team and its allies—led by two liberal interest groups, MoveOn.org and Campaign for America's Future, with help from the all-powerful AARP—also had to stop senators and congressmen from offering compromise plans that might drive a wedge into the caucus. In this way, Democrats had decided to follow the example of Bill Kristol, the Republican strategist who had urged his party (shrewdly, as it turned out) to refrain from proposing any alternatives to Clinton's doomed health care plan in 1993. "The minute we introduce a plan, we have to solve the problem" is how one senior Democratic aide explained it to me. "We are the minority party. It's not our job to fix things."

As it happened, this was where Lakoff himself proved most helpful. In a meeting with House Democrats, some of whom were considering their own versions of private accounts, he urged them to hold firm against Bush's plan. "I pointed out that as soon as you allow them to get a privatization frame in people's minds about retirement and Social Security, it becomes an unintelligible difference," he recalled. "People will not be able to tell the difference between your plan and the other guy's." Referring to Pelosi, he added, "Nancy was saying the same thing, and so they stopped." As Democrats stood firm, Bush's idea for private accounts, which was never all that popular with voters to begin with, seemed to slowly lose altitude. A Gallup tracking poll conducted for CNN and *USA Today* showed the president's plan losing support, from 40 percent of voters in January to 33 percent in April.

Bush had tried to recast his proposed "private accounts" as "personal accounts" after it became clear to both sides that privatization, as a concept, frightened voters. But as they did on the filibuster, Democrats had managed to trap the president in his own linguistic box. "We branded them

with privatization, and they can't sell that brand anywhere," Pelosi bragged
when I spoke with her in May. "It's down to, like, 29 percent or something.
At the beginning of this debate, voters were saying that the president was
a *president* who had new ideas. Now he's a *guy* who wants to cut my benefits." At this, Pelosi laughed loudly.

What had Democrats learned about framing? In the end, the success of
the Social Security effort—and, for that matter, the filibuster campaign—
may have had something to do with language or metaphor, but it probably
had more to do with the elusive virtue of party discipline. Pelosi explained it
to me this way: for years, the party's leaders had tried to get restless Democrats to stay "on message," to stop freelancing their own rogue proposals, and
to continue reading from the designated talking points even after it got excru-
ciatingly boring to do so. Consultants like Garin and Margolis had been
saying the same thing, but Democratic congressmen, skeptical of the in-
crowd of D.C. strategists, had begun to tune them out. "Listening to people
inside Washington did not produce any victories," Pelosi said.

But now there were people from outside Washington—experts from the
worlds of academia and Silicon Valley—who were making the same case.
What the framing experts had been telling Democrats on the Hill, aside
from all this arcane stuff about narratives and neural science, was that they
needed to stay unified and repeat the same few words and phrases over and
over again. And these "outsiders" had what Reid and Pelosi and their legion
of highly paid consultants did not: the patina of scientific credibility. Culturally, this made perfect sense. If you wanted Republican lawmakers to
buy into a program, you brought in a guy like Frank Luntz, an unapolo-
getically partisan pollster who dressed like the head of the College Republicans. If you wanted Democrats to pay attention, who better to do the job
than an egghead from Berkeley with an armful of impenetrable journal
studies on the workings of the brain?

You might say that Lakoff and the others managed to give the old concept of message discipline a new, more persuasive frame—and that frame
was called "framing." "The framing validates what we're trying to say to
them," Pelosi said. "You have a Berkeley professor saying, 'This is how the
mind works; this is how people perceive language; this is how you have to
be organized in your presentation.' It gives me much more leverage with
my members."

*   *   *   *   *

On a recent morning in his Virginia office, seated next to one of those one-way glass walls that you find only in the offices of cops and pollsters, Frank Luntz explained why George Lakoff and his framing theory were leading the Democratic Party astray. In recent years, Luntz's penchant for publicity—he is a frequent commentator on cable television—has earned him no small amount of scorn and ridicule from fellow Republicans; that Lakoff's little book had suddenly elevated Luntz to a kind of mythic villain seemed to amuse him. "In some ways, the Democrats appreciate me more than the Republicans do," Luntz, forty-three, told me with a trace of self-pity.

The problem with Lakoff, Luntz said, is that the professor's ideology seemed to be driving his science. Luntz, after all, has never made for a terribly convincing conservative ideologue. (During our conversation, he volunteered that the man he admired most was the actor Peter Sellers, for his ability to disappear into whatever role he was given.) Luntz sees Lakoff, by contrast, as a doctrinaire liberal who believes viscerally that if Democrats are losing, it has to be because of the words they use rather than the substance of the argument they make. What Lakoff didn't realize, Luntz said, was that poll-tested phrases like "tax relief" were successful only because they reflected the values of voters to begin with; no one could sell ideas like higher taxes and more government to the American voter, no matter how they were framed. To prove it, Luntz, as part of his recent polling for the U.S. Chamber of Commerce, specifically tested some of Lakoff's proposed language on taxation. He said he found that even when voters were reminded of the government's need to invest in education, health care, national security, and retirement security, 66 percent of them said the United States overtaxed its citizenry and only 14 percent said we were undertaxed. Luntz presented this data to chamber officials on a slide with the headline "George Lakoff Is Wrong!!"

"He deserves a lot of credit," Luntz said of Lakoff. "He's one of the very few guys who understands the limits of liberal language. What he doesn't understand is that there are also limits on liberal philosophy. They think that if they change all the words, it'll make a difference. Won't happen." (Last month, after we talked, Luntz challenged Lakoff, through me, to a "word-off" in which each man would try to "move" a roomful of thirty swing voters. Lakoff responded by counterchallenging Luntz to an "on-the-spot conceptual analysis." Since I had no idea what either of them was talking about, I let it go.)

Luntz's dismissiveness is what you might expect to hear about Lakoff from a Republican, of course. But the same complaint has surfaced with growing ferocity among skeptical Democrats and in magazines like *The Atlantic Monthly* and *The New Republic*. An antiframing backlash has emerged, and while it is, on the surface, an argument about Lakoff and his theories, it is clearly also a debate about whether the party lacks only for language or whether it needs a fresher agenda. Lakoff's detractors say that it is he who resembles the traveling elixir salesman, peddling comforting answers at a time when desperate Democrats should be admitting some hard truths about their failure to generate new ideas. "Every election defeat has a charlatan, some guy who shows up and says, 'Hey, I marketed the lava lamp, and I can market Democratic politics,'" says Kenneth Baer, a former White House speechwriter who wrote an early article attacking Lakoff's ideas in *The Washington Monthly*. "At its most basic, it represents the Democratic desire to find a messiah."

In a devastating critique in *The Atlantic*'s April issue, Marc Cooper, a contributing editor at *The Nation*, skillfully ridiculed Lakoff as the new progressive icon. "Much more than an offering of serious political strategy, *Don't Think of an Elephant!* is a feel-good, self-help book for a stratum of despairing liberals who just can't believe how their common-sense message has been misunderstood by eternally deceived masses," Cooper wrote. In Lakoff's view, he continued, American voters are "redneck, chain-smoking, baby-slapping Christers desperately in need of some gender-free nurturing and political counseling by organic-gardening enthusiasts from Berkeley."

Lakoff doesn't have much patience for criticism (he's a tenured professor, after all), and he keeps at his disposal a seemingly bottomless arsenal of linguistic and philosophical theories with which to refute such attacks. In response to Cooper's article and another in *The Atlantic*, by Joshua Green, Lakoff fired off a nine-page draft response to a long e-mail list of friends and journalists in which he accused Cooper and Green of living in the "rationalist-materialist paradigm" (that's RAM for short), an outdated belief system that mistakenly assumes the rationality of other human beings. He also pointed out that they had cleverly, but unsuccessfully, tried to trap him in the "guru frame," a story line about one individual who passes himself off as having all the answers to other people's problems.

Lakoff has some valid points. In his writing, at least, he explains framing in a way that is more intellectually complex than his critics have admitted. His essential insight into politics—that voters make their decisions based on larger frames rather than on the sum of a candidate's positions—is hard to refute. And Lakoff does say in *Don't Think of an Elephant!* albeit very briefly, that Democrats need not just new language but also new thought; he told me the party suffers from "hypocognition," or a lack of ideas. What's more, when it comes to the language itself, Lakoff has repeatedly written that the process of reframing American political thought will take years, if not decades, to achieve. He does not suggest in his writing that a few catchy slogans can turn the political order on its head by the next election.

The message Lakoff's adherents seem to take away from their personal meetings with him, however, is decidedly more simplistic. When I asked Senator Richard Durbin of Illinois, the minority whip and one of Lakoff's strongest supporters, whether Lakoff had talked to the caucus about this void of new ideas in the party, Durbin didn't hesitate. "He doesn't ask us to change our views or change our philosophy," Durbin said. "He tells us that we have to recommunicate." In fact, Durbin said he now understood, as a result of Lakoff's work, that the Republicans have triumphed "by repackaging old ideas in all new wrapping," the implication being that this was not a war of ideas at all, but a contest of language.

The question here is whether Lakoff purposely twists his own academic theories to better suit his partisan audience or whether his followers are simply hearing what they want to hear and ignoring the rest. When I first met Lakoff in Los Angeles, he made it clear, without any prompting from me, that he was exasperated by the dumbing down of his intricate ideas. He had just been the main attraction at a dinner with Hollywood liberals, and he despaired that all they had wanted from him were quick fixes to long-term problems. "They all just want to know the magic words," he told me. "I say: 'You don't understand, there aren't any magic words. It's about ideas.' But all everyone wants to know is: 'What three words can we use? How do we win the next election?' They don't get it."

And yet Lakoff had spoken for twelve minutes and then answered questions at the UCLA forum with Huffington and Frank, and not once had he even implied that the Democratic problem hadn't been entirely caused by

Republicans or that it couldn't be entirely fixed by language. The more time I spent with Lakoff, in fact, the more I began to suspect that his complaint about "magic words" was another example of framing; in this case, Lakoff was consciously framing himself in his conversations with me as a helpless academic whose theories were being misused. The reality seemed to be that Lakoff was enjoying his sudden fame and popularity too much to bother his followers with troubling details—like, say, the notion that their problem might be bigger than mere words or that it might take decades to establish new political frames. After all, Lakoff is selling out theaters and making more money than he ever thought possible; in 2006, Farrar, Straus & Giroux will publish his next book, on how conservatives have changed the meaning of the word "freedom." At one point, Lakoff told me he would like to appear as the host of a regular TV segment on framing.

Peter Teague, who oversees environmental programs at the liberal Nathan Cummings Foundation, was Lakoff's most important patron in the days after he wrote *Moral Politics*. When I spoke with Teague about Lakoff a few months ago, he sounded a little depressed. "There's a cartoon version of Lakoff out there, and everyone's responding to the cartoon," Teague said. "It's not particularly useful. As much as we talk about having a real dialogue and a deeper discussion, we really end up having a very superficial conversation.

"I keep saying to George, 'You're reinforcing the very things you're fighting against.'"

I asked Lakoff, during an afternoon walk across the Berkeley campus, if he felt at all complicit in the superficiality that Teague was describing. "I do," he said thoughtfully. "It's a complicated problem. Of course it bothers me. But this is just Stage One, and there are stages of misunderstanding. People have to travel a path of understanding."

His celebrity may yet prove to be his undoing. When I visited him in Berkeley in April, Lakoff, who until then had done all his work with Washington Democrats on a volunteer basis, had submitted a proposal to leaders in the House for a consulting contract. Although the details were closely guarded, it had something to do with a project to use focus groups to study narrative. In May, House Democrats decided not to finalize the deal after some members and senior aides wondered out loud if Lakoff mania had gotten out of hand. Lakoff, it seemed, was experiencing a common Washington phenomenon to which Frank Luntz could easily

relate: the more famous an adviser gets, the more politicians begin to suspect him of trying to further himself at their expense. A friend of Lakoff's
suggested to me that we were witnessing the beginning of an all-too-
familiar frame: the meteoric rise and dizzying fall of a political sensation.

If that were true, it seemed, then the whole notion of framing might just be
a passing craze, like some postelection macarena. It certainly sounded like
that might be the case when I visited Harry Reid just before Memorial Day.
Reid waved away the suggestion that language had much to do with the
party's recent successes. "If you want my honest opinion, and I know you
do, I think people make too much out of that," he said. "I'm not a person
who dwells on all these people getting together and spending hours and
days coming up with the right words. I know that my staff thinks, 'Oh, why
don't you tell him about all this great work we've done on framing?' But
honestly, that's not it."

Reid credited the "team effort" and message discipline of the caucus for
its victory on the filibuster issue. At one point, when I asked Reid, a former
boxer, about Lakoff's theories, he seemed to equate them with psy-
chotherapy. "I'm not going to waste a lot of time sitting in a room talking
about how my parents weren't good to me or something like that," Reid
said firmly. "I'm not involved in any of that gimmickry."

After leaving Reid, I walked across the Capitol to see Nancy Pelosi, who
told a different story. She assured me that Lakoff's ideas had "forever
changed" the way Democratic House members thought about politics. "He
has taken people here to a place, whether you agree or disagree with his
particular frame, where they know there has to be a frame," she told me.
"They all agree without any question that you don't speak on Republican
terms. You don't think of an elephant."

I suggested that maybe she and Reid had different views on the value of
framing as a strategy. "Oh, no," she said emphatically, drawing out the last
word. "He's been a leader on it! The two of us know better than anyone
what's at stake here. In fact, he sort of initiated our abuse-of-power frame."

It was hard to know what to make of these conflicting conversations. Perhaps Reid feared that if he admitted to caring about framing, he would be

framed as one of those clueless Democrats seeking easy answers. Perhaps Pelosi was covering for him by suggesting they were unified when in fact they weren't. But it seemed more likely that the disconnect between the party's two elected leaders reflected a broader confusion among Democrats about what they actually mean by framing. There is no doubt that having a central theme and repeating it like robots has made Democrats a respectable opposition force in Congress. To Pelosi and a lot of other Democrats, that is the miracle of this thing called framing. To Reid, it is just an intuitive part of politics, and he doesn't need some professor to give it a name or tell him that Democrats haven't been very good at it.

Whatever you call it, this kind of message discipline will be a crucial piece of what will most likely become, in the weeks ahead, a Democratic push to block Bush's designs on the Supreme Court. In order to stop a nominee, Democrats will have to frame the filibuster battle in the public arena all over again, and this time, they will have to convince voters that it is Bush's specific choice for the nation's highest court—and not simply a slate of faceless judges—who represents the reckless arrogance of Republican rule. Even in the hours after O'Connor made her announcement, you could see in Democratic responses the first stirrings of this new campaign. "If the president abuses his power and nominates someone who threatens to roll back the rights and freedoms of the American people," said Ted Kennedy, lifting lines directly from Garin's latest polling memo, "then the American people will insist that we oppose that nominee, and we intend to do so." Meanwhile, Susan McCue, Reid's powerful chief of staff, offered me a preview of the theory to come: "It goes beyond 'abuse of power.' It's about arrogance, irresponsibility, being out of touch and catering to a narrow, narrow slice of their ideological constituency at the expense of the vast majority of Americans."

It is not inconceivable that such an argument could sway public opinion; Americans are congenitally disposed to distrust whichever party holds power. The larger question—too large, perhaps, for most Democrats to want to consider at the moment—is whether they can do more with language and narrative than simply snipe at Bush's latest initiative or sink his nominees. Here, the Republican example may be instructive. In 1994, Republican lawmakers, having heeded Bill Kristol's advice and refused to engage in the health care debate, found themselves in a position similar to where Democrats are now; they had weakened the president and spiked his trademark proposal, and they knew from Luntz's polling that the public harbored serious reservations about the Democratic majority in Congress. What they did next changed the course of American politics. Rather than continue merely to deflect Clinton's agenda, Republicans came up with their own, the Contract with America, which promised ten major legislative acts that were, at the time, quite provocative. They included reforming welfare, slashing budget deficits, imposing harsher criminal penalties, and cutting taxes on small businesses. Those ten items, taken as a whole, encapsulated a rigid conservative philosophy that had been taking shape for thirty years—and that would define politics at the end of the twentieth century.

By contrast, consider the declaration that House Democrats produced after their session with John Cullinane, the branding expert, last fall. The pamphlet is titled, "The House Democrats' New Partnership for America's Future: Six Core Values for a Strong and Secure Middle Class." Under each of the six values—"prosperity, national security, fairness, opportunity, community and accountability"—is a wish list of vague notions and familiar policy ideas. ("Make health care affordable for every American," "Invest in a fully funded education system that gives every child the skills to succeed" and so on.) Pelosi is proud of the document, which—to be fair—she notes is just a first step toward repackaging the party's agenda. But if you had to pick an unconscious metaphor to attach to it, it would probably be a cotton ball.

Consider, too, George Lakoff's own answer to the Republican mantra. He sums up the Republican message as "strong defense, free markets, lower taxes, smaller government and family values," and in *Don't Think of an Elephant!* he proposes some Democratic alternatives: "Stronger America, broad prosperity, better future, effective government and mutual responsibility." Look at the differences between the two. The Republican version is an argument, a series of philosophical assertions that require voters to make concrete choices about the direction of the country. Should we spend more or less on the military? Should government regulate industry or leave it unfettered? Lakoff's formulation, on the other hand, amounts to a vague collection of the least objectionable ideas in American life. Who out there wants to make the case against prosperity and a better future? Who doesn't want an effective government?

What all these middling generalities suggest, perhaps, is that Democrats are still unwilling to put their more concrete convictions about the country into words, either because they don't know what those convictions are or because they lack confidence in the notion that voters can be persuaded to embrace them. Either way, this is where the power of language meets its outer limit. The right words can frame an argument, but they will never stand in its place.

The Bush-Cheney Era Ends Here
Ryan Lizza

New York magazine | April 10, 2006

For all the talk about the two major political parties' policy positions, embrace of "values," competing visions for the nation, and so on, elections always come down to contests between individuals—and they often end up going the most talented politician, regardless of party affiliation. In this fascinating account, which originally appeared in New York *magazine, political reporter Ryan Lizza analyzes how the Democrats, led by New York's senior senator, Chuck Schumer, have launched a painstaking, state-by-state recruiting effort that has just one aim in mind: to regain control of the Senate this November.*

Democrats have a dream. They dream that they will wake up on November 8 and that West Virginia Senator Robert Byrd, the eighty-eight-year-old antiwar firebrand, will be in charge of appropriating every dollar spent in Iraq. They dream that Patrick Leahy, the Vermont senator who led the effort against Samuel Alito, will be the man deciding which Bush judges get considered. They dream that a senator from South Dakota named Tim Johnson will be running the now-dormant Ethics Committee, aggressively investigating GOP lobbyists looting their way through Washington. They dream of a vote on a minimum-wage increase and public hearings on global warming. And Democrats soothe themselves to sleep every night with visions of beating six years' worth of secrets out of the Bush administration—on pre-9/11 intelligence, the

Plame affair, Katrina, Dubai Ports World, Halliburton—through the fear-some power of the subpoena.

Democrats dream that they will once again matter in Washington. In short, they dream of taking control of the United States Senate.

In an election year that offers Democrats a target-rich environment, no goal is more coveted than that of reclaiming the upper chamber of Congress. Democrats are poised to take back governor's mansions scattered from coast to coast, but those races are local ones and will have almost no impact on Bush or his agenda. The party needs a net gain of fifteen seats to regain the House of Representatives, and while that is starting to look less impossible than it did just a few months ago, deftly gerrymandered districts serve as powerful structural impediments to a Democratic takeover.

The Senate is different. It has forty-four Democrats and one independent who votes with them. Because ties are broken by Dick Cheney, six seats need to change hands to bring the body under Democratic control. Unlike reclaiming the House, or the far-off presidential race, it is a goal that seems tangible, achievable. Any Democrat in Washington can rattle off the six states of greatest opportunity—Pennsylvania, Missouri, Ohio, Montana, Rhode Island, and Tennessee—and explain how each can be won. And if Election Day were tomorrow, according to the latest polls, the Democrats would stand a reasonable chance of sweeping all six. Such a colossal victory would spell the end of the Bush era.

The man orchestrating the Senate takeover is New York's senior senator, Charles Schumer, who is the head of the Democratic Senatorial Campaign Committee and has already managed the unlikely task of out-fund-raising his Republican counterparts.

Despite the intensity of this moment, Schumer has a disarmingly casual air when I meet him at his Capitol Hill office. He's kicked off his shoes and sits with his feet propped up on a coffee table. Aides march in and out without knocking, always addressing him as Chuck. One tosses him an apple across the room.

Although he has never been as captivated by the trappings of the Senate as some of his colleagues, and hasn't quite brushed off the scrappiness of his eighteen years in the House, Schumer brings to the DSCC a mastery of the two basics of modern politics: money and media. He is, famously, the

Senate's greatest fund-raiser and greatest TV hound, important qualifications for his new job. Schumer thought about running for governor this year but instead leveraged the threat of leaving the Senate to secure a spot on the powerful Finance Committee, which writes the nation's tax laws and, not insignificant, is a perch that puts him in constant contact with the political donor class. "That was my dream," he says. "I always wanted to be on the Finance Committee."

Agreeing to run the DSCC was a tougher call. The job is not always considered a great gig for a senator. Schumer calls it "a lemon." But he took it, he insists, leaning forward and getting animated for the first time in our interview, because the GOP coalition of what he delicately calls "theocrats" and "economic royalists" is on the cusp of total victory in Washington. "The only barrier between these people and the America we've all come to know and love are the 45 Democrats in the Senate. And if we were to lose 3 seats, which looked very possible in December of 2004, it would be gone, because the magic number in the Senate is 41, not 51. So I said I had to take the job."

On the Republican side, the lemon was awarded to North Carolina Senator Elizabeth Dole. As head of the National Republican Senatorial Committee, she is the anti-Schumer. He relishes politics and is his own best consultant, while Dole can hardly get dressed in the morning without an adviser. Schumer's most rehearsed lines seem to be off the cuff, while Dole's every utterance is a robotic drone. Schumer envelops the press with love. Dole rarely submits to on-the-record interviews. He has shattered fund-raising records. She has failed to keep pace.

In another year, her mistakes wouldn't matter much because much of the NRSC's political work would actually be done by Karl Rove—she'd just be the one with her name on the stationery. But 2005 happened to be the year Rove was waylaid by the Plame-leak investigation, forcing Dole to run the committee on her own and making Schumer shine by comparison.

Part of the reason Schumer took the job is that he was able to join Minority Leader Harry Reid's Senate leadership team, which allows him to craft the party's message with an eye toward the Senate races. He has embraced that job as if he'd spent his career representing Dubuque rather than Brooklyn. He is obsessed with the health of what he calls his "marginals," red-state Democrats who live in fear of being too closely associated with, well, New York liberals like Schumer. He treats the marginals like fragile vases in constant danger of being knocked off their pedestals.

Schumer considers every Washington debate in terms of how it will affect the marginals. "There were some in our caucus that wanted to let the Patriot Act lapse," he tells me. "I said that I think we got to change it, and I'll work to change it, but to let it lapse would be a disaster, particularly for our Democrats in red states. You know, when I go to a drawing room in Manhattan and they say, 'You got to appeal to our base!' I say, 'There is no base in North Dakota!'"

When Schumer took the helm of the DSCC last year, he became personally immersed in the weeds of the operation, hiring his own team, messing around in primaries, recruiting candidates, and personally lecturing them about how to run a campaign using what he calls the Schumer Method. That's his secret recipe for his own New York victory, and he is now franchising it out. He instructs his candidates to very carefully define the prototypical swing voters in their home states—for him, it's the imaginary Joe and Ilene O'Reilly from Massapequa—and then craft a campaign to meet their needs. To reach these local Joes and Ilenes regularly, he also coaches his candidates to get home and hit every media market in their state at least once a month. "The head of the DSCC used to be just a fund-raiser," says Schumer's communications director, Phil Singer. "He's become more of a strategist and tactician."

Schumer hired a top party fund-raiser, Julianna Smoot, and a well-respected political director, Guy Cecil. To do press, he brought in Singer, a wound-up master opposition researcher and favorite of Washington reporters, who looks like a trim, thirty-year-old version of Schumer. He installed J. B. Poersch as executive director. A dead-ringer for the late comedian Chris Farley, Poersch is a coveted operative whose last stint was running the Kerry campaign in Ohio, the Waterloo for Democrats in 2004. After that searing near-victory, Poersch, like Schumer, gravitated to the DSCC out of a sense of foreboding about what would happen if the Democrats lost three more seats. "This is the place of last refuge," he says.

Even with this new team in place, the DSCC was still weighted down by the past, including $4 million in debt. Nothing is more depressing to donors than being called after a humiliating defeat and begged to pay off the old credit-card bill. "They hated that," Schumer says. "Because they were paying for past mistakes." Instead, Schumer and Reid demanded that Democratic senators themselves retire the debt. In a month, the DSCC was solvent.

And still things looked fairly grim. Democrats hold eighteen seats up for reelection this year, while Republicans hold fifteen. Most sitting senators glide to victory; their reelection rate is 80 percent. Open seats are where the genuine battles tend to be waged. In 2002 and 2004, the greatest predictor of who would win a competitive Senate race was how well Bush had fared in the state. Compounding the problem for Democrats in 2004 was that several red-state senators, some elected decades earlier, retired and were replaced with fresh new Republicans. In 2002, Democrats lost seats in Georgia and Missouri. In 2004, they lost another Georgia seat and ones in South Dakota, North Carolina, South Carolina, Florida, and Louisiana. Since there are thirty-one red states and nineteen blue states, this is a very unhappy trend for Senate Democrats.

Schumer's first job was to put a finger in this dike. He badgered the five Democrats up for reelection this year in red states—New Mexico, North Dakota, Florida, Nebraska, and West Virginia—not to retire. One by one, Schumer and Reid sat down with these five men and played *Let's Make a Deal*. "We basically begged them to stay," says Schumer. "They came to Harry's office and we said, 'What do you need?'" Some got a seat on a prized committee. Others received assurances that their pet legislative issues or pork-barrel requests would be given priority. And everyone was promised that the DSCC would help out aggressively with fund-raising and that Schumer would talk up the candidates to his donors.

Octogenarian Robert Byrd was flirting with retirement, and keeping him on became an especially crucial mission. Once a reliably Democratic state, West Virginia has, through the Bush years, grown steadily more con-servative. In 2000, Bush captured it with 52 percent of the vote, and in 2004 with 56 percent. If Byrd had left this year, the seat would almost surely have been lost to Republican congresswoman Shelley Moore Capito, a young up-and-comer in the state whose father was governor. Schumer and other Democrats persuaded Byrd to stick around partly by promising him that they would do most of his fund-raising for him. Schumer, Reid, Dick Durbin, and former majority leader Tom Daschle all held early fund-raisers for Byrd to convince him they were serious. By September, with almost $2 million banked, Byrd announced his reelection bid. Similar horse trading persuaded his four red-state colleagues to do the same.

Schumer had less success keeping all his blue-state senators. Three are retiring. Independent Jim Jeffords is leaving, though his Vermont seat is likely to be won by a Democrat. Maryland's Paul Sarbanes is also quitting, producing a long-shot opportunity for Republicans in that state. More worrisome for Democrats is holding onto the seat of Minnesota's Mark Dayton. Schumer's relentlessness helped push Dayton out. Best known as the only senator to vacate his Washington office last fall after a vague terrorism threat, Dayton retired partly because he couldn't stomach the fund-raising pace demanded by Schumer. "Every time I'd see Chuck Schumer . . . he'd say, 'Raise money, Mark. Go raise money. Raise money,'" Dayton told his hometown paper after announcing his retirement. According to sources close to Schumer, the senator privately believed Dayton was a sitting duck who had lost the hunger to serve. He wanted Dayton to quit, and he quickly recruited a less-vulnerable replacement. "That was the one retirement they were actually happy about," says Jennifer Duffy, who analyzes Senate races for *The Cook Political Report*.

In exchange for helping candidates raise money, Schumer makes a demand: no amateurs. Anybody who wants DSCC help must have a campaign manager, a finance director, and a communications director personally approved by Schumer and his aides. "To preapprove the top three spots is about as hands-on as I've ever heard," says Duffy.

But the truth is that an incumbent senator's great hope is that he never has to use that campaign staff. "The goal is not to win your race," says Phil Singer. "The goal is not to have a race." And the first year of Schumer's DSCC service was devoted to making sure that vulnerable Democrats faced no serious opposition in 2006. Through a mix of luck, heavy fund-raising, hardball politics, Elizabeth Dole's anemic performance, and a major assist from Bush's deteriorating political situation, the top Republicans in state after state decided not to challenge weak Democrats. In North Dakota, Republicans tried to get popular governor John Hoeven to run against Democratic senator Kent Conrad. "He voted against the war," says Schumer, explaining how worried he was about Conrad, one of his marginals, "and against the anti-gay-marriage amendment. And Kent, amazingly enough, to his everlasting credit, was the thirty-fourth vote blocking a constitutional amendment banning flag-burning, which would have been the first time the Bill of Rights had ever been amended. In North Dakota! That would have been hard to do in any state."

Bush twisted Hoeven's arm aboard Air Force One and fêted him during a two-night sleepover at the White House, but Hoeven declined to jump into the race. Conrad now has $3 million in the bank and no serious Republican opponent.

In Nebraska, another vulnerable red-stater, Ben Nelson, wanted to scare off a challenge from Governor Mike Johanns. Nelson came to Schumer and Reid in late 2004 and told them that if he could raise $1 million in one month, Johanns wouldn't challenge him. Schumer personally tapped his own base of New York donors, many of whom had never heard of Nelson. They coughed up tens of thousands of dollars. In his last Senate election campaign, Nelson raised a total of $50,395 from New Yorkers; this cycle, he's already netted $130,500. His ratio of Nebraska money to New York money used to be thirteen to one. Now it's three to one. Sure enough, a month after the fund-raising blitz began, and with $1 million in the bank, Johanns decided to join the Bush administration as secretary of agriculture, and other top Republicans in the state declined to enter the race.

In West Virginia, nudging Capito out of the race became a matter of some urgency. Byrd is in no shape to campaign around the state. One of his first radio interviews after he announced he was running turned into a rambling, semicoherent soliloquy about how much he loved the people of West Virginia. So Byrd, Schumer, and the DSCC, working with West Virginia's Democratic governor, Joe Manchin, sought to scare off potential sources of Republican funding, threatening and browbeating state donors into not giving a dime to Capito. Their efforts may have had only a marginal impact, but combined with Bush's slipping popularity and the NRSC's paltry fund-raising, that did the trick. Capito decided not to run.

The story was similar in Washington, Michigan, and Florida. In the top six races targeted by Republicans, the Democratic incumbents didn't retire and their toughest adversaries declined to run. "Every one of the six candidates faced down their major opponent," Schumer boasts.

Schumer's early success at preventing retirements and strengthening his most vulnerable colleagues puts Senate Democrats in their strongest defensive position since the 2000 election. Their most at-risk seat is in Minnesota, though Washington's Senator Maria Cantwell is also facing a spirited challenge. In six other states targeted by the GOP—Florida, Michigan, Nebraska, New Jersey, Maryland, and Vermont—Democrats currently look safe. This surprisingly strong start has allowed Schumer to play offense and concentrate his firepower on the six states Democrats recite in their dreams: Pennsylvania, Missouri, Ohio, Montana, Rhode Island, and Tennessee.

Schumer has spent an inordinate amount of his time recruiting candidates to challenge the five vulnerable incumbent Republicans in these states (Tennessee has an open seat). He set the tone early last year in Pennsylvania when he risked the wrath of prochoice Democrats by begging prolifer Bob Casey Jr. to run against Senator Rick Santorum, whom Democrats call "our Daschle," referring to the zeal with which Republicans attacked and defeated Tom Daschle in 2004. "I must admit there's probably a degree of payback," says Schumer. In 2005, every poll showed Casey as Santorum's toughest opponent, but he was planning to run for governor instead. Meanwhile, a prochoice Democrat, Barbara Hafer, was already in the race. Schumer plotted with outgoing governor Ed Rendell, who persuaded Hafer not to run. Schumer then worked on Casey, luring him into the race with assurances that he could win and a promise that he would be rewarded with the DSCC's best campaign manager. ("J.B. has a stable of these guys," says Schumer, who allocates them according to need.) Schumer knew that the full fury of prochoice Democrats would rain down on him when Casey announced his candidacy. But that was exactly the point. By pissing off the party's most loyal supporters, Schumer sent a message that he was serious about winning, one that rippled into other states and helped persuade reluctant recruiting targets to run. "I said, 'Hey, we have to win!' If we had fifty-eight seats, maybe you wouldn't do this, but our back is against the wall," Schumer says.

Casey now enjoys double-digit leads over Santorum, who is surely the Republican senator most likely to be unemployed come November. Santorum dodged Bush on a recent presidential visit to the state, something unthinkable for a Republican senator two years ago. And instead of running strictly on national security, Santorum has been forced to woo suburban women by softening his religious-conservative image. One of his first ads, "Dreamers," stars his fourteen-year-old daughter praising her father's commitment to education.

In Missouri, a onetime swing state that has become redder and redder in the Bush era, the plan to beat incumbent Jim Talent called for finding a Democrat who could reconnect with the state's rural, religious population outside the Democratic islands of Kansas City and St. Louis. Once

Schumer decided that state auditor Claire McCaskill was that candidate, he courted her with all the ardor of a love-struck teenager. There was rarely a day he didn't talk to her or send her something. "The Number One word that I can use to describe a successful recruiter is *relentless*," Schumer says. "You just have to keep calling and calling and calling."

He learned that McCaskill's new husband, Joseph Shepard, was the problem. So when Schumer heard that the whole McCaskill family would be in London at the same time as the Schumers, he sought them out and organized a dinner, planting himself beside Shepard, a wealthy businessman who invested a good chunk of his real-estate fortune into his wife's losing 2004 campaign for governor, an office they both still covet. Schumer weaned them off their obsession with the gubernatorial race and assured Shepard that his wife's Senate job would still have her home to him at a reasonable hour every night, a somewhat dubious promise considering Schumer's wife lives in New York and most weekdays in Washington he works until midnight. But within two weeks of the London dinner, McCaskill decided to run. "You have to gently envelop the candidate and show them that the Senate is just an incredibly good job," Schumer says, explaining the recruiting of McCaskill. "I instinctively felt that if we did it with our families, we could make it happen."

The Missouri race is crucial to understanding the challenge Democrats face this year. Bush's approval rating may be in the thirties nationally, but it's higher in Missouri. Washington Democrats may talk of censure, but McCaskill's campaign wants nothing to do with any of that. Recently, McCaskill has pointedly distanced herself from Howard Dean and Hillary Clinton, and, though prochoice, has proclaimed, "I am not for abortion." Races like Missouri will force Senate Democrats in Washington to be extremely vigilant about how bold their agenda gets this year and how much Bush-bashing they do. Although "check on Bush" is the mantra Schumer uses to pull money out of Democratic donors, it's not necessarily a winning message for all his candidates. In essence, national Democrats can move only as far left as their most conservative Senate candidate in the six target states, four of which were carried by Bush in 2000 and 2004.

So far, McCaskill and her Washington-based colleagues are navigating these shoals effectively. Recent polls show her with a narrow lead over Talent. She has even found a wedge issue to confound Republicans: stem cells. Talent wanted to criminalize a type of stem-cell research requiring embryonic cloning, a position he reversed in February. For weeks, the campaign has been about little else. And taking a page from the Republican playbook of 2004, when the GOP added a gay-marriage initiative to the ballot in Ohio to help maximize conservative turnout, Democrats have added a stem-cell initiative to the ballot in Missouri.

These red-state political moves aren't just helping Democrats this cycle. They are serving as a road test for the potential platform of the party's 2008 presidential nominee, whoever that turns out to be. Democratic victories in red states this year will be seized upon by party strategists as pointing the way forward for 2008. In that way, Schumer is helping the party define a kind of centrism that, if successful, could also help win the White House.

In Ohio, Schumer's aggressive recruiting proved too successful. Iraq veteran Paul Hackett became the darling of liberal Democrats last year by nearly defeating a Republican in a special House election in an extremely pro-Bush Ohio district. He was then pushed into the Senate race by Schumer and Reid, whose first and second choices decided not to run. Schumer's hard sell even included a call from his wife to Hackett's wife to allay any spousal concerns. But months later, when the second-choice candidate, Sherrod Brown, changed his mind, Schumer changed his mind about Hackett. Hackett, in turn, quit the race, angrily firing away at Schumer as he left the stage. "Schumer, in particular," he wrote in a newspaper column, "actively sought to undermine my insurgent campaign, in part by calling up my donors and telling them not to raise money for me, which is like a doctor cutting off oxygen to a patient. He also worked through others to get state and local politicians to publicly urge me to quit." It worked.

Ohio is now the test case for how much harm corruption scandals have inflicted on the GOP. The Republican governor has pleaded no contest to misdemeanor charges for taking gifts. A byzantine scandal regarding a Bush donor who invested part of Ohio's workers' compensation fund into rare coins has tarred almost every Republican in the state. Meanwhile, conservatives are fuming at the already vulnerable Republican senator Mike DeWine for signing on to the so-called Gang of Fourteen deal, which prevented Republicans from banning the use of a filibuster to block judicial nominees. The Democratic strategy is simple: a relentless focus on corruption, punctuated more recently by almost Pat Buchanan-like attacks on Arab-owned firms that have anything to do with American security. Brown is a fairly liberal candidate for the state—think a more polished Dennis Kucinich—but the scandals, the Dubai issue, and declining support for Bush and the war have combined to give him a 50-50 chance at victory.

Montana has been a showcase for another skill that Schumer's DSCC has elevated to an art this cycle—the ability to inject anti-GOP stories into the state press. "This is what the DSCC is good at," says the *Cook Report*'s Duffy. "They are good at taking little things and beating them to death."

In Montana, the story of lobbyist Jack Abramoff has been transformed from an obscure inside-Washington tale into a local Montana feeding frenzy. Republican Senator Conrad Burns assisted Abramoff's Indian clients, and, with some help from Singer at the DSCC, the Montana press has explored every cranny of Burns's connection to the lobbyist. In 2000, Burns won with only 51 percent, pushed over the edge by Bush's strong showing in the state. He's a mediocre campaigner and has been slow to organize. In late March, rumors flew around Washington that he was quitting the race.

But he hasn't dropped out. Like other GOP candidates, Burns has decided to run on state micro-issues rather than national ones. His latest TV ad isn't about Iraq but the "scourge [that] is threatening Montana's children: methamphetamine addiction." As in Ohio, Democrats are drilling away at GOP scandals, but as in Missouri, they tread carefully around social issues and eschew Bush-bashing. After Santorum, Burns is the most likely Republican to go down this year.

In Rhode Island, Schumer failed to recruit his top candidate. He wanted prolife Congressman Jim Langevin, but a second prolifer proved to be too much for many Democrats to take, especially in liberal Rhode Island, and Langevin declined to run. The Republican incumbent is Lincoln Chafee, one of the last GOP moderates from New England left in Congress. Chafee famously refused to vote for Bush in 2004, writing in the name of the president's father instead. That and other heresies have attracted a conservative primary opponent who is sure to send him into the general election bloodied and weakened. To his credit, Chafee has been unwilling to shift rightward in response. He even said he would consider backing Senator Russ Feingold's resolution to censure Bush (though he later offered a tortuous clarification). Rhode Island is the bluest state in America with a Republican senator. Bush lost there in 2004 by twenty-one points, and it is looking increasingly doubtful that Chafee's storied name (his dad was a senator) or fierce independence can save him in a year with such an anti-Republican undertow.

Finally, in Tennessee, where Majority Leader Bill Frist is retiring to pursue an increasingly quixotic campaign for president, the Republicans have abjectly failed to be as ruthless and top-down as Schumer has been. Instead of handpicking their strongest candidate, the party has allowed a raucous primary to break out, one that won't end until August 3, which won't give the eventual winner much time to regroup. Still, it will be a difficult seat for the Democrats to claim. Their nominee, Congressman Harold Ford Jr., has a reputation in Washington for being more of a show horse than a workhorse, and questions of maturity have long dogged him. He seems preoccupied about whether Tennessee is enlightened enough to send a black man to represent it in the Senate or whether he might be blamed for the sins of an uncle caught up in a bribery scandal. Like McCaskill, he has been forced to distance himself from Washington Democrats and stress his opposition to gay marriage and "partial birth" abortion.

Winning all six of these races as well as the open seat in Minnesota while holding on to all their vulnerable incumbents is hardly a sure thing for Democrats. But the national climate is getting more poisonous for the GOP, and polls show that the mood of the country is as sour now as it was at this point in 1994 when Democrats were turned out of power. But it is still a dream.

Some Democrats, however, have been flirting with a slightly altered version of the dream. Wouldn't it be better, they wonder, if they came close to winning back the Senate this year, but accomplished the task only in 2008? After all, a slim Senate majority would make it difficult to govern, perhaps giving Bush the opportunity to turn the new Senate leadership into a useful foil, just as Bill Clinton did to Newt Gingrich and Bob Dole, and thereby revive his presidency. Furthermore, this alternate dream scenario goes, in 2008, there are twenty-one Republicans up for reelection and only twelve Democrats. Wouldn't that be the moment for Democrats to come sweeping back into power?

It would be unusual, but people who have watched Schumer over the past year and a half as he has become increasingly consumed by his DSCC work believe that he would be willing to stay in the job for another two years if he falls short this year. Aides close to him agree. Asked about that scenario, Schumer will only say, "Let's see how I do this time."

Not as Lame as You Think: Democrats Learn the Art of Opposition

Amy Sullivan

The Washington Monthly | May 2006

Republicans have seemingly out-campaigned and outmaneuvered Democrats for so long now, it's become something of a truism that the Dems are simply out-matched by the GOP when it comes to electoral and legislative strategizing. But in this Washington Monthly *article, Amy Sullivan argues that the Democrats' political skills have grown a lot sharper lately. As she points out, from the Dubai port scandal to the crash-and-burn of President Bush's Social Security privatization plan to the growing public discontent over the Iraq War, "On virtually all of the major slips this White House has made in the past year, there have been unnoticed Democrats putting down the banana peels."*

The first week of March should have been a bright spot for Democrats in an otherwise bleak five years. With the president's approval numbers reaching Nixon-esque lows, and Democrats outpolling Republicans by fifteen points—the party's largest lead in a midterm election since 1982—it was beginning to look like the long-suffering Democrats had rediscovered their mojo.

But you wouldn't know it if you picked up a newspaper that week. "For Democrats, Many Verses, but No Chorus," declared the headline on the *New York Times'* front page on Monday. Reporting that "Democratic candidates for Congress are reading from a stack of different scripts these days," political writer Adam Nagourney described targeted local campaign strategies as "scattershot messages" that "reflect splits within the party." The next day, *The Washington Post* featured a story that declared, "Democrats Struggle to Seize Opportunity," and questioned whether congressional Democrats could regain power without "the hard-charging, charismatic figurehead that Gingrich represented for the House GOP in 1994." Picking up that theme on Wednesday, *Slate's* Jacob Weisberg lambasted Rep. Nancy Pelosi (D-Calif.), Harry Reid (D-Nev.), and Howard Dean, calling them "The Three Stooges" and indicting them as "useless and disastrous." And as if on cue, the Republican National Committee released a web video on Friday titled "Find the Democratic Leader."

Democrats are lame, feckless, timid, and hopelessly divided, with no ideas, no vision, no message, and no future: You'll never fall flat at a Washington party by repeating this bit of conventional wisdom because everyone "knows" it to be true. Jon Stewart compares congressional Democrats to the fuzzy-but-not-fearsome Ewoks. *The Onion* gets an easy laugh from a parody headlined "Democrats Vow Not to Give Up Hopelessness."

Of course, we chuckle because the jokes contain an element of truth. On some of the defining issues of the day, Democrats are indeed conflicted and divided. Most Americans and virtually the entire Democratic base wants universal health care, and yet congressional Democrats compete to offer marginal changes to the system. On a key economic issue like bankruptcy, too many Democrats sell out to lobbying interests, making it hard for the party as a whole to attack Republicans over it. Iraq has dominated the political scene for nearly four years, but Democrats couldn't agree whether to get into it, and now they can't agree on how to get out.

It's understandable that pundits take one look at congressional Democrats today and declare them to be a far cry from the mighty mighty Gingrich revolutionaries of 1994. The implosion of the Bush administration and congressional Republicans has led to speculation not about whether Democrats could regain power but about how they will muff up the opportunity. Turn on a television these days, and you won't have to count to ten before you hear, "Where is the Democrats' Newt?" or "Why don't Democrats have a Contract with America?"

But the truth is that Newt Gingrich and his Contract loom so large—and today's D.C. Democrats seem so small—largely because of the magic of hindsight. Back in 1994, Republicans were at least as divided as Democrats are now, if not more so. Traditional statesmen like Robert Michel, Howard Baker, and Robert Dole were constantly at loggerheads with the conservative bomb-throwers like Gingrich, Bob Walker, and Rep. Tom DeLay (R-Texas). As for unity of message, the now-revered Contract with America didn't make its debut until just six weeks before the election; Democratic pollster Mark Mellman recently pointed out that one week before Election Day, 71 percent of Americans said they hadn't heard anything about it. And while political journalists rushed to hail Gingrich's genius after the election, before November they were more likely to describe Republicans in terms we associate with Democrats today. "Republicans have taken to personal attacks on President Clinton because they have no ideas of their own to run on," wrote Charles Krauthammer in the summer of 1994, while a George F. Will column in the fall ran under the headline, "Timid GOP Not Ready for Prime Time."

What the GOP did so brilliantly in 1994 was exploit Clinton's weaknesses (his 1993 tax increase, his wife's failed health care initiative), as well as the sense among voters that reigning congressional Democrats had become complacent and corrupt (reviving the Keating Five and House banking scandals). Well, guess what? This is precisely what congressional Democrats have been getting better at doing over the past eighteen months. And just as most observers missed the coming Republican revolution in 1994, so they're missing a similar insurgency today.

Rolling Grenades

On virtually all of the major slips this White House has made in the past year, there have been unnoticed Democrats putting down the banana peels. One of the best examples—and certainly the issue that sent Bush's poll numbers southward—was the Dubai port deal. The little-noticed administration decision to contract with a United Arab Emirate–owned company to run terminals at six ports around the United States mushroomed into a public relations disaster for which the Bush administration was uncharacteristically unprepared. Within a week of the story breaking, congressional Republicans had vowed to pass legislation undoing the deal, Bush angrily declared he would veto such legislation, and polls showed that three-quarters of Americans were concerned the deal would jeopardize American security. Even more damaging, the issue shifted public opinion about who can best protect the country from future acts of terrorism. For the first time since 9/11, Democrats pulled even with Republicans on this question.

If you read the press coverage of the story, you would have thought the issue surfaced on its own. In fact, however, the story was a little grenade rolled into the White House bunker by Senator Charles Schumer (D-N.Y.). No one was aware of the port deal until Schumer—who had been tipped off by a source in the shipping industry—held a press conference, and another, and another until the press corps finally paid attention. As for Schumer, he popped up in news reports about the deal, but almost always as a "critic of the administration," not as the initiator of the entire episode.

This is not a lone example. In the winter of 2005, Bush unveiled his Social Security privatization plan, the domestic centerpiece of his second term. The president invested a tremendous amount of personal political capital in the effort, featuring it in his 2005 State of the Union address and holding carefully choreographed town meetings to simulate public support for the idea.

Most of the press corps expected the debate to be a painful defeat for Democrats. Not only were moderates predicted to jump ship and join with Republicans to support the president's plan, but Social Security—one of the foundational blocks of the New Deal social compact—would be irrevocably changed. But then a funny thing happened. Reid and Pelosi managed to keep the members of their caucuses united in opposition. Day after day they launched coordinated attacks on Bush's "risky" proposal. Without a single Democrat willing to sign on and give a bipartisanship veneer of credibility, the private accounts plan slowly came to be seen by voters for what it was: another piece of GOP flimflam.

As the privatization ship began sinking, Republicans challenged Democrats to develop their own plan, and when none was forthcoming, pundits whacked the minority party for being without ideas. But not putting forth a plan was the plan. It meant that once the bottom fell out on public support for Bush's effort—which it did by early summer—Democrats couldn't be pressured to work with Republicans to form a compromise proposal. It was a brilliant tactical maneuver that resulted in a defeat at least as decisive as the Republicans' successful effort to kill Clinton's health care plan.

One reason many were unable to appreciate the brilliance of Democrats' Social Security strategy was that they view Reid and Pelosi as ineffective party spokespeople, and therefore ineffective leaders. Reid, with his slight frame and round glasses, looks like he should be running a mercantile in the Old West, not a major political party. Even Democrats find themselves wincing when Pelosi appears on camera, perpetually wide-eyed and on-message, whatever the message may be. Neither has Gingrich's charisma, strategic vision, or propensity to quote Clausewitz. And that leads reporters to airbrush their tactical successes out of news reports.

Consider, for instance, what happened last fall when Rep. Jack Murtha (D-Pa.), a Vietnam veteran and hawk who initially supported the Iraq War, called for immediate troop withdrawal from Iraq. When reporters asked Pelosi what she thought of Murtha's statement, she replied that the congressman spoke for himself, not the caucus. Her response was immediately denounced by liberal critics and portrayed by reporters as evidence of Democrats' lack of message, discipline, and shared conviction. In fact, as Howard Fineman would later report, Pelosi had worked behind the scenes to convince Murtha to go public with his change of heart and orchestrated the timing of his announcement. Knowing that the credibility of Murtha's position would be damaged if it looked like he was the token hawk being used by "cut and run" liberal Democrats, Pelosi made the strategic calculation to put Murtha in the spotlight by himself for a few weeks before stepping forward to endorse his suggestion.

The strategy worked, and it allowed Murtha to visibly establish Democrats as the advocates of what now looks like the position toward which our Iraq policy is headed. A late February Zogby poll showed that fully 72 percent of American troops think that the United States should leave Iraq within the year; 25 percent say they should leave immediately. In addition, Pelosi's party now holds the advantage on Iraq. As with Social Security, critics have charged that Democrats can't win without a plan for Iraq, but a mid-March Gallup poll showed that voters think Democrats would better handle the situation (they hold a forty-eight to forty advantage over Republicans), even though only one-quarter of them think that Democrats have a plan for dealing with the country.

Over in the Senate, Reid temporarily silenced his critics when he staged a showdown last fall, shutting down the Senate to compel Republicans to discuss prewar intelligence. GOP promises to pursue inquiries into how the intelligence was gathered, interpreted, and used had gone nowhere, and Democrats had no institutional means to conduct their own investigation. So Reid forced the issue, invoking an obscure parliamentary procedure that sent the Senate into a closed session. Republicans were furious, but they were also backed into a corner. Reluctantly, the leadership agreed to restart the investigations, putting the issue of intelligence back in the national spotlight. The in-your-face move signaled that Reid had the inclination, and the electoral security, to push Republicans around in a way that his predecessor Tom Daschle never could.

"You're out of order"

For years now, one of the knocks on Democrats has been that they don't know how to function as an opposition party, that they still behave as if they're governing. During the first few years of the Bush administration, even stalwart liberals like Senator Ted Kennedy (D-Mass.) worked with

Republicans on legislation like Medicare reform, time and again—like Charlie Brown and Lucy—making a run at impacting policy. And their response to bruising partisanship was, as a rule, puzzling meekness. (So much so that this magazine ran a story in early 2002 called "Why Can't the Democrats Get Tough?")

But that changed with the heartbreaking loss in 2004. The defeat of Daschle, the nice-guy Democratic leader, and the nasty tactics of the campaign against him particularly outraged congressional Democrats. The anger was only compounded by the party's new degree of powerlessness. They didn't control a single thing in Washington—not the House or the Senate or the White House. Autocratic GOP chairmen turned off their microphones at hearings, reporters ignored their press conferences, and late-night comedians used them as the butt of every joke, a kind of institutional Kato Kaelin. And the base was mad as well; everywhere Democrats turned, they got an earful from activists and funders who wanted the party to fight back, to kick some ass. In the end, Democrats snapped.

One clear indication that things had changed came in the fall of 2005 when Republicans went after Jack Murtha. Two years earlier, Democrats had stood silently by while the GOP viciously attacked Daschle, comparing him to Saddam Hussein and Osama bin Laden. But when newly elected Rep. Jean Schmidt (R-Ohio) called Murtha a coward during a House budget debate, Democrats shouted her down and booed. Schmidt was forced to return and ask her remarks be stricken from the record, the parliamentary equivalent of eating her words. Later in the debate, when Rep. Jeb Hensarling (R-Texas) taunted conservative Democrats as "lapdogs," Democratic Rep. Marion Berry (D-Ark.) shot back, calling him a "Howdy-Doody looking nimrod." As the House chair tried to gavel down the fracas that followed, shouting, "The House is out of order," California Democrat Rep. George Miller could be heard yelling back, *You're* out of order!"

Perhaps figuring they have little left to lose, Democrats have begun turning up the heat in countless small ways. When, in the wake of Hurricane Katrina, Bush quietly suspended the Davis-Bacon Act in order to allow federal contractors to avoid paying the prevailing wage to workers involved in cleanup efforts, Miller led Democrats in handing the president a rare defeat. Appalled that "the President has exploited a national tragedy to cut workers' wages," Miller unearthed a little-used provision of a 1976 law that allows Congress to countermand the president's authority to suspend laws after a national emergency. While it is usually nearly impossible for Democrats to get bills through the all-powerful House Rules Committee, Miller's maneuver would have bypassed that step and guaranteed an automatic vote by the full House. Bush, faced with a vote he was sure to lose, reversed his earlier action and reinstated Davis-Bacon.

Democrats aren't shying away from quixotic fights, either. Senator Frank Lautenberg (D-N.J.) introduces an amendment to rename the FY2006 budget bill the "Moral Disaster of Monumental Proportion" Act. Rep. Henry Waxman (D-Calif.) continues his one-man oversight operation, exposing the ineffectiveness of federally funded abstinence-only programs, investigating taxpayer-funded propaganda, and detailing the failure of Iraq reconstruction efforts. A new 527 organization called the Senate Majority Project, started by former Kerry campaign manager Jim Jordan, gets under the skin of several GOP senators in its first week of existence by publicly questioning their ethics (Senator Saxby Chambliss [R-Ga.] took to the Senate floor to defend himself against the group).

Of course, the point of all this is not just to annoy Republicans and stymie their efforts, but to win back Congress in fall elections. Leading that charge for the Democratic Congressional Campaign Committee is Rep. Rahm Emanuel (D-Ill.), a former Clinton White House enforcer much admired for his bare-knuckle approach to politics. The man they call "Rahmbo" has no patience for anyone who would go down without a fight or waste time crying into their chai tea about the odds against them. And so he has scraped, cajoled, and arm-twisted to expand the number of congressional races that Democrats are seriously contesting from a few dozen to nearly fifty this time around. Emanuel has done it by throwing out old ideas about who gets to be a Democratic congressional candidate—career politicians, such as state representatives or city councilmen moving up the ladder—and going after military veterans, sheriffs, ministers, and even one former NFL quarterback. With more Republican retirements being announced every day (not to mention resignations by the stray congressman or two headed off to prison), Emanuel's chances of spearheading the biggest Democratic victory in over a decade look better than ever.

Missing the Story

If the unsung Democratic guerrillas were ever to adopt a mascot, it would have to be Rep. Louise Slaughter (D-N.Y.). The ten-term congresswoman from upstate New York is someone you don't hear about very often because (a) she's a House Democrat, and the media only has room for one of those, if that; and (b) she's far too feisty and interesting. In a different news world that actually covered opposition parties, she'd be a media darling. Slaughter rarely bites her tongue, and she doesn't mind turning the tables on reporters. At age 76, she looks at least 15 years younger and has the energy of someone 50 years her junior. When I met Slaughter at her top-floor office in the Rayburn House Office Building to talk about why no one knows what she's been doing, she was ready to vent.

"There's this assumption that we're the Three Stooges over here, bungling around," she said, rolling her eyes. "I hear it all day and all night." *What's wrong with Democrats?* she mimics. "There's *nothing* wrong with us!" Slaughter herself has waged an ongoing—and largely unnoticed—campaign to highlight the ways in which Republicans have abused the legislative process, locking Democrats out completely and awarding themselves unbridled power. She almost single-handedly forced Republicans to back off on plans to tamper with the Ethics Committee in order to give Tom DeLay a break. The problem she and her colleagues run into over and over, Slaughter tells me, is that "nobody knows what we're doing up here because nobody ever covers it." A perfect example occurred at the beginning of March. Slaughter, who is a ranking member on the House Rules Committee, released the report "America for Sale: The Cost of Republican Corruption," outlining all of the ways that congressional Republicans have not only gamed the system, but created their own legislative system. She followed it up a week later with a legislative package to reform the House rules process, one of the major sources of GOP power.

At a press conference to announce this reform package, Slaughter made her case and then challenged the reporters present, daring them to tell the story of how the Rules Committee had been hijacked. Unsurprisingly, no one did. That is, until Republicans decided to attack Slaughter's report, charging that it constituted campaign activity and was therefore an unlawful use of her office. Once journalists had a Republican angle to cover, it became a story, although the substance of Slaughter's report and its accusations was never mentioned.

The irony of Republicans calling her report about their ethics lapses unethical amused Slaughter, but it wasn't over. A few weeks later, the National Republican Campaign Committee (NRCC) issued a crowing press release claiming that Nancy Pelosi had removed Slaughter's report from her leadership Web site because of GOP pressure. Staff for both Slaughter and Pelosi got a chuckle out of the release because they knew the Web site simply automatically rotated the items featured on the homepage. But liberal bloggers jumped at the bait. To them, it was proof of Democratic cowardice. Using the NRCC release as his source, Matt Stoller at *MyDD.com* complained about Democratic "knuckling-under." David Sirota went further, writing: "[T]he House Democratic Leadership publicly pee[d] down its leg in knee-shaking fright, removing a major report on Republican corruption from its Web site. Why? Because they feared the GOP would yell at them about it."

When reporters do write about Democratic victories, they often omit the protagonists from the story completely, leaving readers to wonder why Republicans would change course out of the blue. A *Washington Post* article about the Ethics Committee rule change simply noted that "House Republicans overwhelmingly agreed to rescind rule changes," in the face, apparently, of phantom opposition. Or journalists give credit to maverick Republicans rather than acknowledge the success of a unified Democratic effort: The Associated Press covered Bush's reversal on Davis-Bacon by writing, "The White House promised to restore the 74-year-old Davis-Bacon prevailing wage protection on Nov. 8, following a meeting between chief of staff Andrew Card and a caucus of pro-labor Republicans." Or Bush is blamed for his own defeats, without any mention of an opposition effort, as with Social Security privatization.

Nor are reporters paying attention to Democratic policy proposals, as the party tries to develop a national agenda to run on. Congressional press secretaries say that reporters won't write about their efforts unless or until Democratic legislation comes up for serious consideration. "A lot of reporters tell me, 'Yeah, I'll write about that when it's on the floor,'" complained the Democratic communications director for a Senate committee. "So then some columnist writes that Democrats have no ideas and everybody in America says, 'You're right—I haven't read about any.'"

As a result, it's easy for talking heads to paint Democrats as a bunch of complainers who attack Republicans while putting forward no ideas of their own. MSNBC's Chris Matthews calls them "kids in the backseat," whining and asking, "are we there yet?" And in a column last winter, the *U.S. News & World Report* columnist Gloria Borger criticized Democrats for being, yes, "reflexively critical," and scolded that it wouldn't kill them to show a little "gratitude" once in a while.

Paradigm Shift

In 2002 and 2003, Joshua Micah Marshall wrote a series of articles for this magazine about the myth of Republican competence. In one of those pieces, he referenced Thomas Kuhn's famous paradigm theory, which maintains that people can hold fast to a theory or narrative even as vast amounts of contradictory evidence piles up. At the time, there were plenty of indications pointing to GOP missteps and policy failures. But Republican message discipline, and a general awe of the Bush White House's corporate authority model, ruled the day. Everyone "knew" the Bush administration was a well-oiled machine. It took three more years, more than 2,300 U.S. troops dead in Iraq, a botched relief effort for Hurricane Katrina victims, and the vice president shooting a guy in the face for the narrative to change. Yes, it is possible for conventional wisdom to be that wrong.

So it is that Democrats can be "hopelessly divided" while voting together 88 percent of the time, according to *Congressional Quarterly*; just one percentage point lower than the vaunted lock-step Republican caucus. They can be "pathetically ineffective" while dealing a humiliating defeat to the president's biggest domestic policy effort. They can be deemed "weak" and "timid" while setting the terms of the debate for pulling troops out of Iraq.

It seems the only way this particular narrative is going to change is with a Democratic victory in November. "They'll have to pay attention to us if we win," Slaughter told me. Taking back either house of Congress while battling the idea that they're a weak, ineffective party with no ideas won't be easy for Democrats. But stranger things have happened. Just ask Newt Gingrich.

Party in Search of a Notion

Michael Tomasky

The American Prospect | May 4, 2006

One of the main reasons why the Republican Party has dominated the political landscape in recent years is that their policies have largely been guided by a coherent set of political ideals. In this essay from The American Prospect, *Michael Tomasky suggests that if the Democrats hope to regain their status as the nation's majority party, they need to relinquish their "interest-group approach to politics" once and for all, and develop an equally overarching political philosophy of their own.*

The Democrats are feeling upbeat these days, and why not? The Republican president and vice president have lost the country's confidence. The Republican-controlled Congress is a sump of corruption, sycophancy, and broken principle. Races in the midterm election that Democratic leaders wouldn't have dreamed of a few months ago are in play (the Senate seat in Tennessee!). A recent poll showed Democrats with a gaping sixteen-point lead over Republicans this fall. Seizing on the issues of corruption and incompetence, the party might even take back the House or the Senate—or both.

The prevailing conventional wisdom in Washington—that the Democrats have no idea what they stand for—has recently been put to the test in persuasive ways. In an important piece in the May [2006] issue of *The Washington Monthly*, Amy Sullivan demonstrates that the Democrats have in fact become a disciplined and effective opposition party. From their Social Security victory to George W. Bush's backing down on his post-Katrina changes to the Davis-Bacon law to the Dubai ports deal, the Democrats have dealt the administration a series of defeats—each of which took a reflexive media, still accustomed to hitting F9, to spit out the words "Democrats in disarray," by complete surprise. More than that, the Democrats *do* have ideas; it's just that no one bothers to cover them.

The party has discipline, a tactical strategy as the opposition, and a more than respectable roster of policy proposals waiting to be considered should Democrats become the majority again. It's quite different from, say, three years ago. But let's not get carried away. There remains a missing ingredient—*the* crucial ingredient of politics, the factor that helps unite a party (always a coalition of warring interests), create majorities, and force the sort of paradigm shifts that happened in 1932 and 1980. It's the factor they need to think about if their goal is not merely to win elections but to govern decisively after winning them.

What the Democrats still don't have is a philosophy, a big idea that unites their proposals and converts them from a hodgepodge of narrow and specific fixes into a vision for society. Indeed, the party and the constellation of interests around it don't even think in philosophical terms and haven't for quite some time. There's a reason for this: They've all been trained to believe—by the media, by their pollsters—that their philosophy is an electoral loser. Like the dogs in the famous "learned helplessness" psychological experiments of the 1960s—the dogs were administered electrical shocks from which they could escape, but from which, after a while, they didn't even try to, instead crouching in the corner in resignation and fear—the Democrats have given up attempting big ideas. Any effort at doing so, they're convinced, will result in electrical (and electoral) shock.

But is that as true as it appears? Certainly, today's Democrats can't simply return to the philosophy that was defeated in the late 1970s. But at the same time, let's recognize a new historical moment when we see one: Today, for the first time since 1980, it is *conservative* philosophy that is being discredited (or rather, is discrediting itself) on a scale liberals wouldn't have dared imagine a few years ago. An opening now exists, as it hasn't in a very long time, for the Democrats to be the visionaries. To seize this moment, the Democrats need to think differently—to stop focusing on their grab bag of small-bore proposals that so often seek not to offend and that accept conservative terms of debate. And to do that, they need to begin by looking to their history, for in that history there is an idea about liberal governance that amounts to more than the million-little-pieces, interest-group approach to politics that has recently come under deserved scrutiny and that can clearly offer the most compelling progressive response to the radical individualism of the Bush era.

For many years—during their years of dominance and success, the period of the New Deal up through the first part of the Great Society—the Democrats practiced a brand of liberalism quite different from today's. Yes, it certainly sought to expand both rights and prosperity. But it did something more: That liberalism was built around the idea—the philosophical principle—that citizens should be called upon to look beyond their own self-interest and work for a greater common interest.

This, historically, is the moral basis of liberal governance—not justice, not equality, not rights, not diversity, not government, and not even prosperity or opportunity. Liberal governance is about demanding of citizens that they balance self-interest with common interest. Any rank-and-file liberal is a liberal because she or he somehow or another, through reading or experience or both, came to believe in this principle. And every leading Democrat became a Democrat because on some level, she or he believes this, too.

I remember my moment of epiphany clearly. It was early 1981; Ronald Reagan had taken office. I was toying, at the time, with some conservative notions—not because I believed them, but mostly to engage in that time-honored sport of twenty-year-old men everywhere: to traduce the old man. Reagan had just fired the air-traffic controllers. Dad and I were in the car, our Ford Granada, driving somewhere; I said (I cringe to confess this in print) something about the strike being illegal—Reagan's line, then being aped on television by such TV loudmouths as existed in that distant age. "Michael," he thundered (and he could thunder, all right!), "*all* strikes are illegal! That's part of the point!" Hmmm. It hadn't quite occurred to me that maybe there was more to the story than the television savants were letting on. He'd overstated the case a bit (all strikes aren't illegal), but in doing so, my father had asked me to *think*, and his request led me to consider things in a light I hadn't before—about the PATCO workers, yes; but about history and money and power, about the mine workers so central to the place where I grew up (Morgantown, West Virginia) and to my father's life (he was a United Mine Workers shop steward as a young man, before he got his law degree); about the precept that real thought and engagement on my part required looking beyond first assumptions, examining a problem from points of view other than my own, and considering any action's impact on the whole society.

This is the only justification leaders can make to citizens for liberal governance, really: That all are being asked to contribute to a project larger than themselves.

In terms of political philosophy, this idea of citizens sacrificing for and participating in the creation of a common good has a name: civic republicanism. It's the idea, which comes to us from sources such as Rousseau's

social contract and some of James Madison's contributions to the Federalist Papers, that for a republic to thrive, leaders must create and nourish
a civic sphere in which citizens are encouraged to think broadly about
what will sustain that republic and to work together to achieve common
goals. This is what Dad asked me to understand that day in our Granada.

This is what Democrats used to ask of people. Political philosophers argue
about when they stopped; Michael Sandel believes that republicanism died
with the New Deal. But for me, it's clear that the great period of liberal
hegemony in this country was, in fact, a period when citizens were asked
to contribute to a project larger than their own well-being. And, crucially,
it was a period when citizens (a majority of them, at least) *reciprocally
understood themselves to have a stake in this larger project*. The New Deal,
despite what conservative critics have maintained since the 1930s, did not
consist of the state (the government) merely handing out benefices to the
nation (the people), turning citizens into dependent wards; it engaged and
ennobled people: Social Security and all the jobs programs and rural elec-
trification plans and federal mortgage-insurance programs were examples
of the state giving people the tools to improve their own lives while
improving the collective life of the country (to say nothing of the way
Franklin Roosevelt rallied Americans to common purpose in fighting
through the Depression and the war). Harry Truman turned the idea of
common purpose outward to the rest of the world, enacting the Marshall
Plan, creating NATO and other regional alliances, exhorting Americans to
understand that they belonged to a community larger than even their
country. John Kennedy engaged Americans precisely at the level of asking
them to sacrifice for a common good, through the things that are obvious
to us—the Peace Corps, and of course "ask not what your country can do
for you, ask what you can do for your country"—and through things that
history's fog has made less obvious (his relentless insistence that victory in
the Cold War could be truly achieved only through improvement at home,
which would require sacrifice and civic engagement).

Lyndon Johnson's Great Society, until it washed up on the bone-strewn
beaches of Vietnam and New Left-driven atomization, fit the paradigm,
too. Consider just the first two sentences of Johnson's remarks upon
signing the Civil Rights Act: "I am about to sign into law the Civil Rights

Act of 1964. I want to take this occasion to talk to you about what that law means to every American." Not black people. Not Southerners. Not even "our nation." Every American—the words gave citizens agency and a stake in seeing that this unprecedented social experiment would succeed. In March 1965, Johnson again emphasized every American's stake in the fight for equal rights: "Should we defeat every enemy, and should we double our wealth and conquer the stars, and still be unequal to this issue, then we will have failed as a people and as a nation. . . . Their cause must be our cause, too. Because it is not just Negroes, but really it's all of us who must overcome the crippling legacy of bigotry and injustice."

What Johnson and his advisers knew, just as Hubert Humphrey down Pennsylvania Avenue in the Senate knew, was that desegregation would fail if the matter were put to the American people only in terms of the rights of those directly affected; it had to be presented as advancing the common good. This was a core belief for these Democrats (besides which, they knew—and their testimony on this point is amply demonstrated in books and memoirs and the like—that their programs would never get through Congress if they lacked this element).

Today's Democratic Party has completely lost connection with this principle. How and when did this happen? Against this small-r republican tradition that posits sacrifice for larger, universalist purposes is another tradition that has propelled American liberalism, that indeed is what the philosophers call liberalism proper: from Locke and Mill up to John Rawls in our time, a greater emphasis on the individual (and, later, the group), on tolerance, on rights, and on social justice. In theory, it is not inevitable that these two traditions must clash. But in the 1960s, it was inevitable that they did. And it is clear which side has won the argument within the Democratic Party.

The old liberalism got America out of depression, won the war against fascism, built the middle class, created global alliances, and made education and health care far closer to universal than they had ever been. But there were things it did not do; its conception of the common good was narrow—completely unacceptable, in fact, to us today. Japanese Americans during World War II and African Americans pretty much ever were not part of that common good; women were only partially included. Because of lack of leadership and political expediency (Roosevelt needing the South, for example), this liberalism had betrayed liberal principle and failed millions of Americans. Something had to give.

At first, some Democrats—Johnson and Humphrey, for example, and even some Republicans back then—tried to expand the American community to include those who had been left behind. But the political process takes time, and compromise; young people and black people and poor people were impatient, and who could blame them? By 1965, '66, '67, the old liberalism's failures, both domestically and in Vietnam, were so apparent as to be crushing. A new generation exposed this "common good" as nothing more than a lie to keep power functioning, so as not to disturb the "comfortable, smooth, reasonable, democratic unfreedom" that Herbert Marcuse described in 1964 in one of the more memorable phrases of the day. Activists at the time were convinced—and they were not particularly wrong—that the old liberalism, far from nurturing a civic sphere in which all could deliberate and whose bounty all could enjoy, had created this unfreedom. The only response was to shatter it.

That was the work, of course, of New Left groups like Students for a Democratic Society, the (post-1965) Student Non-Violent Coordinating Committee, and a host of others. Other activists opposed the shattering—to the contrary, their goal was to make the Democratic Party more inclusive. But even this more salutary impulse could be excessive, as with the famous example of the Cook County delegation to the 1972 Democratic Convention, in which, of the 59 delegates, only three were Poles. Many in the Democratic Party of that era opposed these attempts at inclusion and new social justice efforts vehemently. But in time, the party rid itself of those elements, and some of the sixties activists became Democratic operatives and even politicians. The stance of radical oppositionism dissipated as the sixties flamed out; but the belief system, which devalued the idea of the commons, held fast and became institutionalized within the Democratic Party. The impact on the party was that the liberal impulse that privileged social justice and expansion of rights was now, for the first time, separated entirely from the civic-republican impulse of the common good. By the 1970s, some social programs—busing being the most obvious example—were pursued not because they would be good for every American, but because they would expand the rights of some Americans. The old Johnsonian formulation was gone. Liberalism, and the Democratic Party, lost the language of advancing the notion that a citizen's own interest, even if that citizen did not directly benefit from such-and-such a program, was bound up in the common interest. Democrats were now asking many people to sacrifice for a greater good of which they were not always a part.

Toss in inflation, galloping under a new Democratic president; a public, especially a white urban public, tiring of liberal failures on the matters of crime and decline; the emergence of these new things, social issues, which hadn't been very central to politics before but became a permanent fixture of the landscape now; the Iranian hostage crisis; and the funding on a huge scale, unprecedented in our history, of a conservative intellectual class and polemical apparatus. Toss in also the rise of interest-group pluralism: the proliferation of single-issue advocacy organizations. All supported good causes, but their dominance intensified the stratification. They presented Democrats with questionnaires to fill out, endorsements to battle for, sentences to be inserted into speeches, and favors to be promised—and not just at election time; but even more important, when it came time to govern.

By 1980, Reagan had seized the idea of the common good. To be sure, it was a harshly conservative variant that quite actively depended on white middle-class resentment. But to its intended audience, his narrative was powerful, a clean punch landed squarely on the Democratic glass jaw. The liberals had come to ask too much of regular people: You, he said to the middle-class (and probably white) American, have to work hard and pay high taxes while welfare cheats lie around the house all day, getting the checks liberal politicians make sure they get; you follow the rules while the criminals go on their sprees and then get sprung by shifty liberal lawyers. For a lot of (white) people, it was powerful. And, let's face it, manipulative as it was, it wasn't entirely untrue, either!

Bill Clinton took several important steps to address this, and to recapture the notion of the common good. He was quite attuned to the sometimes heated academic debates of the 1980s that pitted liberalism against republicanism and the then-new school of thought called communitarianism. With some programs, Clinton strove toward a kind of civic-republican liberalism: notably AmeriCorps, his program of national and community service that has been a noble attempt to create a sense of civic obligation among young people, even if it has never quite penetrated the national consciousness.

But, after the health care fiasco, he didn't really use political capital (he would argue that he didn't have any, and he'd have a point) to try to build a liberalism of the common good. Here, the Democratic Leadership Council (DLC) enters the story. The DLC did have its own conception of the common good; indeed, the DLC, along with the communitarians, introduced the vocabulary of "rights and responsibilities" as a way to restore a civic-republican impulse to Democratic politics. Adding that word "responsibilities" was seen by many liberals as racial code, but, to be fair, the DLC also proposed, for example, an aggressive corporate-welfare program in the 1990s (that is, responsibility for the corporate body, too).

On balance, adding "responsibilities" was a useful rhetorical corrective. But in the real world, it ended up applying chiefly to poor black women (i.e., welfare reform); the corporate-welfare plans went nowhere. Why? Because what the DLC gave up on, by and large, was government—a belief in public sector answers to large and pressing problems. If the rights-based activists of the 1960s were guilty of defenestrating the idea of the common good, then the centrists of the 1980s and early 1990s were guilty of pushing too far in the other direction—the direction of a too extreme reticence about state interventionism, and of trying to make the rights crowd just shut up. Also— of dressing up small and innocuous proposals in the garb of world-historical significance. The common good was said to be waiting to be rekindled not in the idea that capital should be taxed just as highly as wages, or in large-scale investments in public infrastructure, but in the form of the V-chip.

For all his important successes, Clinton's broadest appeal was to people's self-interest; "I feel your pain." (Let's stop and appreciate that this was quite an achievement at the time, to make voters identify their self-interest with a Democrat!) Meanwhile, even though the party controlled the presidency, it lost the Senate, the House, many State Houses, and several state legislatures. In philosophical terms, the 1990s was really a decade of conservative advancement—checked and meliorated by the presence of a reasonably progressive president, but an age when the attacks on liberal governance that started in the late 1970s really took root, well below the level of the presidency, creating this thing "Red America," making the Gingrich revolution possible, and laying the groundwork for the second Bush era. Then came September 11, and Iraq, and a bulldozing Congress. Democrats were lost in the woods, completely disconnected from their mission and history.

*   *   *   *   *

So where does this leave today's Democrats? A more precise way to ask the question is this: What principle or principles unites them all, from Max Baucus to Maxine Waters and everyone in between, and what do they demand that citizens believe?

As I've said, they no longer ask them to believe in the moral basis of liberal governance, in demanding that citizens look beyond their own self-interest. They, or many of them, don't really ask citizens to believe in government anymore. Or taxes, or regulation—oh, sort of in regulation, but only some of them, and only occasionally, when something happens like the mining disasters in my home state earlier this year. They do ask Americans to believe that middle-income people should get a fair shake, but they lack the courage to take that demand to the places it should logically go, like universal health coverage. And, of course, on many issues the party is ideologically all over the place; if you were asked to paint the party's belief system, the result would resemble a Pollock.

At bottom, today's Democrats from Baucus to Waters are united in only two beliefs, and they demand that American citizens believe in only two things: diversity and rights.

Sometime last fall, after John Roberts' Senate Judiciary Committee nomination hearings but before the full vote, I was on a conference call set up by Senate Minority Leader Harry Reid with a few reporters and bloggers. *The Nation*'s Eric Alterman wanted to know whether Reid would make the Roberts nomination a party-line vote. No, he said; but he himself would be opposing Roberts. His stated reason: Roberts' refusal to apologize to Chuck Schumer during the hearings for his use of the phrase "illegal amigos" in a 1983 White House memo. Let's agree that Roberts should have apologized, said it was a poor attempt at humor. Let's even say that it does demonstrate a certain attitude that is inappropriate to this day and age. But honestly—of all the many reasons to oppose Roberts' elevation to the chief justice's chair, *this* is the main one cited by the top-ranking Democrat in the country? Like a bungling politician in a Milan Kundera novel, here is brave Reid, ready to defend the polity, not against reactionary interpretations of the establishment clause or executive power, but against a twenty-year-old politically incorrect joke!

Don't misunderstand me. It's one of the transcendent victories of contemporary liberalism, in an era when victories have been few, to consecrate
diversity as a societal end, a legitimate measure of a good and complete
society. Far from having been an invention of sixties radicals, it is in fact
rooted deep in the liberal tradition, in that Lockean tradition of tolerance.
It's a marvelous thing that this is one historical battle we seem (for now at
least, as we brace for the Roberts-Alito era) to have won. Here I think back
to 1995, when the Gingrich revolutionaries, and Bob Dole, wanted to pass
legislation banning or curtailing affirmative action. Sharpening their
knives, they went to their friends in corporate America: The time is right,
they said; let's scuttle these racial preferences. To their consternation, they
didn't have many takers. Corporate leaders said, well, we've spent a lot of
time (and money) developing diversity policies, and they're working rather
nicely. Imagine! The principle of diversity supported by a mostly Republican group to such an extent that Congress was taken aback. The revolutionaries dropped it, left it to the courts. These corporations were in fact
making a common-good argument to the revolutionaries: Diversity has
served us well as a whole, enriched us. And it's not just corporate America:
All over the country, white attitudes on race, straight peoples' attitudes
toward gay people, have changed dramatically for the better. These attitudes have changed because liberals and (most) Democrats decided that
diversity was a principle worth defending on its own terms. Put another
way, they decided to *demand* of citizens that they come to terms with diversity. So it can work, this demanding.

On the question of rights, the story is more mixed. Liberals were cha-
grined, after 9/11, to see the percentages of Americans who told pollsters
they were willing to sacrifice some liberties for security, and more recently
that only a very slim majority thought warrantless spying was a bad idea.
But even this narrative isn't all bad. Majorities support all manner of rights,
if with asterisks—to an abortion under many conditions, to privacy unless
you're a terrorist, to a fair trial even if you *are* a terrorist, to free speech
unless you're inciting to riot. Americans are actually better about this than
the French or the British, or just about anyone, really. Again, liberals (with
an assist from the Founders) placed this demand on citizens, and a
majority of citizens responded.

But diversity and rights cannot be the *only* goods that Democrats demand
citizens accept. For liberalism to succeed, they have to exist alongside an

idea of a common good. When they don't, things are out of balance, corrupted; and liberalism is open to the sort of attack made by Stanley Fish on the *New York Times* op-ed page back in February [2006]. Liberalism, he wrote, is "the religion of letting it all hang out"; its "first tenet" is that "everything (at least in the realm of expression and ideas) is to be permitted, but nothing is to be taken seriously."

This is preposterous, and the column drew many angry (and intelligent) letters. But unfortunately, I suspect that many Americans—not just people on the right, many not-terribly-political people—believe that Fish described liberalism precisely. Anything goes, man, because we don't really think about how a given action affects the community; we just care about whether, in questioning that action, the community is trampling on the actor's rights. We're in an age today—the age of Guantanamo, of withdrawal from the Geneva Conventions, and of illegal spying justified as executive necessity—when rights must be guarded with special care. But to think of every mode of action in terms of whether it can be enshrined as a right is a habit of mind that can lead our fellow citizens not to take us as seriously as we want them to when we talk about these other very real infringements on rights.

Liberals and Democrats of the 1960s had to abandon common-good conceptions in favor of rights and social justice ideas when they decided that the older liberalism had failed on too many fronts and they could no longer delay the work of securing the full rights of those Americans who hadn't had them. Their decision was necessary and courageous, even if some of them and their followers did spin off into radical and profoundly antimajoritarian directions.

But that decision is now *forty years old*. And, yet, that mode of thought still governs much about the way the Democratic Party, its interest groups, and liberal activists think and act today. And many of those who don't think and act this way, those Democrats who fight this brand of liberalism, have gone too far down the *other* road—so chary of anything that smacks of the old-time liberal religion that they too readily embrace a new one so promiscuously ecumenical, so intent on proving that it carries none of that old baggage, that it makes room for things like voting for last year's bankruptcy bill and supporting, still, the war in Iraq. Both roads are philosophical dead ends. They're also political dead ends, the former potentially alienating moderates, the latter giving rise to indifference and disgust in the party's base. It's time for something new that stands a chance of reaching both of those groups.

The Democrats need to become the party of the common good. They need a simple organizing principle that is distinct from Republicans and that isn't a reaction to the Republicans. They need to remember what made liberalism so successful from 1933 to 1966, that reciprocal arrangement of trust between state and nation. And they need to take the best parts of the rights tradition of liberalism and the best parts of the more recent responsibilities tradition and fuse them into a new philosophy that is both civic-republican and liberal—that goes back to the kind of rhetoric Johnson used in 1964 and 1965, that attempts to enlist citizens in large projects to which everyone contributes and from which everyone benefits.

Arguing for it is the only way that Democrats can come to stand for something clear and authoritative again. It's not enough in our age, after the modern conservative ascendancy, to stand for activist government, or necessary taxes and regulation, or gay marriage, or abortion rights, or evolution, or the primacy of science, or universal health care, or affirmative action, or paths to citizenship for illegal immigrants, or college education for all, or environmental protection, or more foreign aid, or a comprehensive plan to foster democracy in the Arab world, or any of the other particular and necessary things that Democrats do or should support; it isn't enough to stand for any of those things per se. Some of them have been discredited to the broad public, while others are highly contentious and leave the Democrats open to the same old charges. And those that aren't contentious or discredited suffer the far worse problem of being uninteresting: They're just policies, and voters don't, and should not be expected to, respond to policies. Voters respond to ideas, and Democrats *can* stand for an idea: the idea that we're all in this—postindustrial America, the globalized world, and especially the post-9/11 world in which free peoples have to unite to fight new threats—together, and that we have to pull together, make some sacrifices, and, just sometimes, look beyond our own interests to solve our problems and create the future.

The common good is common sense, and the historical time is right for it, for two reasons. First, what I'm trying to describe here is postideological in the best sense, a sense that could have broader appeal than what we normally think of as liberal ideology, because what's at the core of this worldview isn't ideology. It's something more innately human: faith. Not religious faith. Faith in America and its potential to do good; faith that we can build a civic sphere in which engagement and deliberation lead to good and rational outcomes; and faith that citizens might once again reciprocally recognize, as they did in the era of Democratic dominance, that they will gain from these outcomes. Maintaining such a faith is extraordinarily difficult in the face of the right-wing noise machine and a conservative movement that, to put it mildly, do not engage in good-faith civic debate. Conservatism can succeed on such a cynical basis; its darker view of human nature accepts discord as a fact of life and exploits it. But for *liberalism*, which is grounded in a more benign view of human nature, to succeed, the most persuasive answer to bad faith, as Martin Luther King showed, is more good faith. All Americans are not Bill O'Reilly fans or *Wall Street Journal* editorialists. While they may not call themselves liberals, many of them—enough of them—are intelligent people who want to be inspired by someone to help their country.

The second reason this could succeed is simple: the Bush years. By 2008, we will have lived through seven-plus years of an administration that has done almost nothing for the common good, that has unleashed the most rapacious social Darwinism we've seen in this country for at least eighty years, and that has catered to its interest groups far more, at once more obsequiously and more arrogantly, than even the Mondale-era Democrats did. Americans are, and will be, ready for something very different.

Here, I can even offer some proof. A March 2006 research project by the Center for American Progress (CAP) asked nine hundred Americans of all political stripes a series of questions about the role of faith and values in public life. The numbers, shared with me and about to be released publicly, support the contention that Americans recognize the absence of a common good in civic life and yearn for some leadership that will do something about it. The survey asked respondents whether they agreed with a series of twelve assertions about American life today; 68 percent strongly agreed with the assertion that "our government should be committed to the common good." This placed second only to "Americans are becoming too materialistic" (71 percent); it tied with "our government should uphold basic decency and dignity," which is a similar sentiment, and it came in well ahead of such conservative chestnuts as "religion is on the decline in

America" (41 percent) and "not enough Americans know right from wrong anymore" (46 percent). Respondents were then given an opportunity to offer open-ended descriptions of what the phrase " 'the common good' means to you personally." As with any open-ended poll question, answers were all over the lot, but the two most frequently volunteered answers used language that could have been plucked from this essay: "Good for all concerned/involved/more than individual" (20 percent), and "Good for the majority/not just for the few" (15 percent). One poll isn't conclusive, of course; but this one strongly suggests a nascent sentiment that Democrats can tap into.

Two things have to happen before the Democrats will be able to do this. First, the way interest-group politics are done in today's Democratic Party just has to change. I'm not the first to observe this recently—indeed, momentum is gathering behind this view, although it's still a long way from being a consensus one. In their controversial 2004 paper, "The Death of Environmentalism," Ted Nordhaus and Michael Shellenberger blasted the environmental movement's tactical narrowness and outdated intellectual frameworks. In their perceptive and passionate new book *Crashing the Gate*, Markos Moulitsas Zuniga and Jerome Armstrong rebuke liberal interest groups for a variety of sins, notably of feeling the need to endorse a few moderate Republicans for Congress even though those Republicans, while they might have acceptable records on issue X, Y, or Z, will go on to make Bill Frist the majority leader and Dennis Hastert the speaker—and with that single vote, more than cancel out whatever nice things they do when nothing's on the line.

This kind of politics is shallow, it's shortsighted, it's antiprogressive, and it nullifies the idea that there might even be a common good. Interest groups need to start thinking in common-good terms. Much of the work done by these groups, and many of their goals, are laudable. But if they can't justify that work and those goals in more universalist terms rather than particularist ones, then they just shouldn't be taken seriously. Immigration policy can't be chiefly about the rights of undocumented immigrants; it needs to be about what's good for the country. Similarly with civil rights policy—affirmative action, say, which will surely be up for review one day again when a case reaches the Roberts court. As I noted above, when talking about Gingrich's failure in 1995, there exist powerful common-good arguments for affirmative action. In addition to the idea that diversity enriches private sector environments, affirmative action has been the most important single factor in the last forty years in the broad expansion of the black middle class, which in turn (as more blacks and whites work and live together) has dramatically improved race relations in this county, which has been good, as LBJ would put it, for every American.

The second thing that has to happen is that Democrats must lead—the interest groups and the rest of us—toward this new paradigm. Someone in the party has to decide to bust the mold. I dream of the Democratic presidential candidate who, in his—or *her*—announcement speech in August 2007 says something like the following: "To the single-issue groups arrayed around my party, I say this. I respect the work you do and support your causes. But I won't seek and don't want your endorsement. My staff and I won't be filling out any questionnaires. You know my track record; decide from it whether I'll be a good president. But I am running to communicate to Americans that I put the common interest over particular interests." Okay, I *said* it was a dream. But there it is—in one bold stroke, a candidate occupies the highest moral ground available to politicians: to be unbought and unbossed.

It's hard for groups to change, and they must be given a reason to do so— a stake in a new paradigm and an assurance that their interests will not be tossed to the side. The answer is that, if Democrats are permitted to adopt a new philosophy and practice their politics differently—and, if Democratic leaders rise to the occasion—the prevailing situation in this country could change dramatically for the better, and that would benefit all their causes in the long run. I can't sketch out the implications of the framework I propose for every policy issue—those implications will be a matter of civic negotiation. But I can say that a new civic-republican liberalism can justify collective action far more powerfully and persuasively than anything the Democrats have done or said in a long time. Such arguments can be constructed on behalf of almost every single thing the party purports to stand for: health care coverage for those without it, the need to protect the planet and take global warming seriously, energy independence, asset-building for African Americans and other disproportionately poor groups, a path to citizenship for undocumented immigrants, and more. Such rhetoric can surely be wedded effectively to core economic matters. Last month in these pages, my colleague Harold Meyerson wrote brilliantly about the crisis of the American economy (see "Not Your Father's Detroit," *The American Prospect*, April 8, 2006)—about the need for an industrial policy that addresses the flight of jobs, the health care and pension crises, and the rest. If the Democrats, when addressing these concerns, sound like they're offering one more sop to big labor, they will inaugurate the same old round of embittered cat-calling; if their proposals are rooted in notions of communal sacrifice toward a greater good in which all citizens will have a stake and a share, the terms of the debate are changed.

There are potential dangers here and they should be noted. A too-aggressive common-good framework can discard liberty and rights; after all, Bush uses a conservative kind of common-good rhetoric to defend his spying program (he's protecting us from attack). Democrats have to guard against this; a common good that isn't balanced by concern for liberty can be quasi-authoritarian ("coercive," as the political philosophers call it). Common-good rhetoric and action must be tethered to progressive ends and must operate within the constitutional framework of individual liberty against state encroachment.

But there's an awful lot of maneuvering room between where the Democratic Party is today and coercion; it's the territory of civic deliberation toward a larger common interest, and there are positive signs that some are exploring it. In South Dakota, where legislators recently passed the country's most draconian abortion ban, prochoice advocates have done something very interesting. They decided *not* to sue. Instead they're circulating petitions to hold a referendum on the law. The *Los Angeles Times* reports that "even in the most conservative corners of this conservative state, both Republicans and Democrats—including a few who say they oppose abortion—are eagerly signing the petition." We don't know that their effort will prevail. But we already know that using the political process in this way is a huge improvement over running yet again to the courts. In the long run, showing faith in this kind of democratically negotiated outcome is far better for liberalism.

Some will say that asking Americans to look beyond their own self-interest and participate in a common good will fail, either because it failed before (the 1960s) or because such a request can succeed only in rare moments—a time of war or of deep domestic crisis. But that isn't what failed in the sixties. The first half of the sixties, the civic-republican liberal half, succeeded beyond our wildest dreams. The second half, the half that ditched the common good, is what failed, and it failed for precisely the reason that it did so. And yes, it may be that the times when such appeals can work are comparatively rare in American history.

But what if, as the CAP poll suggests, this is one of those moments? We are not in a Depression-like crisis, perhaps; but thanks to the efforts of the Bush administration we are on the precipice of several crises, and it's not just liberals who recognize this. Many of our fellow citizens, bitterly disappointed by a leadership in which they had placed an extraordinary amount of trust back in September 2001, recognize it, too.

The Democrats must grasp this, kick some old habits, and realize that we are on the verge of a turning point. The Democratic left wants it to be 1968 in perpetuity; the Democratic center wishes for 1992 to repeat itself over and over again. History, however, doesn't oblige such wishes—it rewards those who recognize new moments as they arise. It might just be that the Bush years, these years of civic destruction and counterfeit morality, have provided the Democrats the opening to argue on behalf of civic reconstruction and genuine public morality. If they do it the right way, they can build a politics that will do a lot more than squeak by in this fall's (or any) elections based on the usual unsatisfying admixture of compromises. It can smash today's paradigm to pieces. The country needs nothing less. The task before today's Democratic Party isn't just to eke out electoral victories; it's to *govern*, and to change our course in profound ways. I'd like to think they can do it. But the Democrats must become republicans first.

Part Five:
Iraq and the War on Terror

Why Iraq Has No Army

James Fallows

The Atlantic Monthly | December 2005

These days, the issues of whether or not Iraq had WMDs or whether it is truly a "front" in the global war on terror are largely beside the point, politically speaking. For whatever reason, we're there now, and committed to the project. That leaves the question: Is the U.S. attempt to prop up a democratic Iraqi government making steady progress, or on a glide path to failure? Like so much about Iraq, the truth seems to be in the eye of the beholder. As this book went to press, Iraq's newly appointed prime minister, Nouri al-Maliki, had finally managed to fill the key leadership positions in the ministries of defense, interior, and security; the leader of Al Qaeda in Iraq, Abu Musab al-Zarqawi, had been killed by an American air strike; a new security crackdown had begun in Baghdad; and President Bush had made a surprise five-hour visit to Iraq's capital to bolster the new government. At the same time, much of western Iraq was reportedly under the control of the Sunni insurgency; sectarian violence between Sunnis and Shiites was creating a de facto partitioning of many areas; an alleged massacre of civilians by U.S. marines in Haditha was threatening to taint U.S.-Iraqi relations; and the daily violence of kidnappings, torture killings, and bombings in the country was continuing unabated.

One thing everyone agrees on, however, is that the only way the United States is going to begin reducing its military presence there (which has been holding fairly steady at around 130,000 troops) is by helping to establish a viable Iraqi army and police force. In this Atlantic Monthly *article, veteran military affairs correspondent James Fallows analyzes why the effort to "stand up" Iraqi security forces has taken so long to gain traction—and asks whether the recent successes in this area (over 250,000 Iraqi troops have now been trained) are coming in time to save the country from descending into civil war.*

When Saddam Hussein fell, the Iraqi people gained freedom. What they didn't get was public order. Looting began immediately, and by the time it abated, signs of an insurgency had appeared. Four months after the invasion the first bomb that killed more than one person went off; two years later, through this past summer, multiple-fatality bombings occurred on average once a day. The targets were not just U.S. troops but Iraqi civilians and, more important, Iraqis who would bring order to the country. The first major attack on Iraq's own policemen occurred in October 2003, when a car bomb killed ten people at a Baghdad police station. This summer an average of ten Iraqi policemen or soldiers were killed each day. It is true, as U.S. officials often point out, that the violence is confined mainly to four of Iraq's eighteen provinces. But these four provinces contain the nation's capital and just under half its people.

The crucial need to improve security and order in Iraq puts the United States in an impossible position. It can't honorably leave Iraq—as opposed to simply evacuating Saigon-style—so long as its military must provide most of the manpower, weaponry, intelligence systems, and strategies being used against the insurgency. But it can't sensibly stay when the very presence of its troops is a worsening irritant to the Iraqi public and a rallying point for nationalist opponents—to say nothing of the growing pressure in the United States for withdrawal.

Therefore one question now trumps others in America's Iraq policy: whether the United States can foster the development of viable Iraqi security forces, both military and police units, to preserve order in a new Iraqi state.

The Bush administration's policy toward Iraq is based on the premise that this job can be done—and done soon enough to relieve the pressures created by the large-scale U.S. presence in Iraq. These include strains on the U.S. military from its long overseas assignments, mounting political resistance in America because of the cost and casualties of the war, and resentment in Iraq about the open-ended presence of foreign occupation troops. This is why President Bush and other officials say so often, "As Iraqis stand up, we will stand down." American maximalists who want to transform Iraq into a democracy, American minimalists who want chiefly to get U.S. troops out as soon as possible, and everyone in between share an interest in the successful creation of Iraq's own military.

If the United States can foster the development of a sufficiently stable political system in Iraq, and if it can help train, equip, and support military and police forces to defend that system, then American policy has a chance of succeeding. The United States can pull its own troops out of Iraq, knowing that it has left something sustainable behind. But if neither of those goals is realistic—if Iraqi politics remains chaotic and the Iraqi military remains overwhelmed by the insurgent threat—then the American strategy as a whole is doomed.

As Iraqi politicians struggle over terms of a new constitution, Americans need to understand the military half of the long-term U.S. strategy: when and whether Iraqi forces can "stand up."

Early in the occupation American officials acted as if the emergence of an Iraqi force would be a natural process. "In less than six months we have gone from zero Iraqis providing security to their country to close to a hundred thousand Iraqis," Donald Rumsfeld said in October 2003. "Indeed, the progress has been so swift that . . . it will not be long before [Iraqi security forces] will be the largest and outnumber the U.S. forces, and it shouldn't be too long thereafter that they will outnumber all coalition forces combined." By the end of this year the count of Iraqi security forces should indeed surpass the total of American, British, and other coalition troops in Iraq. Police officers, controlled by Iraq's Ministry of the Interior, should number some 145,000. An additional 85,000 members of Iraq's army, plus tiny contingents in its navy and air force, should be ready for duty, under the control of Iraq's Ministry of Defense. Since early this year Iraqi units have fought more and more frequently alongside U.S. troops.

But most assessments from outside the administration have been far more downbeat than Rumsfeld's. Time and again since the training effort began, inspection teams from Congress, the Government Accountability Office (GAO), think tanks, and the military itself have visited Iraq and come to the same conclusion: the readiness of many Iraqi units is low, their loyalty and morale are questionable, regional and ethnic divisions are sharp, their reported numbers overstate their real effectiveness.

The numbers are at best imperfect measures. Early this year the American-led training command shifted its emphasis from simple head counts of Iraqi troops to an assessment of unit readiness based on a four-part classification scheme. Level 1, the highest, was for "fully capable" units—those that could plan, execute, and maintain counterinsurgency operations with no help whatsoever. Last summer Pentagon officials said that three Iraqi units, out of a total of 115 police and army battalions, had reached this level. In September the U.S. military commander in Iraq, Army General George Casey, lowered that estimate to one.

Level 2 was for "capable" units, which can fight against insurgents as long as the United States provides operational assistance (air support, logistics, communications, and so on). Marine General Peter Pace, who is now the chairman of the Joint Chiefs of Staff, said last summer that just under one-third of Iraqi army units had reached this level. A few more had by fall. Level 3, for "partially capable" units, included those that could provide extra manpower in efforts planned, led, supplied, and sustained by Americans. The remaining two-thirds of Iraqi army units, and half the police, were in this category. Level 4, "incapable" units, were those that were of no help whatsoever in fighting the insurgency. Half of all police units were so classified.

In short, if American troops disappeared tomorrow, Iraq would have essentially no independent security force. Half its policemen would be considered worthless, and the other half would depend on external help for organization, direction, support. Two-thirds of the army would be in the same dependent position, and even the better-prepared one-third would suffer significant limitations without foreign help.

The moment when Iraqis can lift much of the burden from American troops is not yet in sight. Understanding whether this situation might improve requires understanding what the problems have been so far.

Over the summer and fall I asked a large number of people why Iraq in effect still had no army, and what, realistically, the United States could expect in the future. Most were Americans, but I also spoke with experts from Iraq, Britain, Israel, France, and other countries. Most had served in the military; a large number had recently been posted in Iraq, and a sizable contingent had fought in Vietnam. Almost all those still on active duty insisted that I not use their names. The Army's press office did arrange for me to speak with Lieutenant General Dave Petraeus, who was just completing his year's assignment as commander of the training effort in Iraq, before being replaced by Martin Dempsey, another three-star army general. But it declined requests for interviews with Petraeus's predecessor, Major General Paul Eaton, or others who had been involved in training programs during the first months of the occupation, or with lower-ranking officers and enlisted men. Many of them wanted to talk or correspond anyway.

What I heard amounted to this: The United States has recently figured out a better approach to training Iraqi troops. Early this year it began putting more money, and more of its best people, on the job. As a result, more Iraqi units are operating effectively, and fewer are collapsing or deserting under pressure. In 2004, during major battles in Fallujah, Mosul, and else-where, large percentages of the Iraqi soldiers and policemen supposedly fighting alongside U.S. forces simply fled when the shooting began. But since the Iraqi elections last January, "there has not been a single case of Iraqi security forces melting away or going out the back door of the police station," Petraeus told me. Iraqi recruits keep showing up at police and military enlistment stations, even as service in police and military units has become more dangerous.

But as the training and numbers are getting somewhat better, the prob-lems created by the insurgency are getting worse—and getting worse faster than the Iraqi forces are improving. Measured against what it would take to leave Iraqis fully in charge of their own security, the United States and the Iraqi government are losing ground. Absent a dramatic change—in the insurgency, in American efforts, in resolving political differences in Iraq— America's options will grow worse, not better, as time goes on.

Here is a sampling of worried voices:

"The current situation will NEVER allow for an effective ISF [Iraqi Security Force] to be created," a young marine officer who will not let me use his name wrote in an e-mail after he returned from Iraq this summer. "We simply do not have enough people to train forces. If we shift personnel from security duties to training, we release newly trained ISF into ever-worsening environs."

"A growing number of U.S. military officers in Iraq and those who have returned from the region are voicing concern that the nascent Iraqi army will fall apart if American forces are drawn down in the foreseeable future," Elaine Grossman, of the well-connected newsletter *Inside the Pen-tagon*, reported in September.

"U.S. trainers have made a heroic effort and have achieved some success with some units," Ahmed Hashim, of the Naval War College, told me in an e-mail. "But the Iraqi Security Forces are almost like a black hole. You put a lot in and little comes back out."

"I have to tell you that corruption is eating the guts of this counter-insur-gency effort," a civilian wrote in an e-mail from Baghdad. Money meant to train new troops was leaking out to terrorists, he said. He empathized with "Iraqi officers here who see and yet are powerless to stop it because of the corrupt ministers and their aides."

"On the current course we will have two options," I was told by a marine lieutenant colonel who had recently served in Iraq and who prefers to remain anonymous. "We can lose in Iraq and destroy our army, or we can just lose."

The officer went on to say that of course neither option was acceptable, which is why he thought it so urgent to change course. By "destroy our army" he meant that it would take years for the U.S. military to recover from the strain on manpower, equipment, and—most of all—morale that staying in Iraq would put on it. (Retired Army General Barry McCaffrey had this danger in mind when he told *Time* magazine last winter that "the Army's wheels are going to come off in the next twenty-four months" if it remained in Iraq.) "Losing" in Iraq would mean failing to overcome the violent insurgency. A continuing insurgency would, in the view of the officer I spoke with, sooner or later mean the country's fracture in a bloody civil war. That, in turn, would mean the emergence of a central "Sunni-stan" more actively hostile to the United States than Saddam Hussein's Iraq ever was, which could in the next decade be what the Taliban of Afghanistan was in the 1990s: a haven for al-Qaeda and related terrorists. "In Vietnam we just lost," the officer said. "This would be losing with consequences."

How the Iraq story turns out will not be known for years, but based on what is now knowable, the bleak prospect today is the culmination of a drama's first three acts. The first act involves neglect and delusion. Americans—and Iraqis—will spend years recovering from decisions made or avoided during the days before and after combat began, and through the first year of the occupation. The second act involves a tentative approach to a rapidly worsening challenge during the occupation's second year. We are now in the third act, in which Americans and Iraqis are correcting earlier mistakes but too slowly and too late.

As for the fourth act, it must resolve the tensions created in the previous three.

I. Autumn 2002–Autumn 2003: Taken by Surprise

"It was clear what might happen in a highly militarized society once the regime fell," Anthony Cordesman wrote recently. Cordesman, of the Center for Strategic and International Studies, in Washington, has produced an authoritative series of reports of the new Iraqi military, available at the CSIS Web site. "The U.S. chose to largely ignore these indicators."

In explaining the early failures that plagued the occupation, Cordesman cited factors that have become familiar: an unrealistic expectation of how long Iraqis would welcome a foreign force; a deliberate decision to hold down the size of the invading army; too little preparation for postwar complications; and so on. Before the invasion Saddam Hussein had employed at least half a million soldiers and policemen to keep the lid on Iraq. The United States went in with less than a third that many troops, and because virtually none of them spoke Arabic, they could rarely detect changes in the Iraqi mood or exert influence except by force.

But the explanation of early training problems also leads in some less familiar directions.

One view about why things went so wrong so fast is espoused by Ahmed Chalabi, onetime leader of the Iraqi National Congress, and American supporters of the war such as James Woolsey, a former CIA director, and Richard Perle, a former chairman of the Defense Policy Board. "My view is pretty straightforward," Woolsey told me. "We lost five years, thanks to the State Department and the CIA." The years in question were from 1998, when Congress passed and Bill Clinton signed the Iraq Liberation Act, advocating regime change in Iraq, to 2003, when U.S. troops moved on Baghdad. The act provided $97 million for arms and for training expatriate Iraqi forces. "All we had to do was use some of that money to train mainly Kurdish and Shia units to fight with us, like the Free French in 1944," Woolsey said. The main counterargument is that a Kurdish-Shiite invading army would have made it even harder to deal with Sunnis after Saddam fell.

A different view is strongly held by others among the war's early advocates within the Bush administration. In discussions with former members of the administration I was told they felt truly bad about only one intelligence failure. It did not concern WMD stockpiles in Iraq; the world's other intelligence agencies all made the same mistake, my informants said, and Saddam Hussein would have kept trying to build them anyway. What bothered them was that they did not grasp that he was planning all along to have his army melt away and reemerge as a guerrilla force once the Americans took over. In this view the war against Saddam's "bitter enders" is still going on, and the new Iraqi forces are developing as fast or as slowly as anyone could expect.

But here is the view generally accepted in the military: the war's planners, military and civilian, took the postwar transition too much for granted; then they made a grievous error in suddenly dismissing all members of the Iraqi army; and then they were too busy with other emergencies and routines to think seriously about the new Iraqi army.

"Should we have had training teams ready to go the day we crossed the border?" asks Lieutenant General Jim Mattis, who commanded the 1st Marine Division during the assault on Iraq (and whom Harrison Ford is scheduled to play in a film about the battle of Fallujah). "Of course! The military has one duty in a situation like this, and that is to provide security for the indigenous people. It's the windbreak behind which everything else can happen." Mattis argued before the war that teams of civic advisers should have been ready to flood in: mayors from North America and Europe to work with Iraqi mayors, police chiefs with police chiefs, all with the goal of preparing the locals to provide public order. "But we didn't do it, and the bottom line was the loss of security."

Many other people suggest many other sins of omission in preparations for the war. But at least one aspect of the transition was apparently given careful thought: how to handle the Iraqi military once it had surrendered or been defeated. Unfortunately, that careful thought was ignored or overruled.

After years of misuse under Saddam Hussein, the Iraqi military had severe problems, including bad morale, corrupt leadership, shoddy equipment, and a reputation for brutality. But the regular army numbered some 400,000 members, and if any of them could be put to use, there would be less work for Americans.

By late 2002, after Congress voted to authorize war if necessary, Jay Garner, a retired three-star army general, was thinking about how he might use some of these soldiers if the war took place and he became the first viceroy of Iraq. Garner, who had supervised Kurdish areas after the Gulf War, argued for incorporating much of the military rank-and-file into America's occupation force. Stripping off the top leadership would be more complicated than with, say, the Japanese or German army after World War II, because Iraq's army had more than 10,000 generals. (The U.S. Army, with about the same number of troops, has around three hundred generals.) But, I was told by a former senior official who was closely involved in making the plans, "the idea was that on balance it was much better to keep them in place and try to put them to work, public works-style, on reconstruction, than not to." He continued, "The advantages of using them were: They had organization. They had equipment, especially organic transport [jeeps, trucks], which let them get themselves from place to place. They had a structure. But it was a narrow call, because of all the disadvantages." Garner intended to put this plan into action when he arrived in Baghdad in April 2003. He told me recently that there were few signs of the previous army when he first arrived. "But we sent out feelers, and by the first week in May we were getting a lot of responses back. We had a couple of Iraqi officers come to me and say, 'We could bring this division back, that division.' We began to have dialogues and negotiations."

Then, on May 23, came a decision that is likely to be debated for years: Coalition Provisional Authority Order Number 2, to disband the Iraqi military and simply send its members home without pay.

"I always begin with the proposition that this argument is entirely irrelevant," Walter Slocombe, the man usually given credit or blame for initiating the decision, told me in the summer. During the Clinton administration, Slocombe was undersecretary for policy at the Pentagon, the job later made famous by Douglas Feith. A month after the fall of Baghdad, Slocombe went to the Green Zone as a security adviser to Paul Bremer, who had just replaced Garner as the ranking American civilian.

On arrival Slocombe advocated that the Coalition Provisional Authority, or CPA, should face the reality that the previous Iraqi army had disappeared. "There was no intact Iraqi force to 'disband,'" Slocombe said. "There was no practical way to reconstitute an Iraqi force based on the old army any more rapidly than has happened. The facilities were just destroyed, and the conscripts were gone and not coming back." The Bush administration officials who had previously instructed Garner to reconstitute the military endorsed Slocombe's view: the negative aspects of consorting with a corrupt, brutal force were still there, and the positives seemed to be gone. "All the advantages they had ran away with the soldiers," the senior official involved in the plans said. "The organization, the discipline, the organic transport. The facts had changed."

The arguments about the decision are bitter, and they turn on two points: whether the Iraqi army had in fact irreversibly "disbanded itself," as Slocombe contends, and whether the American authorities could have found some way to avoid turning the hundreds of thousands of discharged soldiers into an armed and resentful opposition group. "I don't buy the argument that there was no army to cashier," says Barak Salmoni, of the Marine Corps Training and Education Command. "It may have not been showing up to work, but I can assure you that they would have if there had been dollars on the table. And even if the Iraqi army did disband, we didn't have to alienate them"—mainly by stopping their pay. Several weeks later the Americans announced that they would resume some army stipends, but by then the damage had been done.

Garner was taken by surprise by the decision, and has made it clear that he considers it a mistake. I asked him about the frequently voiced argument that there was no place to house the army because the barracks had been wrecked. "We could have put people in hangars," he said. "That is where *our* troops were."

The most damaging criticism of the way the decision was made comes from Paul Hughes, who was then an army colonel on Garner's staff. "Neither Jay Garner nor I had been asked about the wisdom of this decree," Hughes recalls. He was the only person from Garner's administration then talking with Iraqi military representatives about the terms of their reengagement. On the eve of the order to disband, he says, more than 100,000 Iraqi soldiers had submitted forms to receive a one-time $20 emergency payment, from funds seized from Saddam's personal accounts, which they would show up to collect.

"My effort was not intended to reactivate the Iraqi military," Hughes says. "Whenever the Iraqi officers asked if they could re-form their units, I was quite direct with them that if they did, they would be attacked and destroyed. What we wanted to do was arrange the process by which these hundred thousand soldiers would register with [the occupation authorities], tell us what they knew, draw their pay, and then report to selected sites. CPA Order Number Two simply stopped any effort to move forward, as if the Iraqi military had ceased to exist. [Walt Slocombe's] statement about the twenty dollars still sticks in my brain: 'We don't pay armies we defeated.' My Iraqi friends tell me that this decision was what really spurred the nationalists to join the infant insurgency. We had advertised ourselves as liberators and turned on these people without so much as a second thought."

*   *   *   *   *

The argument will go on. But about what happened next there is little dispute. Having eliminated the main existing security force, and having arrived with fewer troops than past experience in the Balkans, Germany, and Japan would suggest for so large a territory, American officials essentially wasted the next six months. By the time they thought seriously about reconstituting Iraq's military and police forces, the insurgency was under way, and the challenge of pacifying Iraq had magnified.

There is no single comprehensive explanation for what went wrong. After the tension leading up to the war and the brilliant, brief victory, political and even military leaders seemed to lose interest, or at least intensity. "Once Baghdad was taken, Tommy Franks checked out," Victor O'Reilly, who has written extensively about the U.S. military, told me. "He seemed to be thinking mainly about his book." Several people I spoke with volunteered this view of Franks, who was the CENTCOM commander during the war. (Franks did not respond to interview requests, including those sent through his commercially minded Web site, TommyFranks.com.) In retrospect the looting was the most significant act of the first six months after the war. It degraded daily life, especially in Baghdad, and it made the task of restoring order all the more difficult for the United States or Iraqi forces that would eventually undertake it. But at the time neither political nor military leaders treated it as urgent. Weeks went by before U.S. troops effectively intervened.

In June 2003, as the looting was dying down but the first signs of insurgent violence were appearing, the CSIS sent a team of experts who had worked in past occupations. They were alarmed by what they saw. "There is a general sense of steady deterioration in the security situation, in Baghdad, Mosul, and elsewhere," they reported. "Virtually every Iraqi and most CPA and coalition military officials as well as most contractors we spoke to cited the lack of public safety as their number one concern." At that time, the team pointed out, some five thousand U.S. troops were tied down guarding buildings in Baghdad, with two and a half battalions, representing well over a thousand troops, guarding the American headquarters alone.

Anthony Cordesman, of the CSIS, says there was never a conscious decision to delay or ignore training, but at any given moment in the occupation's first months some other goal always seemed more urgent or more interesting. Through the first six months of the occupation, capturing

Saddam Hussein seemed to be the most important step toward ending the resistance. His two sons were killed in July; he himself was captured in December; and the insurgency only grew. Along the way the manhunt relied on detention, interrogation, and break-down-doors-at-night techniques that hastened resentment of the U.S. presence. "The search for Saddam colored everything," Victor O'Reilly told me. "It is my belief that the insurgency was substantially created by the tactics used by the occupying force, who were initially the saviors, in their search for Saddam. Ambitious generals, who should have known better, created a very aggressive do-what-is-necessary culture. Frustrated troops, with no familiarity with the language or culture, naturally make mistakes. And in a tribal society if you shoot one person it spreads right through the system."

The hunt for WMD troves, conducted in the same way as the search for Saddam and by troops with the same inability to understand what was being said around them, had a similar embittering effect. The junior-level soldiers and marines I interviewed consistently emphasized how debilitating the language barrier was. Having too few interpreters, they were left to communicate their instructions with gestures and sign language. The result was that American troops were blind and deaf to much of what was going on around them, and the Iraqis were often terrified.

General Mattis had stressed to his troops the importance of not frightening civilians, so as not to turn those civilians into enemies. He, too, emphasizes the distractions in the first year that diminished the attention paid to building an Iraqi security force. "There was always something," he told me. "Instead of focusing on security, we were trying to get oil pipelines patched, electrical grids back into position, figure out who the engineers were we could trust, since some of them hated us so much they would do sabotage work. It was going to take a while."

When Americans did think about a new Iraqi army, they often began with fears that it might become too strong too fast. "Everybody assumed that within Iraq it would be peaceful," says T. X. Hammes, the author of *The Sling and the Stone*, who was then in Iraq as a Marine Corps colonel. "So the biggest concern was reassuring all of Iraq's neighbors that Iraq would not be a threat. One of the ways you do that is by building a motor infantry force with no logistics"—that is, an army that can't sustain any large-scale offensive operation. Such an army might assuage concerns in

Syria and Iran, but it would do little to provide internal security, and would not be prepared for domestic counterinsurgency work. (This tension has not been resolved: to this day the Iraqi government complains that the United States will not help it get adequate tanks, armored vehicles, and artillery.) Corrupt use of U.S. aid and domestic Iraqi resources was a constant and destructive factor. Last August the Knight Ridder newspapers revealed that Iraq's Board of Supreme Audit had surveyed arms contracts worth $1.3 billion and concluded that about $500 million had simply disappeared in payoffs, kickbacks, and fraud.

Training the police would be as big a challenge as training the army. "There was no image of a noncorrupt police force anywhere in the country," Mattis says. And to make matters more difficult, the effort began just as the police were coming under attack from insurgents' bombs and grenades.

Throughout the occupation, but most of all in these early months, training suffered from a "B Team" problem. Before the fighting there was a huge glamour gap in the Pentagon between people working on so-called Phase III—the "kinetic" stage, the currently fashionable term for what used to be called "combat"—and those consigned to thinking about Phase IV, postwar reconstruction. The gap persisted after Baghdad fell. Nearly every military official I spoke with said that formal and informal incentives within the military made training Iraqi forces seem like second-tier work.

There were exceptions. The Green Berets and other elite units of the Special Forces have long prided themselves on being able to turn ragtag foreign armies into effective fighting units. But there weren't enough Special Forces units to go around, and the mainstream Army and Marine Corps were far less enthusiastic about training assignments. Especially at the start, training missions were filled mostly by people who couldn't get combat postings, and by members of the Reserves and the National Guard.

Walter Slocombe told me that there could have been a larger structural attempt to deal with the B-Team issue. "If we knew then what we know now," he said—that is, if people in charge had understood that public order would be the biggest postwar problem, and that Iraqis would soon resent the presence of foreigners trying to impose that order—"we would have done things differently. It would have made sense to have had an American military unit assigned this way from the beginning. They would be told, 'You guys aren't going to fight this war. You're not going to get Medals of Honor. But you will get due recognition. Your job is to run the occupation and train the Iraqis.' And we'd configure for that mission."

But of course that didn't happen. "I couldn't believe that we weren't ready for the occupation," Terence Daly, a retired army colonel who learned the tactics of counterinsurgency in Vietnam, told me. "I was horrified when I saw the looting and the American inaction afterward. If I were an Iraqi, it would have shown me these people are not serious."

II. Autumn 2003–Autumn 2004: Overwhelmed

By late 2003 the United States had lost time and had changed identity, from liberator to occupier. But in its public pronouncements and its internal guidance the administration resisted admitting, even to itself, that it now faced a genuine insurgency—one that might grow in strength—rather than merely facing the dregs of the old regime, whose power would naturally wane as its leaders were caught and killed. On June 16, Army General John Abizaid, newly installed as CENTCOM commander, was the first senior American official to say that in fact the United States now faced a "classical guerrilla-type campaign." Two days later, in congressional testimony, Paul Wolfowitz, the deputy secretary of defense, seemed to accept the definition, saying, "There is a guerrilla war there, but . . . we can win it." On June 30, Rumsfeld corrected both of them, saying that the evidence from Iraq "doesn't make it anything like a guerrilla war or an organized resistance." Two days after that President Bush said at a White House ceremony that some people felt that circumstances in Iraq were "such that they can attack us there. My answer is, Bring them on." Meanwhile, the insurgency in Iraq grew worse and worse.

Improving the training of Iraqis suddenly moved up the list of concerns. Karl Eikenberry, an army general who had trained Afghan forces after the fall of the Taliban, was sent to Iraq to see what was wrong. Pentagon briefers referred more and more frequently to the effort to create a new Iraqi military. By early 2004 the administration had decided to spend more money on troop training, and to make it more explicitly part of the U.S. mission in Iraq. It was then that a grim reality hit: how hard this process would actually be.

"Training is not just learning how to fire a gun," I was told by a congressional staff member who has traveled frequently to Afghanistan since

9/11. "That's a part of it, but only a small part." Indeed, basic familiarity with guns is an area in which Iraqis outdo Americans. Walter Slocombe says that the CPA tried to enforce a gun-control law—only one AK-47 per household—in the face of a widespread Iraqi belief that many families needed two, one for the house and one for traveling.

Everyone I interviewed about military training stressed that it was only trivially about teaching specific skills. The real goal was to transform a civilian into a soldier. The process runs from the individual level, to the small groups that must trust one another with their lives, to the combined units that must work in coordination rather than confusedly firing at one another, to the concept of what makes an army or a police force different from a gang of thugs.

"The simple part is individual training," Jay Garner says. "The difficult part is collective training. Even if you do a good job of all that, the really difficult thing is all the complex processes it takes to run an army. You have to equip it. You have to equip all units at one time. You have to pay them on time. They need three meals a day and a place to sleep. Fuel. Ammunition. These sound simple, but they're incredibly difficult. And if you don't have them, that's what makes armies not work."

In countless ways the trainers on site faced an enormous challenge. The legacy of Saddam Hussein was a big problem. It had encouraged a military culture in which officers were privileged parasites, enlisted soldiers were cannon fodder, and noncommissioned officers—the sergeants who make the U.S. military function—were barely known. "We are trying to create a professional NCO corps," Army Major Bob Bateman told me. "Such a thing has never existed anywhere in the region. Not in regular units, not in police forces, not in the military."

The ethnic and tribal fissures in Iraq were another big problem. Half a dozen times in my interviews I heard variants on this Arab saying: "Me and my brother against my cousin; me and my cousin against my village; me and my village against a stranger." "The thing that holds a military unit together is trust," T. X. Hammes says. "That's a society not based on trust." A young marine officer wrote in an e-mail, "Due to the fact that Saddam murdered, tortured, raped, etc. at will, there is a limited pool of 18-35-year-old males for service that are physically or mentally qualified for service. Those that are fit for service, for the most part, have a DEEP hatred for those not of the same ethnic or religious affiliation."

The Iraqi culture of guns was, oddly, not an advantage but another problem. It had created gangs, not organized troops. "It's easy to be a gunman and hard to be a soldier," one expert told me. "If you're a gunman, it doesn't matter if your gun shoots straight. You can shoot it in the general direction of people, and they'll run." Many American trainers refer to an Iraqi habit of "Inshallah firing," also called "death blossom" marksmanship. "That is when they pick it up and start shooting," an officer now on duty in Baghdad told me by phone. "Death just blossoms around them."

The constant attacks from insurgents were a huge problem, and not just in the obvious ways. The U.S. military tries hard to separate training from combat. Combat is the acid test, but over time it can, strangely, erode proficiency. Under combat pressure troops cut corners and do whatever it takes to survive. That is why when units return from combat, the Pentagon officially classifies them as "unready" until they have rested and been retrained in standard procedures. In principle the training of Iraqi soldiers and policemen should take place away from the battlefield, but they are under attack from the moment they sign up. The pressure is increased because of public hostility to the foreign occupiers. "I know an Iraqi brigade commander who has to take off his uniform when he goes home, so nobody knows what he's done," Barak Salmoni told me. The Iraqi commander said to him, "It really tugs at our minds that we have to worry about our families' dying in the insurgency when we're fighting the insurgency somewhere else." The GAO found that in these circumstances security units from "troubled townships" often deserted en masse.

The United States, too, brought its own range of problems. One was legislative. Because U.S. forces had helped prop up foreign dictators, Congress in the 1970s prohibited most forms of American aid to police forces—as distinct from armies—in other countries. For the purposes of containing the insurgency in Iraq the distinction was meaningless. But administration officials used up time and energy through 2004 figuring out an answer to this technical-sounding yet important problem.

Language remained a profound and constant problem. One of the surprises in asking about training Iraqi troops was how often it led to comparisons with Vietnam. Probably because everything about the Vietnam War took longer to develop, "Vietnamization" was a more thought-through, developed strategy than "Iraqization" has had a chance to be. A notable difference is that Americans chosen for training assignments in Vietnam were often given four to six months of language instruction. That was too little to produce any real competence, but enough to provide useful rudiments that most Americans in Iraq don't have.

The career patterns of the U.S. military were a problem. For family reasons, and to keep moving up in rank, American soldiers rotate out of Iraq at the end of a year. They may be sent back to Iraq, but probably on a different assignment in a different part of the country. The adviser who has been building contacts in a village or with a police unit is gone, and a fresh, non-Arabic-speaking face shows up. "All the relationships an adviser has established, all the knowledge he has built up, goes right with him," Terence Daly, the counterinsurgency specialist from the Vietnam War, says. Every manual on counterinsurgency emphasizes the need for long-term personal relations. "We should put out a call for however many officers and NCOs we need," Daly says, "and give them six months of basic Arabic. In the course of this training we could find the ones suited to serve there for five years. Instead we treat them like widgets."

All indications from the home front were that training Iraqis had become a boring issue. Opponents of the war rarely talked about it. Supporters reeled off encouraging but hollow statistics as part of a checklist of successes the press failed to report. President Bush placed no emphasis on it in his speeches. Donald Rumsfeld, according to those around him, was bored by Iraq in general and this tedious process in particular, neither of which could match the challenge of transforming America's military establishment.

The lack of urgency showed up in such mundane ways as equipment shortages. In the spring of 2004 investigators from the GAO found that the Iraqi police had only 41 percent of the patrol vehicles they needed, 21 percent of the handheld radios, and 9 percent of the protective vests. The Iraqi Civil Defense Corps, a branch of the military, had received no protective vests at all. According to the GAO report, "A multinational force assessment noted that Iraqis within the Iraqi Civil Defense Corps felt the multinational force never took them seriously, as exhibited by what they perceived as the broken promises and the lack of trust of the multinational force."

Although most people I spoke with said they had warm relations with many of their Iraqi counterparts, the lack of trust applied on the U.S. side as well. American trainers wondered how many of the skills they were imparting would eventually be used against them, by infiltrators or by soldiers who later changed sides. Iraq's Ministry of Defense has complained that the United States is supplying simpler equipment, such as AK-47s rather than the more powerful M4 rifles, and pickup trucks rather than tanks. Such materiel may, as U.S. officials stress, be far better suited to Iraq's current needs. It would also be less troublesome if Iraq and the United States came to be no longer on friendly terms.

And the biggest problem of all was the kind of war this new Iraqi army had to fight.

"Promoting disorder is a legitimate objective for the insurgent," a classic book about insurgency says:

> It helps to disrupt the economy, hence to produce discontent; it serves to undermine the strength and the authority of the counterinsurgent [that is, government forces]. Moreover, disorder . . . is cheap to create and very costly to prevent. The insurgent blows up a bridge, so every bridge has to be guarded; he throws a grenade in a movie theater, so every person entering a public place has to be searched.

The military and political fronts are so closely connected, the book concludes, that progress on one is impossible without progress on the other: "Every military move has to be weighed with regard to its political effects, and vice versa."

This is not a book about Iraq. The book is *Counterinsurgency Warfare: Theory and Practice*, which was published nearly forty years ago by a French soldier and military analyst, David Galula, and is based on his country's experiences in Algeria and Vietnam.

Counterinsurgency scholarship has boomed among military intellectuals in the 2000s, as it did in the 1960s, and for the same reason: insurgents are the enemy we have to fight. "I've been reading a lot of T. E. Lawrence, especially through the tough times," Dave Petraeus said when I asked where he had looked for guidance during his year of supervising training efforts. An influential book on counterinsurgency by John Nagl, an army lieutenant colonel who commanded a tank unit in Iraq, is called *Learning to Eat Soup with a Knife*. That was Lawrence's metaphor for the skills needed to fight Arab insurgents.

"No modern army using conventional tactics has ever defeated an insurgency," Terence Daly told me. Conventional tactics boil down to killing the enemy. At this the U.S. military, with unmatchable firepower and precision, excels. "Classic counterinsurgency, however, is not primarily about killing insurgents; it is about controlling the population and creating a secure environment in which to gain popular support," Daly says.

From the vast and growing literature of counterinsurgency come two central points. One, of course, is the intertwining of political and military objectives: in the long run this makes local forces like the Iraqi army more potent than any foreigners; they know the language, they pick up subtle signals, they have a long-term stake. The other is that defeating an insurgency is the very hardest kind of warfare. The United States cannot win this battle in Iraq. It hopes the Iraqis can.

Through the second year of occupation most of the indications were dark. An internal Pentagon report found,

> The first Iraqi Army infantry battalions finished basic training in early 2004 and were immediately required in combat without complete equipment. . . . Absent-without-leave rates among regular army units were in double digits and remained so for the rest of the year.

I asked Robert Pape about the AWOL and desertion problems that had plagued Iraqi forces in Mosul, Fallujah, and elsewhere. Pape, of the University of Chicago, is the author of *Dying to Win*, a recent book about suicide terrorism. "Really, it was not surprising that this would happen," he said. "You were taking a force that had barely been stood up and asking it to do one of the most demanding missions possible: an offensive mission against a city. Even with a highly loyal force you were basically asking them to sacrifice themselves. Search and destroy would be one of the last things you would want them to do."

A GAO report showed the extent of the collapse. Fifty percent of the Iraqi Civil Defense Corps in the areas around Baghdad deserted in the first half of April. So did 30 percent of those in the northeastern area around Tikrit and the southeast near al-Kut. And so did 80 percent of the forces around Fallujah.

This was how things still stood on the eve of America's presidential election and the beginning of a new approach in Baghdad.

III. Autumn 2004–Autumn 2005: Progress but No Urgency

At the end of June 2004 Ambassador Bremer went home. His Coalition Provisional Authority ceased to exist, and an interim Iraqi government, under a prime minister selected by the Americans, began planning for the first nationwide elections, which were held in January of this year. The first U.S. ambassador to postwar Iraq, John D. Negroponte, was sworn in as Bremer left. And a new American army general arrived to supervise the training of Iraqis: Dave Petraeus, who had just received his third star.

The appointment was noticed throughout the military. Petraeus, who holds a Ph.D. from Princeton, had led the 101st Airborne during its drive on Mosul in 2003 and is one of the military's golden boys. What I heard about him from other soldiers reminded me of what reporters used to hear about Richard Holbrooke from other diplomats: many people marveled at his ambition; few doubted his skills. Petraeus's new assignment suggested that training Iraqis had become a sexier and more important job. By all accounts Petraeus and Negroponte did a lot to make up for lost time in the training program.

Under Petraeus the training command abandoned an often ridiculed way of measuring progress. At first Americans had counted all Iraqis who were simply "on duty"—a total that swelled to more than 200,000 by March 2004. Petraeus introduced an assessment of "unit readiness," as noted above. Training had been underfunded in mid-2004, but more money and equipment started to arrive.

The training strategy also changed. More emphasis was put on embedding U.S. advisers with Iraqi units. Teams of Iraqi foot soldiers were matched with U.S. units that could provide the air cover and other advanced services they needed. To save money and reduce the chance of a coup, Saddam Hussein's soldiers had only rarely, or never, fired live ammunition during training. According to an unpublished study from the U.S. Army War College, even the elite units of the Baghdad Republican Guard were allowed to fire only about ten rounds of ammunition per soldier in the year before the war, versus about 2,500 rounds for the typical U.S. infantry soldier. To the amazement of Iraqi army veterans, Petraeus introduced live-fire exercises for new Iraqi recruits.

At the end of last year, as the Iraqi national elections drew near, Negroponte used his discretion to shift $2 billion from other reconstruction projects to the training effort. "That will be seen as quite a courageous move, and one that paid big dividends," Petraeus told me. "It enabled the purchase of a lot of additional equipment, extra training, and more rebuilding of infrastructure, which helped us get more Iraqi forces out in the field by the January 30 elections."

The successful staging of the elections marked a turning point—at least for the training effort. Political optimism faded with the subsequent deadlocks over the constitution, but "we never lost momentum on the security front," Petraeus told me. During the elections more than 130,000 Iraqi troops guarded more than 5,700 polling stations; there were some attacks, but the elections went forward. "We have transitioned six or seven bases to Iraqi control," he continued, listing a variety of other duties Iraqi forces had assumed. "The enemy recognizes that if Iraqi security forces ever really get traction, they are in trouble. So all of this is done in the most challenging environment imaginable."

Had the training units avoided the "B Team" taint? By e-mail I asked an officer on the training staff about the "loser" image traditionally attached to such jobs within the military. He wrote back that although training slots had long been seen as "career killers," the importance of the effort in Iraq was changing all that. From others not involved in training I heard a more guarded view: If an Iraqi army emerges, the image of training will improve; if it doesn't, the careers of Petraeus and his successor Dempsey will suffer.

Time is the problem. As prospects have brightened inside the training program, they have darkened across the country. From generals to privates, every soldier I spoke with stressed that the military campaign would ultimately fail without political progress. If an army has no stable government to defend, even the best-trained troops will devolve into regional militias and warlord gangs. "I always call myself a qualified optimist, but the qualification is Iraqi leaders muddling through," one senior officer told me. "Certain activities are beyond Americans' control."

Ethnic tensions divide Iraq, and they divide the new army. "Thinking that we could go in and produce a unified Iraqi army is like thinking you could go into the South after the Civil War and create an army of blacks and whites fighting side by side," Robert Pape, of the University of Chicago, told me. "You can pay people to go through basic training and take moderate risks. But unless they're really loyal to a government, as the risks go up, they will run." Almost every study of the new Iraqi military raises doubts about how loyally "Iraqi" it is, as opposed to Kurdish, Shiite, or Sunni. The most impressive successes by "Iraqi" forces have in fact been by units that were really Kurdish *peshmurga* or Shiite militias.

"There is still no sense of urgency," T. X. Hammes says. In August, he pointed out, the administration announced with pride that it had bought two hundred new armored vehicles for use in Iraq. "Two-plus years into the war, and we're proud! Can you imagine if in March of 1944 we had proudly announced two hundred new vehicles?" By 1944 American factories had been retooled to produce 100,000 warplanes. "From the president on down there is no urgency at all."

Since last June, President Bush has often repeated his "As Iraqi forces stand up . . ." formula, but he rarely says anything more specific about American exit plans. When he welcomed Iraq's president, Jalal Talabani, to the White House in September, his total comment on the training issue in a substantial welcoming speech was "Our objective is to defeat the enemies of a free Iraq, and we're working to prepare more Iraqi forces to join the fight." This was followed by the stand up/stand down slogan. Vice President Cheney sounds similarly dutiful. ("Our mission in Iraq is clear," he says in his typical speech. "On the military side we are hunting down the terrorists and training Iraqi security forces so they can take over responsibility for defending their own country." He usually follows with the slogan but with no further details or thoughts.)

Donald Rumsfeld has the same distant tone. Condoleezza Rice and Paul Wolfowitz have moved on to different things. At various times since 9/11 members of the administration have acted as if catching Osama bin Laden, or changing Social Security, or saving Terri Schiavo, or coping with Hurricane Katrina, mattered more than any possible other cause. Creating an Iraqi military actually matters more than almost anything else. But the people who were intent on the war have lost interest in the only way out.

A marine lieutenant colonel said, "You tell me who in the White House devotes full time to winning this war." The answer seems to be Meghan O'Sullivan, a former Brookings scholar who is now the president's special assistant for Iraq. As best I can tell from Nexis, other online news sources, and the White House Web site, since taking the job, late last year, she has made no public speeches or statements about the war.

IV. How to Leave with Honor

Listening to the Americans who have tried their best to create an Iraqi military can be heartening. They send e-mails or call late at night Iraq time to report successes. A Web magazine published by the training command, called *The Advisor*, carries photos of American mentors working side by side with their Iraqi students, and articles about new training techniques. The Americans can sound inspired when they talk about an Iraqi soldier or policeman who has shown bravery and devotion in the truest way—by running toward battle rather than away from it, or rushing to surround a suicide bomber and reduce the number of civilians who will be killed.

But listening to these soldiers and advisers is also deeply discouraging—in part because so much of what they report is discouraging in itself, but even more because the conversations head to a predictable dead end. Sooner or later the question is, What do we do now? or What is the way out? And the answer is that there is no good answer.

Let me suggest a standard for judging endgame strategies in Iraq, given the commitment the United States has already made. It begins with the recognition that even if it were possible to rebuild and fully democratize Iraq, as a matter of political reality the United States will not stay to see it through. (In Japan, Germany, and South Korea we did see it through. But while there were postwar difficulties in all those countries, none had an insurgency aimed at Americans.) But perhaps we could stay long enough to meet a more modest standard.

What is needed for an honorable departure is, at a minimum, a country that will not go to war with itself, and citizens who will not turn to large-scale murder. This requires Iraqi security forces that are working on a couple of levels: a national army strong enough to deter militias from any region and loyal enough to the new Iraq to resist becoming the tool of any faction; policemen who are sufficiently competent, brave, and honest to keep civilians safe. If the United States leaves Iraq knowing that non-American forces are sufficient to keep order, it can leave with a clear conscience—no matter what might happen a year or two later.

In the end the United States may not be able to leave honorably. The pressure to get out could become too great. But if we were serious about reconstituting an Iraqi military as quickly as possible, what would we do? Based on these interviews, I have come to this sobering conclusion: the United States can best train Iraqis, and therefore best help itself leave Iraq, only by making certain very long-term commitments to stay.

Some of the changes that soldiers and analysts recommend involve greater urgency of effort, reflecting the greater importance of making the training succeed. Despite brave words from the Americans on the training detail, the larger military culture has not changed to validate what they do. "I would make advising an Iraqi battalion more career-enhancing than commanding an American battalion," one retired marine officer told me. "If we were serious, we'd be gutting every military headquarters in the world, instead of just telling units coming into the country they have to give up twenty percent of their officers as trainers."

The U.S. military does everything in Iraq worse and slower than it could if it solved its language problems. It is unbelievable that American fighting ranks have so little help. Soon after Pearl Harbor the U.S. military launched major Japanese-language training institutes at universities and was screening draftees to find the most promising students. America has made no comparable effort to teach Arabic. Nearly three years after the invasion of Iraq, the typical company of 150 or so U.S. soldiers gets by with one or two Arabic-speakers. T. X. Hammes says that U.S. forces and trainers in Iraq should have about 22,000 interpreters, but they have nowhere near that many. Some 600,000 Americans can speak Arabic. Hammes has proposed offering huge cash bonuses to attract the needed numbers to Iraq.

In many other ways the flow of dollars and effort shows that the military does not yet take Iraq—let alone the training effort there—seriously. The Pentagon's main weapons-building programs are the same now that they were five years ago, before the United States had suffered one attack and begun two wars. From the Pentagon's policy statements, and even more from its budgetary choices, one would never guess that insurgency was our military's main challenge, and that its main strategic hope lay in the inglorious work of training foreign troops. Planners at the White House and the Pentagon barely imagined before the war that large numbers of U.S. troops would be in Iraq three years later. So most initiatives for Iraq have been stopgap—not part of a systematic effort to build the right equipment, the right skills, the right strategies, for a long-term campaign.

Some other recommended changes involve more explicit long-range commitments. When officers talk about the risk of "using up" or "burning out" the military, they mean that too many arduous postings, renewed too frequently, will drive career soldiers out of the military. The recruitment problems of the National Guard are well known. Less familiar to the public but of great concern in the military is the "third tour" phenomenon: A young officer will go for his first year-long tour in Iraq or Afghanistan, and then his second. Facing the prospect of his third, he may bail out while he still has time to start another, less stressful career.

For the military's sake soldiers need to go to Iraq less often, and for shorter periods. But success in training Iraqis will require some Americans to stay there much longer. Every book or article about counterinsurgency stresses that it is an intimate, subjective, human business. Establishing trust across different cultures takes time. After 9/11 everyone huffed about the shocking loss of "human intelligence" at America's spy agencies. But modern American culture—technological, fluid, transient—discourages the creation of the slow-growing, subtle bonds necessary for both good spy work and good military liaison. The British had their India and East Asia hands, who were effective because they spent years in the field cultivating contacts. The American military has done something similar with its Green Berets. For the training effort to have a chance, many, many more regular soldiers will need to commit to long service in Iraq.

The United States will have to agree to stay in Iraq in another significant way. When U.S. policy changed from counting every Iraqi in uniform to judging how many whole units were ready to function, a triage decision was made. The Iraqis would not be trained anytime soon for the whole range of military functions; they would start with the most basic combat and security duties. The idea, as a former high-ranking administration official put it, was "We're building a spearhead, not the whole spear."

The rest of the spear consists of the specialized, often technically advanced functions that multiply the combat units' strength. These are as simple as logistics—getting food, fuel, ammunition, spare parts, where they are needed—and as complex as battlefield surgical units, satellite-based spy services, and air support from helicopters and fighter planes.

The United States is not helping Iraq develop many of these other functions. Sharp as the Iraqi spearhead may become, on its own it will be relatively weak. The Iraqis know their own territory and culture, and they will be fighting an insurgency, not a heavily equipped land army. But if they can't count on the Americans to keep providing air support, intelligence and communications networks, and other advanced systems, they will never emerge as an effective force. So the United States will have to continue to provide all this. The situation is ironic. Before the war insiders argued that sooner or later it would be necessary to attack, because the U.S. Air Force was being "strained" by its daily sorties over Iraq's no-fly zones. Now that the war is over, the United States has taken on a much greater open-ended obligation.

In sum, if the United States is serious about getting out of Iraq, it will need to reconsider its defense spending and operations rather than leaving them to a combination of inertia, Rumsfeld-led plans for "transformation," and emergency stopgaps. It will need to spend money for interpreters. It will need to create large new training facilities for American troops, as happened within a few months of Pearl Harbor, and enroll talented people as trainees. It will need to make majors and colonels sit through language classes. It will need to broaden the Special Forces ethic to much more of the military, and make clear that longer tours will be the norm in Iraq. It will need to commit air, logistics, medical, and intelligence services to Iraq—and understand that this is a commitment for years, not a temporary measure. It will need to decide that there are weapons systems it does not require and commitments it cannot afford if it is to support the ones that are crucial. And it will need to make these decisions in a matter of months, not years—before it is too late.

America's hopes today for an orderly exit from Iraq depend completely on the emergence of a viable Iraqi security force. There is no indication that such a force is about to emerge. As a matter of unavoidable logic, the United States must therefore choose one of two difficult alternatives: It can make the serious changes—including certain commitments to remain in Iraq for many years—that would be necessary to bring an Iraqi army to maturity. Or it can face the stark fact that it has no orderly way out of Iraq, and prepare accordingly.

Afghanistan: The Other War

Christian Parenti

The Nation | March 27, 2006

In many ways, the U.S. military effort in Afghanistan has been a mirror image of the Iraq conflict. While the necessity of invading Saddam Hussein's Iraq is likely to be debated for years to come, overthrowing the Taliban regime in Aghanistan was clearly essential to our national security, and the project has always had the full backing of the great majority of Americans. Despite a relatively small troop presence, the United States also was able to swiftly establish a democratic Aghani government, which, while it's never had full control over the mountainous nation, has been largely effective in maintaining security.

Lately, however, cracks have begun appearing: recent American air strikes have repeatedly led to civilian deaths, prompting an official complaint from Afghan president Hamid Karzai—and in May, when a U.S. Army truck lost control and crashed into a line of cars, killing five and wounding many more, it touched off anti-American rioting in Kabul that left fourteen dead. Even more ominously, this spring, as the United States prepared to hand over control of military operations to a NATO command, resurgent Taliban forces launched their biggest offensive since being routed in 2001. In response, a U.S.-led coalition of 10,000 troops mounted a counteroffensive called Operation Mountain Thrust, which has included hundreds of air strikes against Taliban positions.

In this Nation *article, filed before the start of the latest offensive, Christian Parenti reports on conditions in the still-volatile nation—including significant reductions in U.S. aid to the country and the growing strength of the Talib fighters.*

Our Humvee jolts and sways against another cold dirt track in Parwan Province, an hour north of Kabul. On the road thin shadows from barren winter orchards lie like dark lacework and flicker across the Humvee's hood and windshield.

A landscape of adobe-walled villages, empty fields, horse carts, and dramatic sharp mountains slides by. Inside the armored Humvee we listen to music on a dusty iPod and two speakers that are jacked into the vehicle's nervous system. Lynyrd Skynyrd's "Sweet Home Alabama" rolls up on the iPod. The lyrics, though older than most of the soldiers on this patrol, capture the squad's mix of homesickness and political cynicism: "Now Watergate does not bother me/Does your conscience bother you?" No one talks much about Afghanistan.

I am riding along with these two Humvees from the 164th Military Police Company to observe the American effort at keeping a lid on the Afghan caldron. I also want to compare U.S. methods with those of the European troops who are taking over an ever larger part of the military mission here.

Specialist Willie Stacey stands in the gun turret on the SAW-249 machine gun. He taps his foot to the music's rhythm, and to the slight twinge of fear that animates us all. Four nights ago this unit was sprayed down with small arms fire, and earlier one of their number lost his leg to a landmine.

Only ninety-eight U.S. troops died in Afghanistan last year; but the ratio of U.S. casualties to overall troop levels makes Afghanistan as dangerous as Iraq. While Iraq's violent disintegration dominates the headlines, Bush touts Afghanistan as a success. During his recent visit, the president told Afghans that their country was "inspiring others . . . to demand their freedom."

But many features of the political landscape here are not so inspiring—for example, the deteriorating security situation. Taliban attacks are up; their tactics have become more aggressive and nihilistic. They have detonated at least twenty-three suicide bombs in the past six months, killing foreign and Afghan troops, a Canadian diplomat, local police, and in some cases crowds of civilians. Kidnapping is on the rise. American contractors are being targeted. Some two hundred schools have been burned or closed down. And Lieutenant General Karl Eikenberry, the senior American military officer here, expects the violence to get worse over the spring and summer.

Even in the once relatively stable northern and western regions of the country, foreign military bases and patrols are coming under sporadic attack, while civilian traffic faces a sharp rise in violent banditry. One security monitoring organization said they had seen a fourfold increase in such crimes over the past year.

The backdrop to this gathering crisis is Afghanistan's shattered economy. The country's 24 million people are still totally dependent on foreign aid, opium poppy cultivation, and remittances sent home by the

5 million Afghans living abroad. Yes, there is a new luxury hotel in Kabul, but Afghanistan ranks fifth from the bottom on the UNDP's Human Development Index. Only a few sub-Saharan semi-failed states are more destitute, more broken down.

Since late 2001 the international community—that consortium of highly industrialized nations, international financial institutions, aid organizations, and UN agencies that in concert manage the world's disaster zones—has spent $8 billion on emergency relief and reconstruction in Afghanistan. That's a lot of money, perhaps, but given what the World Bank has called the aid sector's "sky-high wastage" and the country's endemic poverty, it's simply not enough.

In the face of Afghanistan's deepening troubles, the U.S. government is now slashing its funding for reconstruction from a peak of $1 billion in 2004 to a mere $615 million this year. And thanks to the military's recruitment problems, the United States is drawing down its troops from 19,000 to 16,000. In short, despite Bush's feel-good rhetoric, the United States is giving every impression that it is slowly abandoning sideshow Afghanistan.

To pick up the slack, the primarily European- and Canadian-staffed, NATO-led International Security Assistance Force is increasing its troop levels from about 9,000 to 15,000. On the economic front an additional $10.5 billion in aid has been pledged for the next five years—$1.1 billion of that promised by the United States; the rest from Japan, the European Union, international institutions, and seventy other donor nations.

Many European states see America's unsuccessful wars in Iraq and Afghanistan as an opportunity to impress upon Uncle Sam that he must cooperate more with his junior partners—that he must give a bit more to the interests of the other rich economies. So they are moving in to help the United States by taking over as much responsibility as they can in Afghanistan. But the Europeans look at this opportunity with tremendous trepidation.

As one French diplomat working with the EU in Kabul put it: "The European powers all had to be dragged in one by one, kicking and screaming. They want to be the good allies and create obligation with the U.S., show their power, but they are very worried about casualties, about domestic fallout and about the costs and possible failure."

Many observers hope that a European-led counterinsurgency strategy will be more sophisticated and effective than current American methods, which are rightly criticized as heavy-handed, overly focused on military means, inflexible, culturally insensitive, and badly marred by the torture and murder of prisoners at the Bagram detention facility. The next five years—with a new round of funding and an infusion of fresh European troops—are seen as Afghanistan's last chance to stanch the growing Taliban insurgency and build a functioning state. Will it work?

The MPs from the 164th have a relatively straightforward but important job: to secure the Shomali Plain and the mountains surrounding the Bagram Air Base so that no one fires rockets into the base or shoots down any of its air traffic. To do this, the MPs use information-oriented tactics common throughout Afghanistan.

Counterinsurgency doctrine, such at it is, holds that military action must be guided by accurate knowledge: not just "actionable intelligence" about specific threats but also a generalized, almost ethnographic, understanding of everyday life in the area of operations. What are the local grievances? Who is in charge? Where are the wells?

Learn these things, and the occupying forces can map not only the physical terrain but also the social world they must control, the community power structures and local economies. With this knowledge the occupying forces can effectively direct both economic development and, when necessary, military repression. Thus, part of what these MPs do is conduct village surveys to create an overview of life on the Shomali Plain. Or at least that's the idea.

When I chat with the MPs' platoon leader, a lieutenant who has spent almost eleven months patrolling this valley, I am shocked that he doesn't even know its ethnic makeup. "I think they're Dari," he says. Informed that Dari is a language, not an ethnicity, he tells me to ask one of the Afghan interpreters. "The 'terps know. These guys are smart."

Moments later an MP learns that the 'terps have suddenly been barred from the dining facilities on security grounds. "What the fuck? They've been eating there for a year," says a GI. "They're gonna be pissed."

The prepatrol briefing is perfunctory; little information about recent activity is passed on to the troops. Two days earlier the Bagram Air Base had been attacked by a mob infuriated by the Danish Muhammad cartoons. Someone in the crowd opened fire on the gates. Three protesters were killed when Afghan forces and American MPs returned fire. The meaning or possible implications of these events are not mentioned before we roll out.

After a day of meandering through the valley, we reach the village of Kham Rubah Pan, where the patrol leader, Sergeant Chesley, has decided to do a village survey. One side of the road is hemmed in by a high mud wall, the other by a small creek and a line of tall, naked trees.

The survey questions range from "Who is the local leader?" to "Where is the closest clinic?" to "Are there any ACM [anticoalition militants] in the area?" The answers are pretty bleak: no good well, no school, no clinic, no work. But at least there are no ACM reported in the village.

One of the older men answering the survey, a returnee from the refugee camps in Pakistan, launches into a long tirade. "We have seen nothing from this government. We can't get to Karzai. The ministries do nothing."

As consolation, Sergeant Chesley begins an aid handout. All the GIs on this patrol have mixed feelings about aid giveaways. "There are villages where they throw themselves in front of our Humvees demanding food and blankets because we've created a welfare mentality," says Chesley. But his instructions are to occasionally give things away, especially in villages where no previous surveys have been conducted.

As the windup radios, blankets and gloves come out, the gaggle of men listening to the survey conversation suddenly swells to a boisterous crowd. The narrow road between the mud wall and the small creek is now full of men and children. There are no women over fifteen in sight. Pandemonium is immediate.

Chesley and a village elder attempt to impose order, but it's useless. Every object handed out is seized by several competing men. Shouting children squirm around underfoot. Two younger men start punching each other over a pair of gloves; Chesley and a local intervene to break it up. Now the loser, a skinny guy in a loose shaweer kamis and a Nike ski cap, not only lacks gloves but has hurt pride. More goods come out of the Humvee. A teenager assaults an older man who has just grabbed a blanket; the elder emerges with the blanket but loses his turban. People press in as the victors carry off their trophies.

I jump up on one of the Humvees and shoot video from the safety of the roof. The crowd below is a churning mass of desperation, poverty, hunger and the broken-up pieces of traditional, hierarchical Afghan society.

When we finally pull out of the village, a trail of young boys and men jogging and riding bicycles follows us for about half a mile. Occasionally, one of the GIs throws an MRE [meal ready to eat] out the window. I ride in the gun turret with Specialist Stacey. As far as I can see, the whole pathetic spectacle of the aid handout has had no positive political or cultural impact. "They call us infidels, but they're begging for blankets," says Stacey in his Alabama drawl. He shakes his head and tips a bag of M&Ms into his mouth.

Can the Europeans do any better than the U.S. forces? Attempting to find out, I fly to a Lithuanian base called a PRT, for Provincial Reconstruction Team. These small military bases aim to mix peacekeeping and reconnaissance with development work and political support for fledgling local government institutions like the police and the provincial governor's offices.

I board a huge Dutch-operated C-130 transport plane and fly from Kabul over the rocky snowbound peaks of the central highlands to a rolling plateau in the middle of the country. Strapped into the flip-down seats along the sides of the plane's dark cargo bay is a motley assortment of bearded European soldiers, clean-cut American GIs, private contractors, and mysterious armed men in civilian clothes. Landing at Chagcharan, Ghor Province, is like stepping out onto the moon: Not a tree or bush can be seen for miles.

The largest, poorest, least-populated province in Afghanistan, Ghor is a frozen, muddy desert inaccessible by road for much of the winter. Isolation sends local prices soaring and leaves Ghor's population in permanent debt to merchants and landlords. A thousand years ago this place was heavily forested, but its hills also held mineral deposits, so Ghor's trees were felled and burned to smelt the ore. Then the denuded region became the heart of Afghanistan's medieval cattle industry. Now Ghor is so stripped down that the only fuel available to most people are small bushes gathered during the summer from faraway hills. At an altitude of 9,000 feet, even the air is thin.

The Lithuanian-run PRT also includes a small Danish contingent. I am assigned to one of their squads, called a Mobile Liaison and Observation Team, or MLOT. These teams of six soldiers riding in two SUVs are the PRT's main means of operation. Their job is similar to that of the American squad I had been embedded with on the Shomali Plain. The MLOTs here comb their terrain of operations, driving for up to a week at a time, patrolling from village to village, gathering information, mapping the region's strengths and weaknesses, building links to the local population, and letting people know that the foreign supporters of the central government are out and about with their guns, grenade launchers, and who knows what else.

The information collected by the MLOTs is all digested by the PRT's intelligence and civil affairs sections and plotted on large maps and computer spreadsheets. "This will create institutional memory!" says a huge, enthusiastic Lithuanian civil affairs officer named Aleksiejus Gaizevsis. His databases track the whole province's vast array of needs, and he correlates all this on the wall-mounted maps. In the intelligence tent the walls contain a tree graph of the local power structure, illustrated with snapshots of Ghor's warlords. If violence flares, this information will help guide the military response. The accumulated knowledge is also supposed to help coordinate the efforts of NGOs [non-governmental organizations] and help avoid redundant efforts. But there are hardly any NGOs here.

One of the most difficult parts of the mission is collaborating with local authorities. The Danish intelligence chief describes the police commander as "the biggest crook out here." The governor, on the other hand, is seen as honest but weak.

The next morning, we set out across the empty hills in the SUVs of the Danish MLOT. A year ago two local warlords fought a pitched battle in Chagcharan, but the area has been quiet since then. The Danes are out to do a village survey and distribute some newspapers.

Unlike the American patrol, with its sloppy, halfhearted, ultimately divisive handouts, the Danes and Lithuanians limit their aid work to a few well-thought-out emergency-response projects: heat for an orphanage, shoes for the children of a displaced persons' camp, a few other things.

The European troops work hard to build bridges to the locals, growing beards, taking off their boots for indoor meetings, learning some Dari. And their sympathy seems genuine.

"I understand why everyone is armed," says Captain Bo Jepsen while we wait for one of his vehicles to be towed out of the mud. "There is no law and order out here. They have to protect themselves."

At points on our patrol through the moonscape dotted with villages, I interview several local people. All are brutally frank: It's been four years with no real change. They desperately want a better road so they can reach

Herat to the west and Kabul to the east. Their sense of isolation borders on panic.

Later, in the civil affairs tent, a young USAID rep tells me he's lobbying his superiors to set up a microcredit scheme. The guy, who is not supposed to be talking to me, has a bunch of other ideas. But in the past four years this province of around 670,000 people has received only $6 million in USAID funding. With so little money invested here, many of the NGOs that arrived in the first wave after the U.S. intervention have now pulled out.

This, ultimately, is the problem: Afghanistan is very poor, and the international occupation here is not doing enough to change that. Even if the Europeans go in with a sensitive approach and deploy their best troops, limited money will mean little or no progress.

Back in Kabul I get an interview at the U.S. Embassy, where the official mood is all clean-shaven, fresh-pressed optimism, backed up by Power-Point presentations and development-speak gibberish about stakeholders, capacity-building, business clusters and empowerment. I am allowed to meet a man who knows lots about USAID but whose handler insists he must be identified only as "a U.S. government official." It's a ridiculous inside-the-compound contrivance. The unidentified "U.S. government official" says several interesting things: Yes, USAID has problems with bureaucratic ossification. Yes, there is corruption in Afghanistan. But his final candid point is most important: USAID money for Afghanistan this year will be half what it was last year, and because of Iraq and Katrina, everyone in Kabul is "pessimistic" about the size of any midyear supplemental.

As the empire drifts, the Taliban grow stronger. But who are the Taliban, and why are they placing bombs, attacking foreign troops, infiltrating ever deeper into Afghanistan and provoking a crisis for the international occupation? Some say the Taliban are fragmented beyond coherence and don't even exist. Others say they are controlled by Al Qaeda. Still others say both are controlled by the Pakistani intelligence service.

Western reporters rarely make contact with the insurgents. But my colleague and interpreter, Ajmal, thinks we can meet them. He and I hook up with an Afghan TV journalist who was in the Taliban's ministry of information and still maintains contact with the Taliban in both Afghanistan and Pakistan. He is a rogue and a lush with no real political beliefs. We'll call him Mr. TV.

The plan goes like this: We drive the rather sketchy but newly paved road south into Zabul Province, to the countryside just outside Kandahar. There we bribe the local security commander to get safe passage into a canyon where we meet the Taliban. The security commander is supposed to tell the local American base that any armed men in a certain canyon are paramilitary police and should not be fired on by passing airplanes.

The trip south is hard, and our truck's alignment is badly out of whack. In Ghazni City we switch to a taxi driven by a young, innocent-looking cabbie. I am wearing a shaweer kamis, and he thinks I am Tajik like Ajmal. When I start speaking English, the kid seems nervous. After a few hours Mr. TV tells the kid to proceed to a police commander's compound, where we drop off a payment and some Jim Beam. Then we head out into the desert. Now the kid is really nervous. Mr. TV tells him to drive the cab into a canyon, then to hide the vehicle in a wash. Ajmal, Mr. TV and I bail out and start hiking.

And suddenly there they are: The first Talib is perched up on a slope, dressed in black, cradling an RPG launcher. He's straight from central casting.

There are five of them. They usher us up the side of the canyon into the shade against a wall. I wait for one of them to join us; instead they stand back, their guns trained on our chests. There is an awkward, somewhat terrifying moment. Then the head Talib, acting as if this is normal, says, "You can start asking your questions." I switch on my little video camera and we begin to talk.

"We are fighting because we won't let the American troops in our land," says the Taliban leader. "If their objectives were to rebuild our country we would not fight against them. But that is not their goal." He thinks America is here to "destroy our country" and "not leave."

How is the Taliban organized? "We are under one leadership. We have several groups, but we work together under one leadership. We have one command, but we have to operate in groups of five or six, because if we gather in groups of fifty we are afraid of the aircrafts. They would destroy us in big groups." This jibes with what an officer in the Afghan National Security Directorate tells me. The NSD officer says the Taliban have three fronts but all answer to one Pakistan-supported and -based leadership.

And what about support from Pakistan? "Yes, Pakistan stands with us," says the leader. "And on that side of the border we have our offices. Pakistan is supporting us, they supply us. Our leaders are there collecting help. The people on this side of the border also support us."

Notably, the Taliban have not adopted full-on Iraq-style tactics of targeting the UN, NGOs, and journalists. I ask why they don't attack NGOs. "We don't have any problem with the NGOs that come to help our people. Those who are doing destructive action in our country, we do jihad against them." This appears to confirm the suspicions of many internationals in Afghanistan that the Taliban do not launch all-out attacks on NGOs for fear of alienating the many southern Pashtun Taliban supporters who, though hating foreigners, rely on NGO-funded clinics, drink from NGO-built wells, or work as NGO drivers and staff.

The man firmly disavows the recent spate of suicide bombings and the school burnings. And what of Al Qaeda? "They are not with us. They fight, but they are elsewhere."

At one point, sounding like a classic peasant guerrilla with reformist aims, he says: "The central government must assist us, then we will put down our weapons. We are not against everyone. Our main concern is the government. The foreign troops must leave, and there must be an Islamic government."

Then we hear a quiet droning, high in the empty blue sky. "That is a detective aircraft. You should go," says the Taliban leader. We snap a few last photos and beat a hasty retreat out of the canyon.

A few days later Mr. TV, Ajmal and I reach Dr. Mohammed Hanif, one of two Taliban spokesmen who give out their satellite phone numbers to select journalists. The spokesman contradicts the fighters from Zabul on several key points. He claims responsibility for the suicide bombings. "We are changing our tactics. These martyrs are our Taliban." He also takes responsibility for the school burnings, explaining that they want education for women but only when it is "safe." Mixed schools will be burned. His main message is that the Taliban is unified and ramping up its tactics. None of this bodes well for the spring and summer.

Toward the end of my stay I meet a European "contractor" who is in fact a Western intelligence agent in charge of several important dossiers pertaining to Afghan security. All of this is confirmed through Afghan intelligence sources. But my "contractor" friend maintains his pretenses and I remain respectful of that, and we proceed with otherwise very frank conversations.

To my surprise, this agent to the great powers, this builder of empire, is the most cynical person I've met my whole trip. Highly intellectual, he talks of Afghanistan as doomed, a hostage to history and to the idiocy, arrogance, and Iraq obsession of the Bush clique. He passes me a series of "red gaming papers"—intentionally dissenting analyses of the Afghan situation written by and for the coalition.

The papers paint an arrestingly bleak picture of Afghanistan as a political "fiction," a buffer state that no longer buffers, a collection of fiefdoms run by brutal local warlords. The coalition's mission is portrayed as a fantasy game managed by sheltered careerists. One of the papers is by an American. It ends on this note: Nothing short of an open-ended blank check from the United States will keep Afghanistan from returning to chaos.

One of our meetings takes place at a dinner party. The contractor and I get rather drunk and talk politics by a big outdoor fire pit. He sums up the situation with a Kipling poem: "When you're wounded and left on Afghanistan's plains / And the women come out to cut up what remains / Just roll to your rifle and blow out your brains / An' go to your Gawd like a soldier."

I can't believe how grim his view of things is (though he is cheerful), and I keep pushing him to test for exaggeration. "I know an Afghan commander who is with the government and has been at this for quite a long time," says the contractor. "He described the current situation as 1983: The Taliban can't take on armored columns yet, but they are building momentum."

This analogy between the present and 1983 seems a bit unfair. "The mujahedeen had U.S. backing," I suggest. "The Taliban have no superpower patron."

"Yes, but neither does Afghanistan," says the contractor. He fills my glass once more with dark red wine and stares into the flames.

Taking Stock of the Forever War

Mark Danner

The New York Times Magazine | September 11, 2005

With the Iraq War dominating the news, and the resurgence of the Taliban in Afghanistan beginning to creep back into the headlines as well, it's all too easy to overlook those whose actions drew us into both conflicts: Osama bin Laden and his loose-knit terrorist organization, Al Qaeda. In this essay, published on the fourth anniversary of the 9/11 attacks on the World Trade Center and the Pentagon, journalist Mark Danner reexamines the motivations and aims of Al Qaeda and other Islamist extremist movements, and how these have been impacted by America's "war on terror" and the military interventions associated with it. He suggests that "Al Qaedaism" continues to flourish, despite our successful efforts to incapacitate its leadership—and that the U.S. invasion of Iraq has played a particularly energizing role in this process. "Instead of fighting the real war that was thrust upon us on that incomprehensible morning four years ago," he concludes, ". . . we have finished . . . by fighting precisely the kind of war they wanted us to fight."

I.

Seldom has an image so clearly marked the turning of the world. One of man's mightiest structures collapses into an immense white blossom of churning, roiling dust, metamorphosing in fourteen seconds from hundred-story giant of the earth into towering white plume reaching to heaven. The demise of the World Trade Center gave us an image as newborn to the world of sight as the mushroom cloud must have appeared to those who first cast eyes on it. I recall vividly the seconds flowing by as I sat gaping at the screen, uncomprehending and unbelieving, while Peter Jennings's urbane, perfectly modulated voice murmured calmly on about flights being grounded, leaving unacknowledged and unexplained—*unconfirmed*—the incomprehensible scene unfolding in real time before our eyes. "Hang on there a second," the famously unflappable Jennings finally stammered—the South Tower had by now vanished into a boiling caldron of white smoke—"I just want to check one thing . . . because . . . we now have. . . . What *do* we have? We don't. . . ?" Marveling later that "the most powerful image was the one I actually didn't notice while it was occurring," Jennings would say simply that "it was *beyond our imagination*."

Looking back from this moment, precisely four years later, it still seems almost inconceivable that ten men could have done *that*—could have *brought those towers down*. Could have *imagined* doing what was "beyond our imagination." When a few days later, the German composer Karlheinz Stockhausen remarked that this was "the greatest work of art in the history of the cosmos," I shared the anger his words called forth but couldn't help sensing their bit of truth: "What happened there—spiritually—this jump out of security, out of the everyday, out of life, that happens sometimes *poco a poco* in art." No "little by little" here: however profoundly evil the art, the sheer immensity and inconceivability of the attack had forced Americans instantaneously to "jump out of security, out of the everyday, out of life" and had thrust them through a portal into a strange and terrifying new world, where the inconceivable, the unimaginable, had become brutally possible.

In the face of the unimaginable, small wonder that leaders would revert to the language of apocalypse, of crusade, of "moral clarity." Speaking at the National Cathedral just three days after the attacks, President Bush declared that while "Americans do not yet have the distance of history . . . our responsibility to history is already clear: to answer these attacks and *rid the world of evil*." Astonishing words—imaginable, perhaps, only from an American president, leading a people given naturally in times of crisis to enlisting national power in the cause of universal redemption. "The enemy is not a single political regime or person or religion or ideology," declared the National Security Strategy of the United States of America for 2002. "The enemy is terrorism—premeditated, politically motivated violence perpetrated against innocents." Not Islamic terrorism or Middle Eastern terrorism or even terrorism directed against the United States: terrorism itself. "Declaring war on 'terror,'" as one military strategist later remarked to me, "is like declaring war on air power." It didn't matter; apocalypse, retribution, redemption were in the air, and the grandeur of the goal must be commensurate with the enormity of the crime. Within days of the attacks, President Bush had launched a "global war on terror."

Today marks four years of war. Four years after the attack on Pearl Harbor, U.S. troops ruled unchallenged in Japan and Germany. During those forty-eight months, Americans created an unmatched machine of war and decisively defeated two great enemies.

How are we to judge the global war on terror four years on? In this war, the president had warned, "Americans should not expect one battle but a lengthy campaign." We could expect no "surrender ceremony on a deck of a battleship," and indeed, apart from the president's abortive attempt on the USS *Lincoln* to declare victory in Iraq, there has been none. Failing such rituals of capitulation, by what "metric"—as the generals say—can we measure the progress of the global war on terror?

Four years after the collapse of the towers, evil is still with us and so is terrorism. Terrorists have staged spectacular attacks, killing thousands, in Tunisia, Bali, Mombasa, Riyadh, Istanbul, Casablanca, Jakarta, Madrid, Sharm el Sheik, and London, to name only the best known. Last year, they mounted 651 "significant terrorist attacks," triple the year before, and the highest since the State Department started gathering figures two decades ago. One hundred ninety-eight of these came in Iraq, Bush's "central front of the war on terror"—nine times the year before. And this does not include the hundreds of attacks on U.S. troops. It is in Iraq, which was to serve as the first step in the "democratization of the Middle East," that insurgents have taken terrorism to a new level, killing well over 4,000 people since April in Baghdad alone; in May, Iraq suffered ninety suicide bombings. Perhaps the "shining example of democracy" that the administration promised will someday come, but for now Iraq has become a grotesque advertisement for the power and efficacy of terror.

As for the "terrorist groups of global reach," Al Qaeda, according to the president, has been severely wounded. "We've captured or killed two-thirds of their known leaders," he said last year. And yet however degraded Al Qaeda's operational capacity, nearly every other month, it seems, Osama bin Laden or one of his henchmen appears on the world's television screens to expatiate on the ideology and strategy of global jihad and to urge followers on to more audacious and more lethal efforts. This, and the sheer number and breadth of terrorist attacks, suggest strongly that Al Qaeda has now become Al Qaedaism—that under the American and allied assault, what had been a relatively small, conspiratorial organization has mutated into a worldwide political movement, with thousands of followers eager to adopt its methods and advance its aims. Call it viral Al Qaeda, carried by strongly motivated next-generation followers who download from the Internet's virtual training camp a perfectly adequate trade-craft in terror. Nearly two years ago, Secretary of Defense Donald H. Rumsfeld, in a confidential memorandum, posed the central question about the war on terror: "Are we capturing, killing or deterring and dissuading more terrorists every day than the madrassas and the radical clerics are recruiting, training and deploying against us?" The answer is clearly no. "We have taken a ball of quicksilver," says the counterinsurgency specialist John Arquilla, "and hit it with a hammer."

What has helped those little bits of quicksilver grow and flourish is, above all, the decision to invade and occupy Iraq, which has left the United States bogged down in a brutal, highly visible counterinsurgency war in the heart of the Arab world. Iraq has become a training ground that will temper and prepare the next generation of jihadist terrorists and a televised stage from which the struggle of radical Islam against the "crusader forces" can be broadcast throughout the Islamic world. "Islamic extremists are exploiting the Iraqi conflict to recruit new anti-U.S. jihadists," Porter J. Goss, director of the CIA, told the Senate in February. "These jihadists who survive will leave Iraq experienced in, and focused on, acts of urban terrorism. They represent a potential pool of contacts to build transnational terrorist cells, groups and networks in Saudi Arabia, Jordan and other countries."

As the Iraq War grows increasingly unpopular in the United States— scarcely a third of Americans now approve of the president's handling of the war, and four in ten think it was worth fighting—and as more and more American leaders demand that the administration "start figuring out how we get out of there" (in the words of Senator Chuck Hagel, a Republican), Americans confront a stark choice: whether to go on indefinitely fighting a politically self-destructive counterinsurgency war that keeps the jihadists increasingly well supplied with volunteers or to withdraw from a post-Saddam Hussein Iraq that remains chaotic and unstable and beset with civil strife and thereby hand Al Qaeda and its allies a major victory in the war on terror's "central front."

Four years after we watched the towers fall, Americans have not succeeded in "ridding the world of evil." We have managed to show ourselves, our friends, and most of all our enemies the limits of American power. Instead of fighting the real war that was thrust upon us on that incomprehensible morning four years ago, we stubbornly insisted on fighting a war of the imagination, an ideological struggle that we defined not by frankly appraising the real enemy before us but by focusing on the mirror of our own obsessions. And we have finished—as the escalating numbers of terrorist attacks, the grinding Iraq insurgency, the overstretched American military, and the increasing political dissatisfaction at home show—by fighting precisely the kind of war they wanted us to fight.

II.

Facing what is beyond imagination, you find sense in the familiar. Standing before Congress on September 20, 2001, George W. Bush told Americans why they had been attacked. "They hate our freedoms," the president declared. "Our freedom of speech, our freedom to vote and assemble and disagree with each other." As for Al Qaeda's fundamentalist religious mission: "We are not deceived by their pretenses to piety. We have seen their kind before. They are the heirs of all the murderous ideologies of the 20th century. By sacrificing human life to serve their radical visions—by abandoning every value except the will to power—they follow in the path of fascism, and Nazism, and totalitarianism. And they will follow that path all the way, to where it ends: in history's unmarked grave of discarded lies."

Stirring words, and effective, for they domesticated the unthinkable in the categories of the accustomed. The terrorists are only the latest in a long line of "evildoers." Like the Nazis and the Communists before them, they are Americans' evil twins: tyrants to our free men, totalitarians to our democrats. The world, after a confusing decade, had once again split in two. However disorienting the horror of the attacks, the "war on terror" was simply a reprise of the Cold War. As Harry S. Truman christened the Cold War by explaining to Americans how, "at the present moment in world history, nearly every nation must choose between alternative ways of life," George W. Bush declared his global war on terror by insisting that "every nation, in every region, now has a decision to make. Either you are with us, or you are with the terrorists." The echo, as much administration rhetoric since has shown, was not coincidental. Terrorists, like Communists, despised America not because of what our country did but because of who we are. Hating "our values" and "our freedoms," the evildoers were depicted as deeply irrational and committed to a nihilistic philosophy of obliteration, reawakening for Americans the sleeping image of the mushroom cloud. "This is not aimed at our policies," Henry Kissinger intoned. "This is aimed at our existence."

Such rhetoric not only fell easily on American ears. It provided a familiar context for a disoriented national-security bureaucracy that had been created to fight the Cold War and was left, at its ending, without clear purpose. "Washington policy and defense cultures still seek out cold-war models," as members of the Defense Science Board, a Defense Department task force commissioned to examine the war on terror, observed in a report last year. "With the surprise announcement of a new struggle, the U.S. government reflexively inclined toward cold-war-style responses to the new threat, without a thought or a care as to whether these were the best responses to a very different strategic situation."

Al Qaeda was not the Nazis or the Soviet Communists. Al Qaeda controlled no state, fielded no regular army. It was a small, conspiratorial organization, dedicated to achieving its aims through guerrilla tactics, notably a kind of spectacular terrorism carried to a level of apocalyptic brutality the world had not before seen. Mass killing was the necessary but not the primary aim, for the point of such terror was to mobilize recruits for a political cause—to move sympathizers to act—and to tempt the enemy into reacting in such a way as to make that mobilization easier. And however extreme and repugnant Al Qaeda's methods, its revolutionary goals were by no means unusual within Islamist opposition groups throughout the Muslim world. "If there is one overarching goal they share," wrote the authors of the Defense Science Board report, "it is the overthrow of what Islamists call the 'apostate' regimes: the tyrannies of Egypt, Saudi Arabia, Pakistan, Jordan and the gulf states. . . . The United States finds itself in the strategically awkward—and potentially dangerous—situation of being the longstanding prop and alliance partner of these authoritarian regimes. Without the U.S., these regimes could not survive. Thus the U.S. has strongly taken sides in a desperate struggle that is both broadly cast for all Muslims and country-specific."

The broad aim of the many-stranded Salafi movement, which includes the Muslim Brotherhood of Egypt and the Wahhabis of Saudi Arabia and of which Al Qaeda is one extreme version, is to return Muslims to the ancient ways of pure Islam—of Islam as it was practiced by the Prophet Muhammad and his early followers in the seventh century. Standing between the more radical Salafi groups and their goal of a conservative Islamic revolution are the "apostate regimes," the "idolators" now ruling in Riyadh, Cairo, Amman, Islamabad, and other Muslim capitals. All these authoritarian regimes

oppress their people: on this point Al Qaeda and those in the Bush administration who promote "democratization in the Arab world" agree. Many of
the Salafists, however, see behind the "near enemies" ruling over them a
"far enemy" in Washington, a superpower without whose financial and military support the Mubarak regime, the Saudi royal family, and the other
conservative autocracies of the Arab world would fall before their attacks.
When the United States sent hundreds of thousands of American troops to
Saudi Arabia after Saddam Hussein invaded Kuwait, Al Qaeda seized on
the perfect issue: the "far enemy" had actually come and occupied the Land
of the Two Holy Places and done so at the shameful invitation of the "near
enemy"—the corrupt Saudi dynasty. As bin Laden observed of the Saudis in
his 1996 "Declaration of Jihad": "This situation is a curse put on them by
Allah for not objecting to the oppressive and illegitimate behavior and measures of the ruling regime: ignoring the divine Shariah law; depriving people
of their legitimate rights; allowing the Americans to occupy the Land of the
Two Holy Places."

But how to "re-establish the greatness of this Ummah"—the Muslim
people—"and to liberate its occupied sanctities"? On this bin Laden is practical and frank: because of "the imbalance of power between our armed
forces and the enemy forces, a suitable means of fighting must be adopted,
i.e., using fast-moving light forces that work under complete secrecy. In
other words, to initiate a guerrilla warfare." Such warfare, depending on
increasingly spectacular acts of terrorism, would be used to "prepare and
instigate the Ummah . . . against the enemy." The notion of "instigation,"
indeed, is critical, for the purpose of terror is not to destroy your enemy
directly but rather to spur on your sleeping allies to enlightenment, to
courage, and to action. It is a kind of horrible advertisement, meant to
show those millions of Muslims who sympathize with Al Qaeda's view of
American policy that something can be done to change it.

III.

Fundamentalist Islamic thought took aim at America's policies, not at its
existence. Americans tend to be little interested in these policies or their
history and thus see the various Middle East cataclysms of the last decades
as sudden, unrelated explosions lighting up a murky and threatening landscape, reinforcing the sense that the 9/11 attacks were not only deadly and
appalling but also irrational, incomprehensible: that they embodied pure

evil. The central strand of American policy—unflinching support for the conservative Sunni regimes of the Persian Gulf—extends back sixty years, to a legendary meeting between Franklin D. Roosevelt and King Saud aboard an American cruiser in the Great Bitter Lake in Egypt. The American president and the Saudi king agreed there on a simple bond of interest: the Saudis, rulers over a sparsely populated but incalculably wealthy land, would see their power guaranteed against all threats, internal and external. In return, the United States could count on a stable supply of oil, developed and pumped by American companies. This policy stood virtually unthreatened for more than three decades.

The eruption of Iran's Islamic revolution in 1978 dealt a blow to this compact of interests and cast in relief its central contradictions. The shah, who owed his throne to a covert CIA intervention that returned him to power in 1953, had been a key American ally in the gulf, and the Islamic revolution that swept him from power showed at work what was to become a familiar dynamic: "friendly" autocrats ruling over increasingly impatient and angry peoples who evidence resentment if not outright hostility toward the superpower ally, in whom they see the ultimate source of their own repression.

Iran's Islamic revolution delivered a body blow to the Middle East status quo not unlike that landed by the French Revolution on the European autocratic order two centuries before; it was ideologically aggressive, inherently expansionist, and deeply threatening to its neighbors—in this case, to the United States' Sunni allies, many of whom had substantial Shia minorities, and to Iraq, which, though long ruled by Sunnis, had a substantial Shia majority. Ayatollah Khomeini's virulent and persistent calls for Saddam Hussein's overthrow, and the turmoil that had apparently weakened the Iranian armed forces, tempted Saddam Hussein to send his army to attack Iran in 1980. American policy makers looked on this with favor, seeing in the bloody Iran-Iraq War the force that would blunt the revolutionary threat to America's allies. Thus President Reagan sent his special envoy Donald Rumsfeld to Baghdad in 1983 to parlay with Hussein, and thus the administration supported the dictator with billions of dollars of agricultural credits, supplied the Iraqis with hundreds of millions of dollars in advanced weaponry through Egypt and Saudi Arabia, and provided Hussein's army with satellite intelligence that may have been used to direct chemical weapons against the massed infantry charges of Iranian suicide brigades.

The Iraqis fought the Iranians to a standstill but not before ripples from Iran's revolution threatened to overwhelm American allies, notably the Saudi dynasty, whose rule was challenged by radicals seizing control of the Grand Mosque in Mecca in November 1979, and the Egyptian autocracy, whose ruler, Anwar el-Sadat, was assassinated by Islamists as he presided over a military parade in October 1981. The Saudis managed to put down the revolt, killing hundreds. The Egyptians, under Hosni Mubarak, moved with ruthless efficiency to suppress the Islamists, jailing and torturing thousands, among them Osama bin Laden's current deputy, Ayman al-Zawahiri. Merciless repression by both autocracies' effective security services led thousands to flee abroad.

Many went to Afghanistan, which the Soviet Red Army occupied in 1979 to prop up its own tottering client, then under threat from Islamic insurgents—mujahedeen, or "holy warriors," who were being armed by the United States. "It was July 3, 1979, that President Carter signed the first directive for secret aid to the opponents of the pro-Soviet regime in Kabul," Zbigniew Brzezinski, Carter's national security adviser, recalled in 1998. "And that very day, I wrote a note to the president in which I explained to him that in my opinion this aid was going to induce a Soviet military intervention." It was a strategy of provocation, for the gambit had the effect of "drawing the Russians into the Afghan trap. . . . The day that the Soviets officially crossed the border, I wrote to President Carter: We now have the opportunity of giving to the U.S.S.R. its Vietnam War."

If, to the Americans, supporting the Afghan mujahedeen seemed an excellent way to bleed the Soviet Union, to the Saudis and other Muslim regimes, supporting a "defensive jihad" to free occupied Muslim lands was a means to burnish their tarnished Islamic credentials while exporting a growing and dangerous resource (frustrated, radical young men) so they would indulge their taste for pious revolution far from home. Among the thousands of holy warriors making this journey was the wealthy young Saudi Osama bin Laden, who would set up the Afghan Services Bureau, a "helping organization" for Arab fighters that gathered names and contact information in a large database—or "qaeda"—which would eventually lend its name to an entirely new organization. Though the Afghan operation was wildly successful, as judged by its American creators—"What is most important to the history of the world?" Brzezinski said in 1998, "some stirred-up Muslims or the liberation of Central Europe and the end of the cold war?"—it had at least one unexpected result: it created a global jihad movement, led by veteran fighters who were convinced that they had defeated one superpower and could defeat another.

The present jihad took shape in the backwash of forgotten wars. After the Soviet Army withdrew in defeat, the United States lost interest in Afghanistan, leaving the mujahedeen forces to battle for the ruined country in an eight-year blood bath from which the Taliban finally emerged victorious. In the gulf, after eight years of fantastically bloody combat, Saddam Hussein forced the Iranians to sign a cease-fire, a "victory" that left his regime heavily armed, bloodied and bankrupt. To pay for his war, Hussein had borrowed tens of billions of dollars from the Saudis, Kuwaitis and other neighbors, and he now demanded that these debts be forgiven—he had incurred them, as he saw it, defending the lenders from Khomeini—and that oil prices be raised. The Kuwaitis' particularly aggressive refusal to do either led Hussein, apparently believing that the Americans would accept a fait accompli, to invade and annex the country.

The Iraqi Army flooding into Kuwait represented, to bin Laden, the classic opportunity. He rushed to see the Saudi leaders, proposing that he defend the kingdom with his battle-tested corps of veteran holy warriors. The Saudis listened patiently to the pious young man—his father, after all, had been one of the kingdom's richest men—but did not take him seriously. Within a week, King Fahd had agreed to the American proposal, carried by Richard Cheney, then the secretary of defense, to station American soldiers—"infidel armies"—in the Land of the Two Holy Places. This momentous decision led to bin Laden's final break with the Saudi dynasty.

The American presence, and the fatal decision to leave American forces stationed in Saudi Arabia as a trip wire or deterrent even after Hussein had been defeated, provided bin Laden with a critical propaganda point, for it gave to his worldview, of a Muslim world under relentless attack, and its central argument, that the "unjust and renegade ruling regimes" of the Islamic world were in fact "enslaved by the United States," a concrete and vivid reality. The "near enemies" and their ruthless security services had proved resistant to direct assault, and the time had come to confront directly the one antagonist able to bring together all the jihadists in a single great battle: the "far enemy" across the sea.

IV.

The deaths of nearly 3,000 people, the thousands left behind to mourn them, the great plume hanging over Lower Manhattan carrying the stench of the vaporized buildings and their buried dead: mass murder of the most abominable, cowardly kind appears to be so at the heart of what happened on this day four years ago that it seems beyond grotesque to remind ourselves that for the attackers those thousands of dead were only a means to an end. Not the least disgusting thing about terrorism is that it makes objects of human beings, makes use of them, exploits their deaths as a means to accomplish something else: to send a message, to force a concession, to advertise a cause. Though such cold instrumentality is not unknown in war—large-scale bombing of civilians, "terror bombing," as it used to be known, does much the same thing—terrorism's ruthless and intimate randomness seems especially appalling.

Terror is a way of talking. Those who employed it so unprecedentedly on 9/11 were seeking not just the large-scale killing of Americans but to achieve something by means of the large-scale killing of Americans. Not just large-scale, it should be added: spectacular.

The asymmetric weapons that the nineteen terrorists used on 9/11 were not only the knives and box cutters they brandished or the fuel-laden airliners they managed to commandeer but, above all, that most American of technological creations: the television set. On 9/11, the jihadists used this weapon with great determination and ruthlessness to attack the most powerful nation in the history of the world at its point of greatest vulnerability: at the level of spectacle. They did it by creating an image, to repeat Peter Jennings's words, "beyond our imagination."

The goal, first and foremost, was to diminish American prestige—showing that the superpower could be bloodied, that for all its power, its defeat was indeed conceivable. All the major attacks preceding 9/11 attributed at least in part to Al Qaeda—the shooting down of U.S. Army helicopters in Mogadishu in 1993, the truck bombing of American military housing at Khobar in 1996, the car bombing of the American embassies in Nairobi and Dar es Salaam in 1998, the suicide bombing of the U.S.S. *Cole* in Aden in 2000—were aimed at the same goal: to destroy the aura of American power. Power, particularly imperial power, rests not on its use but on its credibility; U.S. power in the Middle East depends not on ships and missiles but on the certainty that the United States is invincible and stands behind its friends. The jihadis used terrorism to create a spectacle that would remove this certainty. They were by no means the first guerrilla group to adopt such a strategy. "History and our observation persuaded us," recalled Menachem Begin, the future Israeli prime minister who used terror with great success to drive the British out of Palestine during the mid-1940s, "that if we could succeed in destroying the government's prestige in Eretz Israel, the removal of its rule would follow automatically. Thenceforward, we gave no peace to this weak spot. Throughout all the years of our uprising, we hit at the British government's prestige, deliberately, tirelessly, unceasingly." In its most spectacular act, in July 1946, the Irgun guerrilla forces led by Begin bombed the King David Hotel, killing ninety-one people, most of them civilians.

The 9/11 attacks were a call to persuade Muslims who might share bin Laden's broad view of American power to sympathize with, support, or even join the jihad he had declared against the "far enemy." "Those young men," bin Laden said of the terrorists two months after the attacks, "said in deeds, in New York and Washington, speeches that overshadowed all other speeches made everywhere else in the world. The speeches are understood by both Arabs and non-Arabs—even by Chinese. . . . [I]n Holland, at one of the centers, the number of people who accepted Islam during the days that followed the operations were more than the people who accepted Islam in the last 11 years." To this, a sheik in a wheelchair shown in the videotape replies: "Hundreds of people used to doubt you, and few only would follow you until this huge event happened. Now hundreds of people are coming out to join you." Grotesque as it is to say, the spectacle of 9/11 was meant to serve, among other things, as an enormous recruiting poster.

But recruitment to what? We should return here to the lessons of Afghanistan, not only the obvious one of the defeat of a powerful Soviet Army by guerrilla forces but the more subtle one taught by the Americans, who by clever use of covert aid to the Afghan resistance tempted the Soviets to invade the country and thereby drew "the Russians into an Afghan trap." Bin Laden seems to have hoped to set in motion a similar strategy. According to a text attributed to Saif al-Adel, a former Egyptian Army colonel now generally identified as bin Laden's military chief, "the ultimate objective was to prompt" the United States "to come out of its hole" and take direct military action in an Islamic country. "What we had wished for actually happened. It was crowned by the announcement of Bush Jr. of his crusade against Islam and Muslims everywhere." ("This is a new kind of evil," the president said five days after the attacks, "and we understand . . . this crusade, this war on terrorism, is going to take a while.")

The 9/11 attacks seem to have been intended at least in part to provoke an overwhelming American response: most likely an invasion of Afghanistan, which would lead the United States, like the Soviet Union before it, into an endless, costly and politically fatal quagmire. Thus, two days before the attacks, Qaeda agents posing as television journalists taping an interview murdered Ahmed Shah Massoud, the charismatic leader of the Northern Alliance, with a bomb concealed in a video camera—apparently a preemptive strike intended to throw into confusion the United States' obvious ally in the coming invasion of Afghanistan.

For the jihadists, luring the Americans into Afghanistan would accomplish at least two things: by drawing the United States into a protracted guerrilla war in which the superpower would occupy a Muslim country and kill Muslim civilians—with the world media, including independent Arab networks like Al Jazeera, broadcasting the carnage—it would leave increasingly isolated those autocratic Muslim regimes that depended for their survival on American support. And by forcing the United States to prosecute a long, costly and inconclusive guerrilla war, it would severely test, and ultimately break, American will, leading to a collapse of American prestige and an eventual withdrawal—first, physically, from Afghanistan and then, politically, from the "apostate regimes" in Riyadh, Cairo, and elsewhere in the Islamic world.

In his "Declaration of Jihad" in 1996, bin Laden focused on American political will as the United States' prime vulnerability, the enemy's "center of gravity" that his guerrilla war must target and destroy. "The defense secretary of the crusading Americans had said that 'the explosions at Riyadh and Al-Khobar had taught him one lesson: that is, not to withdraw when attacked by cowardly terrorists.' We say to the defense secretary, Where was this false courage of yours when the explosion in Beirut took place in 1983?

"But your most disgraceful case was in Somalia. . . . When tens of your soldiers were killed in minor battles and one American pilot was dragged in the streets of Mogadishu, you left the area carrying disappointment, humiliation, defeat and your dead with you. . . . The extent of your impotence and weaknesses became very clear."

In Afghanistan, bin Laden would be disappointed. The U.S. military initially sent in no heavy armor but instead restricted the American effort to aerial bombardment in support of several hundred Special Operations soldiers on the ground who helped lead the Northern Alliance forces in a rapid advance. Kabul and other cities quickly fell. America was caught in no Afghan quagmire, or at least not in the sort of protracted, highly televisual bloody mess bin Laden had envisioned. But bin Laden and his senior leadership, holed up in the mountain complex of Tora Bora, managed to survive the bombing and elude the Afghan forces that the Americans commissioned to capture them. During the next months and years, as the United States and its allies did great damage to Al Qaeda's operational cadre, arresting or killing thousands of its veterans, its major leadership symbols survived intact, and those symbols, and their power to lead and to inspire, became Al Qaeda's most important asset.

After Tora Bora, the Qaeda fighters who survived regrouped in neighboring countries. "We began to converge on Iran one after the other," Saif al-Adel recalled in a recent book by an Egyptian journalist. "We began to form some groups of fighters to return to Afghanistan to carry out well-prepared missions there." It is these men, along with the reconstituted Taliban, that 16,000 American soldiers are still fighting today.

Not all the fighters would return to Afghanistan. Other targets of opportunity loomed on the horizon of the possible. "Abu Mus'ab and his Jordanian and Palestinian comrades opted to go to Iraq," al-Adel recalled, for, he said, an "examination of the situation indicated that the Americans would inevitably make a mistake and invade Iraq sooner or later. Such an invasion would aim at overthrowing the regime. Therefore, we should play an important role in the confrontation and resistance."

Abu Mus'ab is Abu Mus'ab al-Zarqawi—or A.M.Z. to the American troops who are pursuing him and his Qaeda in Mesopotamia forces all over the shattered landscape of occupied Iraq. The United States, as Al Qaeda had hoped, had indeed come out of its hole.

V.

It was strangely beautiful, the aftermath of the explosion in Baghdad: two enormous fires, bright orange columns of flame rising perhaps twenty feet into the air, and clearly discernible in the midst of each a cage of glowing metal: what remained of 2 four-wheel-drive vehicles. Before the flames, two bodies lay amid a scattering of glass and sand; the car bomb had toppled the sandbags piled high to protect the building, collapsing the facade and crushing a dozen people. It was October 27, 2003, and I stood before what remained of the Baghdad office of the International Committee of the Red Cross. In the distance, I heard a second huge explosion, saw rising the great plume of oily smoke; within the next forty-five minutes, insurgents attacked four more times, bombing police stations throughout the capital, killing at least thirty-five. Simultaneity and spectacle: Qaeda trademarks. I was gazing at Zarqawi's handiwork.

Behind me, the press had gathered, a jostling crowd of aggressive, mostly young people bristling with lenses short and long, pushing against the line of young American soldiers, who, assault rifles leveled, were screaming at them to stay back. The scores of glittering lenses were a necessary part of the equation, transforming what in military terms would have been a minor engagement into a major defeat.

"There is no war here," an American colonel told me a couple of days before in frustration and disgust. "There's no division-on-division engagements, nothing really resembling a war. Not a real war anyway."

It was not a war the Americans had been trained or equipped to fight. With fewer than 150,000 troops—and many fewer combat soldiers—they were trying to contain a full-blown insurgency in a country the size of California. The elusive enemy—an evolving, loose coalition of a score or so groups, some of them ex-Baathists from Saddam Hussein's dozen or so security agencies, some former Iraqi military personnel, some professional Islamic insurgents like Zarqawi, some foreign volunteers from Saudi Arabia or Kuwait or Syria come to take the jihad to the Americans—attacked not with tanks or artillery or infantry assaults but with roadside bombs and suicide car bombers and kidnappings. Iraq, bin Laden declared, had become a "golden opportunity" to start a "third world war" against "the crusader-Zionist coalition."

Amid the barbed wire and blast walls and bomb debris of postoccupation Iraq, you could discern a clear strategy behind the insurgent violence. The insurgents had identified the Americans' points of vulnerability: their international isolation; their forced distance, as a foreign occupier, from Iraqis; and their increasing disorientation as they struggled to keep their footing on the fragile, shifting, roiling political ground of post-Hussein Iraq. And the insurgents hit at each of these vulnerabilities, as Begin had urged his followers to do, "deliberately, tirelessly, unceasingly."

When, during the summer of 2003, the Bush administration seemed to be reaching out to the United Nations for political help in Iraq, insurgents struck at UN headquarters in Baghdad, killing the talented envoy Sergio Vieira de Mello and twenty-one others and driving the United Nations from the country. When the Americans seemed to be trying to attract Arab forces to come to Iraq to help, the insurgents struck at the Jordanian Embassy, killing seventeen. When the Turks offered to send troops, the insurgents bombed the Turkish Embassy. When nongovernmental organizations seemed the only outsiders still working to ease the situation in Iraq, insurgents struck at the Red Cross, driving it and most other nongovernmental organizations from the country.

Insurgents in Iraq and jihadists abroad struck America's remaining allies. First they hit the Italians, car bombing their base in Nasiriyah in November 2003, killing 28. Then they struck the Spanish, bombing commuter trains in Madrid on March 11, 2004, killing 191. Finally they struck the British, bombing three London Underground trains and a double-decker bus this July, killing 56. It is as if the insurgents, with cold and patient precision, were severing one by one the fragile lines that connected the American effort in Iraq to the rest of the world.

With car bombs and assassinations and commando attacks, insurgents have methodically set out to kill any Iraqi who might think of cooperating with the Americans, widening the crevasse between occupiers and occupied. They have struck at water lines and electricity substations and oil pipelines, interrupting the services that Iraqis depended on, particularly during the unbearably hot summers, keeping electrical service in Baghdad far below what it was under Saddam Hussein—often only a few hours a day this summer—and oil exports 300,000 barrels a day below their prewar peak (helping to double world oil prices). Building on the chaotic unbridled looting of the first weeks of American rule, the insurgents have worked to destroy any notion of security and to make clear that the landscape of apocalyptic destruction that is Baghdad, with its omnipresent concrete blast walls and rolls of concertina wire and explosions and gunshots, should be laid at the feet of the American occupier, that unseen foreign power that purports to rule the country from behind concrete blast walls in the so-called Green Zone but dares to venture out only in tanks and armored cars.

"With . . . officials attempting to administrate from behind masses of barbed wire, in heavily defended buildings, and . . . living in pathetic seclusion in 'security zones,' one cannot escape the conclusion that the government . . . is a hunted organization with little hope of ever being able to cope with conditions in this country as they exist today." However vividly these words fit contemporary Baghdad, they are in fact drawn from the report of the American consul general in Jerusalem in 1947, describing what Begin's guerrilla forces achieved in their war against the British. "The very existence of an underground," as Begin remarked in his memoirs, "must, in the end, undermine the prestige of a colonial regime that lives by the legend of its omnipotence. Every attack which it fails to prevent is a blow to its standing."

In Iraq, the insurgents have presided over a catastrophic collapse in confidence in the Americans and a concomitant fall in their power. It is difficult to think of a place in which terror has been deployed on such a scale: there have been suicide truck bombs, suicide tanker bombs, suicide police cars, suicide bombers on foot, suicide bombers posing as police officers, suicide bombers posing as soldiers, even suicide bombers on bicycles. While the American death toll climbs steadily toward 2,000, the number of Iraqi dead probably stands at ten times that and perhaps many more; no one knows. Conservative unofficial counts put the number of Iraqi dead in the war at somewhere between 25,000 and 30,000, in a country a tenth the size of the United States.

Civil wars, of course, are especially bloody, and a civil war is now being fought in Iraq. The country is slowly splitting apart along the lines where French and British negotiators stitched it together early in the last century out of three Ottoman provinces—Mosul, Baghdad, and Basra—and it is doing so with the enthusiastic help of the Islamists, who are doing all they can to provoke a Shia-Sunni regionwide war.

The Kurds in the north, possessed of their own army and legislature, want to secure what they believe are their historic rights to the disputed city of Kirkuk, including its oil fields, and be quit of Iraq. The Shia in the south, now largely ruled by Islamic party militias trained by the Iranians and coming under the increasingly strict sway of the clerics on social matters, are evolving their oil-rich ministate into a paler version of the Islamic republic next door. And in the center, the Baathist elite of Saddam Hussein's security services and army—tens of thousands of well-armed professional intelligence operatives and soldiers—have formed an alliance of convenience with Sunni Islamists, domestic and foreign, in order to assert their rights in a unitary Iraq. They are in effective control of many cities and towns, and they have the burdensome and humiliating presence of the foreign occupier to thank for the continuing success of their recruitment efforts. In a letter to bin Laden that was intercepted by American forces in January 2004, Zarqawi asked: "When the Americans disappear . . . what will become of our situation?"

As Zarqawi described in his letter and in subsequent broadcasts, his strategy in Iraq is to strike at the Shia—and thereby provoke a civil war. "A nation of heretics," the Shia "are the key element of change," he wrote. "If we manage to draw them onto the terrain of partisan war, it will be possible to tear the Sunnis away from their heedlessness, for they will feel the weight of the imminence of danger." Again a strategy of provocation—which plays on an underlying reality: that Iraq sits on the critical sectarian fault line of the Middle East and that a conflict there gains powerful momentum from the involvement of neighboring states, with Iran strongly supporting the Shia and with Saudi Arabia, Kuwait, Jordan, and Syria strongly sympathetic to the Sunnis. More and more, you can discern this outline in the chaos of the current war, with the Iranian-trained militias of the Shia Islamist parties that now control the Iraqi government battling Sunni Islamists, both Iraqi and foreign born, and former Baathists.

In the midst of it all, increasingly irrelevant, are the Americans, who have the fanciest weapons but have never had sufficient troops, or political will, to assert effective control over the country. If political authority comes from achieving a monopoly on legitimate violence, then the Americans, from those early days when they sat in their tanks and watched over the wholesale looting of public institutions, never did achieve political authority in Iraq. They fussed over liberalizing the economy and writing constitutions and achieving democracy in the Middle East when in fact there was really only one question in Iraq, emerging again and again in each successive political struggle, most recently in the disastrously managed writing of the constitution: how to shape a new political dispensation in which the age-old majority Shia can take control from the minority Sunni and do it in a way that minimized violence and insecurity—do it in a way, that is, that the Sunnis would be willing to accept, however reluctantly, without resorting to armed resistance. This might have been accomplished with hundreds of thousands of troops, iron control, and a clear sense of purpose. The Americans had none of these. Instead they relied first on a policy of faith and then on one of improvisation, driven in part by the advice of Iraqi exile "friends" who used the Americans for their own purposes. Some of the most strikingly ideological decisions, like abruptly firing and humiliating the entire Iraqi Army and purging from their jobs many hundreds of thousands of Baath Party members, seemed designed to alienate and antagonize a Sunni population already terrified of its security in the new Iraq. "You Americans," one Sunni businessman said to me in Baghdad last February, shaking his head in wonder, "you have created your own enemies here."

The United States never used what authority it had to do more than pretend to control the gathering chaos, never managed to look clearly at the country and confront Iraq's underlying political dysfunction, of which the tyranny of Saddam Hussein was the product, not the cause. "The illusionists," Ambassador John Negroponte's people called their predecessors, the officials of the Coalition Provisional Authority under L. Paul Bremer III. Now, day by day, the illusion is slipping away, and with it what authority the Americans had in Iraq. What is coming to take its place looks increasingly like a failed state.

VI.

It is an oft-heard witticism in Washington that the Iraq War is over and that the Iranians won. And yet the irony seems misplaced. A truly democratic Iraq was always likely to be an Iraq led not only by Shia, who are the majority of Iraqis, but by those Shia parties that are the largest and best organized— the Supreme Council for the Islamic Revolution in Iraq and the Dawa Islamic Party—which happen to be those blessed by the religious authorities and nurtured in Iran. Nor would it be a surprise if a democratic Saudi Arabia turned out to be a fundamentalist Saudi Arabia and one much less friendly to the United States. Osama bin Laden knows this, and so do American officials. This is why the United States is "friendly" with "apostate regimes." Democratic outcomes do not always ensure friendly governments. Often the contrary is true. On this simple fact depends much of the history of American policy not only in the Middle East but also in Latin America and other parts of the world throughout the Cold War. Bush administration officials, for all their ideological fervor, did the country no favor by ignoring it.

In launching his new cold war, George W. Bush chose a peculiarly ideological version of Cold War history. He opted not for containment, the cautious, status quo grand strategy usually attributed to the late George F. Kennan, but for rollback. Containment, by which the United States determinedly resisted Soviet attempts to expand its influence, would have meant a patient, methodical search for terrorists, discriminating between those groups that threaten the United States and those that do not, pursuing the former with determined, practical policies that would have drawn much from the military and law-enforcement cooperation of our allies and that would have included an effective program of nonproliferation to keep weapons of mass destruction out of terrorist hands. Rollback, on the other hand, meant something quite different; those advocating it during the 1950s considered containment immoral, for it recognized the status quo: Communist hegemony in Eastern Europe and parts of Asia. They wanted instead to destroy Communism entirely by "rolling back" Communists from territory they had gained, as General Douglas MacArthur did briefly and, it turned out, catastrophically, in North Korea, and as President Eisenhower refused to do when he declined to support the Hungarian revolutionaries against the Soviet invasion in 1956.

The original advocates of rollback lost that struggle. In this new cold war, the rollback advocates triumphed and adopted as the heart of their policy a high-stakes, metaphysical gamble to "democratize the Middle East" and thus put an end, once and for all, to terrorism. They relied on a "domino theory" in which the successful implantation of democracy in Iraq would lead to a "democratic revolution" across the region. The ambition of this idea is breathtaking; it depends on a conception of American power as virtually limitless and on an entirely fanciful vision of Iraqi politics, a kind of dogged political wish-fulfillment that no sober analysis could penetrate. Replacing any real willingness to consider whether a clear course existed between here and there, between an invasion and occupation of Iraq and a democratic Middle East, was, at bottom, the simple conviction that since the United States enjoyed a "preponderance of power" unseen in the world since the Roman Empire, and since its cause of democratic revolution was so incontrovertibly just, defeat was inconceivable. One detects here an echo of Vietnam: the inability to imagine that the all-powerful United States might lose.

American power, however, is not limitless. Armies can destroy and occupy, but it takes much more to build a lasting order, especially on the shifting sands of a violent political struggle: another Vietnam echo.

Learning the lesson this time around may prove more costly, for dominoes can fall both ways. "Political engineering on this scale could easily go awry," Stephen D. Biddle, a U.S. Army War College analyst, wrote this past April in a shrewd analysis. "If a democratic Iraq can catalyze reform elsewhere, so a failed Iraq could presumably export chaos to its neighbors. A regionwide Lebanon might well prove beyond our capacity to police, regardless of effort expended. And if so, then we will have replaced a region of police states with a region of warlords and chronic instability. This could easily prove to be an easier operating environment for terrorism than the police states it replaces."

The sun is setting on American dreams in Iraq; what remains now to be worked out are the modalities of withdrawal, which depend on the powers of forbearance in the American body politic. But the dynamic has already been set in place. The United States is running out of troops. By the spring of 2006, nearly every active-duty combat unit is likely to have been deployed twice. The National Guard and Reserves, meanwhile, make up an unprecedented 40 percent of the force, and the Guard is in the "stage of meltdown," as General Barry McCaffrey, retired, recently told Congress. Within twenty-four months, "the wheels are coming off." For all the apocalyptic importance President Bush and his administration ascribed to the Iraq War, they made virtually no move to expand the military, no decision to restore the draft. In the end, the president judged his tax cuts more important than his vision of a "democratic Middle East." The administration's relentless political style, integral to both its strength and its weakness, left it wholly unable to change course and to add more troops when they might have made a difference. That moment is long past; the widespread unpopularity of the occupation in Iraq and in the Islamic world is now critical to insurgent recruitment and makes it possible for a growing insurgent force numbering in the tens of thousands to conceal itself within the broader population.

Sold a war made urgent by the imminent threat of weapons of mass destruction in the hands of a dangerous dictator, Americans now see their sons and daughters fighting and dying in a war whose rationale has been lost even as its ending has receded into the indefinite future. A war promised to bring forth the Iraqi people bearing flowers and sweets in exchange for the beneficent gift of democracy has brought instead a kind of relentless terror that seems inexplicable and unending. A war that had a clear purpose and a certain end has now lost its reason and its finish. Americans find themselves fighting and dying in a kind of existential desert of the present. For Americans, the war has lost its narrative.

Of the many reasons that American leaders chose to invade and occupy Iraq—to democratize the Middle East; to remove an unpredictable dictator from a region vital to America's oil supply; to remove a threat from Israel, America's ally; to restore the prestige sullied on 9/11 with a tank-led procession of triumph down the avenues of a conquered capital; to seize the chance to overthrow a regime capable of building an arsenal of chemical and biological weapons—of all of these, it is remarkable that the Bush administration chose to persuade Americans and the world by offering the one reason that could be proved to be false. The failure to find the weapons of mass destruction, and the collapse of the rationale for the war, left terribly exposed precisely what bin Laden had targeted as the critical American vulnerability: the will to fight.

How that collapse, reflected in poll numbers, will be translated into policy is a more complicated question. One of 9/11's more obvious consequences was to restore to the Republicans the advantage in national security they surrendered with the Cold War's end; their ruthless exploitation of this advantage and the Democrats' compromising embrace of the Iraq War has in effect left the country, on this issue, without an opposition party. Republicans, who fear to face the voters shackled to a leader whose approval ratings have slid into the low forties, are the ones demanding answers on the war. The falling poll numbers, the approaching midterm elections, and the desperate manpower straits of the military have set in motion a dynamic that could see gradual American withdrawals beginning in 2006, as General George W. Casey Jr., the commander in Iraq, acknowledged publicly in July. Unless Iraq's political process, which has turned another downward spiral with Sunni negotiators' rejection of the constitution, can somehow be retrieved, American power in Iraq will go on deteriorating.

Two and a half years into the invasion, for U.S. policy in Iraq, the time of "the illusionists" has finally passed. Since the January elections, which Sunnis largely boycotted, American officials have worked hard to persuade Sunni leaders to take part in the constitutional referendum and elections, hoping thereby to isolate the Baathist and Islamist extremists and drain strength from the insurgency. This effort comes very late, however, when Iraqi politics, and the forces pulling the country apart, have taken on a momentum that waning American power no longer seems able to stop. Even as the constitutional drama came to a climax last month, the president telephoned Abdul Aziz Hakim, the Shia cleric who leads the Sciri Party, appealing for concessions that might have tempted the Sunnis to agree to the draft; the Shia politician, faced with the American president's personal plea, did not hesitate to turn him down flat. Perhaps the best hope now for a gradual American withdrawal that would not worsen the war is to negotiate a regional solution, which might seek an end to Sunni infiltration from U.S. allies in exchange for Shia guarantees of the Sunni position in Iraq and a phased American departure.

For all the newfound realism in the second-term administration's foreign policy, in which we have seen a willingness finally to negotiate seriously with North Korea and Iran, the president seems nowhere close to considering such an idea in Iraq, insisting that there the choice is simple: the United States can either "stay the course" or "cut and run." "An immediate withdrawal of our troops in Iraq, or the broader Middle East, as some have called for," the president declared last month, "would only embolden the terrorists and create a staging ground to launch more attacks against America and free nations." These words, familiar and tired, offering no solution beyond staying a course that seems to be leading nowhere, have ceased to move Americans weary of the rhetoric of terror. That does not mean, however, that they may not be entirely true.

VII.

We cannot know what future Osama bin Laden imagined when he sent off his nineteen suicide terrorists on their mission four years ago. He got much wrong; the U.S. military, light years ahead of the Red Army, would send no tank divisions to Afghanistan, and there has been no uprising in the Islamic world. One suspects, though, that if bin Laden had been told on that day that in a mere forty-eight months he would behold a world in which the United States, "the idol of the age," was bogged down in an endless guerrilla war fighting in a major Muslim country; a world in which its all-powerful army, with few allies and little sympathy, found itself overstretched and exhausted; in which its dispirited people were starting to demand from their increasingly unpopular leader a withdrawal without victory—one suspects that such a prophecy would have pleased him. He had struck at the American will, and his strategy, which relied in effect on the persistent reluctance of American leaders to speak frankly to their people about the costs and burdens of war and to expend the political capital that such frank talk would require, had proved largely correct.

He has suffered damage as well. Many of his closest collaborators have been killed or captured, his training camps destroyed, his sanctuary occupied. "What Al Qaeda has lost," a senior Defense Department official said five months after the attacks, "again, it's lost its center of gravity. . . . The benefits of Afghanistan cannot be overestimated. Again, it was the one state sponsor they had." This analysis seems now a vision of the past. Al Qaeda was always a flexible, ghostly organization, a complex worldwide network made up of shifting alliances and marriages of convenience with other shadowy groups. Now Al Qaeda's "center of gravity," such as it is, has gone elsewhere.

In December 2003, a remarkable document, "Jihadi Iraq: Hopes and Dangers," appeared on the Internet, setting out a fascinating vision of how to isolate the United States and pick off its allies one by one. The truly ripe fruit, concludes the author, is Spain: "In order to force the Spanish government to withdraw from Iraq the resistance should deal painful blows to its forces . . . [and] make utmost use of the upcoming general election. . . . We think that the Spanish government could not tolerate more than two, maximum three blows, after which it will have to withdraw."

Three months later, on March 11, 2004—3/11, as it has come to be known—a cell of North African terrorists struck at the Atocha Train Station in Madrid. One hundred ninety-one people died—a horrific toll but nowhere near what it could have been had all of the bombs actually detonated, simultaneously, and in the station itself. Had the terrorists succeeded in bringing the roof of the station down, the casualties could have surpassed those of 9/11.

In the event, they were quite sufficient to lead to the defeat of the Spanish government and the decision of its successor to withdraw its troops from Iraq. What seems most notable about the Madrid attack, however—and the attack on Jewish and foreign sites in Casablanca on May 17, 2003, among others—is that the perpetrators were "home-grown" and not, strictly speaking, Al Qaeda. "After 2001, when the U.S. destroyed the camps and housing and turned off the funding, bin Laden was left with little control," Marc Sageman, a psychiatrist and former CIA case officer who has studied the structure of the network, has written. "The movement has now degenerated into something like the Internet. Spontaneous groups of friends, as in Madrid and Casablanca, who have few links to any central leadership, are generating sometimes very dangerous terrorist operations, notwithstanding their frequent errors and poor training."

Under this view, Al Qaeda, in the form we knew it, has been subsumed into the broader, more diffuse political world of radical Salafi politics. "The network is now self-organized from the bottom up and is very decentralized," Sageman wrote. "With local initiative and flexibility, it's very robust."

We have entered the era of the amateurs. Those who attacked the London Underground—whether or not they had any contact with Al Qaeda—manufactured their crude bombs from common chemicals (including hydrogen peroxide, bleach, and drain cleaner), making them in plastic food containers, toting them to Luton Station in coolers, and detonating them with cell phone alarms. One click on the Internet and you can pull up a Web site offering a recipe—or, for that matter, one showing you how to make a suicide vest from commonly found items, including a video download demonstrating how to use the device: "There is a possibility that the two seats on his right and his left might not be hit with the shrapnel," the unseen narrator tells the viewer. Not to worry, however: "The explosion will surely kill the passengers in those seats."

During the four years since the attacks of 9/11, while terrorism worldwide has flourished, we have seen no second attack on the United States. This may be owed to the damage done Al Qaeda. Or perhaps planning and preparation for such an attack is going on now. When it comes to the United States itself, the terrorists have their own "second-novel problem"— how do you top the first production? More likely, though, the next attack, when it comes, will originate not in the minds of veteran Qaeda planners but from this new wave of amateurs: viral Al Qaeda, political sympathizers who nourish themselves on Salafi rhetoric and bin Laden speeches and draw what training they require from their computer screens. Very little investment and preparation can bring huge rewards. The possibilities are endless, and terrifyingly simple: rucksacks containing crude homemade bombs placed in McDonald's—one, say, in Times Square and one on Wilshire Boulevard, 3,000 miles away, exploded simultaneously by cell phone. The effort is small, the potential impact overwhelming.

Attacks staged by amateurs with little or no connection to terrorist networks, and thus no visible trail to follow, are nearly impossible to prevent, even for the United States, with all of its power. Indeed, perhaps what is most astonishing about these hard four years is that we have managed to show the world the limits of our power. In launching a war on Iraq that we have been unable to win, we have done the one thing a leader is supposed never to do: issue a command that is not followed. A withdrawal from Iraq, rapid or slow, with the Islamists still holding the field, will signal, as bin Laden anticipated, a failure of American will. Those who will view such a withdrawal as the critical first step in a broader retreat from the Middle East will surely be encouraged to go on the attack. That is, after all, what you do when your enemy retreats. In this new world, where what is necessary to go on the attack is not armies or training or even technology but desire and political will, we have ensured, by the way we have fought this forever war, that it is precisely these qualities our enemies have in large and growing supply.

Big Brother Is Listening
James Bamford

The Atlantic Monthly | April 2006

What a difference thirty years makes! In 1975, when it was revealed that the National Security Agency (NSA), the U.S. government's electronic-surveillance arm, had been intercepting the international communications of American citizens without a court warrant for decades, the resulting uproar led to the passage of the 1978 Foreign Intelligence Surveillance Act (FISA), requiring all such surveillance to be approved by a special court. (In cases where swift action was required, authorities could go to the court after the fact for approval.)

In mid-December 2005, the New York Times *reported that the Bush administration had basically been ignoring the FISA requirements since the attacks of September 11, 2001, after which President Bush signed an executive order allowing the monitoring of Americans' international phone calls and e-mails without a court order. Then in May 2006, in a scoop of its own,* USA Today *reported that over the past several years the NSA has been amassing records of all domestic and international phone calls handled by AT&T, Verizon, and Bell South.*

Congress's initial outrage to both revelations was quickly muted, as the Bush administration staunchly defended both the legality of the surveillance effort and its importance in helping to track Al Qaeda and other terrorist groups. In late May, the Senate easily confirmed General Michael Hayden, who had overseen the warrantless wiretapping program at the NSA, to replace Porter Goss as director of the CIA.

One major reason that congressional fury was so short-lived: Opinion polls revealed that most Americans didn't particularly mind having their phone and e-mail records monitored, if that's what it took to keep the nation safe. This public indifference may be due in part to a widespread sense that electronic privacy is already nonexistent. In this Atlantic Monthly article, James Bamford explores the astonishingly well-developed ability of the U.S. government to listen on our daily communications—often with virtually no judicial oversight whatsoever.

On the first Saturday in April 2002, the temperature in Washington, D.C., had taken a dive. Tourists were bundled up against the cold, and the cherry trees along the Tidal Basin were fast losing their blossoms to the biting winds. But a few miles to the south, in the Dowden Terrace neighborhood of Alexandria, Virginia, the chilly weather was not deterring Royce C. Lamberth, a bald and burly Texan, from mowing his lawn. He stopped only when four cars filled with FBI agents suddenly pulled up in front of his house. The agents were there not to arrest him but to request an emergency court hearing to obtain seven top-secret warrants to eavesdrop on Americans.

As the presiding justice of the Foreign Intelligence Surveillance Court, known as the FISA court, Lamberth had become accustomed to holding the secret hearings in his living room. "My wife, Janis . . . has to go upstairs because she doesn't have a top-secret clearance," he noted in a speech to a group of Texas lawyers. "My beloved cocker spaniel, Taffy, however, remains at my side on the assumption that the surveillance targets cannot make her talk. The FBI knows Taffy well. They frequently play with her while I read some of those voluminous tomes at home." FBI agents will even knock on the judge's door in the middle of the night. "On the night of the bombings of the U.S. embassies in Africa, I started the first emergency hearings in my living room at 3:00 A.M.," recalled Lamberth. "From the outset, the FBI suspected bin Laden, and the surveillances I approved that night and in the ensuing days and weeks all ended up being critical evidence at the trial in New York.

"The FISA court is probably the least-known court in Washington," added Lamberth, who stepped down from it in 2002, at the end of his seven-year term, "but it has become one of the most important." Conceived in the aftermath of Watergate, the FISA court traces its origins to the mid-1970s, when the Senate's Church Committee investigated the intelligence community and the Nixon White House. The panel, chaired by Idaho Democrat Frank Church, exposed a long pattern of abuse, and its work led to bipartisan legislation aimed at preventing a president from unilaterally directing the National Security Agency or the FBI to spy on American citizens. This legislation, the 1978 Foreign Intelligence Surveillance Act, established the FISA court—made up of eleven judges handpicked by the chief justice of the United States—as a secret part of the federal judiciary. The court's job is to decide whether to grant warrants requested by the NSA or the FBI to monitor communications of American citizens and legal residents. The law allows the government up to three days after it starts eavesdropping to ask for a warrant; every violation of FISA carries a penalty of up to five years in prison. Between May 18, 1979, when the court opened for business, until the end of 2004, it granted 18,742 NSA and FBI applications; it turned down only four outright.

Such facts worry Jonathan Turley, a George Washington University law professor who worked for the NSA as an intern while in law school in the 1980s. The FISA "courtroom," hidden away on the top floor of the Justice Department building (because even its location is supposed to be secret), is actually a heavily protected, windowless, bug-proof installation known as a Sensitive Compartmented Information Facility, or SCIF. "When I first went into the FISA court as a lowly intern at the NSA, frankly, it started a lifetime of opposition for me to that court," Turley recently told a group of House Democrats looking into the NSA's domestic spying. "I was shocked with what I saw. I was convinced that the judge in that SCIF would have signed anything that we put in front of him. And I wasn't entirely sure that he had actually *read* what we put in front of him. But I remember going back to my supervisor at NSA and saying, 'That place scares the daylights out of me.'"

Lamberth bristles at any suggestion that his court routinely did the administration's bidding. "Those who know me know the chief justice did not put me on this court because I would be a rubber stamp for whatever the executive branch was wanting to do," he said in his speech. "I ask questions. I get into the nitty-gritty. I know exactly what is going to be done and why. And my questions are answered, in every case, before I approve an application."

It is true that the court has been getting tougher. From 1979 through 2000, it modified only two out of 13,087 warrant requests. But from the start of the Bush administration, in 2001, the number of modifications increased to 179 out of 5,645 requests. Most of those—173—involved what the court terms "substantive modifications."

This friction—and especially the requirement that the government show "probable cause" that the American whose communications they are seeking to target is connected in some way to a terrorist group—induced the administration to begin circumventing the court. Concerned about preventing future 9/11-style attacks, President Bush secretly decided in the fall of 2001 that the NSA would no longer be bound by FISA. Although Judge Lamberth was informed of the president's decision, he was ordered to tell no one about it—not even his clerks or his fellow FISA-court judges.

Why the NSA Might Be Listening to *YOU*

Contrary to popular perception, the NSA does not engage in "wiretapping"; it collects signals intelligence, or "sigint." In contrast to the image we have from movies and television of an FBI agent placing a listening device on a target's phone line, the NSA intercepts entire streams of electronic communications containing millions of telephone calls and e-mails. It runs the intercepts through very powerful computers that screen them for particular names, telephone numbers, Internet addresses, and trigger words or phrases. Any communications containing flagged information are forwarded by the computer for further analysis.

The NSA's task is to listen in on the world outside American shores. During the Cold War, the principal targets were the communications lines used by the Soviet government and military—navy captains calling their ports, fighter pilots getting landing instructions, army commanders out on maneuvers, and diplomats relaying messages to the Kremlin. But now the enemy is one that communicates very little and, when it does, uses the same telecommunications network as everyone else: a complex system of wires, radio signals, and light pulses encircling and crisscrossing the globe like yarn. Picking up just the right thread, and tracing it through the maze of strands, is difficult. Sometimes a thread leads back inside the United States. An internal agency report predicted a few years ago that the NSA's worldwide sigint operation would demand a "powerful and permanent presence" on the global telecommunications networks that carry "protected American communications." The prediction has come true, and the NSA now monitors not only purely "foreign" communications but also "international" ones, where one end of the conversation might be in the United States. As a result, the issue at hand since the revelation last December of the NSA's warrantless spying on American citizens is not the agency's access to the country's communications network—it already has access—but whether the NSA must take legal steps in preparing to target the communications of an American citizen.

It used to be that before the NSA could place the name of an American on its watch list, it had to go before a FISA-court judge and show that it had probable cause—that the facts and circumstances were such that a prudent person would think the individual was somehow connected to terrorism—in order to get a warrant. But under the new procedures put into effect by Bush's 2001 order, warrants do not always have to be obtained, and the critical decision about whether to put an American on a watch list is left to the vague and subjective "reasonable belief" of an NSA shift supervisor. In charge of hundreds of people, the supervisor manages a wide range of sigint specialists, including signals-conversion analysts separating HBO television programs from cell phone calls, traffic analysts sifting through massive telephone data streams looking for suspicious patterns, cryptanalysts attempting to read e-mail obscured by complex encryption algorithms, voice-language analysts translating the gist of a phone call from Dari into English, and cryptolinguists trying to unscramble a call on a secure telephone. Bypassing the FISA court has meant that the number of Americans targeted by the NSA has increased since 2001 from perhaps a dozen per year to as many as 5,000 over the last four years, knowledgeable sources told *The Washington Post* in February. If telephone records indicate that one of the NSA's targets regularly dials a given telephone number, that number and any names associated with it are added to the watch lists and the communications on that line are screened by computer. Names and information on the watch lists are shared with the FBI, the CIA, the Department of Homeland Security, and foreign intelligence services. Once a person's name is in the files, even if nothing incriminating ever turns up, it will likely remain there forever. There is no way to request removal, because there is no way to confirm that a name is on the list.

In December 1997, in a small factory outside the southern French city of Toulouse, a salesman got caught in the NSA's electronic web. Agents working for the NSA's British partner, the Government Communications Headquarters, learned of a letter of credit, valued at more than $1.1 million, issued by Iran's defense ministry to the French company Microturbo. According to NSA documents, both the NSA and the GCHQ concluded that Iran was attempting to secretly buy from Microturbo an engine for the embargoed C-802 antiship missile. Faxes zapping back and forth between Toulouse and Tehran were intercepted by the GCHQ, which sent them on not just to the NSA but also to the Canadian and Australian sigint agencies, as well as to Britain's MI6. The NSA then sent the reports on the salesman making the Iranian deal to a number of CIA stations around the world, including those in Paris and Bonn, and to the U.S. Commerce Department and the Customs Service. Probably several hundred people in at least four countries were reading the company's communications. The question, however, remained: Was Microturbo shipping a missile engine to Iran? In the end, at the insistence of the U.S. government, the French conducted a surprise inspection just before the ship carrying the mysterious crate was set to sail for Iran. Inside were legal generators, not illegal missile engines.

Such events are central to the current debate involving the potential harm caused by the NSA's warrantless domestic eavesdropping operation. Even though the salesman did nothing wrong, his name made its way into the computers and onto the watch lists of intelligence, customs, and other secret and law-enforcement organizations around the world. Maybe nothing will come of it. Maybe the next time he tries to enter the United States or Britain he will be denied, without explanation. Maybe he will be arrested. As the domestic eavesdropping program continues to grow, such uncertainties may plague innocent Americans whose names are being run through the supercomputers even though the NSA has not met the established legal standard for a search warrant. It is only when such citizens are turned down while applying for a job with the federal government—or refused when seeking a Small Business Administration loan, or turned back by British customs agents when flying to London on vacation, or even placed on a "no-fly" list—that they will realize that something is very wrong. But they will never learn why.

More than seventy-five years ago, Supreme Court Justice Louis Brandeis envisioned a day when technology would overtake the law. He wrote:

Subtler and more far-reaching means of invading privacy have become available
to the government. . . . The progress of science in furnishing the government with
means of espionage is not likely to stop with wiretapping. Ways may some day be
developed by which the Government, without removing papers from secret
drawers, can reproduce them in court, and by which it will be enabled to expose
to a jury the most intimate occurrences of the home. . . . Can it be that the Constitution affords no protection against such invasions of individual security?

Brandeis went on to answer his own question, quoting from an earlier
Supreme Court decision, *Boyd v. U.S.* (1886): "It is not the breaking of his
doors, and the rummaging of his drawers that constitutes the essence of
the offence; but it is the invasion of his indefeasible right of personal security, personal liberty, and private property."

Eavesdropping in the Digital Age

Today, the NSA's capability to eavesdrop is far beyond anything ever
dreamed of by Justice Brandeis. With the digital revolution came an explosion in eavesdropping technology; the NSA today has the ability to scan
tens of millions of electronic communications—e-mails, faxes, instant messages, Web searches, and phone calls—every hour. General Michael
Hayden, director of the NSA from 1999 to 2005 and now principal deputy
director of national intelligence, noted in 2002 that during the 1990s, e-
communications "surpassed traditional communications. That is the same
decade when mobile cell phones increased from 16 million to 741 million—an increase of nearly 50 times. That is the same decade when
Internet users went from about 4 million to 361 million—an increase of
over 90 times. Half as many land lines were laid in the last six years of the
1990s as in the whole previous history of the world. In that same decade of
the 1990s, international telephone traffic went from 38 billion minutes to
over 100 billion. This year, the world's population will spend over 180 billion minutes on the phone in international calls alone."

Intercepting communications carried by satellite is fairly simple for the
NSA. The key conduits are the thirty Intelsat satellites that ring the Earth,
22,300 miles above the equator. Many communications from Europe, Africa,
and the Middle East to the eastern half of the United States, for example,
are first uplinked to an Intelsat satellite and then downlinked to AT&T's
ground station in Etam, West Virginia. From there, phone calls, e-mails,

and other communications travel on to various parts of the country. To listen in on that rich stream of information, the NSA built a listening post fifty miles away, near Sugar Grove, West Virginia. Consisting of a group of very large parabolic dishes, hidden in a heavily forested valley and surrounded by tall hills, the post can easily intercept the millions of calls and messages flowing every hour into the Etam station. On the West Coast, high on the edge of a bluff overlooking the Okanogan River, near Brewster, Washington, is the major commercial downlink for communications to and from Asia and the Pacific. Consisting of forty parabolic dishes, it is reportedly the largest satellite antenna farm in the Western Hemisphere. A hundred miles to the south, collecting every whisper, is the NSA's western listening post, hidden away on a 324,000-acre Army base in Yakima, Washington. The NSA posts collect the international traffic beamed down from the Intelsat satellites over the Atlantic and Pacific. But each also has a number of dishes that appear to be directed at domestic telecommunications satellites.

Until recently, most international telecommunications flowing into and out of the United States traveled by satellite. But faster, more reliable undersea fiber-optic cables have taken the lead, and the NSA has adapted. The agency taps into the cables that don't reach our shores by using specially designed submarines, such as the USS *Jimmy Carter*, to attach a complex "bug" to the cable itself. This is difficult, however, and undersea taps are short-lived because the batteries last only a limited time. The fiber-optic transmission cables that enter the United States from Europe and Asia can be tapped more easily at the landing stations where they come ashore. With the acquiescence of the telecommunications companies, it is possible for the NSA to attach monitoring equipment inside the landing station and then run a buried encrypted fiber-optic "backhaul" line to NSA headquarters at Fort Meade, Maryland, where the river of data can be analyzed by supercomputers in near real time.

Tapping into the fiber-optic network that carries the nation's Internet communications is even easier, as much of the information transits through just a few "switches" (similar to the satellite downlinks). Among the busiest are MAE East (Metropolitan Area Ethernet), in Vienna, Virginia, and MAE West, in San Jose, California, both owned by Verizon. By accessing the switch, the NSA can see who's e-mailing with whom over the

Internet cables and can copy entire messages. Last September, the Federal Communications Commission further opened the door for the agency. The 1994 Communications Assistance for Law Enforcement Act required telephone companies to rewire their networks to provide the government with secret access. The FCC has now extended the act to cover "any type of broadband Internet access service" and the new Internet phone services— and ordered company officials never to discuss any aspect of the program.

The NSA won't divulge how many people it employs, but it is likely that more than 38,000 worldwide now work for the agency. Most of them are at Fort Meade. Nicknamed Crypto City, hidden from public view, and located halfway between Washington and Baltimore, the NSA's own company town comprises more than fifty buildings—offices, warehouses, factories, laboratories, and a few barracks. Tens of thousands of people work there in absolute secrecy, and most never tell their spouses exactly what they do. Crypto City also houses the nation's largest collection of powerful computers, advanced mathematicians, and skilled language experts.

The NSA maintains a very close and very confidential relationship with key executives in the telecommunications industry through their membership on the NSA's advisory board. Created shortly after the agency's formation, the board was intended to pull together a panel of science wizards from universities, corporate research labs, and think tanks to advise the agency. They keep the agency abreast of the industry's plans and give NSA engineers a critical head start in finding ways to penetrate technologies still in the development phase.

One of the NSA's strategies is to hire people away from the companies that make the critical components for telecommunications systems. Although it's sometimes difficult for the agency to keep up with the tech sector's pay scale, for many people the chance to deal with the ultimate in cutting-edge technology and aid national security makes working for the NSA irresistible. With the help of such workers, the agency reverse-engineers communication system components. For example, among the most crucial pieces of the Internet infrastructure are routers made by Cisco. "Virtually all Internet traffic," says one of the company's television ads, "travels across the systems of one company: Cisco Systems." For the NSA, this is an opportunity. In 1999, Terry Thompson, then the NSA deputy director for services, said, "[Y]ou can see down the road two or three or five years and say, 'Well, I only need this person to do reverse-engineering on Cisco routers (that's a good example) for about three or five years, because I see Cisco going away as a key manufacturer for routers and so I don't need that expertise. But I really need somebody today and for the next couple of years who knows Cisco routers inside and out and can help me understand how they're being used in target networks.'"

The Temptations of Secrecy

The National Security Agency was born in absolute secrecy. Unlike the CIA, which was created publicly by a congressional act, the NSA was brought to life by a top-secret memorandum signed by President Truman in 1952, consolidating the country's various military sigint operations into a single agency. Even its name was secret, and only a few members of Congress were informed of its existence—and they received no information about some of its most important activities. Such secrecy has lent itself to abuse.

During the Vietnam War, for instance, the agency was heavily involved in spying on the domestic opposition to the government. Many of the Americans on the watch lists of that era were there solely for having protested against the war. Among the names in the NSA's supercomputers were those of the folk singer Joan Baez, the pediatrician Benjamin Spock, the actress Jane Fonda, the civil-rights leader Martin Luther King Jr., and the newspaper editor David Kahn, whose standard history of cryptology, *The Codebreakers*, contained information the NSA viewed as classified. Even so much as writing about the NSA could land a person a place on a watch list. The NSA, on behalf of the FBI, was also targeting religious groups. "When J. Edgar Hoover gives you a requirement for complete surveillance of all Quakers in the United States," recalled Frank Raven, a former senior NSA official, "and when Richard M. Nixon is a Quaker and he's the president of the United States, it gets pretty funny."

Of course, such abuses are hardly the exclusive province of the NSA; history has repeatedly shown that simply having the ability to eavesdrop brings with it the temptation to use that ability—whatever the legal barriers against that use may be. For instance, during World War I, the government read and censored thousands of telegrams—the e-mail of the day—sent hourly by telegraph companies. Though the end of the war brought with it a reversion to the Radio Act of 1912, which guaranteed the secrecy of communications, the State and War Departments nevertheless joined together in May 1919 to create America's first civilian eavesdropping and code-breaking agency, nicknamed the Black Chamber. By arrangement, messengers visited the telegraph companies each morning and took bundles of hard-copy telegrams to the agency's offices across town. These copies were returned before the close of business that day.

A similar tale followed the end of World War II. In August 1945, President Truman ordered an end to censorship. That left the Signal Security Agency (the military successor to the Black Chamber, which was shut down in 1929) without its raw intelligence—the telegrams provided by the telegraph companies. The director of the SSA sought access to cable traffic through a secret arrangement with the heads of the three major telegraph companies. The companies agreed to turn all telegrams over to the SSA, under a plan code-named Operation Shamrock. It ran until the government's domestic spying programs were publicly revealed, in the mid-1970s. The discovery of such abuses in the wake of the Watergate scandal led Congress to create select committees to conduct extensive investigations into the government's domestic spying programs: their origin, extent, and effect on the public. The shocking findings turned up by the Church Committee finally led to the formation of permanent Senate and House intelligence committees, whose primary responsibility was to protect the public from future privacy abuses. They were to be the FISA court's partner in providing checks and balances to the ever-expanding U.S. intelligence agencies. But it remains very much an open question whether these checks are up to the task at hand.

Who Watches the Watchmen?

Today, the NSA has access to more information than ever before. People express their most intimate thoughts in e-mails, send their tax returns over the Internet, satisfy their curiosity and desires with Google searches, let their hair down in chat rooms, discuss every event over cell phones, make appointments with their BlackBerrys, and do business by computer in WiFi hot spots.

NSA personnel, the customs inspectors of the information super-highway, have the ultimate goal of intercepting and reviewing every syllable and murmur zapping into, out of, or through the United States. They are close to achieving it. More than a dozen years ago, an NSA director gave an indication of the agency's capability. "Just one intelligence-collection system," said Admiral William O. Studeman, referring to a listening post such as Sugar Grove, "can generate a million inputs per half hour." Today, with the secret cooperation of much of the telecommunications industry, massive dishes vacuuming the airwaves, and electronic "packet sniffers," software that monitors network traffic, diverting e-mail and other data from fiber-optic cables, the NSA's hourly take is in the tens of millions of communications. One transatlantic fiber-optic cable alone has the capacity to handle close to 10 million simultaneous calls. While most communications flow through the NSA's electronic net unheard and unread, those messages associated with persons on the agency's watch lists—whether guilty or innocent—get kicked out for review.

As history has shown, the availability of such vast amounts of information is a temptation for an intelligence agency. The criteria for compiling watch lists and collecting information may be very strict at the beginning of such a program, but the reality—in a sort of bureaucratic law of expansion—is that it will draw in more and more people whose only offense was knowing the wrong person or protesting the wrong war.

Moreover, as Internet and wireless communications have grown exponentially, users have seen a corresponding decrease in the protections provided by the two institutions set up to shield the public from eavesdroppers. The first, the FISA court, has simply been shunted aside by the executive branch. The second, the congressional intelligence committees, have quite surprisingly abdicated any role. Created to be the watchdogs over the intelligence community, the committees have instead become its most enthusiastic cheerleaders. Rather than fighting for the public's privacy rights, they are constantly battling for more money and more freedom for the spy agencies.

Last November, just a month before the *New York Times* broke the story of the NSA's domestic spying, the American Bar Association publicly expressed concern over Congress's oversight of FISA searches. "The ABA is concerned that there is inadequate congressional oversight of government investigations undertaken pursuant to the Foreign Intelligence Surveillance Act," the group stated, "to assure that such investigations do not violate the First, Fourth, and Fifth Amendments to the Constitution." And while the administration did brief members of Congress on the decision to bypass FISA, the briefings were limited to a "Gang of Eight"—the majority and minority leaders of the House and Senate and the chairmen and ranking members of the two intelligence committees. None of the law-makers insisted that the decision be debated by the joint committees, even though such hearings are closed.

Frank Church, the Idaho Democrat who led the first probe into the National Security Agency, warned in 1975 that the agency's capabilities

> could be turned around on the American people, and no American would have any privacy left, such [is] the capability to monitor everything: telephone conversations, telegrams, it doesn't matter. There would be no place to hide. If this government ever became a tyranny, if a dictator ever took charge in this country, the technological capacity that the intelligence community has given the government could enable it to impose total tyranny, and there would be no way to fight back, because the most careful effort to combine together in resistance to the government, no matter how privately it is done, is within the reach of the government to know. Such is the capacity of this technology.

It was those fears that caused Congress to enact the Foreign Intelligence Surveillance Act three years later. "I don't want to see this country ever go across the bridge," Senator Church said. "I know the capacity that is there to make tyranny total in America, and we must see to it that [the National Security Agency] and all agencies that possess this technology operate within the law and under proper supervision, so that we never cross over that abyss. That is the abyss from which there is no return."

Part Six:
America in an Uncertain World

After Neoconservatism

Francis Fukuyama

The New York Times Magazine | February 19, 2006

While the Bush administration has focused assiduously on courting its conservative base, a maxim of governing holds that keeping all of your supporters happy all the time is an impossible task. Anti-big-government and fiscal conservatives have grown displeased by the ever-increasing levels of government spending and debt under Bush—a complaint voiced in conservative commentator Bruce Bartlett's recent book Impostor: How George W. Bush Bankrupted America and Betrayed the Reagan Legacy. *Other conservatives have expressed disenchantment with the president's backing of amnesty for illegal aliens, or his less-than-enthusasitc support for an amendment banning same-sex marriages. Still others, like Pat Buchanan and William Buckley, have split with the administration over the Iraq War, which Buckley recently termed an outright failure.*

Another dissent over the Bush administration's foreign policy that's caused waves in intellectual circles has been that of the influential neoconservative thinker Francis Fukuyama, who coined the phrase "the end of history." In this essay, adapted from his recent book America at the Crossroads: Democracy, Power, and the Neoconservative Legacy, *Fukuyama explains why, in his view, America's effort in Iraq marks the demise of the neoconservative movement as we know it. "The problem with neoconservatism's agenda lies not in its ends, which are as American as apple pie," he notes, "but rather in the overmilitarized means by which it has sought to accomplish them."*

As we approach the third anniversary of the onset of the Iraq War, it seems very unlikely that history will judge either the intervention itself or the ideas animating it kindly. By invading Iraq, the Bush administration created a self-fulfilling prophecy: Iraq has now replaced Afghanistan as a magnet, a training ground and an operational base for jihadist terrorists, with plenty of American targets to shoot at. The United States still has a chance of creating a Shiite-dominated democratic Iraq, but the new government will be very weak for years to come; the resulting power vacuum will invite outside influence from all of Iraq's neighbors, including Iran. There are clear benefits to the Iraqi people from the removal of Saddam

Hussein's dictatorship, and perhaps some positive spillover effects in Lebanon and Syria. But it is very hard to see how these developments in themselves justify the blood and treasure that the United States has spent on the project to this point.

The so-called Bush Doctrine that set the framework for the administration's first term is now in shambles. The doctrine (elaborated, among other places, in the 2002 National Security Strategy of the United States) argued that, in the wake of the September 11 attacks, America would have to launch periodic preventive wars to defend itself against rogue states and terrorists with weapons of mass destruction; that it would do this alone, if necessary; and that it would work to democratize the greater Middle East as a long-term solution to the terrorist problem. But successful preemption depends on the ability to predict the future accurately and on good intelligence, which was not forthcoming, while America's perceived unilateralism has isolated it as never before. It is not surprising that in its second term, the administration has been distancing itself from these policies and is in the process of rewriting the National Security Strategy document.

But it is the idealistic effort to use American power to promote democracy and human rights abroad that may suffer the greatest setback. Perceived failure in Iraq has restored the authority of foreign policy "realists" in the tradition of Henry Kissinger. Already there is a host of books and articles decrying America's naïve Wilsonianism and attacking the notion of trying to democratize the world. The administration's second-term efforts to push for greater Middle Eastern democracy, introduced with the soaring rhetoric of Bush's second Inaugural Address, have borne very problematic fruits. The Islamist Muslim Brotherhood made a strong showing in Egypt's parliamentary elections in November and December. While the holding of elections in Iraq this past December was an achievement in itself, the vote led to the ascendance of a Shiite bloc with close ties to Iran (following on the election of the conservative Mahmoud Ahmadinejad as president of Iran in June). But the clincher was the decisive Hamas victory in the Palestinian election last month, which brought to power a movement overtly dedicated to the destruction of Israel. In his second inaugural, Bush said that "America's vital interests and our deepest beliefs are now one," but the charge will be made with increasing frequency that the Bush administration made a big mistake when it stirred the pot, and that the United States would have done better to stick by its traditional authoritarian friends in the Middle East. Indeed, the effort to promote democracy around the world has been attacked as an illegitimate activity both by people on the left like Jeffrey Sachs and by traditional conservatives like Pat Buchanan.

The reaction against democracy promotion and an activist foreign policy may not end there. Those whom Walter Russell Mead labels Jacksonian conservatives—red-state Americans whose sons and daughters are fighting and dying in the Middle East—supported the Iraq War because they believed that their children were fighting to defend the United States against nuclear terrorism, not to promote democracy. They don't want to abandon the president in the middle of a vicious war, but down the road the perceived failure of the Iraq intervention may push them to favor a more isolationist foreign policy, which is a more natural political position for them. A recent Pew poll indicates a swing in public opinion toward isolationism; the percentage of Americans saying that the United States "should mind its own business" has never been higher since the end of the Vietnam War.

More than any other group, it was the neoconservatives both inside and outside the Bush administration who pushed for democratizing Iraq and the broader Middle East. They are widely credited (or blamed) for being the decisive voices promoting regime change in Iraq, and yet it is their idealistic agenda that in the coming months and years will be the most directly threatened. Were the United States to retreat from the world stage, following a drawdown in Iraq, it would in my view be a huge tragedy, because American power and influence have been critical to the maintenance of an open and increasingly democratic order around the world. The problem with neoconservatism's agenda lies not in its ends, which are as American as apple pie, but rather in the overmilitarized means by which it has sought to accomplish them. What American foreign policy needs is not a return to a narrow and cynical realism, but rather the formulation of a "realistic Wilsonianism" that better matches means to ends.

The Neoconservative Legacy

How did the neoconservatives end up overreaching to such an extent that they risk undermining their own goals? The Bush administration's first-term foreign policy did not flow ineluctably from the views of earlier generations of people who considered themselves neoconservatives, since those views were themselves complex and subject to differing interpretations.

Four common principles or threads ran through much of this thought up through the end of the Cold War: a concern with democracy, human rights, and, more generally, the internal politics of states; a belief that American power can be used for moral purposes; a skepticism about the ability of international law and institutions to solve serious security problems; and, finally, a view that ambitious social engineering often leads to unexpected consequences and thereby undermines its own ends.

The problem was that two of these principles were in potential collision. The skeptical stance toward ambitious social engineering—which in earlier years had been applied mostly to domestic policies like affirmative action, busing, and welfare—suggested a cautious approach toward remaking the world and an awareness that ambitious initiatives always have unanticipated consequences. The belief in the potential moral uses of American power, on the other hand, implied that American activism could reshape the structure of global politics. By the time of the Iraq War, the belief in the transformational uses of power had prevailed over the doubts about social engineering.

In retrospect, things did not have to develop this way. The roots of neoconservatism lie in a remarkable group of largely Jewish intellectuals who attended City College of New York (CCNY) in the mid to late 1930s and early 1940s, a group that included Irving Kristol, Daniel Bell, Irving Howe, Nathan Glazer, and, a bit later, Daniel Patrick Moynihan. The story of this group has been told in a number of places, most notably in a documentary film by Joseph Dorman called *Arguing the World*. The most important inheritance from the CCNY group was an idealistic belief in social progress and the universality of rights, coupled with intense anti-Communism.

It is not an accident that many in the CCNY group started out as Trotskyites. Leon Trotsky was, of course, himself a Communist, but his supporters came to understand better than most people the utter cynicism and brutality of the Stalinist regime. The anti-Communist left, in contrast to the traditional American right, sympathized with the social and economic aims of Communism, but in the course of the 1930s and 1940s came to realize that "real existing socialism" had become a monstrosity of unintended consequences that completely undermined the idealistic goals it espoused. While not all of the CCNY thinkers became neoconservatives, the danger of good intentions carried to extremes was a theme that would underlie the life work of many members of this group.

If there was a single overarching theme to the domestic social policy critiques issued by those who wrote for the neoconservative journal *The Public Interest*, founded by Irving Kristol, Nathan Glazer, and Daniel Bell in 1965, it was the limits of social engineering. Writers like Glazer, Moynihan, and, later, Glenn Loury argued that ambitious efforts to seek social justice often left societies worse off than before because they either required massive state intervention that disrupted preexisting social relations (for example, forced busing) or else produced unanticipated consequences (like an increase in single-parent families as a result of welfare). A major theme running through James Q. Wilson's extensive writings on crime was the idea that you could not lower crime rates by trying to solve deep underlying problems like poverty and racism; effective policies needed to focus on shorter-term measures that went after symptoms of social distress (like subway graffiti or panhandling) rather than root causes.

How, then, did a group with such a pedigree come to decide that the "root cause" of terrorism lay in the Middle East's lack of democracy, that the United States had both the wisdom and the ability to fix this problem, and that democracy would come quickly and painlessly to Iraq? Neoconservatives would not have taken this turn but for the peculiar way that the Cold War ended.

Ronald Reagan was ridiculed by sophisticated people on the American left and in Europe for labeling the Soviet Union and its allies an "evil empire" and for challenging Mikhail Gorbachev not just to reform his system but also to "tear down this wall." His assistant secretary of defense for international security policy, Richard Perle, was denounced as the "prince of darkness" for this uncompromising, hard-line position; his proposal for a double-zero in the intermediate-range nuclear arms negotiations (that is, the complete elimination of medium-range missiles) was attacked as hopelessly out of touch by the *bien-pensant* centrist foreign-policy experts at places like the Council on Foreign Relations and the State Department. That community felt that the Reaganites were dangerously utopian in their hopes for actually winning, as opposed to managing, the Cold War.

And yet total victory in the Cold War is exactly what happened in 1989–91. Gorbachev accepted not only the double zero but also deep cuts in conventional forces, and then failed to stop the Polish, Hungarian and East German defections from the empire. Communism collapsed within a couple of years because of its internal moral weaknesses and contradictions, and with regime change in Eastern Europe and the former Soviet Union, the Warsaw Pact threat to the West evaporated.

The way the Cold War ended shaped the thinking of supporters of the Iraq war, including younger neoconservatives like William Kristol and Robert Kagan, in two ways. First, it seems to have created an expectation that all totalitarian regimes were hollow at the core and would crumble with a small push from outside. The model for this was Romania under the Ceausescus: once the wicked witch was dead, the munchkins would rise up and start singing joyously about their liberation. As Kristol and Kagan put it in their 2000 book *Present Dangers*: "To many the idea of America using its power to promote changes of regime in nations ruled by dictators rings of utopianism. But in fact, it is eminently realistic. There is something perverse in declaring the impossibility of promoting democratic change abroad in light of the record of the past three decades."

This overoptimism about postwar transitions to democracy helps explain the Bush administration's incomprehensible failure to plan adequately for the insurgency that subsequently emerged in Iraq. The war's supporters seemed to think that democracy was a kind of default condition to which societies reverted once the heavy lifting of coercive regime change occurred, rather than a long-term process of institution-building and reform. While they now assert that they knew all along that the democratic transformation of Iraq would be long and hard, they were clearly taken by surprise. According to George Packer's recent book on Iraq, *The Assassins' Gate*, the Pentagon planned a drawdown of American forces to some 25,000 troops by the end of the summer following the invasion.

By the 1990s, neoconservatism had been fed by several other intellectual streams. One came from the students of the German Jewish political theorist Leo Strauss, who, contrary to much of the nonsense written about him by people like Anne Norton and Shadia Drury, was a serious reader of philosophical texts who did not express opinions on contemporary politics or policy issues. Rather, he was concerned with the "crisis of modernity" brought on by the relativism of Nietzsche and Heidegger, as well as the fact that neither the claims of religion nor deeply held opinions about the nature of the good life could be banished from politics, as the thinkers of the European Enlightenment had hoped. Another stream came from Albert Wohlstetter, a Rand Corporation strategist who was the teacher of Richard Perle, Zalmay Khalilzad (the current American ambassador to Iraq), and

Paul Wolfowitz (the former deputy secretary of defense), among other people. Wohlstetter was intensely concerned with the problem of nuclear proliferation and the way that the 1968 Nonproliferation Treaty left loopholes, in its support for "peaceful" nuclear energy, large enough for countries like Iraq and Iran to walk through.

I have numerous affiliations with the different strands of the neoconservative movement. I was a student of Strauss's protégé Allan Bloom, who wrote the best-seller *The Closing of the American Mind*; worked at Rand and with Wohlstetter on Persian Gulf issues; and worked also on two occasions for Wolfowitz. Many people have also interpreted my book *The End of History and the Last Man* (1992) as a neoconservative tract, one that argued in favor of the view that there is a universal hunger for liberty in all people that will inevitably lead them to liberal democracy, and that we are living in the midst of an accelerating, transnational movement in favor of that liberal democracy. This is a misreading of the argument. *The End of History* is in the end an argument about modernization. What is initially universal is not the desire for liberal democracy but rather the desire to live in a modern— that is, technologically advanced and prosperous—society, which, if satisfied, tends to drive demands for political participation. Liberal democracy is one of the byproducts of this modernization process, something that becomes a universal aspiration only in the course of historical time.

The End of History, in other words, presented a kind of Marxist argument for the existence of a long-term process of social evolution, but one that terminates in liberal democracy rather than communism. In the formulation of the scholar Ken Jowitt, the neoconservative position articulated by people like Kristol and Kagan was, by contrast, Leninist; they believed that history can be pushed along with the right application of power and will. Leninism was a tragedy in its Bolshevik version, and it has returned as farce when practiced by the United States. Neoconservatism, as both a political symbol and a body of thought, has evolved into something I can no longer support.

The Failure of Benevolent Hegemony

The Bush administration and its neoconservative supporters did not simply underestimate the difficulty of bringing about congenial political outcomes in places like Iraq; they also misunderstood the way the world would react to the use of American power. Of course, the Cold War was replete with instances of what the foreign policy analyst Stephen Sestanovich calls American maximalism, wherein Washington acted first and sought legitimacy and support from its allies only after the fact. But in the post-Cold War period, the structural situation of world politics changed in ways that made this kind of exercise of power much more problematic in the eyes of even close allies. After the fall of the Soviet Union, various neoconservative authors like Charles Krauthammer, William Kristol and Robert Kagan suggested that the United States would use its margin of power to exert a kind of "benevolent hegemony" over the rest of the world, fixing problems like rogue states with WMD, human rights abuses, and terrorist threats as they came up. Writing before the Iraq War, Kristol and Kagan considered whether this posture would provoke resistance from the rest of the world, and concluded, "It is precisely *because American foreign policy is infused with an unusually high degree of morality* that other nations find they have less to fear from its otherwise daunting power." (Italics added.)

It is hard to read these lines without irony in the wake of the global reaction to the Iraq War, which succeeded in uniting much of the world in a frenzy of anti-Americanism. The idea that the United States is a hegemon more benevolent than most is not an absurd one, but there were warning signs that things had changed in America's relationship to the world long before the start of the Iraq War. The structural imbalance in global power had grown enormous. America surpassed the rest of the world in every dimension of power by an unprecedented margin, with its defense spending nearly equal to that of the rest of the world combined. Already during the Clinton years, American economic hegemony had generated enormous hostility to an American-dominated process of globalization, frequently on the part of close democratic allies who thought the United States was seeking to impose its antistatist social model on them.

There were other reasons as well why the world did not accept American benevolent hegemony. In the first place, it was premised on American exceptionalism, the idea that America could use its power in instances where others could not because it was more virtuous than other countries. The doctrine of preemption against terrorist threats contained in the 2002 National Security Strategy was one that could not safely be generalized through the international system; America would be the first country to object if Russia, China, India, or France declared a similar right of unilateral action. The United States was seeking to pass judgment on others while being unwilling to have its own conduct questioned in places like the International Criminal Court.

Another problem with benevolent hegemony was domestic. There are sharp limits to the American people's attention to foreign affairs and willingness to finance projects overseas that do not have clear benefits to American interests. September 11 changed that calculus in many ways, providing popular support for two wars in the Middle East and large increases in defense spending. But the durability of the support is uncertain: although most Americans want to do what is necessary to make the project of rebuilding Iraq succeed, the aftermath of the invasion did not increase the public appetite for further costly interventions. Americans are not, at heart, an imperial people. Even benevolent hegemons sometimes have to act ruthlessly, and they need a staying power that does not come easily to people who are reasonably content with their own lives and society.

Finally, benevolent hegemony presumed that the hegemon was not only well intentioned but competent as well. Much of the criticism of the Iraq intervention from Europeans and others was not based on a normative case that the United States was not getting authorization from the United Nations Security Council, but rather on the belief that it had not made an adequate case for invading Iraq in the first place and didn't know what it was doing in trying to democratize Iraq. In this, the critics were unfortunately quite prescient.

The most basic misjudgment was an overestimation of the threat facing the United States from radical Islamism. Although the new and ominous possibility of undeterrable terrorists armed with weapons of mass destruction did indeed present itself, advocates of the war wrongly conflated this with the threat presented by Iraq and with the rogue state/proliferation problem more generally. The misjudgment was based in part on the massive failure of the American intelligence community to correctly assess the state of Iraq's WMD programs before the war. But the intelligence community never took nearly as alarmist a view of the terrorist/WMD threat as the war's supporters did. Overestimation of this threat was then used to justify the elevation of preventive war to the centerpiece of a new security strategy, as well as a whole series of measures that infringed on civil liberties, from detention policy to domestic eavesdropping.

What to Do

Now that the neoconservative moment appears to have passed, the United States needs to reconceptualize its foreign policy in several fundamental ways. In the first instance, we need to demilitarize what we have been calling the global war on terrorism and shift to other types of policy instruments. We are fighting hot counterinsurgency wars in Afghanistan and Iraq and against the international jihadist movement, wars in which we need to prevail. But "war" is the wrong metaphor for the broader struggle, since wars are fought at full intensity and have clear beginnings and endings. Meeting the jihadist challenge is more of a "long, twilight struggle" whose core is not a military campaign but a political contest for the hearts and minds of ordinary Muslims around the world. As recent events in France and Denmark suggest, Europe will be a central battleground in this fight.

The United States needs to come up with something better than "coalitions of the willing" to legitimate its dealings with other countries. The world today lacks effective international institutions that can confer legitimacy on collective action; creating new organizations that will better balance the dual requirements of legitimacy and effectiveness will be the primary task for the coming generation. As a result of more than two hundred years of political evolution, we have a relatively good understanding of how to create institutions that are rule bound, accountable and reasonably effective in the vertical silos we call states. What we do not have are adequate mechanisms of horizontal accountability among states.

The conservative critique of the United Nations is all too cogent: while useful for certain peacekeeping and nation-building operations, the United Nations lacks both democratic legitimacy and effectiveness in dealing with serious security issues. The solution is not to strengthen a single global body, but rather to promote what has been emerging in any event, a "multi-multilateral world" of overlapping and occasionally competing international institutions that are organized on regional or functional lines. Kosovo in 1999 was a model: when the Russian veto prevented the Security Council from acting, the United States and its NATO allies simply shifted the venue to NATO, where the Russians could not block action.

The final area that needs rethinking, and the one that will be the most contested in the coming months and years, is the place of democracy promotion in American foreign policy. The worst legacy that could come from the Iraq War would be an anti-neoconservative backlash that coupled a sharp turn toward isolation with a cynical realist policy aligning the United States with friendly authoritarians. Good governance, which involves not just democracy but also the rule of law and economic development, is critical to a host of outcomes we desire, from alleviating poverty to dealing with pandemics to controlling violent conflicts. A Wilsonian policy that pays attention to how rulers treat their citizens is therefore right, but it needs to be informed by a certain realism that was missing from the thinking of the Bush administration in its first term and of its neoconservative allies.

We need in the first instance to understand that promoting democracy and modernization in the Middle East is not a solution to the problem of jihadist terrorism; in all likelihood it will make the short-term problem worse, as we have seen in the case of the Palestinian election bringing Hamas to power. Radical Islamism is a byproduct of modernization itself, arising from the loss of identity that accompanies the transition to a modern, pluralist society. It is no accident that so many recent terrorists, from September 11's Mohamed Atta to the murderer of the Dutch filmmaker Theo van Gogh to the London subway bombers, were radicalized in democratic Europe and intimately familiar with all of democracy's blessings. More democracy will mean more alienation, radicalization, and—yes, unfortunately—terrorism.

But greater political participation by Islamist groups is very likely to occur whatever we do, and it will be the only way that the poison of radical Islamism can ultimately work its way through the body politic of Muslim communities around the world. The age is long since gone when friendly authoritarians could rule over passive populations and produce stability indefinitely. New social actors are mobilizing everywhere, from Bolivia and Venezuela to South Africa and the Persian Gulf. A durable Israeli-Palestinian peace could not be built upon a corrupt, illegitimate Fatah that constantly had to worry about Hamas challenging its authority. Peace might emerge, sometime down the road, from a Palestine run by a formerly radical terrorist group that had been forced to deal with the realities of governing.

If we are serious about the good governance agenda, we have to shift our focus to the reform, reorganization and proper financing of those institutions of the United States government that actually promote democracy, development and the rule of law around the world, organizations like the State Department, USAID, the National Endowment for Democracy and the like. The United States has played an often decisive role in helping along many recent democratic transitions, including in the Philippines in 1986; South Korea and Taiwan in 1987; Chile in 1988; Poland and Hungary in 1989; Serbia in 2000; Georgia in 2003; and Ukraine in 2004-5. But the overarching lesson that emerges from these cases is that the United States does not get to decide when and where democracy comes about. By definition, outsiders can't "impose" democracy on a country that doesn't want it; demand for democracy and reform must be domestic. Democracy promotion is therefore a long-term and opportunistic process that has to await the gradual ripening of political and economic conditions to be effective.

The Bush administration has been walking—indeed, sprinting—away from the legacy of its first term, as evidenced by the cautious multilateral approach it has taken toward the nuclear programs of Iran and North Korea. Condoleezza Rice gave a serious speech in January about "transformational diplomacy" and has begun an effort to reorganize the nonmilitary side of the foreign-policy establishment, and the National Security Strategy document is being rewritten. All of these are welcome changes, but the legacy of the Bush first-term foreign policy and its neoconservative supporters has been so polarizing that it is going to be hard to have a reasoned debate about how to appropriately balance American ideals and interests in the coming years. The reaction against a flawed policy can be as damaging as the policy itself, and such a reaction is an indulgence we cannot afford, given the critical moment we have arrived at in global politics.

Neoconservatism, whatever its complex roots, has become indelibly associated with concepts like coercive regime change, unilateralism and American hegemony. What is needed now are new ideas, neither neoconservative nor realist, for how America is to relate to the rest of the world—ideas that retain the neoconservative belief in the universality of human rights, but without its illusions about the efficacy of American power and hegemony to bring these ends about.

The Iran Plans

Seymour Hersh

The New Yorker | April 17, 2006

Since it was first established nearly three decades ago, the Shiite Islamic theocracy of Iran has always been a foreign-policy thorn in the side of the United States. But when reports surfaced that Iran was actively seeking to build nuclear weapons, the country—long known to be a leading supporter of various terrorist organizations—abruptly morphed from an irritant into a potentially serious threat, both to the region and the world. Following the collapse of a 2004 agreement to suspend its nuclear program, Iran has expelled International Atomic Energy Agency investigators from the country and publicly affirmed its right to possess enriched uranium—all the while insisting that its nuclear aims are strictly peaceful.

As this book went to press, a six-country negotiating group—consisting of the United States, Russia, China, Britain, France, and Germany—had formally offered Iran a set of incentives to freeze its nuclear enrichment program. Iran, in turn, had given a tentatively positive response. In this New Yorker *article, Seymour Hersh reports on an alternative option being considered by the United States: that of military strikes against Iran's nuclear sites—which, according to Hersh's sources, could potentially include the use of nuclear weapons.*

The Bush administration, while publicly advocating diplomacy in order to stop Iran from pursuing a nuclear weapon, has increased clandestine activities inside Iran and intensified planning for a possible major air attack. Current and former American military and intelligence officials said that Air Force planning groups are drawing up lists of targets, and teams of American combat troops have been ordered into Iran, under cover, to collect targeting data and to establish contact with antigovernment ethnic-minority groups. The officials say that President Bush is determined to deny the Iranian regime the opportunity to begin a pilot program, planned for this spring, to enrich uranium.

American and European intelligence agencies, and the International Atomic Energy Agency (IAEA), agree that Iran is intent on developing the capability to produce nuclear weapons. But there are widely differing estimates of how long that will take, and whether diplomacy, sanctions, or military action is the best way to prevent it. Iran insists that its research is for peaceful use only, in keeping with the Nuclear Non-Proliferation Treaty, and that it will not be delayed or deterred.

There is a growing conviction among members of the U.S. military, and in the international community, that President Bush's ultimate goal in the nuclear confrontation with Iran is regime change. Iran's president, Mahmoud Ahmadinejad, has challenged the reality of the Holocaust and said that Israel must be "wiped off the map." Bush and others in the White House view him as a potential Adolf Hitler, a former senior intelligence official said. "That's the name they're using. They say, 'Will Iran get a strategic weapon and threaten another world war?'"

A government consultant with close ties to the civilian leadership in the Pentagon said that Bush was "absolutely convinced that Iran is going to get the bomb" if it is not stopped. He said that the president believes that he must do "what no Democrat or Republican, if elected in the future, would have the courage to do," and "that saving Iran is going to be his legacy."

One former defense official, who still deals with sensitive issues for the Bush administration, told me that the military planning was premised on a belief that "a sustained bombing campaign in Iran will humiliate the religious leadership and lead the public to rise up and overthrow the government." He added, "I was shocked when I heard it, and asked myself, 'What are they smoking?'"

The rationale for regime change was articulated in early March by Patrick Clawson, an Iran expert who is the deputy director for research at the Washington Institute for Near East Policy and who has been a supporter of President Bush. "So long as Iran has an Islamic republic, it will have a nuclear-weapons program, at least clandestinely," Clawson told the Senate Foreign Relations Committee on March 2. "The key issue, therefore, is: How long will the present Iranian regime last?"

When I spoke to Clawson, he emphasized that "this administration is putting a lot of effort into diplomacy." However, he added, Iran had no choice other than to accede to America's demands or face a military attack. Clawson said that he fears that Ahmadinejad "sees the West as wimps and thinks we will eventually cave in. We have to be ready to deal with Iran if the crisis escalates." Clawson said that he would prefer to rely on sabotage and other clandestine activities, such as "industrial accidents." But, he said, it would be prudent to prepare for a wider war, "given the way the Iranians are acting. This is not like planning to invade Quebec."

One military planner told me that White House criticisms of Iran and the high tempo of planning and clandestine activities amount to a campaign of "coercion" aimed at Iran. "You have to be ready to go, and we'll see how they respond," the officer said. "You have to really show a threat in order to get Ahmadinejad to back down." He added, "People think Bush has been focused on Saddam Hussein since 9/11," but, "in my view, if you had to name one nation that was his focus all the way along, it was Iran." (In response to detailed requests for comment, the White House said that it would not comment on military planning but added, "As the president has indicated, we are pursuing a diplomatic solution"; the Defense Department also said that Iran was being dealt with through "diplomatic channels" but wouldn't elaborate on that; the CIA said that there were "inaccuracies" in this account but would not specify them.)

"This is much more than a nuclear issue," one high-ranking diplomat told me in Vienna. "That's just a rallying point, and there is still time to fix it. But the administration believes it cannot be fixed unless they control the hearts and minds of Iran. The real issue is who is going to control the Middle East and its oil in the next ten years."

A senior Pentagon adviser on the war on terror expressed a similar view. "This White House believes that the only way to solve the problem is to change the power structure in Iran, and that means war," he said. The danger, he said, was that "it also reinforces the belief inside Iran that the only way to defend the country is to have a nuclear capability." A military conflict that destabilized the region could also increase the risk of terror: "Hezbollah comes into play," the adviser said, referring to the terror group that is considered one of the world's most successful, and which is now a Lebanese political party with strong ties to Iran. "And here comes Al Qaeda."

In recent weeks, the president has quietly initiated a series of talks on plans for Iran with a few key senators and members of Congress, including at least one Democrat. A senior member of the House Appropriations Committee, who did not take part in the meetings but has discussed their content with his colleagues, told me that there had been "no formal briefings," because "they're reluctant to brief the minority. They're doing the Senate, somewhat selectively."

The House member said that no one in the meetings "is really objecting" to the talk of war. "The people they're briefing are the same ones who led the charge on Iraq. At most, questions are raised: How are you going to hit all the sites at once? How are you going to get deep enough?" (Iran is building facilities underground.) "There's no pressure from Congress" not to take military action, the House member added. "The only political pressure is from the guys who want to do it." Speaking of President Bush, the House member said, "The most worrisome thing is that this guy has a messianic vision."

"The planning is enormous," the former senior intelligence official said, referring to the activity at the U.S. Central Command headquarters, in Florida; the Joint Warfare Analysis Center, in Virginia; and the U.S. Strategic Command, in Nebraska. "Space assets, SLBMs"—submarine-launched ballistic missiles—"tactical air, and sabotage, cooperation from the Turks and the Russians." He added that the plans include "significant air attacks on their countermeasures and anti-aircraft missiles—a huge takedown." He depicted the planning as hectic, and far beyond the contingency work that is routinely done. "These are operational plans," the former official said.

Some operations, apparently aimed in part at intimidating Iran, are already under way. American Naval tactical aircraft, operating from carriers in the Arabian Sea, have been flying simulated nuclear-weapons delivery missions—rapid ascending maneuvers known as "over the shoulder" bombing—since last summer, the former official said, within range of Iranian coastal radars.

Last month, in a paper given at a conference on Middle East security in Berlin, Colonel Sam Gardiner, a military analyst who taught at the National War College before retiring from the Air Force, in 1987, provided an estimate of what would be needed to destroy Iran's nuclear program. Working from satellite photographs of the known facilities, Gardiner estimated that at least four hundred targets would have to be hit. He added:

> I don't think a U.S. military planner would want to stop there. Iran probably has two chemical-production plants. We would hit those. We would want to hit the medium-range ballistic missiles that have just recently been moved closer to Iraq. There are fourteen airfields with sheltered aircraft. . . . We'd want to get rid of that threat. We would want to hit the assets that could be

used to threaten Gulf shipping. That means targeting the cruise-missile sites and the Iranian diesel submarines. . . . Some of the facilities may be too difficult to target even with penetrating weapons. The U.S. will have to use Special Operations units.

One of the military's initial option plans, as presented to the White House by the Pentagon this winter, calls for the use of a bunker-buster tactical nuclear weapon, such as the B61-11, against underground nuclear sites. One target is Iran's main centrifuge plant, at Natanz, nearly two hundred miles south of Tehran. Natanz, which is no longer under IAEA safeguards, reportedly has underground floor space to hold 50,000 centrifuges, and laboratories and workspaces buried approximately seventy-five feet beneath the surface. That number of centrifuges could provide enough enriched uranium for about twenty nuclear warheads a year. (Iran has acknowledged that it initially kept the existence of its enrichment program hidden from IAEA inspectors, but claims that none of its current activity is barred by the Non-Proliferation Treaty.) The elimination of Natanz would be a major setback for Iran's nuclear ambitions, but the conventional weapons in the American arsenal could not insure the destruction of facilities under seventy-five feet of earth and rock, especially if they are reinforced with concrete.

There is a Cold War precedent for targeting deep underground bunkers with nuclear weapons. In the early 1980s, the American intelligence community watched as the Soviet government began digging a huge underground complex outside Moscow. Analysts concluded that the underground facility was designed for "continuity of government"—for the political and military leadership to survive a nuclear war. (There are similar facilities, in Virginia and Pennsylvania, for the American leadership.) The Soviet facility still exists, and much of what the United States knows about it remains classified. "The 'tell'"—the giveaway—"was the ventilator shafts, some of which were disguised," the former senior intelligence official told me. At the time, he said, it was determined that "only nukes" could destroy the bunker. He added that some American intelligence analysts believe that the Russians helped the Iranians design their underground facility. "We see a similarity of design," specifically in the ventilator shafts, he said.

A former high-level Defense Department official told me that, in his view, even limited bombing would allow the United States to "go in there and do enough damage to slow down the nuclear infrastructure—it's feasible." The former defense official said, "The Iranians don't have friends, and we can tell them that, if necessary, we'll keep knocking back their infrastructure. The United States should act like we're ready to go." He added, "We don't have to knock down *all* of their air defenses. Our stealth bombers and standoff missiles really work, and we can blow fixed things up. We can do things on the ground, too, but it's difficult and very dangerous—put bad stuff in ventilator shafts and put them to sleep."

But those who are familiar with the Soviet bunker, according to the former senior intelligence official, "say 'No way.' You've got to know what's underneath—to know which ventilator feeds people, or diesel generators, or which are false. And there's a lot that we don't know." The lack of reliable intelligence leaves military planners, given the goal of totally destroying the sites, little choice but to consider the use of tactical nuclear weapons. "Every other option, in the view of the nuclear weaponeers, would leave a gap," the former senior intelligence official said. " 'Decisive' is the key word of the Air Force's planning. It's a tough decision. But we made it in Japan."

He went on, "Nuclear planners go through extensive training and learn the technical details of damage and fallout—we're talking about mushroom clouds, radiation, mass casualties, and contamination over years. This is not an underground nuclear test, where all you see is the earth raised a little bit. These politicians don't have a clue, and whenever anybody tries to get it out"—remove the nuclear option—"they're shouted down."

The attention given to the nuclear option has created serious misgivings inside the offices of the Joint Chiefs of Staff, he added, and some officers have talked about resigning. Late this winter, the Joint Chiefs of Staff sought to remove the nuclear option from the evolving war plans for Iran—without success, the former intelligence official said. "The White House said, 'Why are you challenging this? The option came from you.'"

The Pentagon adviser on the war on terror confirmed that some in the administration were looking seriously at this option, which he linked to a resurgence of interest in tactical nuclear weapons among Pentagon civilians and in policy circles. He called it "a juggernaut that has to be stopped." He also confirmed that some senior officers and officials were considering resigning over the issue. "There are very strong sentiments within the military against brandishing nuclear weapons against other countries," the adviser told me. "This goes to high levels." The matter may soon reach a decisive point, he said, because the Joint Chiefs had agreed to give President Bush a formal recommendation stating that they are strongly opposed to considering the nuclear option for Iran. "The internal debate on this has hardened in recent weeks," the adviser said. "And, if senior Pentagon officers express their opposition to the use of offensive nuclear weapons, then it will never happen."

The adviser added, however, that the idea of using tactical nuclear weapons in such situations has gained support from the Defense Science Board, an advisory panel whose members are selected by Secretary of Defense Donald Rumsfeld. "They're telling the Pentagon that we can build the B61 with more blast and less radiation," he said.

The chairman of the Defense Science Board is William Schneider Jr., an undersecretary of state in the Reagan administration. In January 2001, as President Bush prepared to take office, Schneider served on an ad hoc panel on nuclear forces sponsored by the National Institute for Public Policy, a conservative think tank. The panel's report recommended treating tactical nuclear weapons as an essential part of the U.S. arsenal and noted their suitability "for those occasions when the certain and prompt destruction of high priority targets is essential and beyond the promise of conventional weapons." Several signers of the report are now prominent members of the Bush administration, including Stephen Hadley, the national-security adviser; Stephen Cambone, the undersecretary of defense for intelligence; and Robert Joseph, the undersecretary of state for Arms Control and International Security.

The Pentagon adviser questioned the value of air strikes. "The Iranians have distributed their nuclear activity very well, and we have no clue where some of the key stuff is. It could even be out of the country," he said. He warned, as did many others, that bombing Iran could provoke "a chain reaction" of attacks on American facilities and citizens throughout the world: "What will 1.2 billion Muslims think the day we attack Iran?"

With or without the nuclear option, the list of targets may inevitably expand. One recently retired high-level Bush administration official, who is also an expert on war planning, told me that he would have vigorously argued against an air attack on Iran, because "Iran is a much tougher target" than Iraq. But, he added, "If you're going to do any bombing to stop the nukes, you might as well improve your lie across the board. Maybe hit some training camps, and clear up a lot of other problems."

The Pentagon adviser said that, in the event of an attack, the Air Force intended to strike many hundreds of targets in Iran but that "ninety-nine percent of them have nothing to do with proliferation. There are people who believe it's the way to operate"—that the administration can achieve its policy goals in Iran with a bombing campaign, an idea that has been supported by neoconservatives.

If the order were to be given for an attack, the American combat troops now operating in Iran would be in position to mark the critical targets with laser beams, to insure bombing accuracy and to minimize civilian casualties. As of early winter, I was told by the government consultant with close ties to civilians in the Pentagon, the units were also working with minority groups in Iran, including the Azeris, in the north, the Baluchis, in the southeast, and the Kurds, in the northeast. The troops "are studying the terrain, and giving away walking-around money to ethnic tribes, and recruiting scouts from local tribes and shepherds," the consultant said. One goal is to get "eyes on the ground"—quoting a line from *Othello*, he said, "Give me the ocular proof." The broader aim, the consultant said, is to "encourage ethnic tensions" and undermine the regime.

The new mission for the combat troops is a product of Defense Secretary Rumsfeld's long-standing interest in expanding the role of the military in covert operations, which was made official policy in the Pentagon's Quadrennial Defense Review, published in February. Such activities, if conducted by CIA operatives, would need a Presidential Finding and would have to be reported to key members of Congress.

" 'Force protection' is the new buzzword," the former senior intelligence official told me. He was referring to the Pentagon's position that clandestine activities that can be broadly classified as preparing the battlefield or protecting troops are military, not intelligence, operations, and are therefore not subject to congressional oversight. "The guys in the Joint Chiefs of Staff say there are a lot of uncertainties in Iran," he said. "We need to have more than what we had in Iraq. Now we have the green light to do everything we want."

*   *   *   *   *

The president's deep distrust of Ahmadinejad has strengthened his determination to confront Iran. This view has been reinforced by allegations that Ahmadinejad, who joined a special-forces brigade of the Revolutionary Guards in 1986, may have been involved in terrorist activities in the late eighties. (There are gaps in Ahmadinejad's official biography in this period.) Ahmadinejad has reportedly been connected to Imad Mughniyeh, a terrorist who has been implicated in the deadly bombings of the U.S. Embassy and the U.S. Marine barracks in Beirut, in 1983. Mughniyeh was then the security chief of Hezbollah; he remains on the FBI's list of most-wanted terrorists.

Robert Baer, who was a CIA officer in the Middle East and elsewhere for two decades, told me that Ahmadinejad and his Revolutionary Guard colleagues in the Iranian government "are capable of making a bomb, hiding it, and launching it at Israel. They're apocalyptic Shiites. If you're sitting in Tel Aviv and you believe they've got nukes and missiles—you've got to take them out. These guys are nuts, and there's no reason to back off."

Under Ahmadinejad, the Revolutionary Guards have expanded their power base throughout the Iranian bureaucracy; by the end of January, they had replaced thousands of civil servants with their own members. One former senior United Nations official, who has extensive experience with Iran, depicted the turnover as "a white coup," with ominous implications for the West. "Professionals in the Foreign Ministry are out; others are waiting to be kicked out," he said. "We may be too late. These guys now believe that they are stronger than ever since the revolution." He said that, particularly in consideration of China's emergence as a superpower, Iran's attitude was "To hell with the West. You can do as much as you like."

Iran's supreme religious leader, Ayatollah Khamenei, is considered by many experts to be in a stronger position than Ahmadinejad. "Ahmadinejad is not in control," one European diplomat told me. "Power is diffuse in Iran. The Revolutionary Guards are among the key backers of the nuclear program, but, ultimately, I don't think they are in charge of it. The Supreme Leader has the casting vote on the nuclear program, and the Guards will not take action without his approval."

The Pentagon adviser on the war on terror said that "allowing Iran to have the bomb is not on the table. We cannot have nukes being sent downstream to a terror network. It's just too dangerous." He added, "The whole internal debate is on which way to go"—in terms of stopping the Iranian program. It is possible, the adviser said, that Iran will unilaterally renounce its nuclear plans—and forestall the American action. "God may smile on us, but I don't think so. The bottom line is that Iran cannot become a nuclear-weapons state. The problem is that the Iranians realize that only by *becoming* a nuclear state can they defend themselves against the United States. Something bad is going to happen."

While almost no one disputes Iran's nuclear ambitions, there is intense debate over how soon it could get the bomb, and what to do about that. Robert Gallucci, a former government expert on nonproliferation who is now the dean of the School of Foreign Service at Georgetown, told me, "Based on what I know, Iran could be eight to ten years away" from developing a deliverable nuclear weapon. Gallucci added, "If they had a covert nuclear program and we could prove it, and we could not stop it by negotiation, diplomacy, or the threat of sanctions, I'd be in favor of taking it out. But if you do it"—bomb Iran—"without being able to show there's a secret program, you're in trouble."

Meir Dagan, the head of Mossad, Israel's intelligence agency, told the Knesset last December that "Iran is one to two years away, at the latest, from having enriched uranium. From that point, the completion of their nuclear weapon is simply a technical matter." In a conversation with me, a senior Israeli intelligence official talked about what he said was Iran's duplicity: "There are two parallel nuclear programs" inside Iran—the program declared to the IAEA and a separate operation, run by the military and the Revolutionary Guards. Israeli officials have repeatedly made this argument, but Israel has not produced public evidence to support it. Richard Armitage, the deputy secretary of state in Bush's first term, told me, "I think Iran has a secret nuclear-weapons program—I believe it, but I don't know it."

In recent months, the Pakistani government has given the United States new access to A. Q. Khan, the so-called father of the Pakistani atomic bomb. Khan, who is now living under house arrest in Islamabad, is accused of setting up a black market in nuclear materials; he made at least one clandestine visit to Tehran in the late 1980s. In the most recent interrogations, Khan has provided information on Iran's weapons design and its time line for building a bomb. "The picture is of 'unquestionable danger,'" the former senior intelligence official said. (The Pentagon adviser also confirmed that Khan has been "singing like a canary.") The concern, the former senior official said, is that "Khan has credibility problems. He is suggestible, and he's telling the neoconservatives what they want to hear"— or what might be useful to Pakistan's president, Pervez Musharraf, who is under pressure to assist Washington in the war on terror.

"I think Khan's leading us on," the former intelligence official said. "I don't know anybody who says, 'Here's the smoking gun.' But lights are beginning to blink. He's feeding us information on the time line, and targeting information is coming in from our own sources—sensors and the covert teams. The CIA, which was so burned by Iraqi WMD, is going to the Pentagon and the vice president's office saying, 'It's all new stuff.' People in the administration are saying, 'We've got enough.'"

The administration's case against Iran is compromised by its history of promoting false intelligence on Iraq's weapons of mass destruction. In a recent essay on the *Foreign Policy* Web site, titled "Fool Me Twice," Joseph Cirincione, the director for nonproliferation at the Carnegie Endowment for International Peace, wrote, "The unfolding administration strategy appears to be an effort to repeat its successful campaign for the Iraq war." He noted several parallels:

> The vice president of the United States gives a major speech focused on the threat from an oil-rich nation in the Middle East. The U.S. Secretary of State tells Congress that the same nation is our most serious global challenge. The Secretary of Defense calls that nation the leading supporter of global terrorism.

Cirincione called some of the administration's claims about Iran "questionable" or lacking in evidence. When I spoke to him, he asked, "What do we know? What is the threat? The question is: How urgent is all this?" The answer, he said, "is in the intelligence community and the IAEA." (In August, *The Washington Post* reported that the most recent comprehensive National Intelligence Estimate predicted that Iran was a decade away from being a nuclear power.)

Last year, the Bush administration briefed IAEA officials on what it said was new and alarming information about Iran's weapons program which had been retrieved from an Iranian's laptop. The new data included more than a thousand pages of technical drawings of weapons systems. *The Washington Post* reported that there were also designs for a small facility that could be used in the uranium-enrichment process. Leaks about the laptop became the focal point of stories in the *Times* and elsewhere. The stories were generally careful to note that the materials could have been fabricated, but also quoted senior American officials as saying that they appeared to be legitimate. The headline in the *Times'* account read, "RELYING ON COMPUTER, U.S. SEEKS TO PROVE IRAN'S NUCLEAR AIMS."

I was told in interviews with American and European intelligence officials, however, that the laptop was more suspect and less revelatory than it had been depicted. The Iranian who owned the laptop had initially been recruited by German and American intelligence operatives, working together. The Americans eventually lost interest in him. The Germans kept on, but the Iranian was seized by the Iranian counterintelligence force. It is not known where he is today. Some family members managed to leave Iran with his laptop and handed it over at a U.S. embassy, apparently in Europe. It was a classic "walk-in."

A European intelligence official said, "There was some hesitation on our side" about what the materials really proved, "and we are still not convinced." The drawings were not meticulous, as newspaper accounts suggested, "but had the character of sketches," the European official said. "It was not a slam-dunk smoking gun."

The threat of American military action has created dismay at the headquarters of the IAEA, in Vienna. The agency's officials believe that Iran wants to be able to make a nuclear weapon, but "nobody has presented an inch of evidence of a parallel nuclear-weapons program in Iran," the high-ranking diplomat told me. The IAEA's best estimate is that the Iranians are five years away from building a nuclear bomb. "But, if the United States does anything militarily, they will make the development of a bomb a matter of Iranian national pride," the diplomat said. "The whole issue is America's risk assessment of Iran's future intentions, and they don't trust the regime. Iran is a menace to American policy."

In Vienna, I was told of an exceedingly testy meeting earlier this year between Mohamed ElBaradei, the IAEA's director-general, who won the Nobel Peace Prize last year, and Robert Joseph, the undersecretary of state for arms control. Joseph's message was blunt, one diplomat recalled: "We cannot have a single centrifuge spinning in Iran. Iran is a direct threat to the national security of the United States and our allies, and we will not tolerate it. We want you to give us an understanding that you will not say anything publicly that will undermine us."

Joseph's heavy-handedness was unnecessary, the diplomat said, since the IAEA already had been inclined to take a hard stand against Iran. "All of the inspectors are angry at being misled by the Iranians, and some think the Iranian leadership are nutcases—one hundred percent totally certified nuts," the diplomat said. He added that ElBaradei's overriding concern is that the Iranian leaders "want confrontation, just like the neocons on the other side"—in Washington. "At the end of the day, it will work only if the United States agrees to talk to the Iranians."

The central question—whether Iran will be able to proceed with its plans to enrich uranium—is now before the United Nations, with the Russians and the Chinese reluctant to impose sanctions on Tehran. A discouraged former IAEA official told me in late March that, at this point, "there's nothing the Iranians could do that would result in a positive outcome. American diplomacy does not allow for it. Even if they announce a stoppage of enrichment, nobody will believe them. It's a dead end."

Another diplomat in Vienna asked me, "Why would the West take the risk of going to war against that kind of target without giving it to the IAEA to verify? We're low cost, and we can create a program that will force Iran to put its cards on the table." A Western ambassador in Vienna expressed similar distress at the White House's dismissal of the IAEA. He said, "If you don't believe that the IAEA can establish an inspection system—if you don't trust them—you can only bomb."

There is little sympathy for the IAEA in the Bush administration or among its European allies. "We're quite frustrated with the director-general," the European diplomat told me. "His basic approach has been to describe this as a dispute between two sides with equal weight. It's not. We're the good guys! ElBaradei has been pushing the idea of letting Iran have a small nuclear-enrichment program, which is ludicrous. It's not his job to push ideas that pose a serious proliferation risk."

The Europeans are rattled, however, by their growing perception that President Bush and Vice President Dick Cheney believe a bombing campaign will be needed, and that their real goal is regime change. "Everyone is on the same page about the Iranian bomb, but the United States wants regime change," a European diplomatic adviser told me. He added, "The Europeans have a role to play as long as they don't have to choose between going along with the Russians and the Chinese or going along with Washington on something they don't want. Their policy is to keep the Americans engaged in something the Europeans can live with. It may be untenable."

"The Brits think this is a very bad idea," Flynt Leverett, a former National Security Council staff member who is now a senior fellow at the Brookings Institution's Saban Center, told me, "but they're really worried we're going to do it." The European diplomatic adviser acknowledged that the British Foreign Office was aware of war planning in Washington but that, "short of a smoking gun, it's going to be very difficult to line up the Europeans on Iran." He said that the British "are jumpy about the Americans going full bore on the Iranians, with no compromise."

The European diplomat said that he was skeptical that Iran, given its record, had admitted to everything it was doing, but "to the best of our knowledge the Iranian capability is not at the point where they could successfully run centrifuges" to enrich uranium in quantity. One reason for pursuing diplomacy was, he said, Iran's essential pragmatism. "The regime acts in its best interests," he said. Iran's leaders "take a hard-line approach on the nuclear issue and they want to call the American bluff," believing that "the tougher they are the more likely the West will fold." But, he said, "From what we've seen with Iran, they will appear superconfident until the moment they back off."

The diplomat went on, "You never reward bad behavior, and this is not the time to offer concessions. We need to find ways to impose sufficient costs to bring the regime to its senses. It's going to be a close call, but I think if there is unity in opposition and the price imposed"—in sanctions—"is sufficient, they may back down. It's too early to give up on the UN route." He added, "If the diplomatic process doesn't work, there is no military 'solution.' There may be a military option, but the impact could be catastrophic."

Tony Blair, the British prime minister, was George Bush's most dependable ally in the year leading up to the 2003 invasion of Iraq. But he and his party have been racked by a series of financial scandals, and his popularity is at a low point. Jack Straw, the foreign secretary, said last year that military action against Iran was "inconceivable." Blair has been more circumspect, saying publicly that one should never take options off the table.

Other European officials expressed similar skepticism about the value of an American bombing campaign. "The Iranian economy is in bad shape, and Ahmadinejad is in bad shape politically," the European intelligence official told me. "He will benefit politically from American bombing. You can do it, but the results will be worse." An American attack, he said, would alienate ordinary Iranians, including those who might be sympathetic to the United States. "Iran is no longer living in the Stone Age, and the young people there have access to U.S. movies and books, and they love it," he said. "If there was a charm offensive with Iran, the mullahs would be in trouble in the long run."

Another European official told me that he was aware that many in Washington wanted action. "It's always the same guys," he said, with a resigned shrug. "There is a belief that diplomacy is doomed to fail. The timetable is short."

A key ally with an important voice in the debate is Israel, whose leadership has warned for years that it viewed any attempt by Iran to begin enriching uranium as a point of no return. I was told by several officials that the White House's interest in preventing an Israeli attack on a Muslim country, which would provoke a backlash across the region, was a factor in its decision to begin the current operational planning. In a speech in Cleveland on March 20, President Bush depicted Ahmadinejad's hostility toward Israel as a "serious threat. It's a threat to world peace." He added, "I made it clear, I'll make it clear again, that we will use military might to protect our ally Israel."

Any American bombing attack, Richard Armitage told me, would have to consider the following questions: "What will happen in the other Islamic countries? What ability does Iran have to reach us and touch us globally—that is, terrorism? Will Syria and Lebanon up the pressure on Israel? What does the attack do to our already diminished international standing? And what does this mean for Russia, China, and the UN Security Council?"

Iran, which now produces nearly 4 million barrels of oil a day, would not have to cut off production to disrupt the world's oil markets. It could blockade or mine the Strait of Hormuz, the thirty-four-mile-wide passage through which Middle Eastern oil reaches the Indian Ocean. Nonetheless, the recently retired defense official dismissed the strategic consequences of such actions. He told me that the U.S. Navy could keep shipping open by conducting salvage missions and putting minesweepers to work. "It's impossible to block passage," he said. The government consultant with ties to the Pentagon also said he believed that the oil problem could be managed, pointing out that the United States has enough in its strategic reserves to keep America running for sixty days. However, those in the oil business I spoke to were less optimistic; one industry expert estimated that the price per barrel would immediately spike, to anywhere from ninety to a hundred dollars per barrel, and could go higher, depending on the duration and scope of the conflict.

Michel Samaha, a veteran Lebanese Christian politician and former cabinet minister in Beirut, told me that the Iranian retaliation might be focused on exposed oil and gas fields in Saudi Arabia, Qatar, Kuwait, and the United Arab Emirates. "They would be at risk," he said, "and this could begin the real jihad of Iran versus the West. You will have a messy world."

Iran could also initiate a wave of terror attacks in Iraq and elsewhere, with the help of Hezbollah. On April 2, *The Washington Post* reported that the planning to counter such attacks "is consuming a lot of time" at U.S. intelligence agencies. "The best terror network in the world has remained neutral in the terror war for the past several years," the Pentagon adviser on the war on terror said of Hezbollah. "This will mobilize them and put us up against the group that drove Israel out of southern Lebanon. If we move against Iran, Hezbollah will not sit on the sidelines. Unless the Israelis take them out, they will mobilize against us." (When I asked the government consultant about that possibility, he said that, if Hezbollah fired rockets into northern Israel, "Israel and the new Lebanese government will finish them off.")

The adviser went on, "If we go, the southern half of Iraq will light up like a candle." The American, British, and other coalition forces in Iraq would be at greater risk of attack from Iranian troops or from Shiite militias operating on instructions from Iran. (Iran, which is predominantly Shiite, has close ties to the leading Shiite parties in Iraq.) A retired four-star general told me that, despite the 8,000 British troops in the region, "the Iranians could take Basra with ten mullahs and one sound truck."

"If you attack," the high-ranking diplomat told me in Vienna, "Ahmadinejad will be the new Saddam Hussein of the Arab world, but with more credibility and more power. You must bite the bullet and sit down with the Iranians."

The diplomat went on, "There are people in Washington who would be unhappy if we found a solution. They are still banking on isolation and regime change. This is wishful thinking." He added, "The window of opportunity is now."

North Korea: The War Game
Scott Stossel

The Atlantic Monthly | July/August 2005

While Iran's nuclear ambitions got most of the headlines during the past year, North Korea's nuclear program is even more advanced and, in the view of many experts, poses a significantly greater potential threat to the United States and its allies. To date, the Bush administration has refused to deal with Kim Jong Il one on one, opting instead to isolate North Korea with financial sanctions while calling for regime change—an approach undercut by the continuing flow of aid from South Korea and China to the Jong Il government. Meanwhile, six-nation talks (involving the United States, North and South Korea, China, Russia, and Japan) resulted last September in the signing of a vague commitment on the part of North Korea to disarm its nuclear arsenal, but since then negotiations have stalled.

It's the sort of dilemma that keeps the president's foreign policy advisers up at night. In this fascinating article, The Atlantic Monthly *brought together a number of foreign affairs experts to walk through a simulated policy summit on how best to deal with the North Korean threat, while editor Scott Stossel kept score. Interestingly, one of the ideas advocated in this simulation—that the United States agree to sign a peace treaty with North Korea, at last putting an official end to the Korean War—is reportedly now under serious consideration by administration officials. One other disturbing note: As this book went to press, it was announced that North Korea was on the verge of test firing a long-range missile capable of reaching parts of the continental United States.*

*   *   *   *   *

On the third weekend in March, while America was transfixed by the most exciting NCAA basketball tournament in years, Secretary of State Condoleezza Rice was in the Far East, in the midst of a series of meetings with her opposite numbers in six Asian countries. Arriving in Seoul, South Korea, on Saturday, she boarded a U.S. Army Black Hawk helicopter and flew to Command Post Tango, the underground bunker that would be the nerve center for the U.S. military in the event of a war against North Korea. While not quite on the order of Ariel Sharon's parading around the Temple Mount in Israel, Rice's move was undeniably provocative. No high-ranking American official had ever visited the bunker before—and the choice of a military site as the secretary of state's first stop seemed to represent a gentle rattling of the sword. What's more, Rice spoke against a backdrop of computers and television screens monitoring the 20,000 South Korean and American soldiers who were at that very moment engaging in one of their regular war-game exercises—practicing, in effect, to fight a war with North Korea no sane person hopes ever to see.

The North Koreans responded by rattling their sword right back. First they announced they were boosting their nuclear arsenal, as a "deterrent" against U.S. attack. And then, apparently, they began to act: a few weeks after Rice's visit, U.S. spy satellites detected a reduction in activity at the Yongbyon nuclear reactor. Possibly this meant that the reactor had run into mechanical trouble; more probably, it meant that the North Koreans had shut down the plant to withdraw spent fuel rods in order to reprocess them into fissile material for nuclear weapons. What was clear was that the situation represented a grave international crisis.

Last year *The Atlantic* addressed a similar crisis—this one centering on Iran's nuclear ambitions—by conducting a war game that simulated preparations for a U.S. assault ("Will Iran Be Next?" by James Fallows, December 2004). As Sam Gardiner, the retired Air Force colonel who ran the simulation, put it, the exercise was designed to produce a "clarifying effect" by compelling participants to think through the implications of certain decisions and plans of action. The result was a bracing corrective to the notion that Iran's nuclear capacity could be taken out with a quick military strike.

The North Korean situation is also ripe for war-game treatment, because of the extraordinarily difficult military and diplomatic challenges it presents. Iran, considered an urgent national-security priority, is thought to be three to five years away from possessing even a single nuclear device. North Korea is widely believed to have as many as ten already, and to be producing more every year. (It is also the first developing nation thought to be capable of striking the continental United States with a long-range ballistic missile.) And whereas Iraq did not, after all, have weapons of mass destruction, North Korea is believed to have large stockpiles of chemical weapons (mustard gas, sarin, VX nerve agent) and biological weapons (anthrax, botulism, cholera, hemorrhagic fever, plague, smallpox, typhoid, yellow fever). An actual war on the Korean peninsula would almost certainly be the bloodiest America has fought since Vietnam—possibly since World War II. In recent years Pentagon experts have estimated that the first ninety days of such a conflict might produce 300,000 to 500,000 South Korean and American military casualties, along with hundreds of thousands of civilian deaths. The damage to South Korea alone would rock the global economy.

All-out war, however, is not the only—or even the gravest—threat North Korea currently poses to U.S. security. For some years now the fear that has kept homeland-defense experts awake at night is that terrorists will detonate a nuclear bomb in an American city. In fact, the danger that Saddam Hussein would sell nukes to terrorists was a basic rationale for invading Iraq in at least some of the Bush administration's iterations of it. But North Korea is, if anything, more likely than Saddam to do so, if it hasn't already. The country's weak economy has owed its continued functioning in part to the income from vast smuggling networks (primarily for drugs and counterfeit foreign currency) and sales of missiles and other arms to such fellow outlaw nations as Libya, Iran, Syria, and Iraq. At some point the North Koreans may decide they have more than enough nuclear weapons for their own purposes and sell the extras for cash. The longer North Korea keeps producing nukes, in other words, the greater the likelihood that one will find its way to New York or Washington.

Unfortunately, trying to take out the regime's nuclear sites with surgical strikes—an iffy proposition at best, since we don't know where some of the sites are—might provoke a horrific war. And trying to create regional nuclear deterrence by allowing South Korea, Japan, and even Taiwan to become nuclear powers would undermine the global nonproliferation system that has been in place for more than forty years. The North Korean regime may be fundamentally undeterrable anyway: President Kim Jong Il has reportedly said that he would "destroy the world" or "take the world with me" before accepting defeat on the battlefield. And as bad as Kim is, what comes after him could be worse. A complete collapse of the regime might lead not only to enormous refugee problems for China and South Korea but also, in effect, to a weapons-of-mass-destruction yard sale for smugglers.

There are still other dangers. If we did successfully invade, our troops would be likely to eventually find themselves near North Korea's Chinese border. The last time that happened, in 1950, the Chinese counterinvaded. (A 1961 treaty obliges China to do so again in the event of an attack on North Korea.) Meanwhile, other nations—most notably Iran—are watching carefully to see whether North Korea will be allowed to become an official nuclear power without reprisal.

All of which is to say that any move in North Korea is fraught with potentially disastrous implications. Time is not on our side, as the shut-down of the Yongbyon reactor in April makes clear; the longer we wait to take action, the more nuclear weapons Kim Jong Il may build, and the more threatening he will become. Something needs to be done. But what?

The seeds of the current crisis were planted late in the winter of 1993, when North Korea declared that proposed International Atomic Energy Agency inspections of two of its nuclear sites represented an unwarranted violation of sovereignty. The Kim regime subsequently threatened to begin con-verting 8,000 spent fuel rods from its Yongbyon plant into weaponizable nuclear material. As tensions rose, Pyongyang became more belligerent, at one point reminding the South Koreans that it wouldn't be hard to turn Seoul into "a sea of fire." The United States, for its part, contemplated pre-emptive strikes on Yongbyon.

By the spring of 1994 the United States was probably closer to nuclear war than it had been since the Cuban Missile Crisis. On June 15 President Clinton and others sat in the White House Cabinet Room listening to Secretary of Defense William Perry present an array of military options against North Korea. Clinton was preparing to evacuate American civil-ians from the country when word came that Jimmy Carter—who was in Pyongyang as an independent citizen, not as an official emissary of the Clinton administration—had reached a preliminary deal with the North

Koreans and was about to go on CNN to announce the terms. The parties returned to the negotiating table, and in October 1994 they signed the so-called Agreed Framework. In exchange for North Korea's freezing nuclear weapons development, the United States, South Korea, and Japan would supply Pyongyang with light-water nuclear reactors and with 500,000 metric tons of heavy fuel oil annually.

Congressional Republicans attacked the agreement, calling it "appeasement." The North Koreans eventually cheated on it, a fact nobody disputes; but some have argued that the Agreed Framework was a success despite the cheating. It averted an imminent war, and it shut down the North Korean plutonium program for nine years—thereby limiting Pyongyang's arsenal to one or two nuclear weapons as of 2002, rather than the nearly one hundred it might otherwise have been able to develop by then.

In the summer of 2002, U.S. intelligence discovered that the North Koreans had secretly restarted their weapons development using highly enriched uranium. When Assistant Secretary of State James Kelly went to Pyongyang in October of 2002 to confront the North Koreans, he expected them to deny the existence of the uranium program. They didn't; in fact, evidently they soon restarted their plutonium program, by continuing to reprocess the 8,000 spent fuel rods from Yongbyon (which had been in storage since the signing of the Agreed Framework). In October 2003 the North Koreans said they had finished the reprocessing—meaning, if true, that they had enough fissile material for up to six new nuclear weapons. The Bush administration, not wanting to appear to reward bad behavior, has since adamantly refused to negotiate directly with the North Koreans. Six-party talks involving China, Japan, Russia, and South Korea—regional powers that the Bush administration hoped could help hold the Kim regime to account—began in August 2003, but after the third round of talks, last June, the North Koreans pulled out, demanding direct bilateral negotiations with the United States.

All this loomed in the background when, six days after Condoleezza Rice's visit to Command Post Tango, *The Atlantic* convened a North Korea war game of its own, in Washington, D.C. The assembled knowledge was extensive, and the range of Washington viewpoints more or less complete—hawk to dove, right to left, neocon to realist.

As in our Iran war game, Colonel Sam Gardiner led the proceedings.

(Gardiner has run war games for more than twenty years at the National War College and various other military institutions; the strategy that General Tommy Franks used to seize Baghdad in 2003 had its origins in a game Gardiner had designed some fifteen years earlier.) And once again the premise of the game was a meeting of the "Principals Committee"—the highest-ranking national-security officials of an imaginary U.S. presidential administration—to generate recommendations for the president. Gardiner explained that he would be presenting to the principals a military briefing from the perspective of the commander of the U.S. Pacific Command (PACOM).

Playing the part of the CIA director was David Kay—a man well equipped for this job. In the early 1990s Kay served as the chief nuclear weapons inspector for the IAEA and the United Nations Special Commission in Iraq, and in June 2003 he was asked by the actual CIA director to lead the Iraq Survey Group that searched for (and never found) WMD in Iraq after the U.S. invasion.

The secretary of state in this exercise was Robert Gallucci. The dean of the Edmund A. Walsh School of Foreign Service, at Georgetown University, Gallucci has extensive real-world experience in dealing with North Korea. In 1994 he served as the Clinton administration's chief negotiator with the North Koreans during the crisis that ultimately produced the Agreed Framework. Gallucci did not have to overtax his imagination for this simulation: he had been present at the real versions of such meetings in the White House, including one in June 1994, when the president considered ordering military strikes on the Yongbyon reactor.

Lieutenant General Thomas McInerney, who spent thirty-five years in the U.S. Air Force as a pilot, a commander, and a strategic planner, played the role of chairman of the Joint Chiefs of Staff. McInerney conducted flight reconnaissance missions during the Cuban Missile Crisis, and later completed four tours of duty in Vietnam. From the late 1970s to the early 1990s, he served predominantly in the Pacific theater. While there he watched by means of satellite photography as the North Koreans constructed bunkers and artillery installations in the mountains north of Seoul. A military analyst for Fox News, McInerney last year argued in *Endgame: The Blueprint for Victory in the War on Terror* (written with Paul E. Vallelly) that the key to stopping the spread of terrorism is regime change. McInerney thinks we should invade not only North Korea (if it doesn't give up its nuclear program) but also Syria (if it doesn't end its support of terrorism and surrender the WMD that he believes were smuggled there from Iraq) and Saudi Arabia (if Islamic radicals seize power there).

Filling the newly created position of director of national intelligence was Jessica Mathews, the president of the Carnegie Endowment for International Peace. (Mathews and McInerney had clashed over Iraq, and their animosity was easy to see; this lent extra verisimilitude to the exercise, since personal disputes over policy often color debates within administrations.) Mathews directed the National Security Council's Office of Global Issues from 1977 to 1979, and served as deputy to the undersecretary of state for global affairs under President Clinton.

Rounding out the Principals Committee was Kenneth Adelman, who would be serving as secretary of defense. A current member of the Defense Policy Board, Adelman has held a number of positions in Republican administrations. In the mid-1970s he was assistant to President Ford's secretary of defense, Donald Rumsfeld; later he was a key member of Ronald Reagan's foreign-policy team, serving for two years as deputy UN ambassador and for four years as head of the Arms Control and Disarmament Agency. Like Gallucci and Mathews, Adelman is a veteran of real NSC meetings.

"Let's play," Sam Gardiner said. He announced that he had a memo from the Pentagon asking for a review of the status of our plans for North Korea. He reminded the group that it had been two and a half years since we had told the North Koreans we knew about their clandestine uranium-enrichment program, and nearly two years since international six-party talks had begun—yet the crisis had if anything only deepened.

Gardiner reviewed some of the basic facts about North Korea's conventional military capabilities. The North Korean People's Army, he observed, is the fifth biggest military in the world, with more than 1.2 million active-duty troops and 7 million reservists. One of the most notable components of the People's Army is its highly trained Special Operations Forces—the North Korean equivalent of Saddam Hussein's elite Republican Guard. Consisting of some 125,000 troops, the SOF may be the largest such force in the world. In the event of a conflict on the peninsula, Gardiner said, we would find ourselves not only engaging these troops along the border but also combating their sneak attacks from the rear. Displaying a PowerPoint slide that depicted North Korean tunneling operations along the demilitarized zone since the 1970s, Gardiner observed that the SOF would get behind the front lines not only through hidden tunnels that U.S. and South Korean intelligence agencies have yet to find (one of them, according to the journalist Jasper Becker's new book, *Rogue Regime: Kim Jong Il and the Looming Threat of North Korea*, is large enough for 30,000 infantrymen to pass through in an hour) but also in small aircraft, boats, and midget submarines. We're improving our ability to contend with the SOF, Gardiner said. But it remains a "big deal."

Next he summarized the North Korean missile program: the medium-range No-Dong missiles that can hit Japan; the 1,200-mile Taepo Dong 1 missiles; and the Taepo Dong 2, which could theoretically strike the continental United States. The Taepo Dong 2, Gardiner said, "changes the strategic equation significantly."

Gardiner paused to get initial assessments from the Principals Committee. CIA Director David Kay responded first, noting that what confounds policy making on North Korea is how little anyone actually knows about the country. "We *believe* a lot," he observed. "We actually *know* very little." Kay thought that the principal objective of U.S. intelligence at this point should be to determine the extent of any connection between North Korea's nuclear program and groups outside the country.

Secretary of State Gallucci spoke next. "This is a country," he said, "that has exported ballistic missiles when no other country on earth is exporting ballistic missiles—a country that has threatened explicitly to export nuclear material." What is so frightening about this prospect, Gallucci said, is that traditional deterrent methods won't work. "If there's an incident," he continued, "the worst we can imagine, the detonation of a weapon in an American city, will we have attribution? Will we be able to track it back to North Korea? Is there any deterrence against [the export of nuclear materials] by a desperate state?"

Secretary of Defense Adelman disagreed with the idea that we don't know what North Korea's intentions are. "We *do* know what North Korea's strategy is: it is obviously to deter us from attacking them like we attacked Iraq." Adelman said he thought there was "no hope" of changing North Korea's behavior through conventional diplomacy. "Having talks as an objective of U.S. policy is a diplomatic move that gets you nothing," he said. "I know Winston Churchill said it's better to jaw-jaw than to war-war, but there's lots of jaw-jawing that leads to war-war, or that has nothing to do with war-war. So let's not spend time on whether we should get back to 'talks.'" Instead, Adelman said, we should try to induce the Chinese to lean on the North Koreans to give up their nuclear program. How? By scaring them with the prospect of a nuclear South Korea, a nuclear Japan, and possibly a nuclear Taiwan. Once the Chinese recognize that they'll soon be looking at multiple nuclear powers in the region if they don't force the North Koreans to disarm, Adelman argued, they'll be compelled to use leverage against North Korea— by, for example, cutting off its food and fuel supplies.

Director of National Intelligence Mathews returned to Kay's point regarding how little we really know of North Korea. We know far less about North Korea's nuclear program than we do about Iran's, she said. "Uncertainty is the thing that has to underlie the rest of our discussion. There's very little we can say that we know with confidence, either politically or technically, about North Korea." She agreed with Kay and Gallucci about the real danger to our national security: "This is a regime that will sell anything." And she disagreed with Adelman about whether the Chinese could effectively influence the North Koreans. The Chinese, she pointed out, would be reluctant to do anything that might topple the regime and cause a huge flow of refugees across their border.

Finally, Mathews said that we have never really tested whether the right combination of political promises, security assurances, and economic aid would induce the North Koreans to give up their nuclear weapons. "I'm not saying they *would* give up their nuclear weapons," she said. "I'm saying we don't know the answer to this absolutely crucial question." Before we resort to more extreme measures, she said, we ought to try to answer it. She proposed that we begin by offering to sign a treaty formally ending the Korean War. (Hostilities ceased in 1953 with the signing of an armistice and the drawing of the DMZ, along the 38th parallel—but no peace treaty was signed, which means that technically the United States and North Korea are still at war.)

"That would say something to a paranoid regime," Mathews continued. "It doesn't mean anything to us; we don't think the Korean War is still going on. But it says something to them. It may be a very valuable bargaining chip, and we've never spent it."

Joint Chiefs Chairman McInerney agreed that the greatest national-security threat posed by North Korea was nuclear transfer, and he echoed Gallucci's concern that deterrence will not protect against nuclear terrorism. General McInerney was more willing than the other principals to contemplate military action, and more sanguine about how easy a war with North Korea would be to win. "I don't think we're concerned that they could overrun the South, because they can't," he said. "Militarily, we are far superior to them. Would there be a lot of carnage? Yes, there'd be a lot of carnage. Would we win? Yes, we would win. Would we win quicker than we did in Operation Iraqi Freedom? Optimistically, I'd say we could. More likely, it would take an extra month. But the fact is, we would win."

To prevent North Korea's nuclear capability from creating an imbalance of power, McInerney proposed stationing U.S. nuclear weapons in South Korea and Japan. During the Cold War, he explained, various NATO countries "sat alert" on U.S. nuclear weapons. The weapons were on European aircraft, but the United States dictated when they could be deployed.

North Korea, he conceded, has the potential to use Seoul, which lies only thirty-five miles south of the DMZ, as a "hostage"—to threaten to turn it into that "sea of fire." But he strenuously disagreed that this means "a military option is not thinkable," as some U.S. policy makers say. "A military option is clearly thinkable, and doable," he argued. "If threatened with the transfer of nuclear weapons from North Korea to terrorists, we *have* to do something."

Gardiner, in his role as PACOM commander, resumed his briefing. He displayed a map of Korea that depicted the expected North Korean attack routes. Because of the mountainous terrain along the border, the conventional forces of the People's Army would be limited to a few corridors that would be highly vulnerable to U.S. air power. The bottom line: we could easily repel a conventional ground attack.

But, he continued, there are two degrees of desirable victory: "swiftly defeating" the bad guys, and "winning decisively." In a swift defeat escalation is controlled; victory is rapid enough that the conflict remains limited and conventional. In winning decisively the scope of the victory and the number of troops on the ground are sufficient to carry out postwar stability operations. In Iraq, U.S. forces swiftly defeated the enemy (the war was quick and didn't metastasize) but did not win decisively (a big reason why the military aftermath of Operation Iraqi Freedom has been so protracted).

Gardiner explained that to control escalation in North Korea, the United

States, using its air power, would first have to take out North Korea's aging air force. Though many enemy aircraft are bunkered in mountain redoubts, this would be easy. But one major problem could keep us from taking rapid control of the peninsula: chemical weapons. Citing congressional testimony given by General Leon LaPorte, the commander of U.S. forces in Korea, Gardiner said that North Korea's chemical weapons could be a "showstopper." "The chemical-weapon thing is big," he said. "We have reason to believe that the chemical weapons are with the forward artillery units that are targeting Seoul. If we don't get those early, we end up with chemicals on Seoul."

Next Gardiner projected a PowerPoint slide showing the range of a Taepo Dong 1 missile overlaid on a map of East Asia. It demonstrated that such a missile launched from the Korean peninsula could reach not only Tokyo, Okinawa, and Beijing but also the U.S. base in Guam. To prevent escalation, Gardiner said, we would need to take out the No-Dong and Taepo Dong missile sites quickly—which would not be easy, because we don't know where those missiles are. Many are hidden in underground bunkers throughout North Korea. The PACOM commander's conclusion: "It's a difficult target set, but we can do it."

We would also, of course, need to take out the nuclear sites. Gardiner flashed a map of North Korea's known nuclear-related facilities on the screen, and then showed a series of satellite photos of various WMD targets. Many of the targets were tucked away in underground tunnels or at least partially obscured by what arrows on the photos labeled as "hill masses." "You begin to see how difficult a target set this is," Gardiner said.

"Is that a euphemism for undoable?" Secretary of Defense Adelman asked.

"No, not at all," Gardiner said. General McInerney practically jumped out of his chair to say "No!"

Gardiner continued, explaining that the first few days of the fight would be critical if we were to have any chance of protecting Seoul. To do so, we would have to get the chemical-delivery systems, the missile sites, and the nuclear sites before the North Koreans had a chance to use them. To accomplish all this we would need to carry out 4,000 air sorties a day in the first days of the conflict. In Iraq, in contrast, we had carried out 800 a day.

Director of National Intelligence Mathews disagreed that Seoul could be shielded: "My understanding is that we *cannot* protect Seoul, at least for the first twenty-four hours of a war, and maybe for the first forty-eight." McInerney disputed this, and Mathews asked him to explain.

> McINERNEY: "There's a difference between 'protecting' Seoul and [limiting] the amount of damage Seoul may take."
>
> MATHEWS: "There are a hundred thousand Americans in Seoul, not to mention ten million South Koreans."
>
> McINERNEY: "A lot of people are going to die, Jessica. But you still prevail."
>
> MATHEWS: "I just think we've got to be really careful. We've got to protect Seoul. If your daughter were living in Seoul, I don't think you would feel the U.S. military could protect her in those first twenty-four hours."
>
> McINERNEY: "No, I do. I believe that we have the capability—whether from preemption or response—to minimize the casualties in Seoul."
>
> MATHEWS: " 'Minimize' to roughly what level? A hundred thousand? Two hundred thousand?"
>
> McINERNEY: "I think a hundred thousand or less."

Only a hard-nosed military strategist, of course, can contemplate 100,000 casualties as coolly as McInerney did. He went on to argue that—assuming 4,000 sorties a day, and given our current targeting technology, combined with the fact that the artillery systems firing on Seoul would be fairly concentrated around the DMZ—we would be able to mitigate the lethality of North Korean strikes on Seoul. Gallucci added that the North Koreans would be foolish to waste their artillery on Seoul. "It is insane for them if they are engaged in ground combat," Gallucci said. "They're going to be in desperate need of that artillery for support of ground operations."

McInerney agreed: "If they try to use Seoul as an artillery target, we would destroy their army that much quicker."

Secretary of Defense Adelman was skeptical that the North Koreans would use the same strategy to "break through" that they had when they successfully overran the South in 1950. David Kay reminded everybody that one key difference between 1950 and today is that North Korea may now have "between one and ten nukes, and adequate delivery methods," meaning "they can take out Seoul without using a single artillery round—and I haven't seen anything here that shows we can mitigate *that*." When

McInerney began to argue that maybe we could disable their nuclear missiles before they were fired, Kay retorted, "Our record of attacking mobile missiles in Iraq is not very good."

"That's why our policy must clearly state that for every nuke they use, we will use a hundred," McInerney said.

The other members of the Principals Committee seemed taken aback by this statement.

Gardiner tried to resume his briefing by summing up the sentiment of the committee. "None of the military options is easy—"

Adelman interrupted. "That's a euphemism. Let's talk directly: it would be disastrous."

Mathews agreed. "We can only reach the targets we know about. You can't target targets you don't know about, and there are a whole bunch of them."

"And some targets we do know about, but we don't know where they are," Kay added. "And that's most of the missile force."

The consensus was that Seoul could not be guaranteed protection. And McInerney, who dissented from that consensus, was projecting up to 100,000 casualties in South Korea in the first few days.

Gardiner moved on to the next phase of his briefing, which involved placing the North Korean situation in the context of the U.S. military's other global commitments. President Bush, he reminded the principals, has said that "all options are on the table" with respect to Iran. But if all options (including invasion) are truly on the table for dealing with Iran, Gardiner announced, "then I have to tell you that we cannot do this operation—either in defense or preemption—on the peninsula." There simply aren't enough available troops. Hundreds of thousands of troops are tied up because of Iraq. Tens or hundreds of thousands more would be required for Iran, even if we intended only to make a credible show of force rather than actually invade.

Gardiner also pointed out that U.S. military planners have called for a drawdown in the number of American troops stationed in South Korea over the next few years—from 37,500 in 2004 to 25,000 by 2008. Because of our overwhelming air and naval superiority, we still have the "overmatching" capability to defeat a conventional attack. But, he said, "I can't assure that we can swiftly defeat or win decisively." He also said that as the size of his force diminished, he was losing his capacity to deter a North Korean attack.

David Kay observed that since the greatest national-security threat, everyone agreed, was not a North Korean invasion of South Korea but, rather, the North Korean transfer of nuclear material to terrorists, the essential question was how big a force was needed for a preemptive attack, not how big a force was needed to deter invasion.

Gardiner argued that we have the capability to deter the North Koreans from either course by threatening to launch nuclear weapons at them. He emphasized that he wasn't recommending that we launch nukes—only saying that a nuclear deterrent might work on the peninsula the way it did with the Soviet Union during the Cold War. McInerney agreed, and once again proposed lending some of our nuclear weapons to South Korea and Japan as a deterrent against the North. Gardiner recommended a strategy short of that: we should announce publicly, he suggested, that we are moving nuclear weapons—along with nuclear-capable aircraft and missiles—to Guam, and then keep them there as a deterrent while so many of our troops are tied down elsewhere.

Adelman said, "We have got to decide in this group whether to recommend to the president that we use the standard deterrence approach we have used for years"—that is, keeping a strong conventional force on the peninsula—"or whether we want to take a different approach and have *less* U.S. involvement in this thing." Adelman recommended the latter course, which he said would compel the South Koreans, the Japanese, and the Chinese to deal with the problem.

"You're forgetting the whole history of U.S. nonproliferation policy," Mathews said. "You're encouraging Japan to go nuclear."

"I'm not forgetting," Adelman said. "I may be overriding it."

Nobody else was comfortable with the idea of a nuclear Japan; Kay and Mathews objected that it would undermine long-standing U.S. policy, and McInerney objected because he thought existing treaties obliged us to keep Japan and South Korea under our own nuclear umbrella. Mathews proposed that they move on to the next item, since it was clear that "on this point we're going to have to go to the president with divided opinion."

Before moving on, however, Gardiner wanted to come to consensus about where to draw the "red line" (or lines), the crossing of which would trigger international sanctions—and perhaps ultimately a preemptive strike by U.S. forces. There was some discussion of whether a nuclear-weapons test would constitute a red-line violation. For Gallucci, it was the transfer of fissile material. "That needs not only to be laid down as a red line but reinforced repeatedly," he said.

"Would you do a preemptive attack if transfer happens?" Adelman asked.

"I would mean what I said: 'We will not tolerate that. And we will act against you.' That's all I would tell them."

"But in this room what would you say?" Gardiner asked.

Gallucci responded haltingly. "I would strike at whatever facility—within the context of our capabilities, the protection of Seoul. And I would ask for good advice on how we would do this to protect ourselves. But I would, either immediately or in the fullness of time, use force to end that regime."

McInerney was blunter. "I would say to the North Koreans, 'If a nuclear weapon or weapons go off in the United States, you are a target'"—even if we don't know for sure that North Korea was responsible.

Gallucci didn't want to do that. "The idea that if a nuclear weapon were detonated in an American city without attribution, we would tell North Korea we were going to attack them, does *not* sound like the United States of America. We have to do better than that. And I don't want to wait, by the way, for the detonation of a weapon. Let me be clear here: the trigger for my action is not detonation; the trigger is incontrovertible evidence that the North Koreans have transferred fissile material to a terrorist group."

"But you'll not get that incontrovertible evidence," McInerney said. "That's my point."

"I believe we have to begin to act before that happens," Gallucci said. "I would advocate—and I am now going to use softer language—moving toward the use of military force to deal with the accumulation of fissile material even *before* transfer. When exactly you do that—I think that's got to be squishy. I'm not prepared to tell you exactly when that is."

After a break in the proceedings, the game resumed. Gardiner explained how our understanding of the North Korean situation has changed in light of our experience in Iraq. Specifically, we now know how catastrophic "victory" can be. If the Kim regime were to collapse, the most urgent national-security priority would be securing all chemical, nuclear, and biological weapons facilities, to prevent smugglers and terrorists from seizing them. There would also be, he said, a monumental refugee and "internally displaced person" problem—North Koreans flooding south toward Seoul and north into China—that could become a large-scale tragedy if chemical weapons had been unleashed. And there would be the additional challenges—now quite familiar to us from Iraq—of restoring public security, figuring out how to reform existing security forces, establishing the basic outlines of a functional national government, and preventing a widespread humanitarian disaster.

Ken Adelman strongly disputed that the collapse of the Kim regime would be a problem. "When you win the lottery, you've got to worry about your tax payment. I'm just saying these are wonderful problems to have."

"*If* you're prepared for them," Kay said.

Gardiner presented some numbers. Given the North Korean population of 23 million, and the number of U.S. troops it has taken to (not very successfully) maintain order and prevent looting in Iraq (population: 26 million), he estimated that it would take 500,000 ground troops to carry out stability operations. "These don't all have to be Americans, but if the historical record is correct we've got to have five hundred thousand somebodies in the North," he said.

Gardiner then came back to the question of timing. He displayed a graph that charted targeting difficulty and threat on the vertical axis against time on the horizontal axis. The graph showed that as time passes, and North Korea develops more nuclear weapons, the targeting challenges for the U.S. military grow considerably. It's hard enough to take out one or two—or eight or ten—nuclear devices if we don't know exactly where they are. The task of destroying fifteen or twenty, or eighty or a hundred, before any of them can be launched becomes substantially harder. And the threat that one of them will be sold to a terrorist greatly increases. "The problem of time is a *very* serious one," Gardiner said.

Gardiner summarized his assessment so far, and gave his PACOM recommendation to the Principals Committee. "The targeting dilemma is growing," he said. "We need to begin to plan seriously for the preemption option."

There was a moment of stunned silence. "What did you just say?" Adelman asked.

"We should prepare to preempt and change the regime in North Korea" within the next twelve to eighteen months, Gardiner said. "From a military perspective, to kick this can down the street doesn't make sense."

McInerney said preemption wouldn't be necessary if we had a strong enough nuclear deterrent. And Mathews said she thought everyone was too obsessively focused on the Korean threat, at the expense of attention to other dangers we risked exacerbating. "We have forty-five years of trying to build a world that's safe from nuclear weapons," she said. "I think we ought to keep in mind that we have an equal threat long-term having five or six nuclear powers in Asia. I think it does mean the collapse of the nonproliferation regime, and that's a serious threat to U.S. interests."

Kay remained more concerned about what would happen if the North Korean government fell. "The collapse of a nuclear, chemical, and biologically armed state is a serious national-security threat not just for us but for the whole world. We ought to have a contingency plan for what happens if that regime collapses. Because if you don't, Iraq is going to look like child's play."

Gardiner asked everyone to summarize. Based on the discussion in this meeting, what would they recommend that the president do?

David Kay went first. "The first thing that's clear to me out of this discussion is the importance of reinvigorating the diplomatic approach. Now, we may disagree to some degree about whether it can be a solo Chinese effort as opposed to a combined effort, but I think we all agree: of all the alternatives we've explored, a diplomatic approach that *led* to something would be far better, and less risky, than any of the others. The president has got to be told he's got to try to do this seriously—and it's better to do it sooner rather than later." Kay also observed that the North Korean crisis places an extraordinarily heavy burden on the intelligence system. If we agree that we would have to respond if North Korea transferred nuclear material to terrorists or accumulated more fissile material, then we've got to be able to know with a high degree of confidence when those things have occurred. To simply say we think the lines *may* have been crossed is not enough.

Once the red line gets crossed, Kay said, "then you do have to start thinking about preemption. You also have to think about what happens if you win."

Robert Gallucci agreed about the need to "do something." He argued that we should use the Chinese "as aggressively as we can, within reason"— as long as we also recognize that for diplomacy to have a chance, we need both carrots and sticks. If diplomatic options do not work, Gallucci added, we need to turn to military ones. He concluded by highlighting Jessica Mathews's point that if we're not careful we could end up in a world that has more nuclear states. "That," he said, "would be catastrophic."

Ken Adelman said again that he didn't think diplomacy could work without more leverage from China, and that he would recommend to the president that we actively draw down our force strength in the region, thereby compelling this to become a Chinese problem. "I don't want the United States to take the traditional approach of reinforcing troops, adding nuclear weapons—all the things we've done over the last forty years. We need to give the region more responsibility."

Jessica Mathews disagreed with Gallucci that evidence of a transfer of nuclear material to terrorists would be grounds for war. "I think we get a real Pyrrhic victory," she said. "I don't think you get support out of South Korea. You're asking them to die, to destroy their country, because of a potential threat that some amount of plutonium or highly enriched uranium [might end up in] Washington."

McInerney asked her whether she would "rather wait until the first nuke goes off in the United States" before attacking.

"I'm just saying we're never going to have South Korean support for that policy," Mathews said. "It's just insanely not in their interest." (Gallucci disagreed, pointing out that in June 1994 he thought the Clinton administration could have won South Korean support for military strikes on the Yongbyon complex, even though no one could have been sure that the conflict wouldn't escalate into a war.) Mathews advised that before we resort to preemption we should make absolutely sure we have truly tried all the diplomatic options. Until we do that, in her view, we won't be able to get international support for preemption. "I come back to a series of steps that would be low-cost," she said. "They want us to sign a treaty ending the Korean War? Just say yes. What on earth does it cost us? I don't think we've used all our diplomatic chips in this at all. Before we try military options that have huge costs associated with them, we should try this and prove to ourselves that [diplomacy] fails."

"The problem with that," Adelman said, "is that you never ever know that it failed. You can always say, 'Give me another five years, Mr. President.' Nothing has ever 'failed' until there's an explosion."

McInerney said the key thing we need is better intelligence, so that we can know when terrorists have acquired nuclear materials, and know where Korea's WMD are located. With better intelligence, he said, North Korea becomes an easy military problem to solve conventionally. He repeated his call for placing U.S. nuclear weapons on South Korean and Japanese planes, as a deterrent against attack. And, addressing David Kay, he remarked that he couldn't afford to put 500,000 troops in North Korea if the Kim regime collapsed. "I would like to do it," he said, "but the resources aren't there."

Kay replied, "General, all I would say is that when [U.S. Army Chief of Staff] General Eric Shinseki told the secretary of defense [Rumsfeld] how many troops it would require in Iraq to maintain stability, he did the nation a great service. The secretary of defense did not [do a great service] by saying, 'We can't do it.' Because the problem was there."

"David, we may or may not agree on that number," McInerney said. "Our problem in Iraq has historically been intelligence. This is a small-unit problem—we need five hundred thousand or a million troops. And we don't have that." This conformed with Gardiner's earlier assessment: our military is in danger of being stretched so thin that the troops simply wouldn't be available.

Gardiner called time out, and the official part of the game was over.

At this point various experts who had been invited to watch the war game were asked to offer their observations. Chris Chyba, a former NSC staffer and the codirector of the Center for International Security and Cooperation, spoke first. "There's a ticking clock," he said. "Unfortunately, we don't know how much time is left on the clock." In his view, the biggest problem was how to deal with a red-line violation (namely, transfer of material to terrorists) that we aren't likely to know has occurred.

The next two observers were active-duty military officers who had also commented on *The Atlantic's* Iran war game. Marine Colonel Thomas X. Hammes, a counterinsurgency expert and the author of *The Sling and the Stone*, pointed out that everyone at the table kept saying it was unacceptable for North Korea to become a nuclear power—but everyone also seemed to believe that it already *is* a nuclear power. "So we're having a really stupid argument," he said. "We're the only people we're fooling."

Hammes disagreed with Ken Adelman's plan to have China pressure the North Koreans by cutting off their food supply. He argued that first, Kim Jong Il has already proved he doesn't care how many people he starves, and second, if we really do crank up the pressure on him we increase the likelihood of a "spasm attack" on Seoul. He also disagreed that we would need to ship 500,000 American troops to the peninsula for stability operations if the regime collapsed. "There are about five hundred thousand South Korean infantrymen who can be mobilized in about four days," he noted—infantrymen who, unlike most American peacekeeping troops, happen to speak Korean.

Army Major Donald Vandergriff, whose most recent book is *The Path to Victory*, worried that we could be caught off guard by a surprise attack on the South. U.S. intelligence has failed spectacularly in this regard before—think not just of Pearl Harbor and 9/11 but also of the North Korean invasion in 1950. And, he asked, what if North Korea doesn't even try to fight a conventional war but resorts instead to "fourth-generation war," relying heavily on commandoes, assassins, and sleeper cells in the South?

Ray McGovern, the cofounder of a group called Veteran Intelligence Professionals for Sanity, wanted to know why the Bush administration seemed so unwilling to use the diplomatic measures at its disposal.

"Let's for goodness' sake make our best effort at this," Gallucci said, responding to McGovern's question. "I remember briefing Jimmy Carter once, and he asked me in the middle of this briefing, just before he went to Pyongyang in June of 1994: 'If we make a deal, will they honor it?' And I said, 'I actually have no idea.' Well, now I do have an idea. You cannot count on it. Any deal we cut has to have verification elements in it. I would argue that we really were not hurt by that deal in 1994, that it actually did pretty well—even though they cheated. So I'm not sorry that we did that deal." Gallucci said we should even be willing to offer the North Koreans a security assurance as part of a deal.

"If you're saying we're going to guarantee a Communist regime in North Korea, that's a pretty lousy idea," Adelman said.

"Is that what I said?" Gallucci responded, his choler rising. "I believe I said a 'security assurance,' and that I have always understood we would not attack them *provided* they abided by the deal. And that's an assurance that

I would be prepared to give. When we talked to them, I had an eye-to-eye opportunity to tell them what I thought of their regime. Kang Sok Ju [the leading North Korean negotiator] said to me, 'You're trying to strangle us.' And I said, 'Don't get two things confused. If this works, we're not going to be trying to strangle you; we're going to be going into a new relationship. But don't misunderstand me. We deplore your regime. We believe it is horrendous. We believe you treat your people horribly.'"

Jessica Mathews suggested that one reason diplomacy has not yet been successful is that our own policy makers have been so divided on how to proceed. (This was most starkly revealed in March 2001, when, one day after announcing that the Bush administration would continue the negotiations begun under Clinton, Secretary of State Colin Powell was humiliatingly contradicted by the president. "We don't negotiate with evil," Vice President Dick Cheney reportedly said in a meeting on North Korea; "we defeat it.") "Any negotiation is a two-part deal," Mathews said. "The first part you have with yourself. I would submit that this conversation makes it clear that we have not had that. We have no sense within this country of what it makes sense to do if you're going to try to engage the North Koreans."

"We used to call that, and still do, 'appeasement,'" General McInerney said.

"I didn't say anything about appeasement," Mathews replied.

"I know, and you won't say anything about it," McInerney said. "One's got to be very careful in taking the diplomatic route. Look, I commend Bob [Gallucci] for the work the Clinton administration tried in '94. But let's not live on the good ship *Lollipop* and think that we're going to be able to do this again once they have shown that they are not going to negotiate [in good faith]. They *cheated* us."

"What they have shown is if they can get away with cheating, they'll cheat," Mathews said. "Our job is to be smarter than that. Their having cheated gives us an opportunity to give them a tougher deal."

"This is *precisely* the discussion that needs to take place," David Kay said as the session ended. "And it is very clear why the president of the United States has to be present at the discussion. Otherwise we have an absolute stalemate. We don't win on a stalemate in this case. And so you've got to decide what risk you're willing to run now to avoid a greater risk later on. And only the president can make that decision."

*   *   *   *   *

During the next few weeks I had conversations with all the members of the Principals Committee. What had they taken away from the war game? Despite the disputatiousness of the proceedings, was there any consensus about the lessons that could be drawn from the exercise?

There was. The first lesson was no surprise: This is not a situation that is going to get better with time. "Anyone who walks through the North Korea crisis comes through absolutely convinced that it is only going to get worse," David Kay told me. He came away from the exercise convinced of the situation's urgency—and convinced that the United States has wasted several years, effectively doing nothing while it hoped the regime would collapse. Kay believes that the administration's reluctance to engage the matter diplomatically is dangerous. And that was the second lesson at least three of the principals agreed on: We need—soon—to make a serious attempt at negotiating. "The Bush administration believes that the North Koreans cannot be relied upon to abide by international agreements," Kay said. "They also believe there are groups so bad that you harm yourself by talking to them. North Korea is a horrible regime—in human-rights terms, one of the worst on earth. But talking to them in no way compromises our moral beliefs." We need to take another crack at direct negotiation before we go the military route, he said.

For Jessica Mathews, this second lesson was the most important. She felt that the administration was hurting itself by insisting on participating only in multilateral talks, as opposed to direct negotiations with North Korea. "There's nothing in our national-security interest that is better served by multilateral versus bilateral talks. That's a shape-of-the-table issue. If we wanted to say, 'Okay, they want to have bilateral talks? Fine. We'll have a bilateral subcommittee within the six-party talks'—how long would that take to figure out? Half an hour." She added, "It's kind of odd that this administration, of all administrations, wants to outsource this policy issue to the Chinese."

A third lesson was that the transfer of nuclear material to terrorists is the biggest danger we face. General McInerney agreed with that, and with the idea that North Korea was an urgent matter (though he thought Iran was more pressing). But he disagreed on the importance of pursuing talks. In his view, people like Mathews and Gallucci, who are willing to pursue bilateral negotiations, are being naive. He also believes that it's important for Kim Jong Il to know what our military capabilities are, and to know we are willing to use them—which is why he believes that the "bleeding hearts" who say "Oh, God, we couldn't do this" about a war with North Korea (because of the threat to Seoul) interfere with our deterrent message to Kim. Kim needs to know that if he sells nuclear technology to terrorists, "he will get nuclear weapons on North Korea."

Ken Adelman seemed less willing than any of the other participants to contemplate preemptive war with Pyongyang. But he remained unwilling to put much stock in negotiations of any kind, and continued to rest his hopes on the Chinese. He thought the North Korean situation was so intractable that it needed an unconventional approach to shake it loose; the analogy he used was the way Ronald Reagan shook loose the arms-control debate in the 1980s by conceiving of "Star Wars" missile defense. For Adelman the most surprising thing about the war game was that the debate didn't come down to a typical right-left divide. He noted in particular that he had been surprised to find himself to the left of Robert Gallucci in terms of willingness to use force.

Gallucci, for his part, said he was "surprised at how surprised Adelman was that we—those of us who favor negotiation—could end up in a position where we would favor the use of military force." Gallucci was emphatic that we urgently have to try to negotiate, as a prelude to possible military action, and was frustrated that the Bush administration and some of the war game principals were unwilling to recognize that. To put his frustration in context, he told me a story.

"When I came back with the Agreed Framework deal and tried to sell it," he said, "I ran into the same people sitting around that table—the general to my right, Ken across from me. They hated the idea of trying to solve this problem with a negotiation.

"And I said, 'What's your—pardon me—your fucking plan, then, if you don't like this?'

" 'We don't like—'

"I said, 'Don't tell me what you don't like! Tell me how you're going to stop the North Korean nuclear program.'

" 'But we wouldn't do it this way—'

" 'Stop! What are you going to do?'

"I could never get a goddamn answer. What I got was 'We wouldn't negotiate.'"

I pointed out that the North Koreans had—as McInerney emphasized—cheated on the 1994 agreement. "Excuse me," Gallucci said, "the Soviets cheated on virtually every deal we ever made with them, but we were still better off with the deal than without it."

To people who say that negotiating with the North Koreans rewards bad behavior, Gallucci says, "Listen, I'm not interested in teaching other people lessons. I'm interested in the national security of the United States. If that's what you're interested in, are you better off with this deal or without it? You tell me what you're going to do *without* the deal, and I'll compare that with the deal."

He was adamant that we were better off under the Agreed Framework— cheating and all—than we are now. "When the Clinton folks went out of office, the North Koreans only had the plutonium they had separated in the previous Bush administration. Now they've got a whole lot more. What did all this 'tough' shit give us? It gave us a much more capable North Korea. Terrific!"

For his part, Sam Gardiner came away with one overriding message. "I left the game with a firm conviction that the United States is focusing on the wrong problem," he told me. "Iran is down the road. Korea is now, and growing. We can't wait to deal with Korea." The president needs to engage the North Korean question for a very simple reason: "The military situation on the peninsula," he said, "is not under control."

The Chinese Are Our Friends
Thomas P. M. Barnett

Esquire | November 2005

While most essays on international affairs tend toward the academic in style, former U.S. Naval War College Professor Thomas P. M. Barnett has the rare ability to make foreign policy both understandable and entertaining. In this Esquire *article— a sequel of sorts to his February 2005 piece advising President Bush on how to use his second term to secure his place in world history (which ran in last year's anthology)—Barnett focuses on how the president should deal with the world's largest nation. Along the way, he explains the concept of "fourth generation warfare," and elaborates on why, in his view, many of our military leaders have a vested interest in keeping China as an enemy—to the detriment of our national security.*

*   *   *   *   *

The greatest threat to America's success in its war on terrorism sits inside the Pentagon. The proponents of Big War (that Cold War gift that keeps on giving), found overwhelmingly in the Air Force and Navy, will go to any length to demonize China in their quest to justify high-tech weaponry (space wars for the flyboys) and superexpensive platforms (submarines and ships for the admirals, and bomber jets for both) in the budget struggles triggered by our costly wars in Afghanistan and Iraq.

With China cast as America's inevitable enemy in war, the Air Force and Navy will hold off the surging demands of the army and marines for their labor-intensive efforts in Southwest Asia, keeping a slew of established defense contractors ecstatic in the process. How much money are we talking about? Adding up various reports of the Government Accountability Office, we're talking about $1.3 trillion that the Pentagon is locked into spending on close to a hundred major programs. So if China can't be sold to Congress and the American people as the next Red menace, then we're looking at a lot of expensive military systems being cut in favor of giving our troops on the ground the simple and relatively cheap gear they so desperately need not only to stay alive but also to win these ongoing conflicts.

You'd think the great search for the replacement for the Soviet threat would have finally ended after 9/11, but sadly that's not the case. Too many profits on the line. Army generals are fed up with being told that the global war on terrorism is the Pentagon's number one priority, because if it were, they and their Marine Corps brethren would be getting a bigger slice of the pie instead of so much being set aside for some distant, abstract threat.

It's bodies versus bucks, folks, and that's a presidential call if ever there was one. So it's time for George W. Bush to make up his mind whether or not he's committed to transforming the Middle East and spreading liberty to those Third World hellholes where terrorists now breed in abundance. If he is, the president will put an end to this rising tide of Pentagon propaganda on the Chinese "threat" and tell Secretary of Defense Donald Rumsfeld in no uncertain terms that our trigger pullers on the ground *today* deserve everything they need to conduct the counterinsurgency operations and nation building that will secure America's lasting victory in his self-declared global war on terrorism. If not, then Bush should just admit that the defense-industrial complex—or maybe just Dick Cheney—is in charge of determining who America's "real enemies" are.

The most important thing you need to know about the Pentagon is that it is not in charge of today's wars but rather tomorrow's wars. Today's wars are conducted by America's combatant commanders, those four-star admirals and generals who sit atop the regional commands such as Central Command, which watches over the Middle East and Central Asia, and Pacific Command, which manages our security interests in Asia from its perch in Honolulu.

Central Command has gotten all the attention since the Soviets went away, and as a result of all those boots being on the ground in places like Afghanistan and Iraq, the Tampa-based command is clearly dominated by a ground-forces mentality. Ask CENTCOM about the military's future needs and you'll get a long laundry list of requirements focused on the war fighter who's forced to walk the beat in some of the world's scariest neighborhoods, playing bad cop in nightly shootouts with insurgents and good cop by day as he oversees sewer-line repairs or doles out aid to the locals.

Nothing fancy here, as most of these unconventional operations are decidedly low tech and cheap. It's what the marines like to call Fourth Generation Warfare, or counterinsurgency operations designed to win over civilians while slowly strangling stubborn insurgencies. Completely unsexy, 4GW typically drags on for decades, generating real-time operational costs that inevitably pinch long-term acquisition programs—and therein lies the rub for the Pentagon's Big War clientele.

During the Cold War, it was easy for the Pentagon to justify its budget, as the Soviets essentially sized our forces for us. We simply counted up their stuff and either bought more of the same or upgraded our technology.

When the Soviets went away, the Pentagon's strategists started fishing around for a replacement, deciding on "rising China" in the mid-1990s, thanks to a showy standoff between Pacific Command and China's military over Taiwan. Since then, the Taiwan Strait scenario has served as the standard of the Pentagon's Big War planning and, by extension, fueled all budgetary justifications for big-ticket weapons systems and delivery platforms—everything from space-based infrared surveillance systems to the next generation of superexpensive strike fighter aircraft.

A key but rather anonymous player in this strategic debate has been Andrew Marshall, legendary Yoda of the super influential Office of Net Assessment, which reports directly to the secretary of defense. Marshall's main claim to fame was convincing the Pentagon in the 1980s that the Soviet Union's Red army was hell-bent on pursuing a revolution in military affairs that would—unless countered—send it leapfrogging ahead of us in high-tech weaponry. It never happened, but never mind, because as the neocons brag, it was Ronald Reagan's massive military buildup that bankrupted the Soviets. Now, apparently, we need to do the same thing to "communist" China because its rapid rise as a freewheeling capitalist economy will inevitably close the gap between their military and ours.

Do the Chinese have a trillion-plus dollars locked up in huge acquisition programs like we do? Are you kidding? We spend more to buy *new* stuff each year than the Chinese spend in total on their entire military. In fact, we spend more on operations in the Middle East each year than China spends on its entire military.

Prior to the September 11, 2001, terrorist strikes, the China threat was being successfully employed to win congressional support for all manner of Big War toys that logically had no real application in the 4GW scenarios that U.S. ground forces routinely found themselves in the post-Cold War world. (Think dirt-poor Haiti or *Black Hawk Down* Somalia.) But 9/11 changed all that, and the Bush administration's global war on terrorism and resulting Big Bang strategy of transforming the Middle East inadvertently shifted the budgetary argument from the capital-intensive navy and air force to the labor-intensive army and marines.

And when did that worm really turn? When army and marine officers began their second tours of duty in Iraq and Afghanistan last year. Program Budget Decision 753, signed by Deputy Secretary of Defense Paul Wolfowitz at the end of 2004, was the budgetary shot across the bow to the Big War crowd, as it announced a substantial shift of more than $25 billion to the army's coffers. That "war tax," as it became known within the Defense Department, swept through the defense community like the Christmas tsunami, as basically every budget program was forced to give it up to the ground-pounders.

This shift was long overdue. During the Cold War, the American military used to engage in nation building every decade or so, but since then it's more like once every two years, with a clear concentration on backward Muslim states. All these operations cost money, and as most drag on for years, either the Pentagon forgoes some of its Big War systems in budget battles, or soldiers and marines on the ground inevitably get shortchanged. Star Wars, say hello to hillbilly armor. Want to know why it's taken so unbearably long for our loved ones currently serving in Iraq to receive the body armor and armored Humvees they so desperately need? Because budget battle after budget battle, year in and year out, the Big War crowd inside the Pentagon has consistently defeated the Small War constituency found in the army and marines. And China has been the hammer the Big War strategists of the Navy and Air Force have used to beat back the Fourth Generation Warfare arguments of the ground-pounders, going all the way back to General Tony Zinni's complaints about all the things his CENTCOM troops were lacking in Somalia in the mid-1990s.

But Zinni's advice was routinely ignored by the Pentagon in the years that ensued, yielding the U.S. military that we have today: a first-half team that plays in a league that insists on keeping score until the end of the game. And of course this all culminated last December when Donald Rumsfeld was asked by an army specialist on his way to Iraq why the soldiers there had to scrounge up scrap armor in garbage dumps to fortify their thin-skinned Humvees, and he responded that "you go to war with the Army you have, not the Army you might want or wish to have."

Well, the army that the Pentagon's Big War machine has been wanting for the past ten years is one that's not properly equipped for such second-half efforts as peacekeeping or nation building. None of that mattered so long as the Powell Doctrine reigned supreme and America couldn't give a rat's ass about what came after the wars it waged (because our troops were already home by then, celebrating their "decisive" victory). But the war on terrorism gives the lie to the notion that drive-by regime change has any lasting impact other than making countries safe for terrorist networks. And so now the Defense Department is faced with a new rule set: Don't plan to win the war unless you plan to win the peace.

The Pentagon's own Defense Science Board noted this profound shortcoming in its recent seminal report on postconflict nation-building efforts in the post-Cold War era, "Transition to and from Hostilities," recommending Rumsfeld "direct the services to reshape and rebalance their forces to provide a stabilization and reconstruction capability," one that will require "substantially more resources" if America is going to become more successful in our overseas military interventions.

How so? Doesn't the fact that America fields the most awesome warfighting force on the planet ensure that we'll win any wars we wage? Wars yes, but not the peace that must inevitably follow. As the DSB report noted, our enemies in this global war on terrorism have already cracked our operational code: Don't fight the Americans in the first-half war; simply wait until the second-half "peace" and then go on the offensive—insurgency-style—against a follow-on U.S. force that's poorly equipped and poorly trained for the job of securing the original victory.

How many $2 billion attack subs did it recently take to recapture Fallujah—yet again!—from the Iraqi insurgents? None, which is not enough as far as the Big War crowd is concerned—not nearly enough.

But how many of our soldiers and marines give up their lives each and every time our ground forces are forced to engage in such desperate urban warfare because the neocons screwed up the Iraq occupation?

Ouch. Let's not go there, because if we do, the Pentagon's Big War propaganda machinery might be exposed for what it really is: an unprincipled scheme to put the long-term profitability of major defense contractors ahead of the equally long-term needs of our troops in the field.

So tell me, which scenario do you think is more likely in the future? More inescapable? That our sons and daughters will get stuck patrolling urban shooting galleries in Africa and the Middle East, or that America will fight some fabulous high-tech war with Wal-Mart's main subsidiary, China, Inc.? And which scenario do you think has more relevance to a global war on terrorism? Met any good Chinese terrorists lately?

Atlantic Monthly writer Robert Kaplan is probably more identified with Fourth Generation Warfare thinking than any other journalist working today. His steady stream of articles and books on the Mad Max battlefields of failed states, where drug-crazed teenage mercenaries rule the day, have done more to popularize the 4GW arguments of army and marine strategists than anything else. And boy, do the ground-pounders love him for it.

Which makes his recent conversion to the China hawks' camp all the more stunning. Writing in the June 2005 issue of *The Atlantic*, the widely respected journalist performed the equivalent of a strategic lap dance for Pacific Command by outlining "how we would fight China," which is the title of the article. Not *why*, mind you, just *how*.

Kaplan takes such an indirect route because the "why" argument on China frankly sucks. I mean, we're going to fight China to prevent it from becoming our biggest trade partner? To punish it for generating such a huge trade deficit, already our largest with any country in the world? To stop Beijing from funneling all those trade dollars back into U.S. Treasury bonds and secondary mortgage markets, thus keeping our interest rates low? Because China's cheap labor exerts deflationary pressure on global prices? Because China's rapid embrace of globalization has lifted hundreds of millions of Asians out of poverty in the last twenty years?

No, Kaplan avoids all such arguments for just that reason—they defy logic. Instead, he simply flips the Taiwan card on the table and then he's off to the races, or, should I say, the many wars—both hot and cold—that he imagines America must inevitably wage against China in the coming decades.

Why? Let Kaplan tell you himself in what constitutes the stunning thesis of his argument: "Pulsing with consumer and martial energy, and boasting a peasantry that, unlike others in history, is overwhelmingly literate, China constitutes the principal conventional threat to America's liberal imperium." Got that?

China's "pulsing" with "consumer energy," which apparently means those "literate peasants" want to buy stuff left and right, and since consumerism and literacy go hand in hand with "martial" tendencies (what the Chinese can't buy, they'll wage war to acquire, yes?), obviously America *must* go to war with them. I mean, a billion-plus Chinese consumers must represent a threat to our "liberal imperium," right?

Having spent a long afternoon in a Wal-Mart in the Chinese city of Nanchang last year, I can personally attest to the horror that is the Chinese consumer: Pushy, demanding, and downright aggressive in their price haggling, these people are not to be trusted under any circumstances. And don't even get me started on their line jumping at the checkout!

But the Chinese threat, we are told, is almost always masterfully indirect, so Beijing's growing economic ties around the planet portend a clear diminution of American military power. Check out how our new Sinophobe cleverly ties "rising China" with the global war on terrorism: "While stateless terrorists fill security vacuums, the Chinese fill economic ones."

Notice that subtle linkage? China and Al Qaeda are basically two sides of the same coin! If there's a vacuum to be found (meaning any place not firmly under America's "liberal imperium," one imagines), we're looking at one of two outcomes: Either Al Qaeda or the Chinese will eventually take over. The former may be committed to killing Americans on sight the world over, but the latter—with their "literate consumerism"—most assuredly want to . . . I dunno . . . sell us low-priced furniture and cars?

Don't get me wrong. I do worry about China's yuan being still overly pegged to the U.S. dollar (despite the recent microrevaluation), and no American shareholder in his right mind doesn't fear the amount of intellectual piracy currently occurring in China ("One for a dolla!" being the martial cry of Chinese street vendors hawking Hollywood DVDs the very day those movies open in theaters back home). And when pressed to describe what I consider to be the biggest threat to international security in the near term, I always cite the threat of a financial panic brewing inside China's far too rickety banking sector.

But how the Pentagon solves any of these economic "conflicts" with China is really beyond me. Our strategic exposure here is financial, not force-on-force war. And outside of the pure Taiwan scenario, upon which China's military buildup is clearly focused, it's not clear to me that U.S. and Chinese interests necessarily clash whatsoever.

Here's another good example of this queer logic: The *Wall Street Journal* recently ran a front-page story that laid out—in rather breathless detail— China's "broad push into Africa." The Chinese are accused of courting African dictatorships to gain access to strategic resources, including—God forbid!—oil.

Good thing America could never be accused of similar motivations and tactics.

But the Chinese aren't waging war in Africa, nor are they establishing military outposts like we are. No, China's "indirectness" comes in the form of building dams and laying roads and "cultivating desperately poor nations to serve as markets for its products decades down the road."

My, that is scary, reflecting, as the *Journal* story points out, "Beijing's policy of actively encouraging its companies and citizens to set up shop in Africa at a record pace."

Hmmm. China's investing and creating business and market opportunities in Africa, a continent long ravaged by civil wars and AIDS and

America's complete indifference to a Holocaust's worth of preventable deaths in the last decade. *And that's considered bad?*

To listen to some fire-breathing congressmen, it sure as hell is, because China will secure long-term access to strategic raw materials, leaving our economy high and dry in the "resource wars" that must inevitably ensue.

This is zero-sum thinking at its worst, reflecting a strategic mind-set that declares a rise in any country's commercial influence around the world as necessarily signaling a decline in American power. If you had proposed in 1980 that the biggest threat to America's "liberal imperium" in 2005 was going to be a China whose rapacious style of capitalism surpassed even our own, you would have been drunk.

Donald Rumsfeld recently did some heavy lifting himself for the Big War crowd, signaling just how powerful it remains in the Bush administration. While in Asia in June for an annual regional security conference, he issued a "sharp rebuke," according to the *New York Times*, to China for its rising military spending. "Since no nation threatens China," Rumsfeld wondered out loud, "why this growing investment?"

Interesting question. Since no "nation" threatens the United States, but merely a transnational terrorist movement, perhaps the Chinese are wondering about America's skyrocketing defense budget of the last four years. Baseline defense spending is up 35 percent since 2001, not including the couple hundred billion extra in supplementals to pay for the wars. The United States routinely spends as much on research and development alone as China, according to the highest estimates, spends on its entire defense budget (approximately $70 billion). Meanwhile, the Rand Corporation's estimates of Chinese defense-spending increases, while routinely registering double-digit annual percentage growth, place China's military spending as a percentage of GDP at far less than that of America's defense burden—roughly 2.5 percent to America's almost 4 percent.

Using George Orwell's "newspeak" from *1984*, I guess you could call our defense hike *doubleplusgood* to China's merely *plusgood*. But who's counting?

The Pentagon is. Its latest annual projection of Chinese defense spending, titled "The Military Power of the People's Republic of China," suggests that in two decades' time, China could, according to our highest estimates, be spending roughly half (as much as $250 billion) of what America's total defense bill was for 2005 (roughly $500 billion)—sort of a *doublehalfbad* prediction, if I may be so bold.

Do such wild projections matter? You bet. They will play heavily into the Pentagon's Quadrennial Defense Review debate, which in recent months, according to a recent article by Greg Jaffe in the *Wall Street Journal*, has "intensified divisions among policy makers over how to approach China." Which means, of course, that the immediate tasks of the army and marines—fighting terrorists and insurgents in Iraq—will be balanced against the hypothetical threat of China, the "driver of U.S. military modernization," according to the navy and air force.

With Rumsfeld—who has seemed committed to transforming the Pentagon from its leaden Cold War thinking—himself sounding the China hawks' alarm, you have to wonder just how committed the Bush administration remains to fighting this global war on terrorism. Prior to 9/11, the Republican neocons were firmly fixated on "rising China." With Saddam gone, has the Pentagon's preferred analysis of China simply resurfaced, suggesting that the war on terrorism was nothing more than an excuse to target Iraq?

Trust me, Mr. President, you don't ever want to have *that* conversation with Cindy Sheehan.

If Rumsfeld's comments in Singapore were designed to test the waters for a redemonization of China, they failed dramatically with our allies there, who told the secretary in no uncertain terms that such fearmongering wasn't welcome. Somewhat chastened, Rumsfeld returned to the Pentagon and, according to department insiders, instructed that the Pentagon's annual assessment of China's military capabilities be rewritten to tone down the hype. The final draft that emerged weeks later certainly couldn't have satisfied the neocons or the Pacific Command's hawks, citing as it did only the long-term possibility that "if current trends persist, [the People's Liberation Army's] capabilities could prove a credible threat to other modern militaries operating in the region." Hardly the red meat the Big War crowd requires, and that alone may give the Army and Marines just enough bureaucratic breathing space to prevail in the QDR debates, which will be fought out—PowerPoint slide by PowerPoint slide—in Pentagon conference rooms throughout the fall and right up to the final report's unveiling to Congress in February 2006.

But don't harbor any illusions that anyone will give up the fight anytime soon. With Chinese companies buying up America's industrial-age crown jewels, like IBM's PC-production unit, and planning to build almost thirty nuclear power plants in coming years with the help of global giants like Westinghouse, rest assured that plenty of old men with military-industrial ties will be keeping a close watch on Beijing's so-called Communists, hoping to spot some "disruptive" technology that justifies that trillion-and-a-half pipeline of Big War products. Check out the new "China caucus" in Congress and count the number of members who likewise sit on the House Armed Services Committee. This game ain't over by a long shot. The winning strategic construct that's likely to emerge in the Quadrennial Defense Review is described by Pentagon insiders as the "one-one-one" strategy of organizing our military's force structure around three main pillars, all seemingly equal: (1) homeland defense; (2) the war on terrorism (and all the nation-building efforts it inevitably triggers); and (3) deterrence, an old term now recast to mean, "China, we've got our eyes on you, so don't try anything . . . you know . . . disruptive!"

But let's be honest here. Homeland defense doesn't generate any force requirements beyond having enough National Guard to save lives in natural disasters and to babysit nuclear power plants on Code Red days. As the response to Hurricane Katrina demonstrated, homeland security requires an emphasis on the very same kind of low-tech, labor-intensive forces we've long neglected. No big programs are won or lost on that "pillar." And we know that the global war on terrorism tends to generate lots of Small War equipment needs, largely for the army and marines. That leaves "deterrence" as the long pole in the tent, and that means the Pentagon *needs* China like Red Sox fans *need* the Yankees.

Business executives who've worked China's increasingly open market over the past decade or so will tell you flat out: If possible, avoid working with older Chinese businesspeople, because that first generation of capitalists is simply too tainted by its socialist upbringing to get anything done according to what we would consider to be normal business standards and practices. Frankly, that crowd you bribe—a lot.

No, if you're smart, you deal with the generation of capitalists that followed, which puts almost all of them under age fifty. This crew came of age after Chairman Mao departed the scene, during the long-running economic boom that began with Deng Xiaoping's "four modernizations" campaign in the early 1980s. Moreover, an amazing number of them got some training or education in the United States, so they get us—and our style of capitalism— in ways we tend to underestimate.

I got a good description of this dynamic when I sat down recently for dinner with a couple of big American distributors of high-end consumer products. This pair of old-school guys told me of their recent attempts to forge a strategic alliance with a Chinese company to import a large volume of Chinese-produced big-ticket goods. Their initial attempts at negotiations were complicated by a lot of previously proposed deals that reflected early Chinese capitalist sensibilities, meaning those deals set up by the original Marco Polos who raced into China in the 1990s. Not surprisingly, few of those deals have gotten off the ground, mired as they are in the usual back-scratching arrangements.

The American executives I spoke to were not willing to grease anyone's palms, and they won't be conned into any questionable investments. But they discovered that when they dealt with younger Chinese managers at the factory level, the attitude was entirely focused on "What do you need" to make a deal work in the American market. Chinese capitalism has matured to the point that the government is starting to back off and say, "Don't talk to us, talk to the factory."

And it is the simple fact that American businessmen will be making billions of dollars either in China or partnered with Chinese businesses that leads us to a new twenty-first-century rule: If you're better off not trusting anyone over fifty in China on a business deal, you're also better off not listening to anyone over fifty in Washington on the "threat of rising China." The Cold Warrior crowd received its ideological imprinting on China decades ago, and no matter how smoothly they may talk about global affairs today (think Condi Rice), they are none of them to be trusted on China. Here's an easy way to spot them: If they *ever* quote Henry Kissinger or Zbigniew Brzezinski, tune them out completely. If they think Ronald Reagan defeated Communism single-handedly, watch your wallet, but if they've ever worked under, or anywhere near, Dick Cheney, then watch your back.

It is no secret that in a generation's time China's influence over the global economy will rival America's, so it requires no great leap of logic for any strategist shy of fifty to realize that China and America are destined to enjoy a deep strategic partnership if globalization is to continue its historic expansion across the twenty-first century. This is probably the biggest strategic choice we've ever faced as a nation, because if we avoid this path, we'll most certainly prevent a future in which all of humanity can benefit from globalization's promise.

Few historic ends will ever come close to justifying such a wide array of means as the strategic alliance of the United States and China in coming decades: In this century, this partnership will define global stability just as much as the U.S.-British "special relationship" of the twentieth century did. It will be that important in its execution, that precious in its bond, that profound in its reach. The blueprint for global peace will be a joint Sino-American document. There is no alternative.

Too big of a paradigm shift for you? Check that birth certificate. If it's dated earlier than 1955, you're excused for the century, and here's why: Cold War babies can't escape the logic that says, "If you resemble America politically, then you must be our friend." That was fine and dandy for the late-twentieth-century version of globalization, limited as it was to the narrowly defined West. But that's not the globalization we face today—much less tomorrow. No, that process is far more defined by the emergence of such new pillars as China, India, Brazil, and Russia than it is by that old-boys' club of North America, Western Europe, and industrialized Asia.

In the future, America will have more in common with China than with Japan, with India than with the United Kingdom, with Brazil than with Canada, and with Russia than either France or Germany. In general, if you're more like us economically, then you're logically America's strongest allies—despite whatever political differences appear to divide us. *That's* realism in the age of globalization—love it or leave it.

If you're an aging Boomer, take a seat, but if you're an Echo Boomer, the largest American age cohort in history (currently aged ten to twenty-five), then please stand up and be counted—now—because your future is on the line in this debate.

And if you're one of those Echo Boomers, like my two nephews, wearing a uniform in Iraq today, your life is on the line in this debate.

Today, more than ever, the question of U.S.-Chinese security relations depends on how the president of the United States chooses to define the global future worth creating. And China's continued emergence as a stable pillar of the global economy is crucial to that vision, whether the Pentagon's advocates of Big War planning realize it or not.

America will expend blood and treasure in coming years no matter which strategic path we take. But a whole lot less of each will be wasted if our leadership in Washington displays the moral courage and the strategic vision to realize that China is our natural strategic partner in any global war on terrorism, and not a strategic excuse to lowball that effort and—by doing so—needlessly sacrifice American lives in the process.

Americans need to demand more from our political leaders than an unimaginative strategy of just waiting around for the next "near-peer competitor" to arise—in effect, keeping our powder dry while the blood of our loved ones is spilled in Southwest Asia. America can't embrace its globalized future until it lets go of its Cold War past.

Get moving, Mr. President.

Contributors

Matt Bai covers national politics for *The New York Times Magazine*, where he is a contributing writer.

James Bamford is a journalist who specializes in writing about U.S. intelligence. A visiting professor at the University of California at Berkeley, he is the author of several books, including two profiles of the National Security Agency, *The Puzzle Palace* and *Body of Secrets*, and, most recently, *A Pretext for War: 9/11, Iraq, and the Abuse of America's Intelligence Agencies*.

Thomas P. M. Barnett is a contributing editor to *Esquire*, and a former professor and senior military analyst at the U.S. Naval War College. He is the author of *The Pentagon's New Map: War and Peace in the Twenty-first Century*.

Joe Conason is a columnist for the *The New York Observer* and *Salon.com*. He is the author of several books, including *Big Lies: The Right-Wing Propaganda Machine and How It Distorts the Truth*.

Mark Danner is a staff writer at *The New Yorker* and a frequent contributor to *The New York Review of Books*. A professor of journalism at U.C. Berkeley and Henry R. Luce Professor of Human Rights and Journalism at Bard College, he is the author of several books including, most recently, *The Secret Way to War: The Downing Street Memo and the Iraq War's Buried History*.

Elizabeth Drew is a regular contributor to *The New York Review of Books*. She is the author of numerous books, including *Corruption of American Politics: What Went Wrong and Why* and, most recently, *Fear and Loathing in George W. Bush's Washington*.

James Fallows is a national correspondent for *The Atlantic Monthly*. He is the author of several books including, most recently, *Blind into Baghdad: America's War in Iraq*.

Francis Fukuyama is Bernard L. Schwartz Professor of International Political Economy at the Paul H. Nitze School of Advanced International Studies of The Johns Hopkins University. He is the author of numerous books, including *The End of History and the Last Man* and, most recently, *America at the Crossroads: Democracy, Power, and the Neoconservative Legacy*.

Seymour Hersh is a staff writer for *The New Yorker* magazine and a contributing editor to *The Atlantic Monthly*. Winner of the 1970 Pulitzer Prize for international reporting for his exposé of the My Lai massacre, he is the author of numerous books including, most recently, *Chain of Command: The Road from 9/11 to Abu Ghraib*.

John B. Judis is a senior editor at *The New Republic*. He has also written for numerous other publications, including *The American Prospect*, *The New York Times Magazine*, *The Washington Post*, *Foreign Affairs*, *The Washington Monthly*, *American Enterprise*, and *Mother Jones*. He is the author of several books, including, most recently, *The Folly of Empire: What George W. Bush Could Learn from Theodore Roosevelt and Woodrow Wilson*.

Ryan Lizza is the White House correspondent for *The New Republic*. His writing has also appeared in *The New York Times Magazine*, *Atlantic Monthly*, *New York*, and *The Washington Monthly*.

Janet Malcolm is a staff writer for *The New Yorker* and the author of several books, including *Inside the Freud Archives* and, most recently, *The Silent Woman: Sylvia Plath and Ted Hughes*.

Mark Crispin Miller is the author of several books, including *The Bush Dyslexicon* and, most recently, *Fooled Again: How the Right Stole the 2004 Election & Why They'll Steal the Next One Too (Unless We Stop Them)*.

Walter Mosley is a novelist and essayist, whose nonfiction work has appeared in *The Nation* and *The New York Times Magazine*. Winner of a 1996 O'Henry Award for short-story writing, he is the author of many books, including the popular Easy Rawlins mystery series.

Christian Parenti writes frequently for *The Nation* on international affairs. He is the author of *The Freedom: Shadows and Hallucinations in Occupied Iraq*.

Evgenia Peretz is a contributing editor to *Vanity Fair*.

Ken Silverstein is a reporter for the *Los Angeles Times*. He is the author of several books, including *Washington on $10 Million a Day: How Lobbyists Plunder the Nation*.

Michael Specter is a staff writer for *The New Yorker*. He has also served as Moscow bureau chief for the *New York Times*, and national science reporter for *The Washington Post*.

Scott Stossel is managing editor of *The Atlantic Monthly*. He has also written for numerous other publications, including *The New Yorker*, *The New Republic*, the *New York Times*, *The Washington Post*, and *The Boston Globe*, and is author of the book *Sarge: The Life and Times of Sargent Shriver*.

Amy Sullivan is a contributing editor to *The Washington Monthly*.

Evan Thomas is assistant managing editor and former Washington bureau chief of *Newsweek*. A frequent television commentator, he is the author of several books including, most recently, *Sea of Thunder: Four Commanders and the Last Great Naval Campaign*.

Michael Tomasky is executive editor of *The American Prospect*. Formerly "The City Politic" columnist for *New York* magazine, his work has appeared in numerous publications, including *The Washington Post*, *Harper's*, and *The Nation*. He is the author of *Hillary's Turn: Inside Her Improbable, Victorious Senate Campaign*.

Benjamin Wallace-Wells is a contributing editor to *The Washington Monthly*.

Sean Wilentz is the Dayton-Stockon Professor of History and director of the Program in American Studies at Princeton University. A contributing editor to *The New Republic*, he is the author of numerous books including, most recently, *The Rise of American Democracy: Jefferson to Lincoln*.

James Q. Wilson is the Ronald Reagan professor of public policy at Pepperdine University, and a frequent contributor to *Commentary*. He is the author of several books, including *American Government: Institutions and Policies* (cowritten with John DiIulio).

Permissions